EYES OF THE STORM

HURRICANES KATRINA AND RITA: THE PHOTOGRAPHIC STORY

BY The Dallas Morning News

SPECIAL INTRODUCTION BY COKIE ROBERTS

EYES OF THE STORM

HURRICANES KATRINA AND RITA: THE PHOTOGRAPHIC STORY

BY **The Dallas Morning News**

SPECIAL INTRODUCTION BY COKIE ROBERTS

TAYLOR TRADE PUBLISHING

LANHAM • NEW YORK • BOULDER • TORONTO • OXFORD

For the victims and heroes of Hurricanes Katrina & Rita

in Louisiana, Mississippi and Texas

Published by Taylor Trade Publishing
An imprint of The Rowman & Littlefield Publishing Group, Inc.
4501 Forbes Boulevard, Suite 200, Lanham, Maryland 20706

Distributed by NATIONAL BOOK NETWORK

Library of Congress Control Number: 2005935309
ISBN 1-58979-359-5 (pbk.: alk. paper)

The paper used in this publication meets the minimum requirements of American
National Standard for Information Sciences-Permanence of Paper for Printed Library
Materials, ANSI/NISO Z39.48-1992.

Manufactured in the United States of America.

TABLE OF CONTENTS

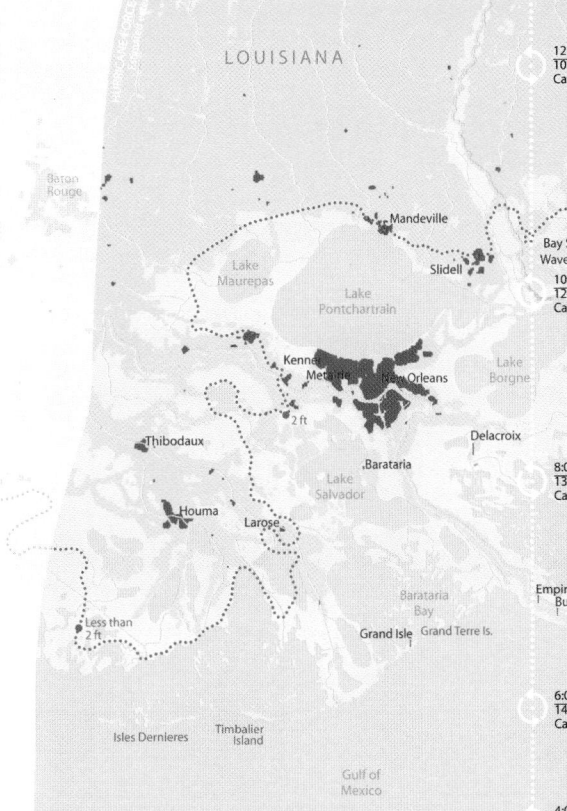

SOURCES: NOAA; LANDSCAN GLOBAL POPULATION DATABASE, OAK RIDGE NATIONAL LABORATORY; STORM SURGE DATA BY NOAA AND MODELED BY INTERNATIONAL HURRICANE RESEARCH CENTER, FLORIDA INTERNATIONAL UNIVERSITY
MAP BY NATIONAL GEOGRAPHIC

COKIE ROBERTS
NPR NEWS SENIOR NEWS ANALYST; ABC NEWS POLITICAL COMMENTATOR

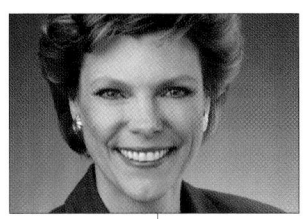

Though for a time they dominated our days, these images of disaster will forever have the power to shock us. A restaurant roof, picked up and blown away like a balsa wood toy, begins this document of devastation. Slabs of foundation where once there was an apartment house, streams of rising water where once there were streets, wary soldiers where once there were joyous revelers - all serve as testaments to destruction. And the chaos caused by the storms comes clear in the scenes of traffic jams and angry evacuees. But it is the simple objects and, especially, the faces caught by the cameras that will keep the stories of Katrina and Rita alive.

Here are two coffins side by side in the ground, a couple of roses thrown on top, holding the remains of her husband and baby found by a woman in Pass Christian, Mississippi. Here also is a woman, drooping from the heat, tending babies as she waits for rescue from a highway overpass. And here is a mother, one solitary tear staining her cheek, unable to find her child. But here, too, are tributes to the human spirit - people praying outside a church in Biloxi, a boy playing with a baby in a shelter in Dallas.

We see in this book heartache and heroism, ruin, and - in the face of a little dog - fur slickened with oil, the hope of resurrection.

Cokie Roberts

THE DALLAS MORNING NEWS

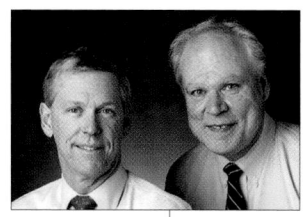

• JIM MORONEY, PUBLISHER AND CHIEF EXECUTIVE OFFICER

• BOB MONG, EDITOR

The beast that would be Katrina bore down on the Gulf Coast with just a hint of mystery. Hurricanes often seem ominous and then suddenly morph into little more than windy rainstorms as they meet the land.

Nevertheless, we planned for the worst, positioning our gifted photographers and writers from Corpus Christi, Texas, to the Mississippi coast. Deep down most of us suspected Katrina would be just another routine hurricane.

By late Saturday the thrashing storm appeared more menacing. New Orleans now seemed Katrina's likely destination -- with all that implied.

For years, New Orleans was deeply aware of its extreme vulnerability to a potent hurricane. The heart of this artistic and iconoclastic city rested in a bowl-like topography below sea level, protected by levees of questionable sturdiness.

Our staff did what reporters and photographers do when such a fierce storm descends: produce until they must hunker down and let it pass through, then emerge to find what they will find.

What they saw was horrifying: a coast strewn with destruction, chaos, pain and death. When the levees failed, our journalists were thrust into the country's most widespread natural disaster.

They attacked the story by land, by boat and by air. Our photos ran on front pages all over the world.

They sloshed through fetid, soupy floodwaters to bring life to the stories closest to the surface. Often, they captured devastation so vivid and striking that it left one breathless.

This work, with all of its many dimensions, helped our readers move beyond the complexity and chaos of catastrophe. It provided, instead, an informed voice and much needed context. We commend it.

Jim Moroney   *R W. Mg/h.*

Karen Brooks
Austin Bureau, The Dallas Morning News

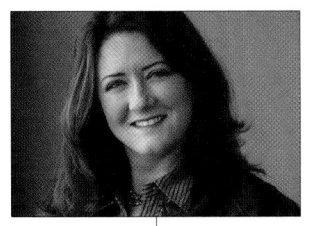

I had been in New Orleans for only a short time when I met the happy-go-lucky "Radio Marigny" gang in a mostly abandoned neighborhood near the French Quarter.

They were holdouts -- surviving on military Meals Ready to Eat and rationed swimming pool water, blasting music through two-foot speakers from the balcony of an apartment that ringleader and self-appointed deejay Kenny Claiborne commandeered from a friend in the Faubourg Marigny.

It had been less than 48 hours since I first drove into this mind-blowing, nightmarish place straight out of a science fiction movie. And yet I could not pry myself from the futon in that sweaty living room, lost in lilting reggae music so loud it didn't permit thought.

The plan had been to drop in for five minutes and then return later to this wild bunch who had formed their own society, hierarchy, way of life. But we stayed for two hours, loath to return to the craziness outside. It felt so good to escape, holed up with these chatty, laughing people who had refused to do just that.

In the days ahead, I would go to places I hope never to be again, like a funeral for a man and his baby -- a scene so painful it still doesn't seem real.

But I kept returning to that balcony. In the middle of the monstrosity, whenever something rocked me to the core, Radio Marigny provided the sanctuary that nobody and nothing else seemed able to give.

Arnold Hamilton
Oklahoma Bureau Chief, The Dallas Morning News

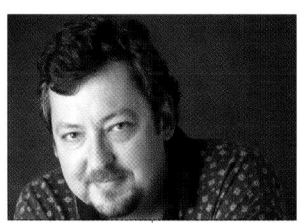

It was like a giant block party.

The sun was shining. The wind was stilled. And thousands of Hurricane Katrina survivors poured out of their storm shelters - in this case, downtown high-rise hotels - onto Canal Street to celebrate.

In the early evening, just hours after Katrina passed, it seemed New Orleans again had dodged The Big One.

Not entirely, of course. Earlier, with the wind still whipping and clouds rolling by, photographer Michael Ainsworth and I stood on an Interstate 10 bridge east of downtown and surveyed the submerged Ninth Ward, an area prone to flooding. A body floated face-down beneath us. A woman clung to her home's guttering, awaiting rescue. Two dogs stretched out on a rooftop, water lapping against the roof-line.

But now, at the edge of the French Quarter, in the Central Business District, there was relief that Katrina left just the usual hurricane remnants: twisted metal awnings, scattered about. Street signs missing. Palm trees uprooted. At our hotel, the Astor Crowne Plaza, workers already were sweeping up broken glass and other debris and making repairs.

In the middle of Canal Street, where cars and streetcars usually run, survivors greeted each other like long-lost friends or relatives - with handshakes and hugs, swapping stories of where and how they endured Katrina's wrath. A couple from Georgia, unable to secure a flight out in the mad scramble to evacuate, talked on a cellphone and snapped pictures of the impromptu party.

Twelve hours later, it was clear the celebration was premature: Water was rushing down Canal Street. The levees had given way. The nightmare was beginning.

Lee Hancock
Staff Writer, The Dallas Morning News

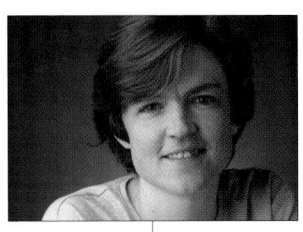

Corpses rotting untended in tropical heat. Generations stuck on roadsides, separated from those who could leave by what wasn't in their gas tanks. Haggard tourists begging strangers to get word out that they'd made it to this trash-strewn stretch of concrete, to this day after Hurricane Katrina turned New Orleans upside down.

The images remain fresh, still charged with the chaos and sweaty fear of that surreal first week after the monster storm. On perhaps the worst section of I-10, overlooking the Superdome, children my daughter's age trailed bewildered parents who had no idea when - or if - help might come. Families struggled to move elders on walkers or in wheelchairs. Women clutched feverish babies they'd toted for miles through the fetid floodwaters. Old men with diabetes and heart conditions went without water for days so their grandkids could drink.

"This is America," a young father said to me, his voice frantic as he scanned the crowds and truckloads of heavily armed soldiers that kept passing them without slowing. "What are all these folks gonna do?"

I wonder what became of him, his wife and sister and their three children, all stranded in a nicer version of the car I drive at home.

I'll probably always wonder about the fates of all on that hellish road, always haunted by how such a storied American city descended so quickly into bedlam.

BRUCE NICHOLS
HOUSTON BUREAU CHIEF, THE DALLAS MORNING NEWS

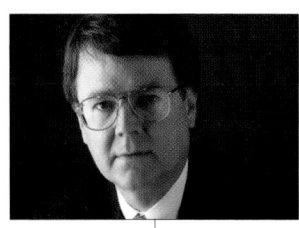

ALONG THE GULF COAST EAST OF NEW ORLEANS — There's nothing quite so depressing as covering a hurricane.

Driving for hours through devastated countryside. Alone, unable to communicate with the outside world because power's out everywhere and telephone lines are down.

Dodging high water, fallen trees and debris in the road. Arguing your way past the occasional police roadblock.

Running over the occasional downed high-voltage line - breathtaking when you remember the extra gasoline in cans in the trunk. Will the car explode?

Wet and dirty. No place to sleep because hotels are either wrecked or booked up.

Living off peanut butter and jelly sandwiches you make in the back seat because there's no place to get food. They taste like gasoline because fumes fill the car. Worrying about finding a working landline or cellular tower that still works so you can file your story.

Worrying about your soul because there's never enough time for a fully human response to the injuries, the loss.

Sometimes telling people's stories feels like stealing.

But not always.

In Slidell, La., Brittany Barbetta, helping recover valuables from her cousin's storm-ravaged shop, worried that relatives would be terrified because they couldn't reach them.

Would I call this number in California and say I saw them and that they were OK?

Of course.

When I made the call, I forgot I wasn't just delivering happy news. The relative in California burst into tears when she heard Ms. Barbetta's home was probably ruined.

I apologized.

She said, "No. I needed to know."

Two weeks later, a card came to the office, postmarked Los Angeles, telling me they'd all relocated to Arizona.

"Words cannot describe the relief I felt when I received your phone call," she wrote. "Thank you."

PETE SLOVER
AUSTIN BUREAU, THE DALLAS MORNING NEWS

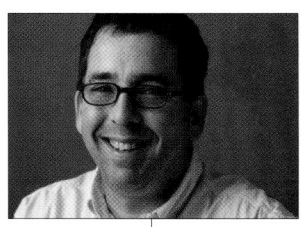

Photographer Irwin Thompson captured pictures of Cajun cowboy Mark Broussard as he helped round up rescued, tired cattle from the flooded marshes of Pecan Island, La., after Hurricane Rita. What his pictures didn't show, as Mr. Broussard led the procession down a high, dry road, was the lead vehicle -- ours. I drove, with photographer Thompson perched atop a cache of loaded gas cans that were strapped to the roof of our rented SUV.

Our vehicle provided more than just a good vantage point, it became another tool in the cattle herding box-of-tricks: As Mr. Broussard cut to the side of the cows to head off a would-be runaway, the leaderless front cattle began to run faster - toward us. Instinctively, we wove our vehicle slowly, left and right in front of the herd, blocking them and - our subject told us later - averting a potential stampede.

Later, nearby, we had the chance to report on the rescue of hundreds of reptiles escaped from tanks at an alligator farm. As we suited up in hip boots to wade into the darkened gator sheds, I asked the farm's owner - sitting on the front stoop of her flood-ruined house: "Are those animals dangerous?" Looking the city boy reporter up and down, she answered in a Cajun deadpan: "They're tired, they're stressed out, they're hungry, and they've got a mouth full of teeth. I guess they could be dangerous." As it turned out, the strays were more gatorlings than gators.

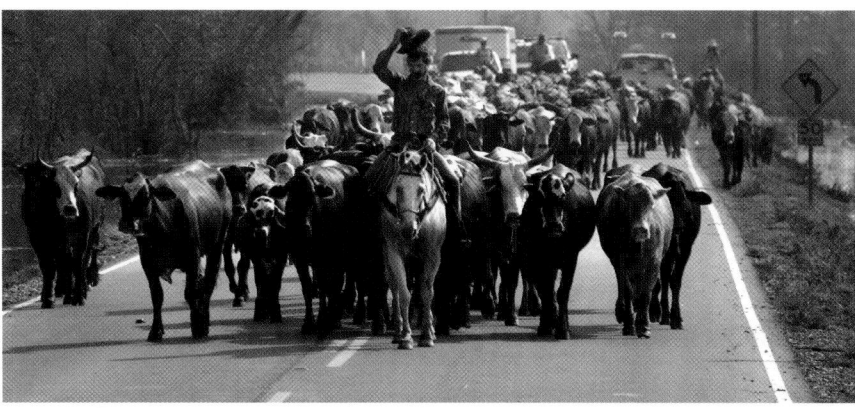

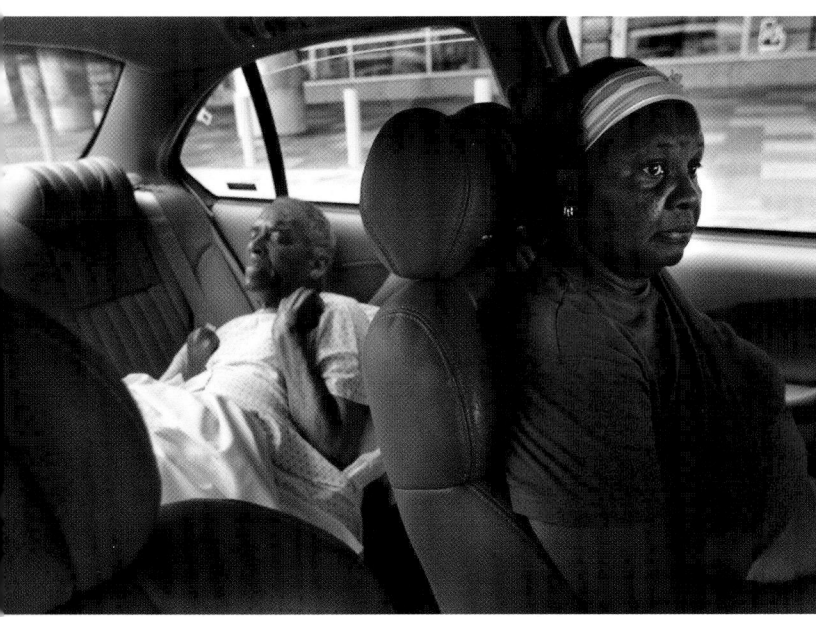

08.28.05 - New Orleans, LA - Many evacuees were elderly or ill. Veronica Jones took husband Joseph Jones, with Alzheimer's disease and an amputated leg, to the Superdome, which literally became a shelter from the storm. After a wait, she got help getting him into the Dome. • MICHAEL AINSWORTH

CENTER

08.28.05 - New Orleans, LA - Hot and frustrated residents of New Orleans endured a painfully slow evacuation on Interstate 10 west of the city that morning, one day before Hurricane Katrina blasted ashore and changed their lives for a long time to come. One man said he traveled five miles in 3 1/2 hours. • MICHAEL AINSWORTH

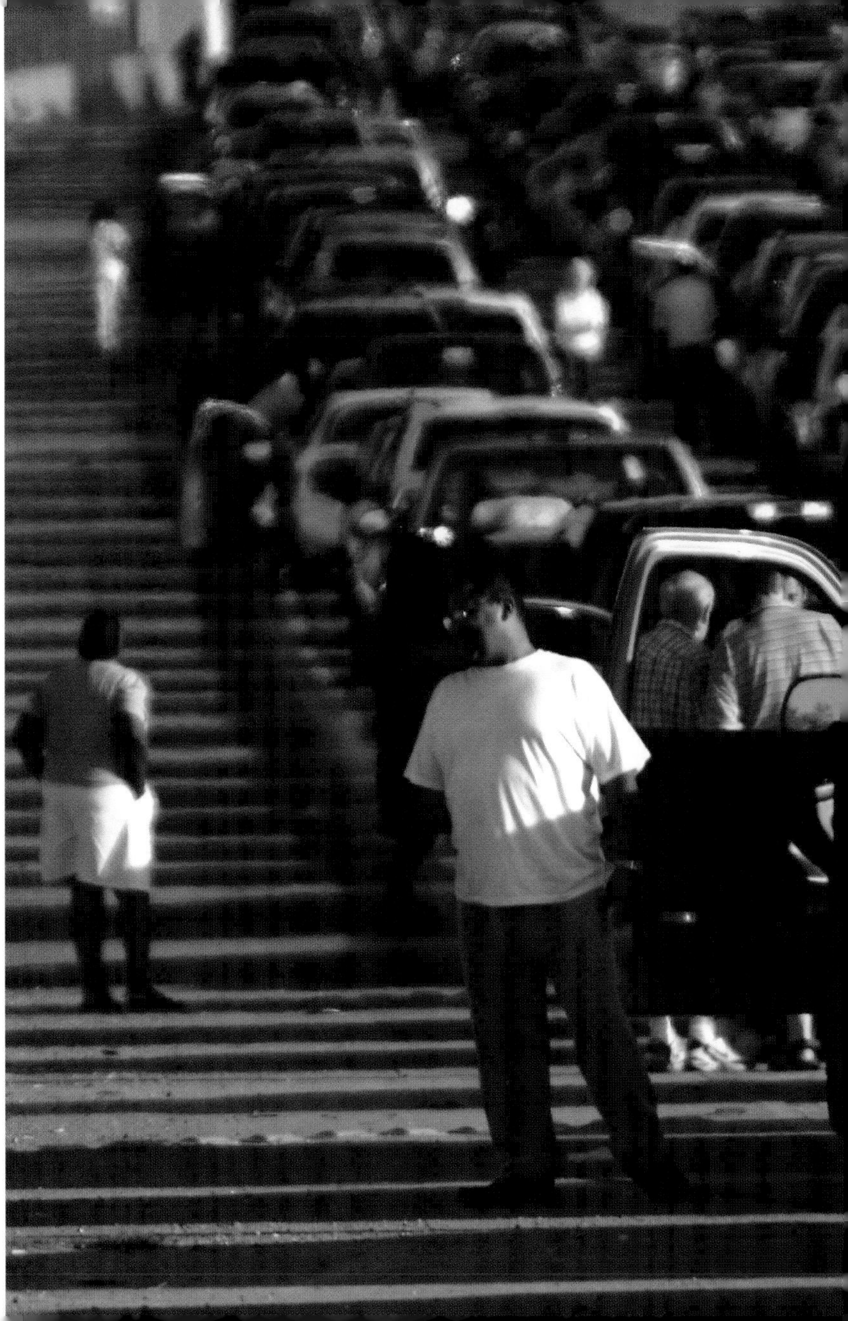

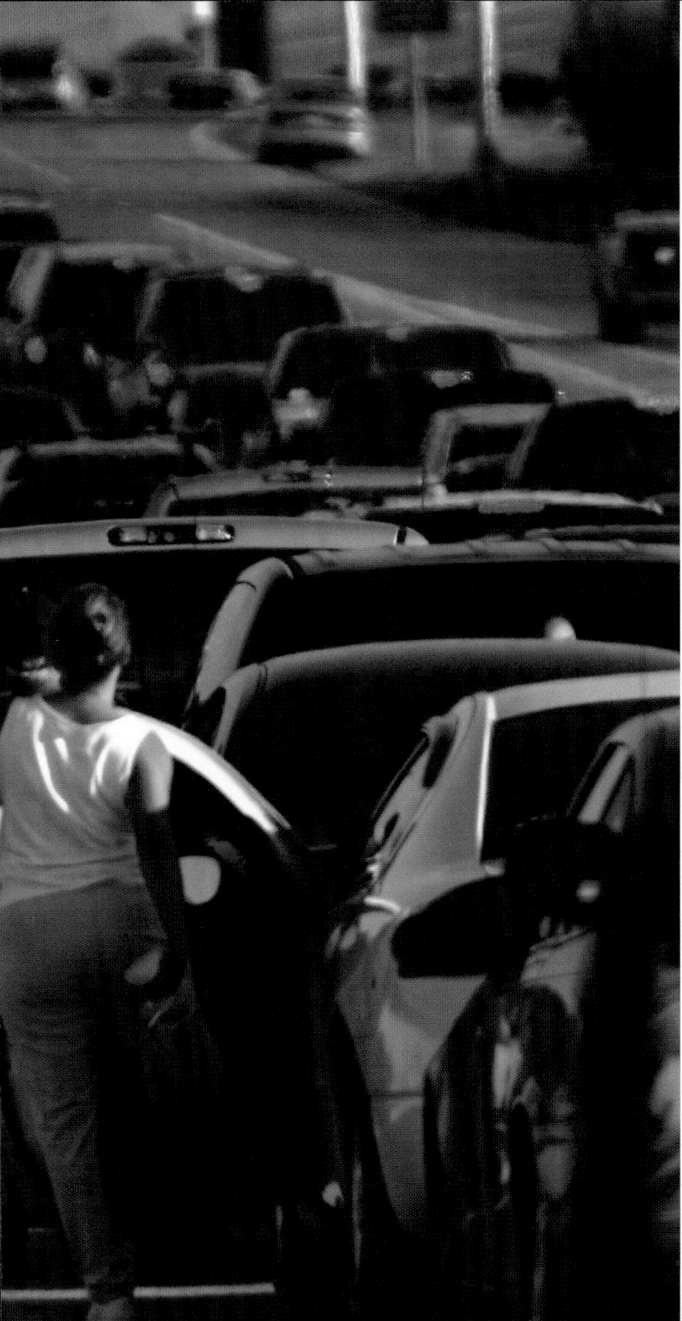

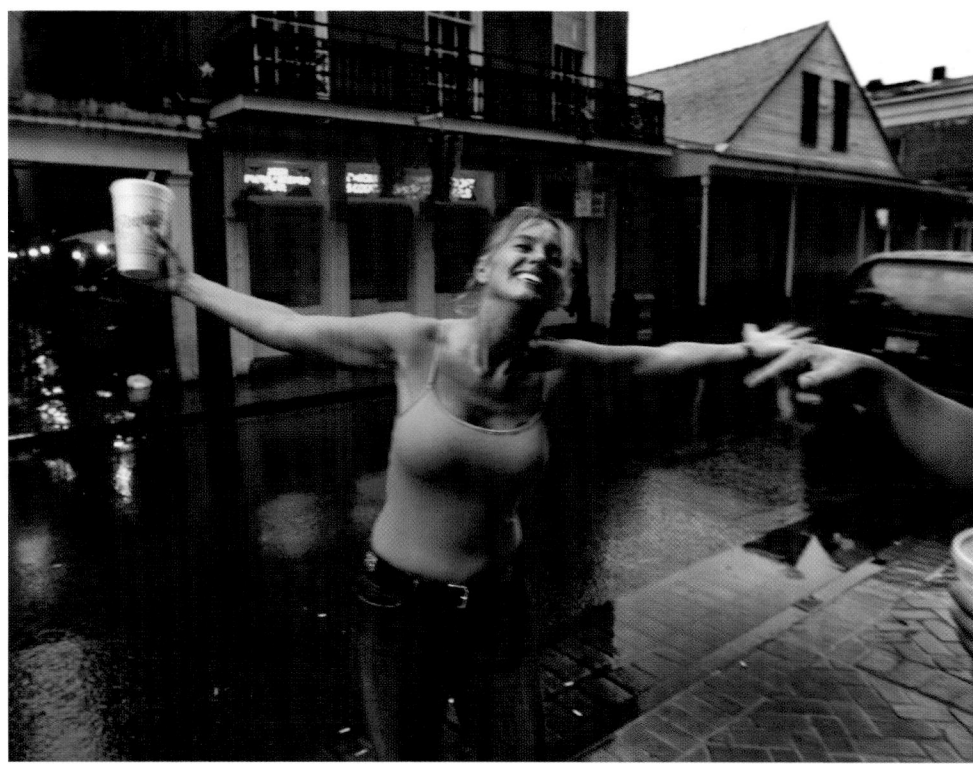

08.28.05 - New Orleans, LA - It was still party time in the French Quarter to some, hurricane or no hurricane. Jackie Esquirol of New Jersey enjoyed the rain and a daiquiri on Bourbon Street the night before Katrina hit. There was a 7 p.m. curfew, but some restaurants and bars remained open. • MICHAEL AINSWORTH

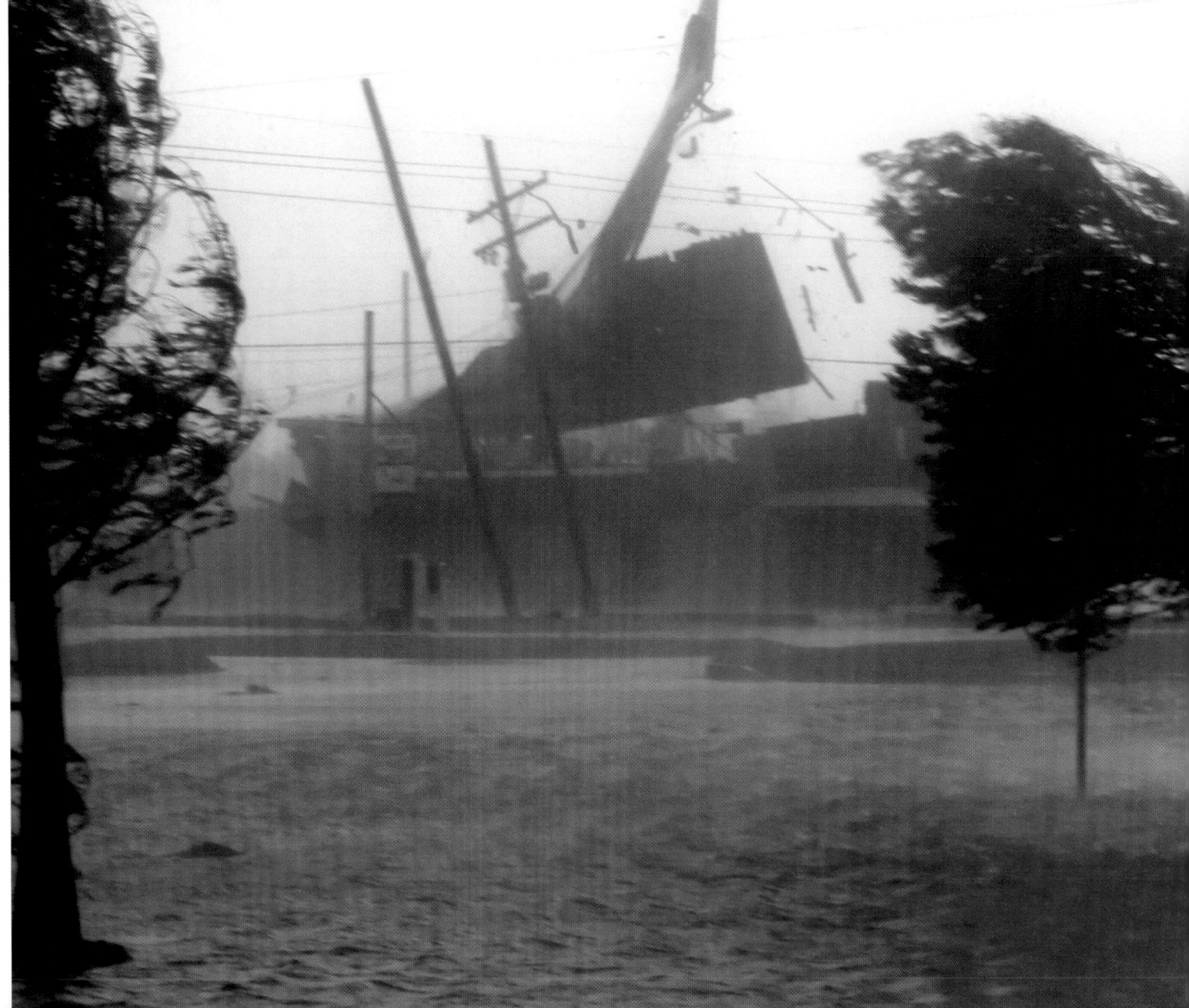

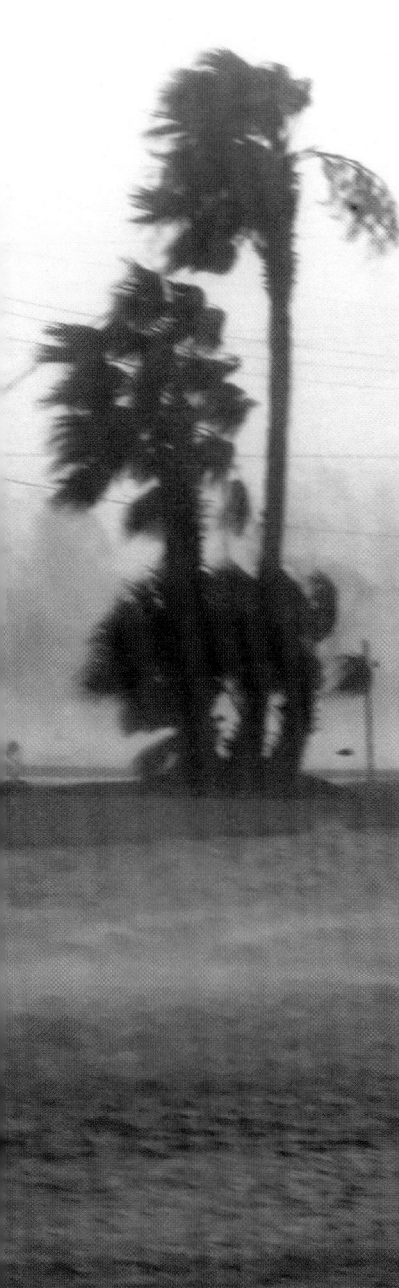

KATRINA UNLEASHES HER FURY

Katrina came ashore early Aug. 29 with howling 145-mph winds as a Category 4 storm, passing just east of New Orleans, sparing the city its full fury, although large stretches of the Mississippi coastline were flattened.

Gulf Coast residents awoke to a hauntingly unfamiliar and uncertain world: storefronts smashed to rubble, streets transformed into muddy rivers, cars submerged, even the roof of the seemingly invincible Louisiana Superdome split open.

But it's what they couldn't see that might prove most frightening in the coming days.

A grim precursor of what could lie ahead in Louisiana: After the storm passed, a body was seen beneath an elevated portion of Interstate 10 just east of downtown New Orleans, floating amid tires, tree limbs and other debris.

There was still plenty of damage in the city, including in the historic French Quarter, where the storm toppled brick walls and trees.

In a particularly low-lying neighborhood on the south shore of Lake Pontchartrain, a levee along a canal gave way and forced dozens of residents to flee or scramble to the roofs when water rose to their gutters. In the eastside Ninth Ward, homes were flooded as far as the eye could see.

And an estimated 40,000 homes were flooded in St. Bernard Parish, east of the city.

"We have 80 percent of our city under water. Basically, everything north of I-10," New Orleans Mayor Ray Nagin told WWL-TV in New Orleans.

Trapped residents called frantically for rescuers to save them or family members from rooftops or in attics. Rescuers struggled to find enough boats to help.

The hurricane's economic impact could prove historic. Estimates of insurance claims ranged from $9 billion to $16 billion, which would make it one of the costliest storms on record.

• LEE HANCOCK and ARNOLD HAMILTON

08.29.05 - Kenner, LA - Hurricane Katrina made landfall with a vengeance, wrenching the roof off Backyard Bar B Que 10 miles west of New Orleans. • IRWIN THOMPSON

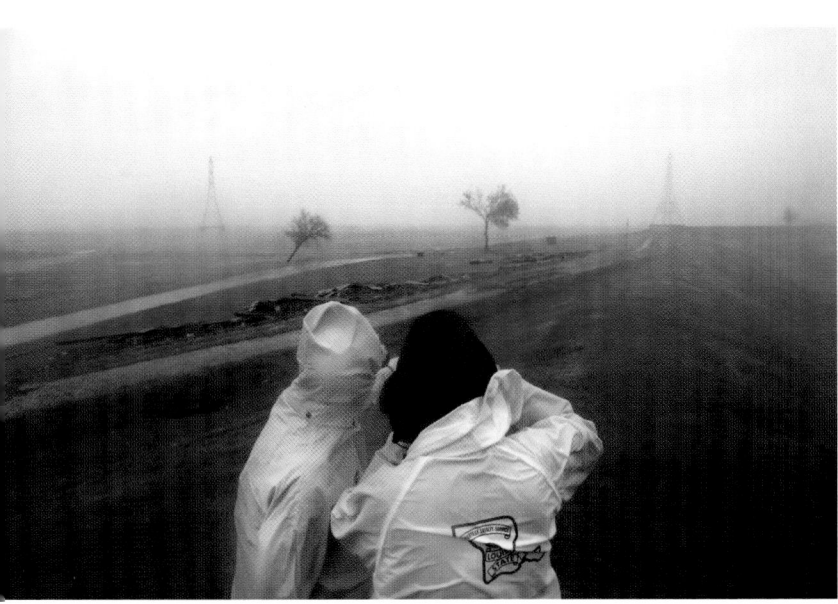

08.29.05 - Kenner, LA - Kenner Police Chief Nick Congemi (left) and Capt. Brian Etland withstood fierce winds as they checked the water level on Lake Pontchartrain in Kenner as the storm blew ashore. • IRWIN THOMPSON

CENTER
08.29.05 - New Orleans, LA - Firefighters waded back to their firehouse in the Ninth Ward after the hurricane passed through the city. Katrina ruined virtually all of the homes in the low-income Ninth Ward. • MICHAEL AINSWORTH

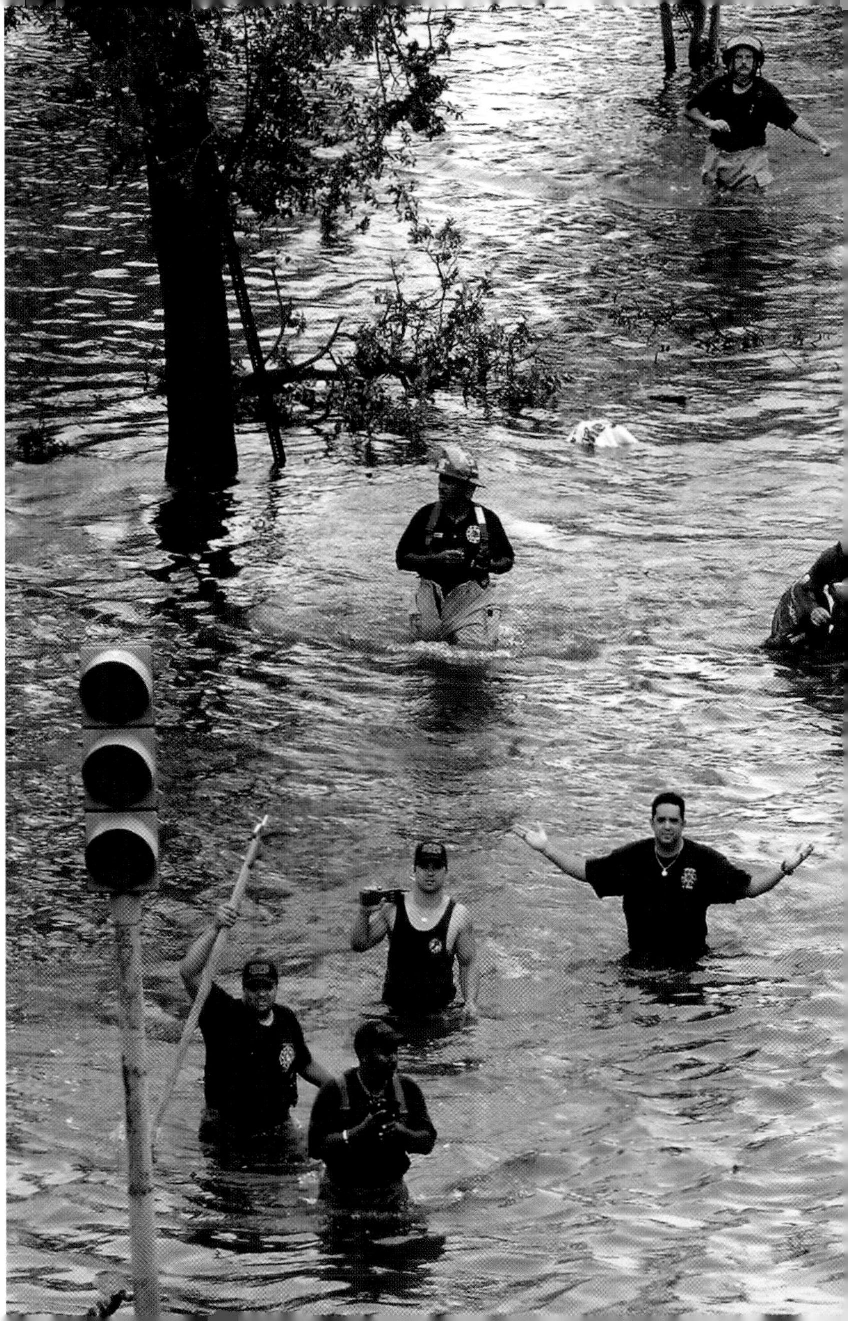

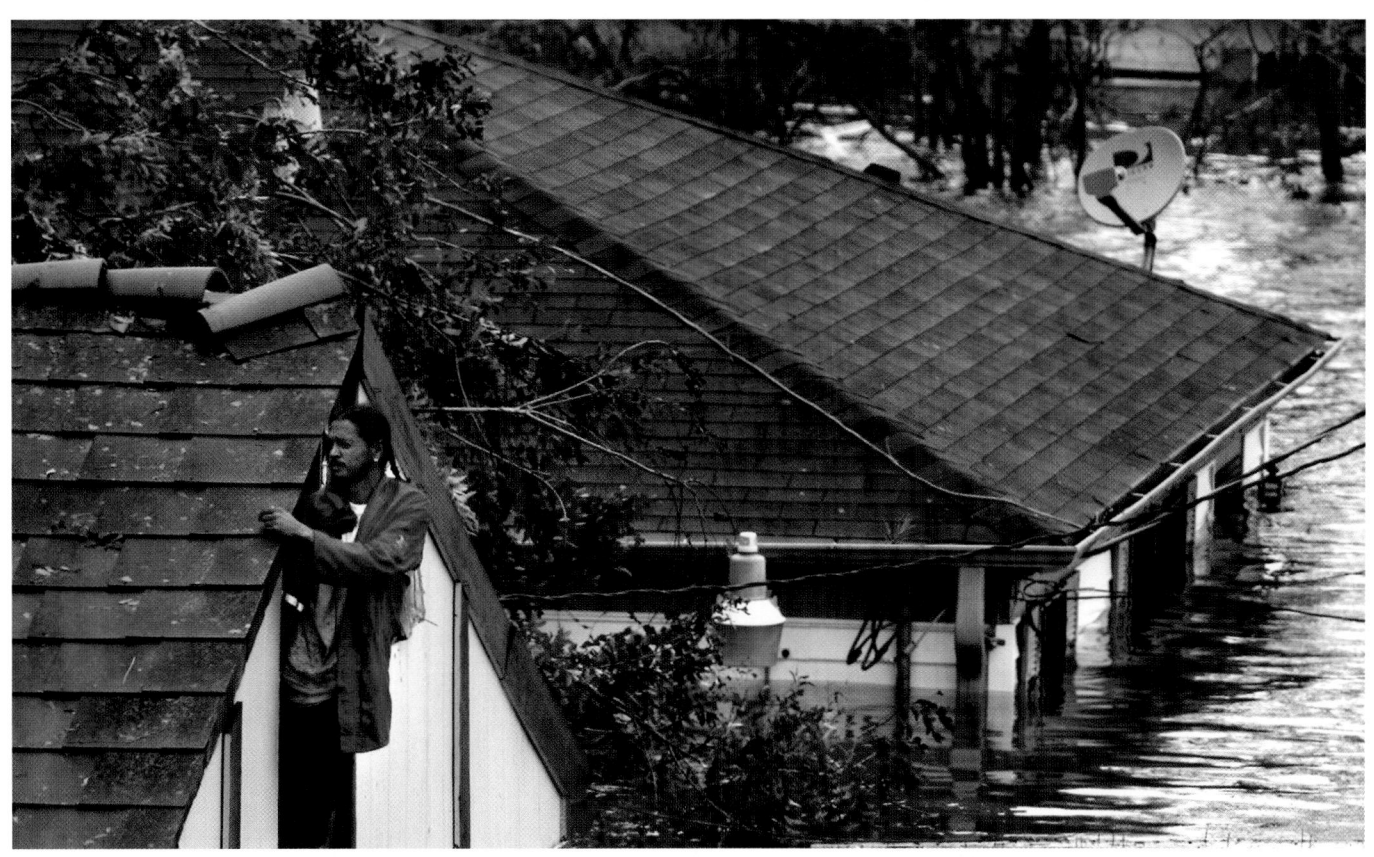

08.29.05 - New Orleans, LA - A man held fast to his home in the Ninth Ward, waiting to be rescued from the attic. • MICHAEL AINSWORTH

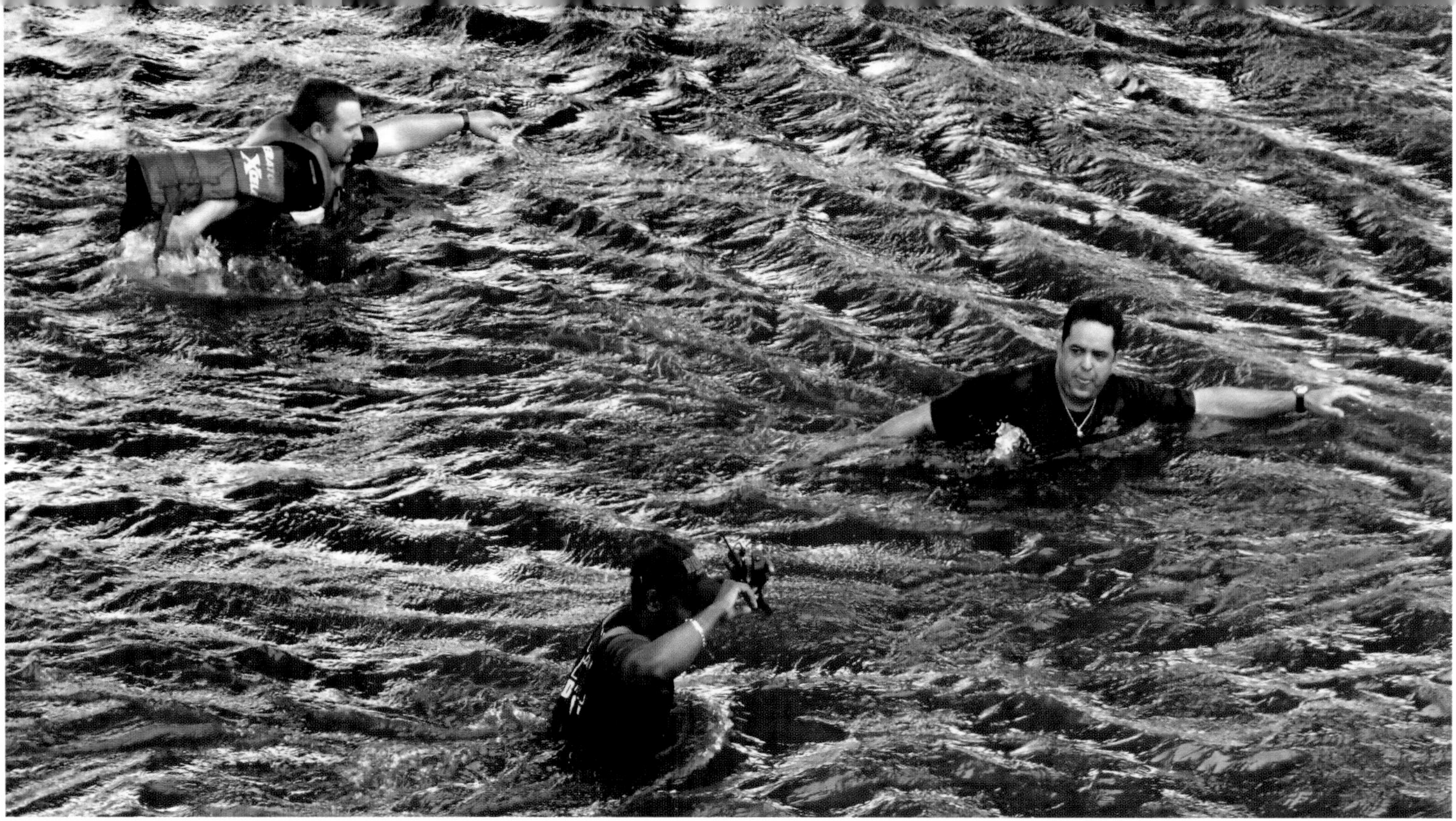

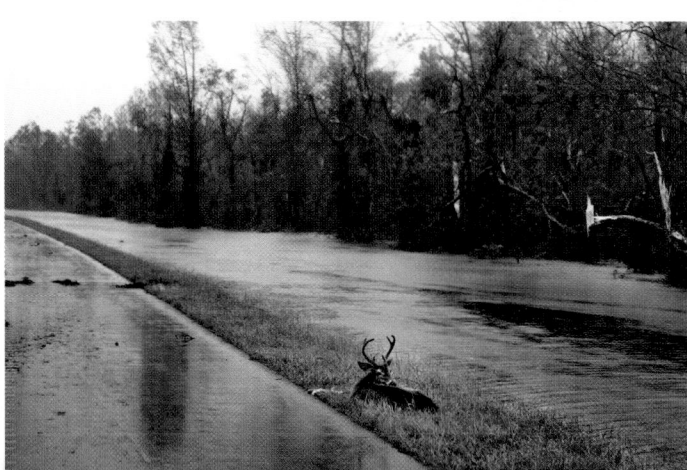

08.29.05 - New Orleans, LA - Firefighters searched for a boat in the choppy floodwaters. Several had brought boats to their station before Hurricane Katrina hit, and they ended up helping about 2,000 people to safety. The storm and the flooding that followed inundated at least half of New Orleans' fire stations and knocked out the emergency communications system for days, undermining firefighting and rescue efforts. • MICHAEL AINSWORTH

CENTER
08.29.05 - East of Slidell, LA - A deer rested on the shoulder of Interstate 10 in the company of floodwaters at the Mississippi state line. • LOUIS DELUCA

RIGHT
08.29.05 - New Orleans, LA - Looting became a major problem in the aftermath of the storm. Residents of a housing project were taken into custody and accused of looting a grocery store. • MICHAEL AINSWORTH

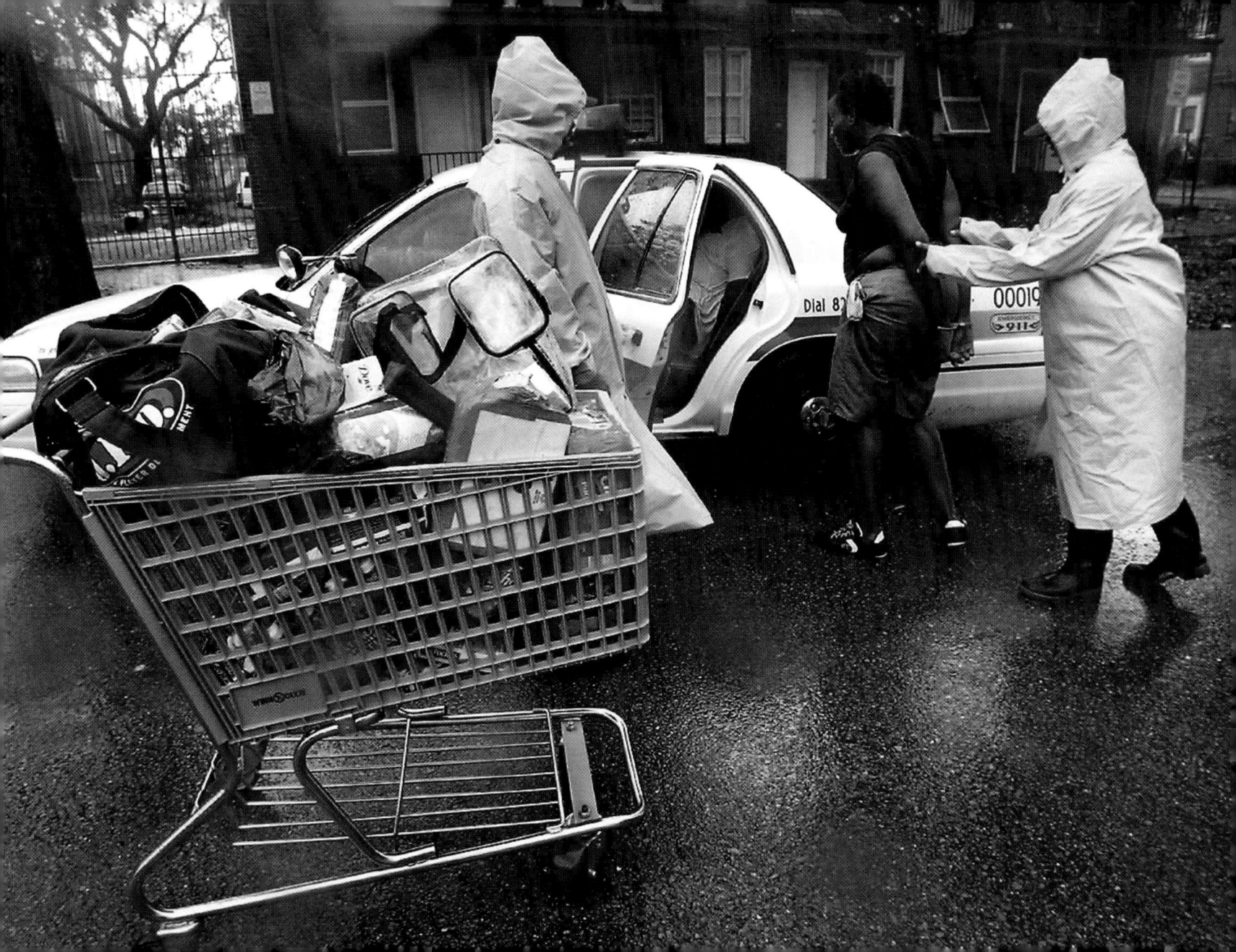

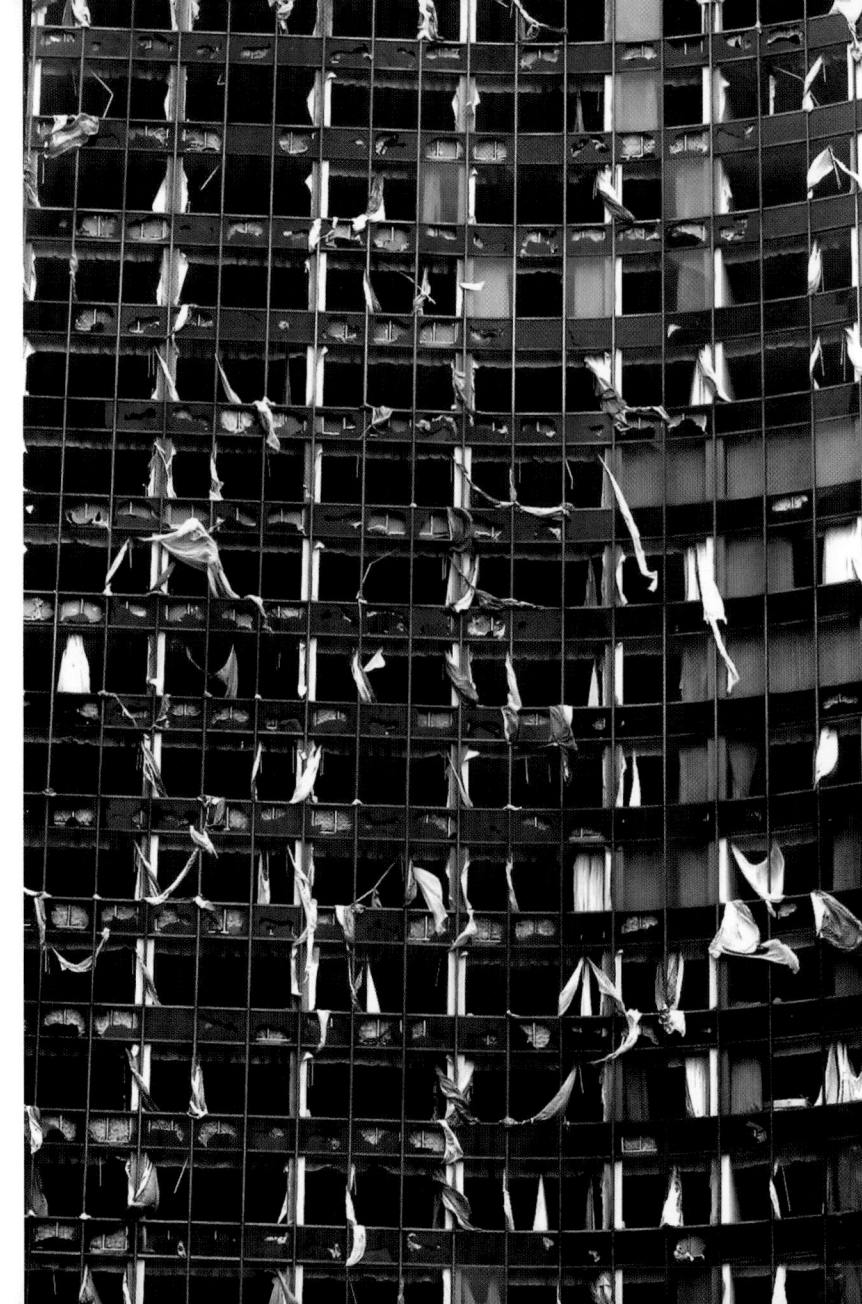

08.29.05 - New Orleans, LA - Curtains billowed from blown-out windows at the Hyatt Regency, the 1,184-room convention hotel near the damaged Louisiana Superdome. Guests had been evacuated to the hotel's ballrooms.
• MICHAEL AINSWORTH

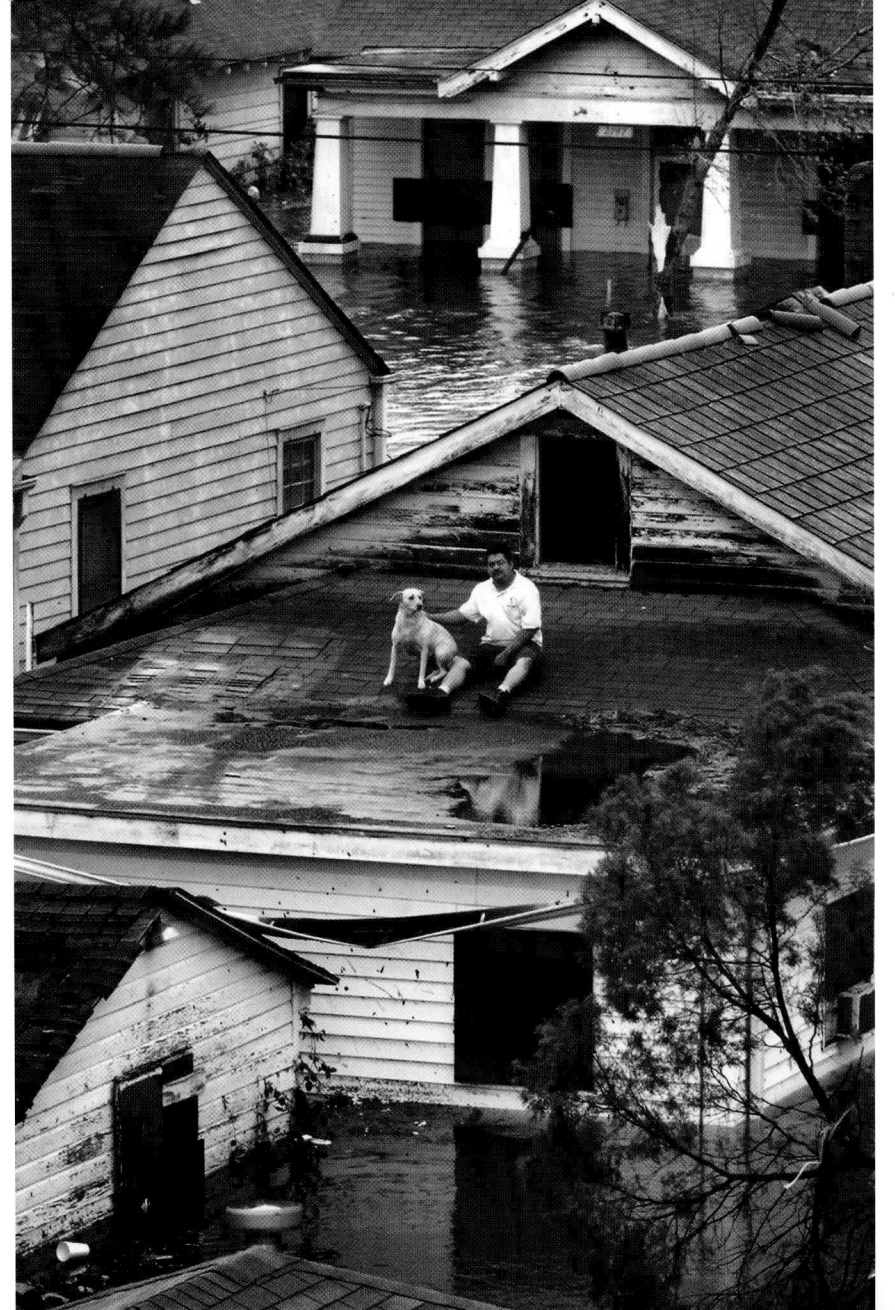

08.29.05 - New Orleans, LA - A man and his dog waited to be rescued from the roof of their Ninth Ward home. Many owners were forced to abandon their pets in the evacuation process, while some refused to leave their companions behind.
• MICHAEL AINSWORTH

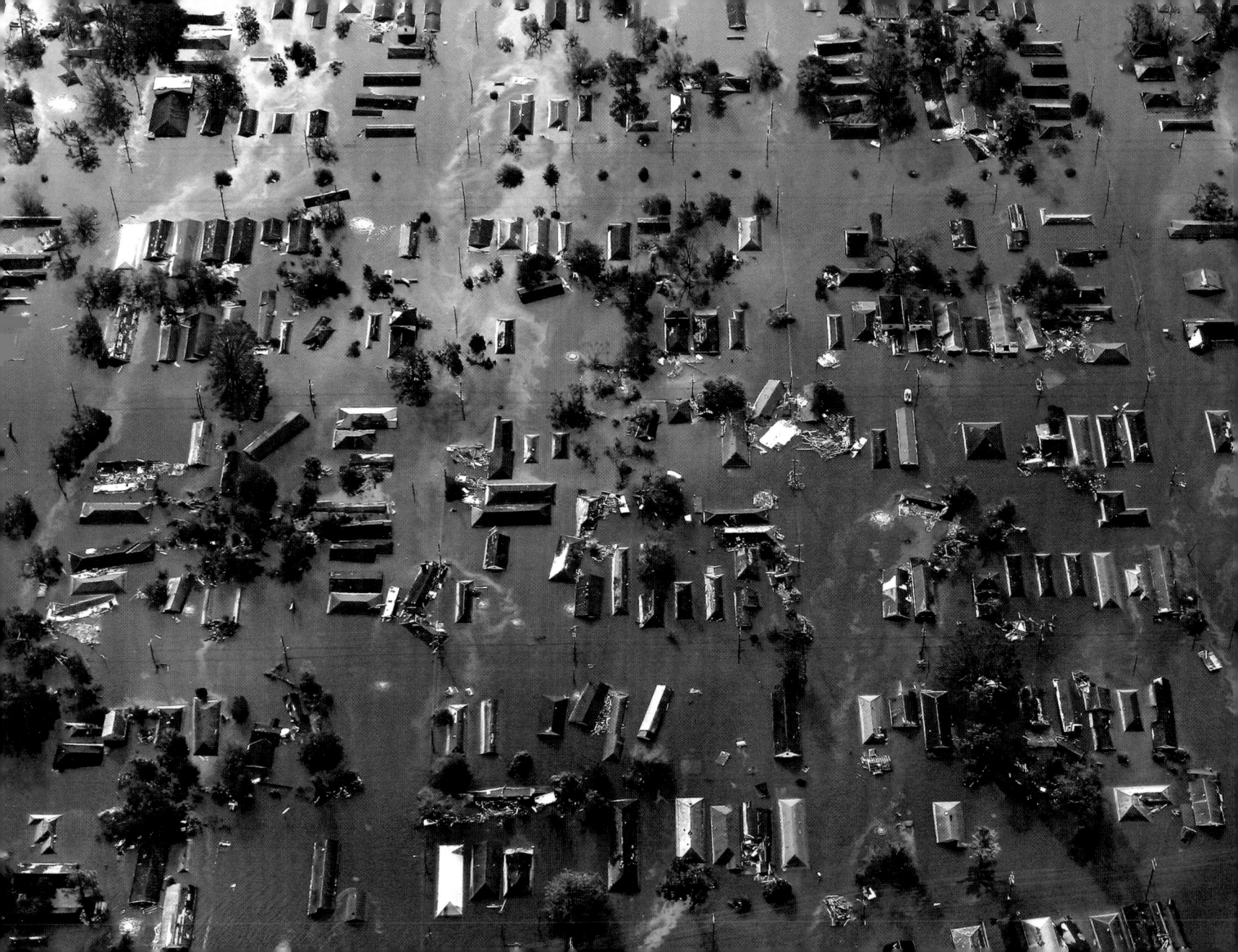

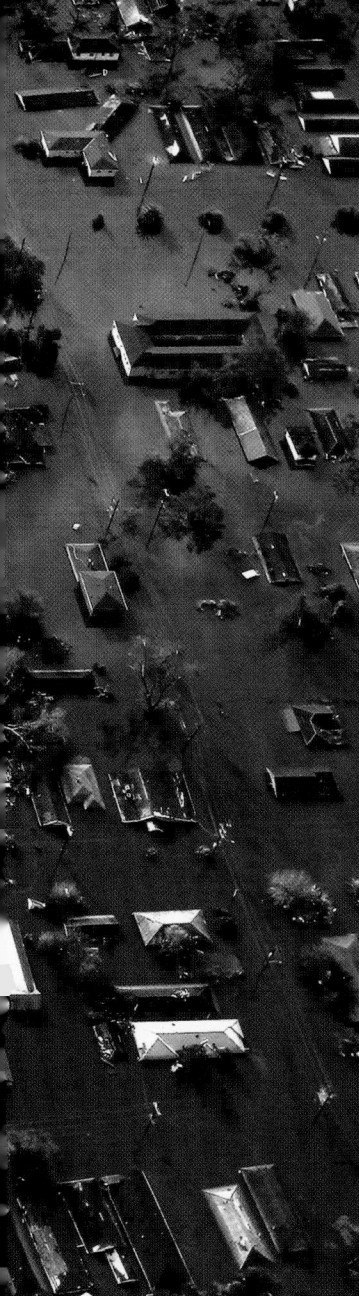

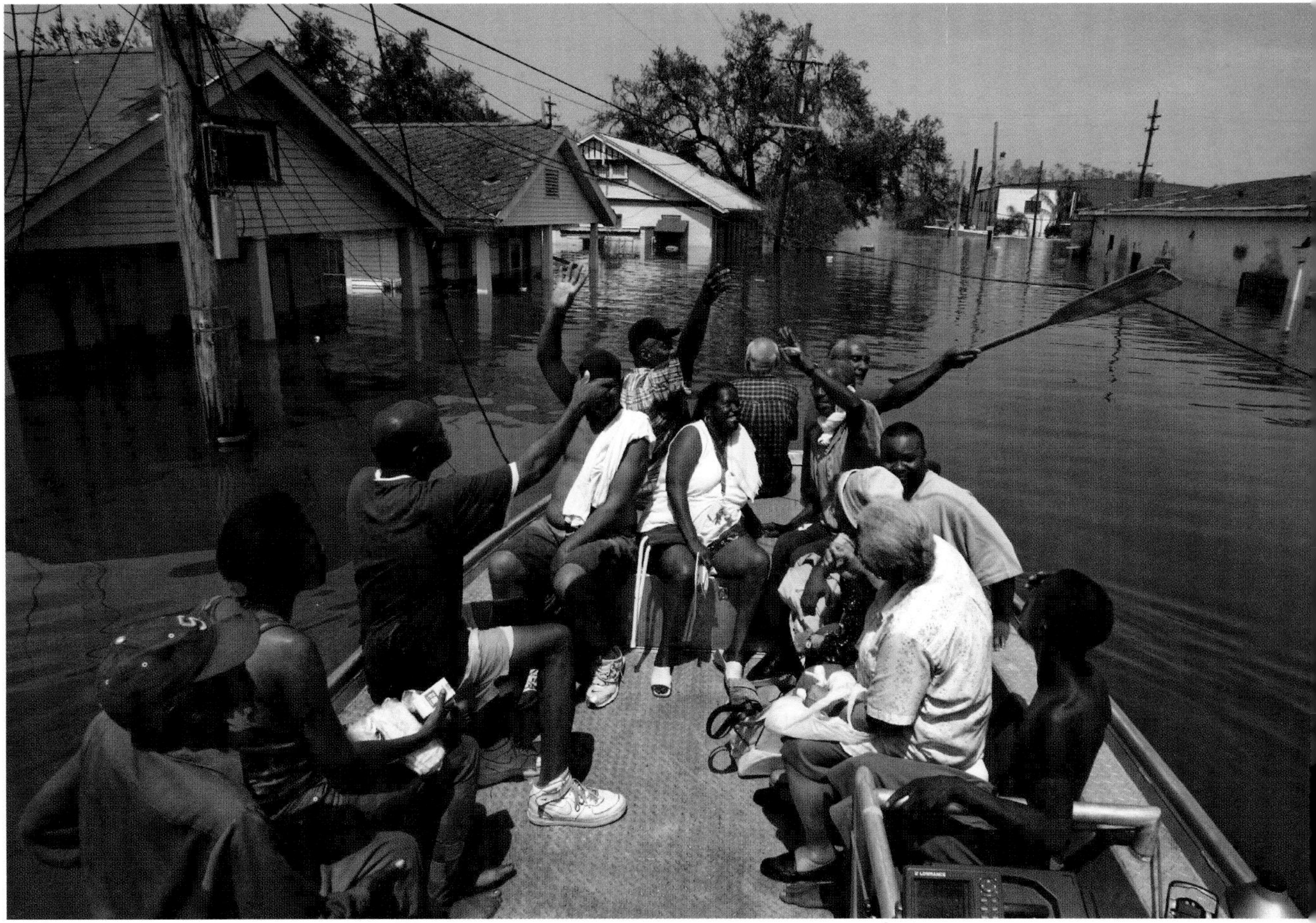

08.30.05 - New Orleans, LA - Residents raised up a dead power line in order to float by after being rescued from a nursing home in the Ninth Ward. • IRWIN THOMPSON

LEFT
08.30.05 - New Orleans, LA - A patchwork of roofs pushed through the floodwaters east of downtown, one day after Hurricane Katrina's march through the Crescent City. Floodwaters left the city a horrific mix of struggling humanity and swamped infrastructure. • SMILEY N. POOL

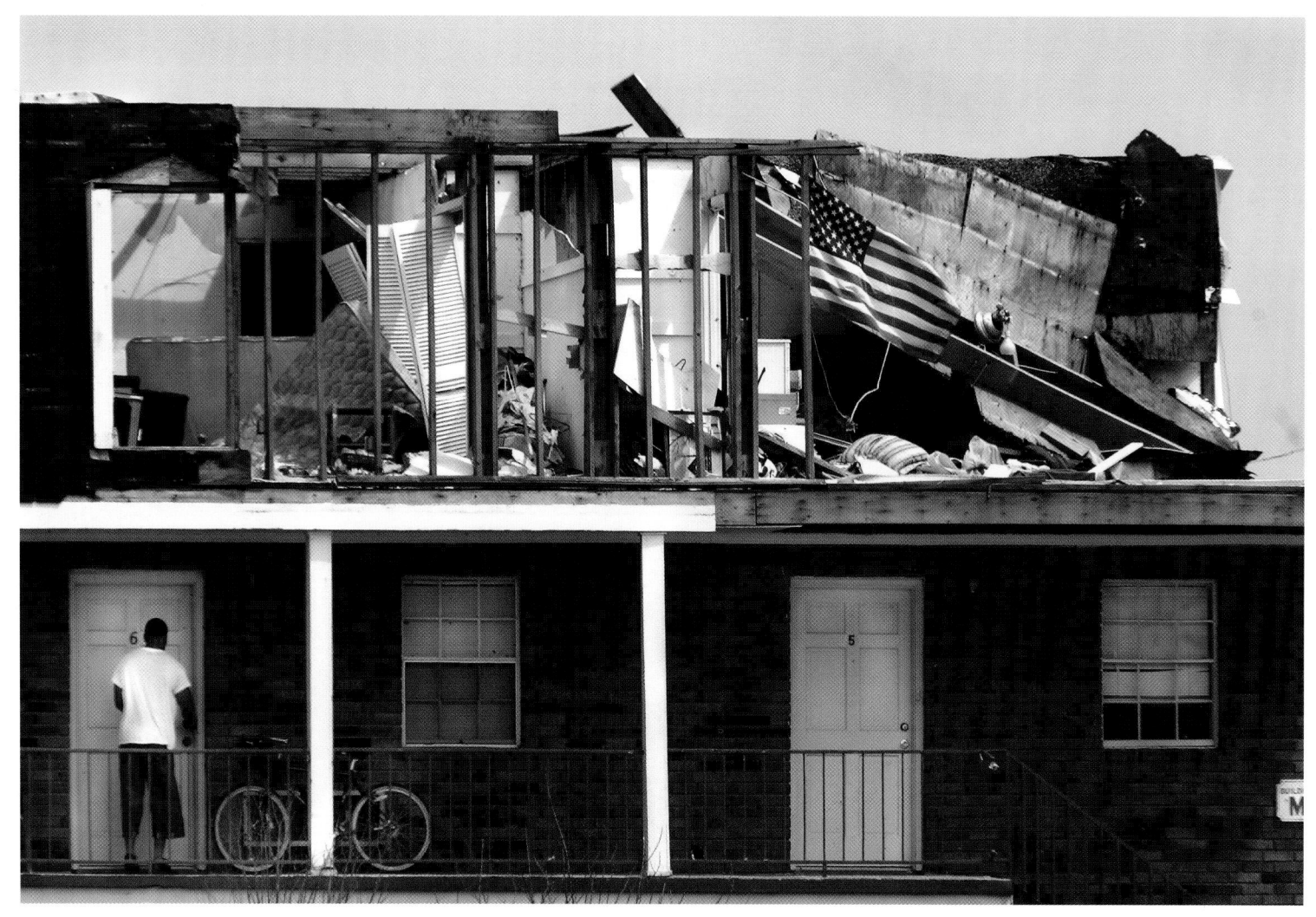

08.30.05 - Gulfport, MS - The American flag fluttered over one of the damaged apartment complexes off U.S. Highway 90. • LOUIS DELUCA

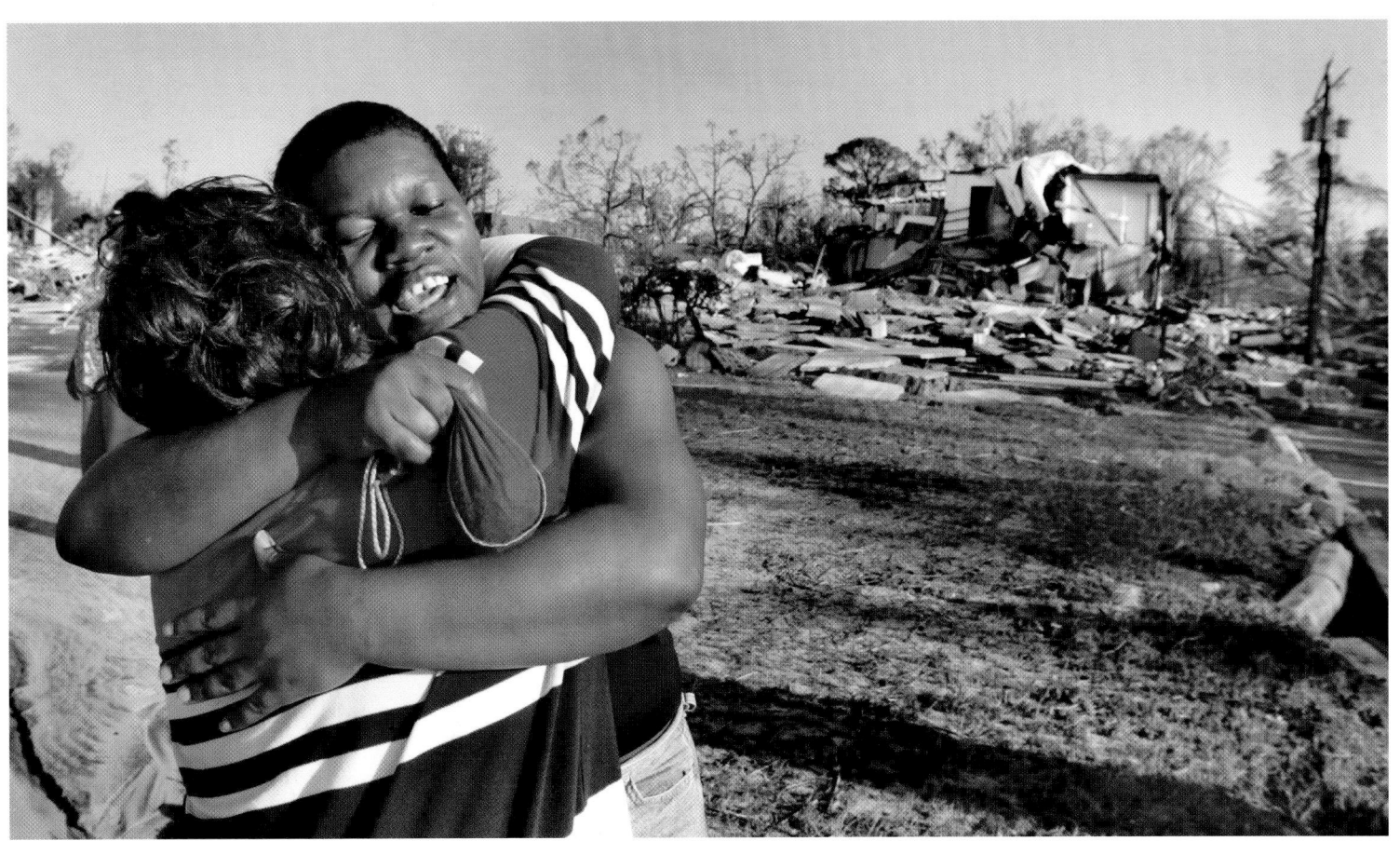

08.30.05 - Gulfport, MS - Roxona Park held fast to her friend Althea Brown as they surveyed the storm's devastation. Their apartments, on U.S. Highway 90 along the coast, were destroyed. "We have nothing left," Ms. Park sobbed. • LOUIS DELUCA

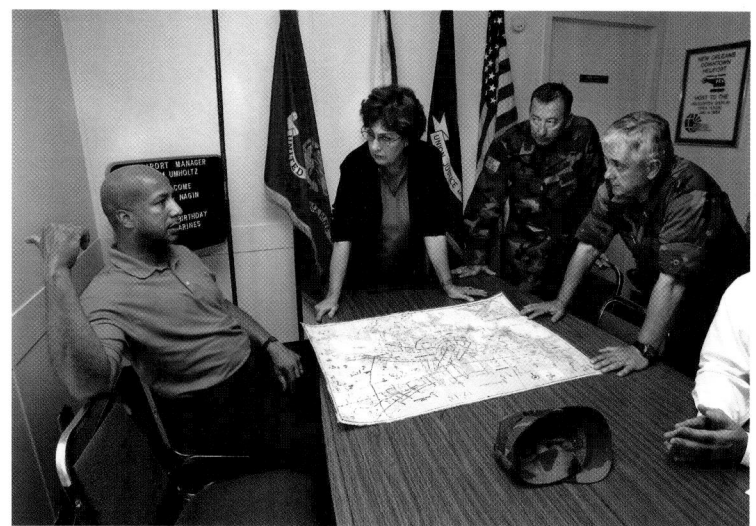

08.30.05 - New Orleans, LA - Mayor Ray Nagin (from left), Louisiana Gov. Kathleen Blanco and Maj. Gen. Bennett Landreneau were briefed by Brig. Gen. Brod Veillon of the Louisiana National Guard about the rising floodwater. • MICHAEL AINSWORTH

RIGHT
08.30.05 - New Orleans, LA - A breach in a levee can be seen in an aerial view of damage one day after Katrina made landfall. • SMILEY N. POOL

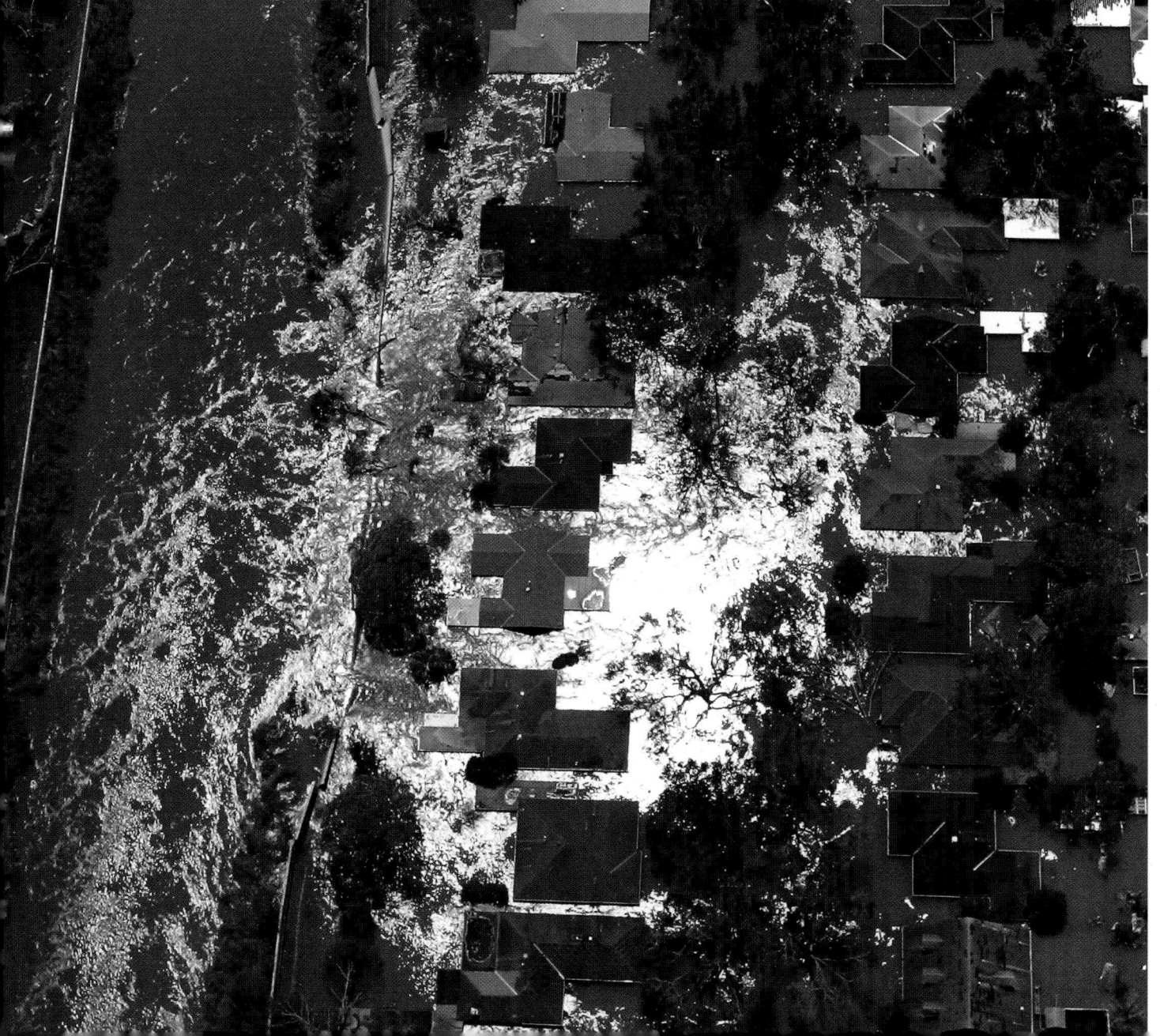

08.30.05 - New Orleans, LA - Residents made their way to the Superdome, though the governor had ordered the stadium evacuated. Inside, the air was sour, and bathrooms were filthy.
• MICHAEL AINSWORTH

OPPOSITE PAGE
08.30.05 - New Orleans, LA - Deraldine Burnett, 61, of New Orleans tried to make herself comfortable at the Superdome after she was evacuated from her flooded home. The stadium was jammed with people who hadn't showered in days.
• MICHAEL AINSWORTH

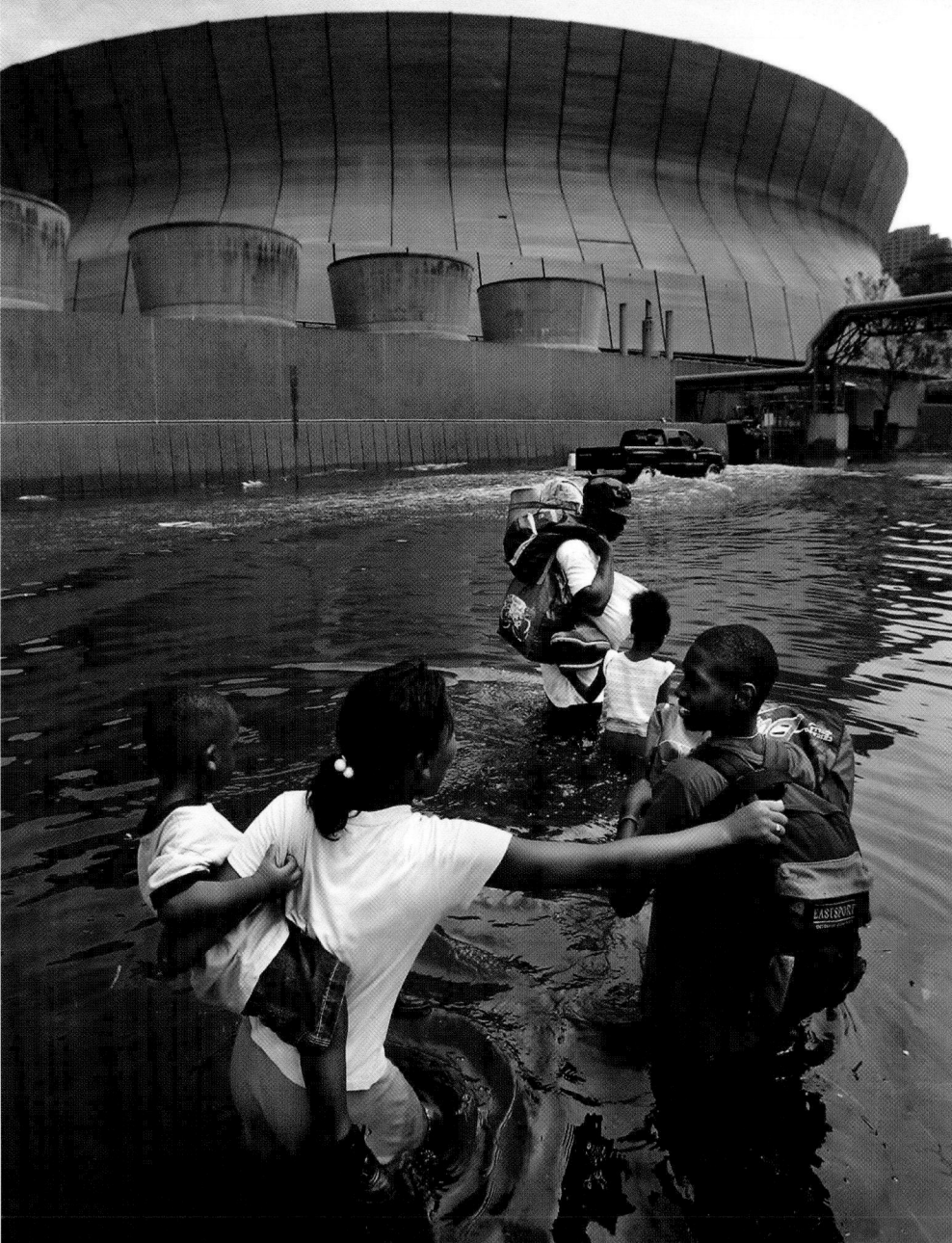

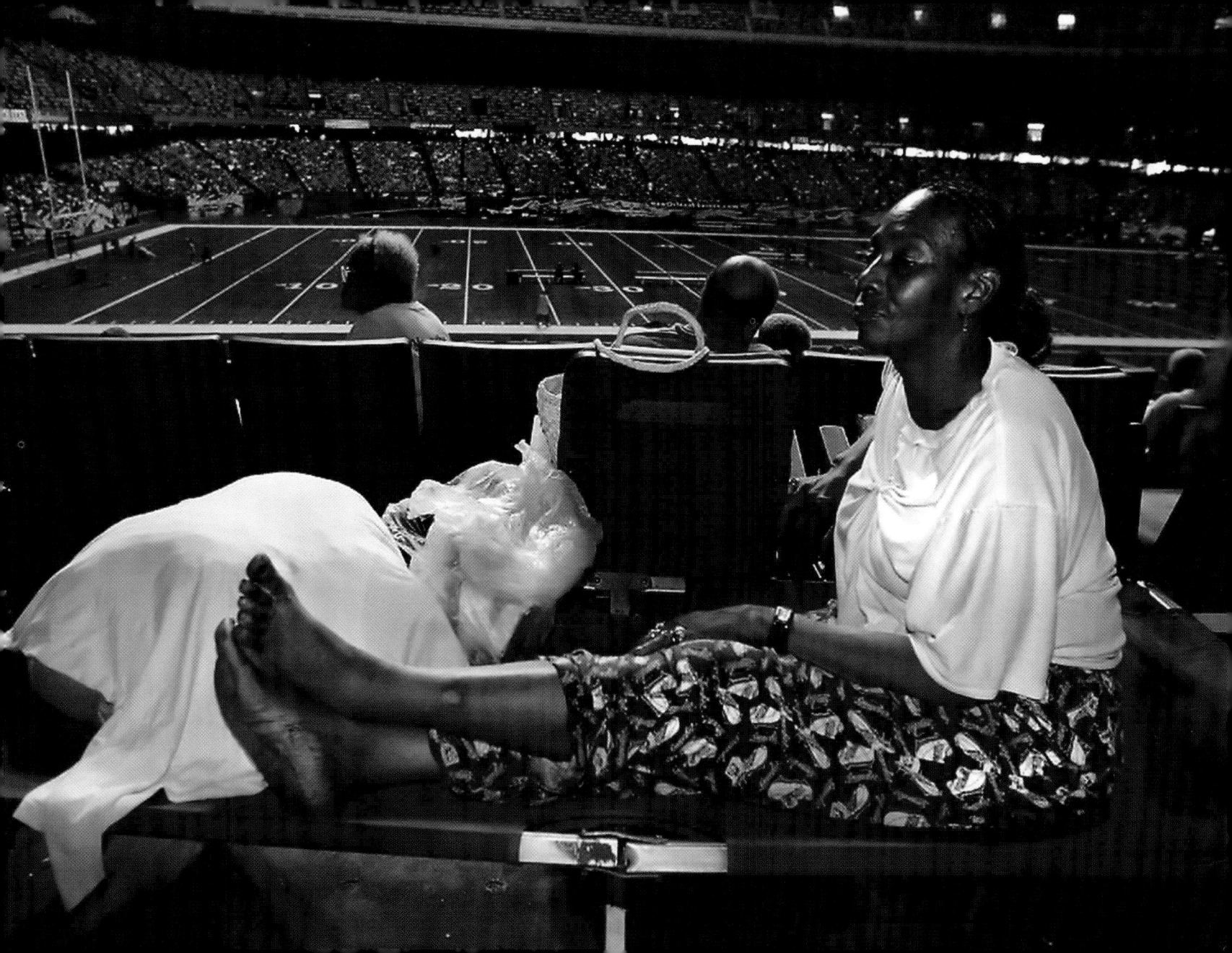

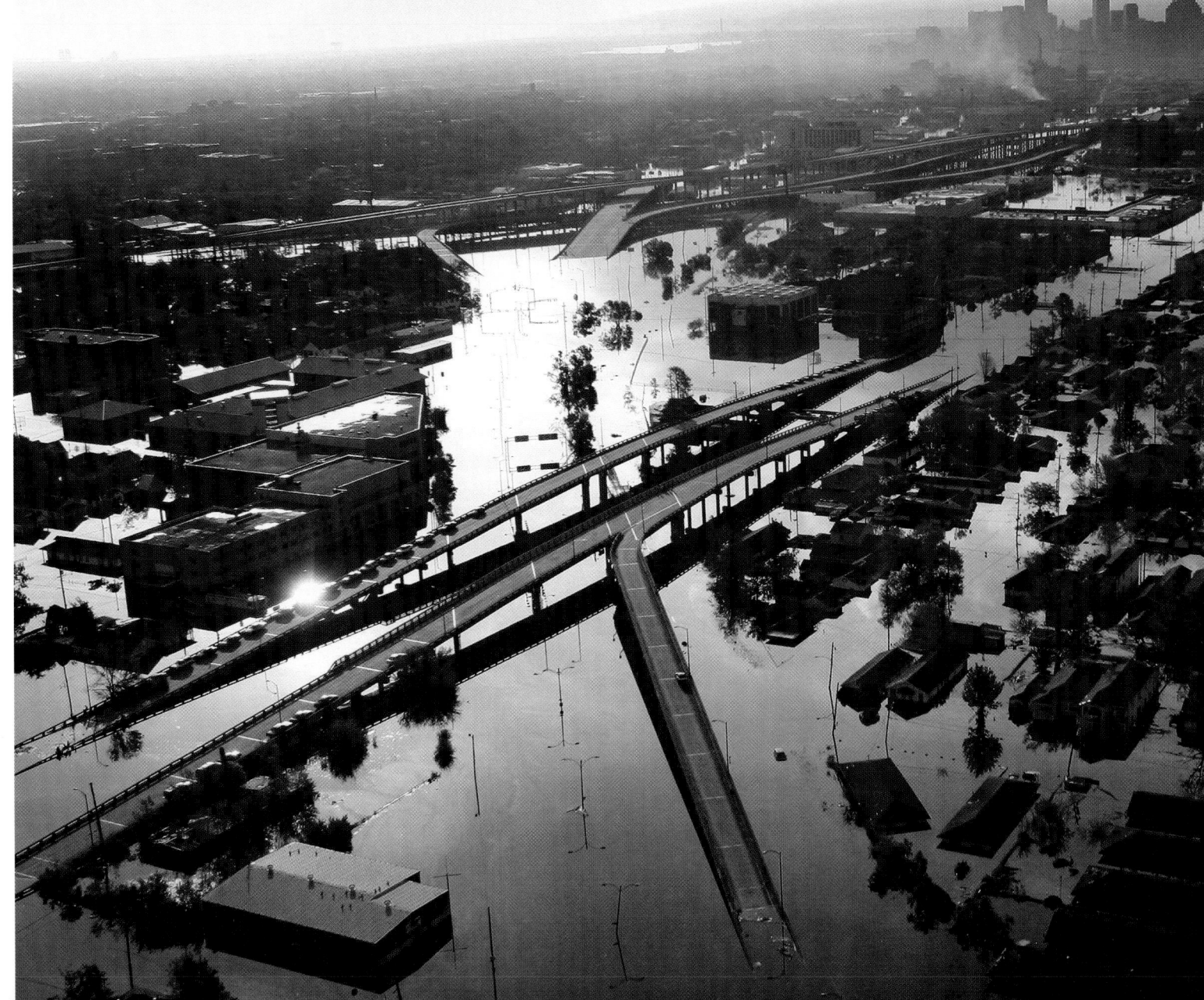

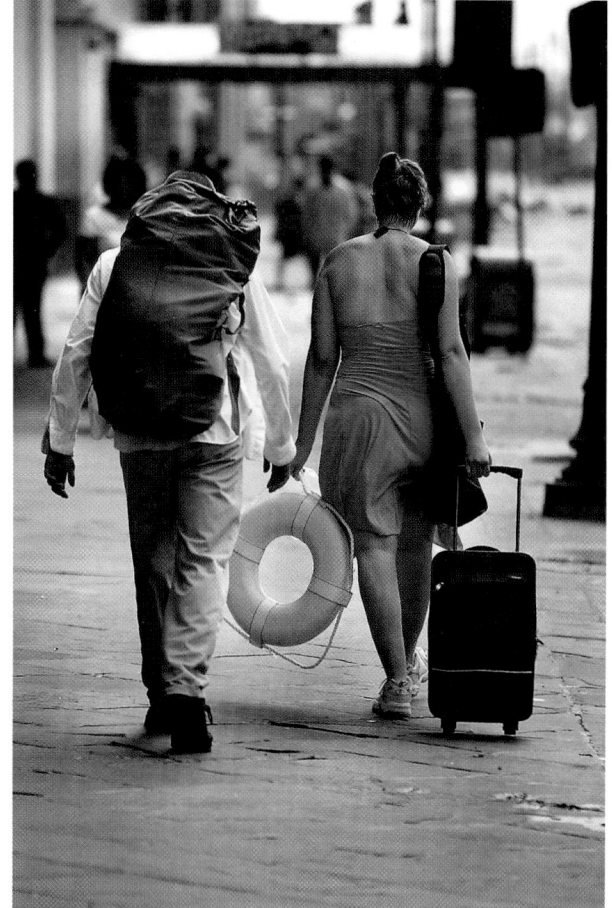

08.30.05 - New Orleans, LA - Highways, homes and buildings were swamped by water in a view of storm damage looking east toward downtown.
• SMILEY N. POOL

08.30.05 - New Orleans, LA - Tourists headed down Canal Street with their life preserver in tow. After the storm, looters rampaged through the Central Business District's main thoroughfare, sloshing through hip-deep water and ripping open the steel gates on the front of several clothing and jewelry stores. • MICHAEL AINSWORTH

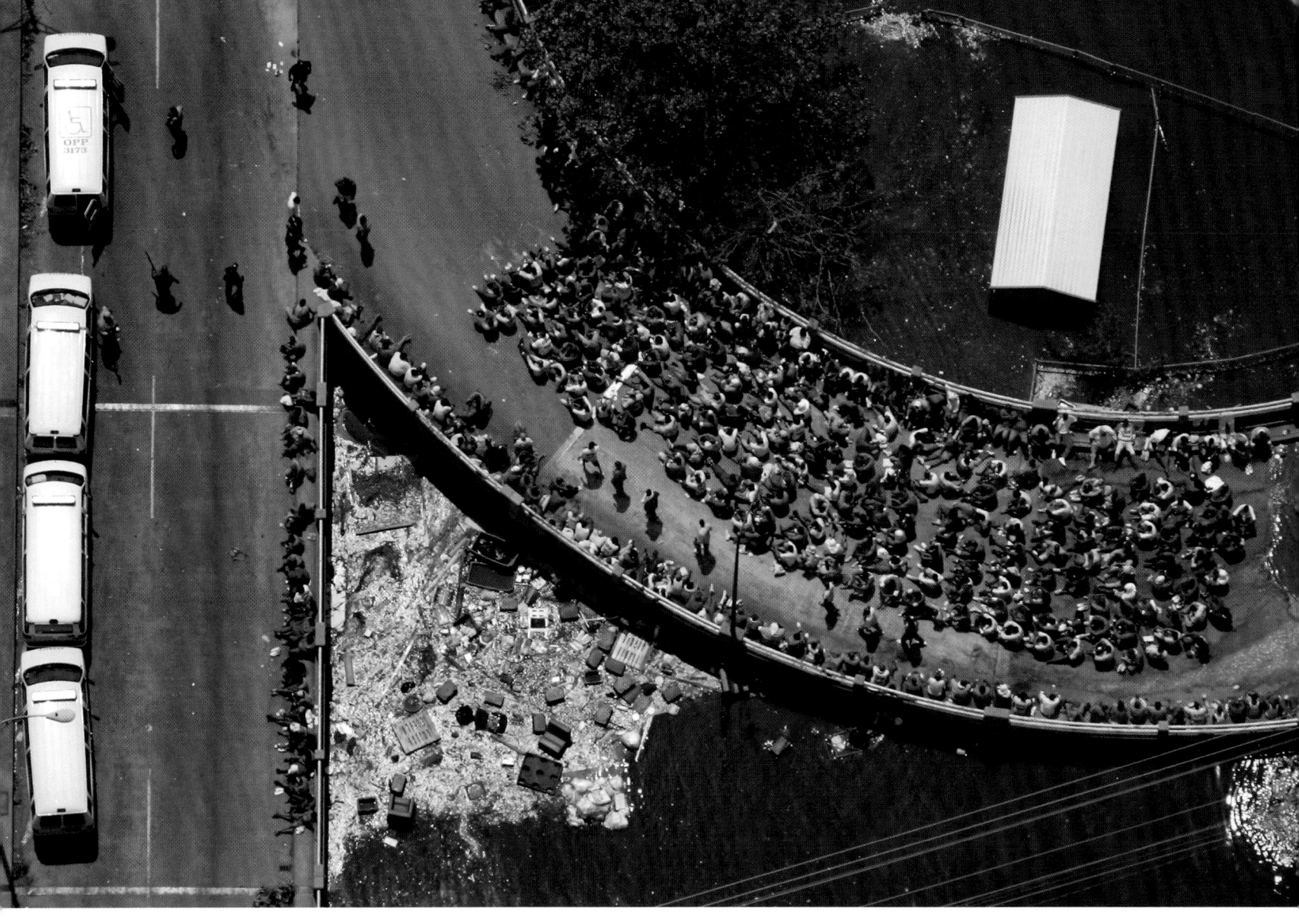

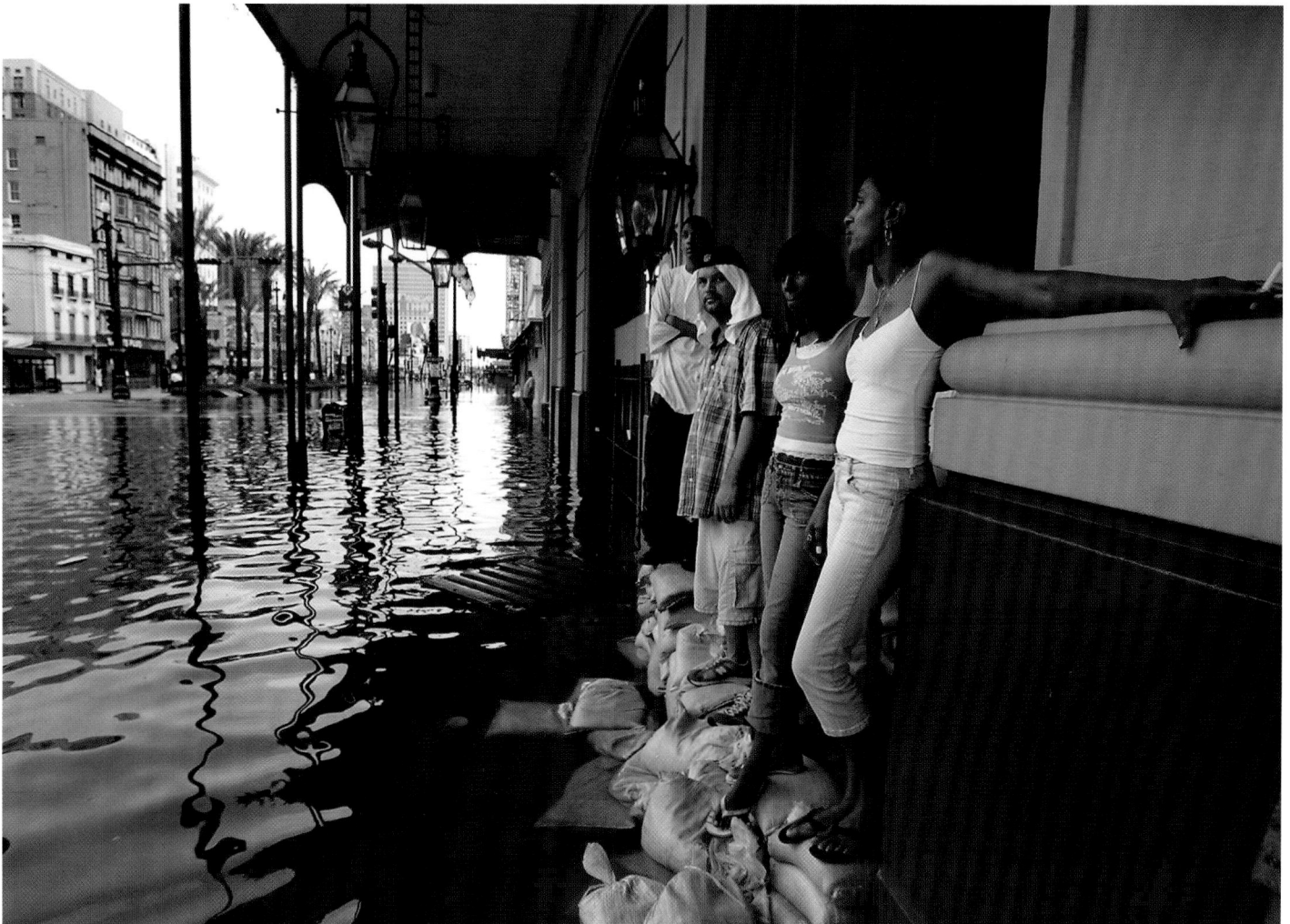

08.30.05 - New Orleans, LA - Guests of the Astor Crown Plaza hotel stood on sandbags and took in the view of a watery Canal Street. • MICHAEL AINSWORTH

08.30.05 - New Orleans, LA - Orleans Parish prisoners were held on a highway overpass and watched over by guards as the water rose beneath them. Some inmates from the Jefferson and Orleans Parish prisons were evacuated as a precaution against possible unrest. "It is an ideal time to have unrest," said Louisiana Attorney General Charles Foti. "They're hot, and they're ready to go." • SMILEY N. POOL

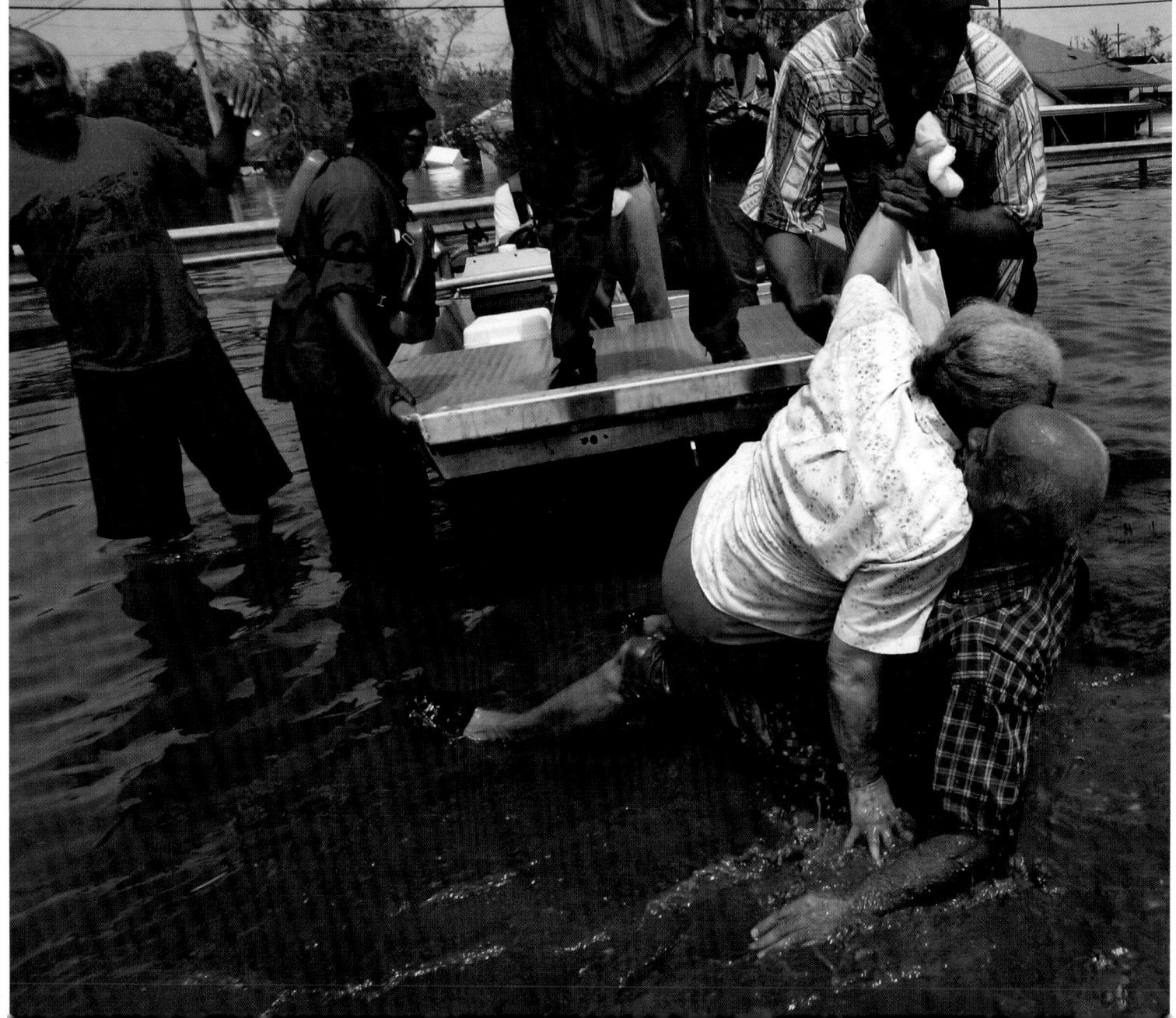

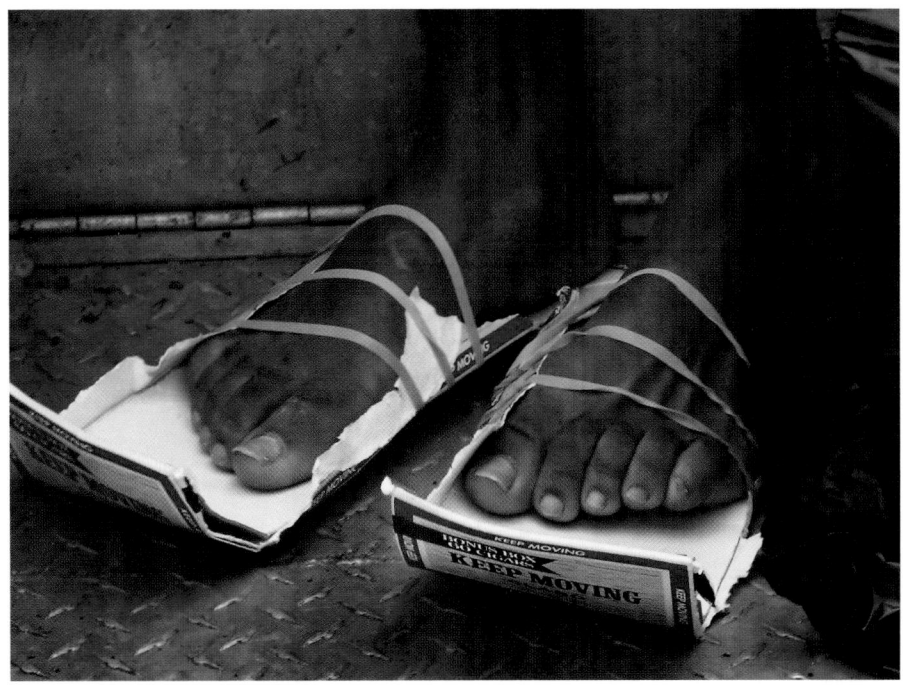

08.30.05 - New Orleans, LA - Jeremiah Ward got by on makeshift shoes after he was rescued in the Ninth Ward. Many storm evacuees had to flee without crucial possessions.
• IRWIN THOMPSON

Left
08.30.05 - New Orleans, LA - Ibry Smith (right) fell as he helped Norma Rankins out of a boat after they were rescued from a nursing home in the Ninth Ward. • IRWIN THOMPSON

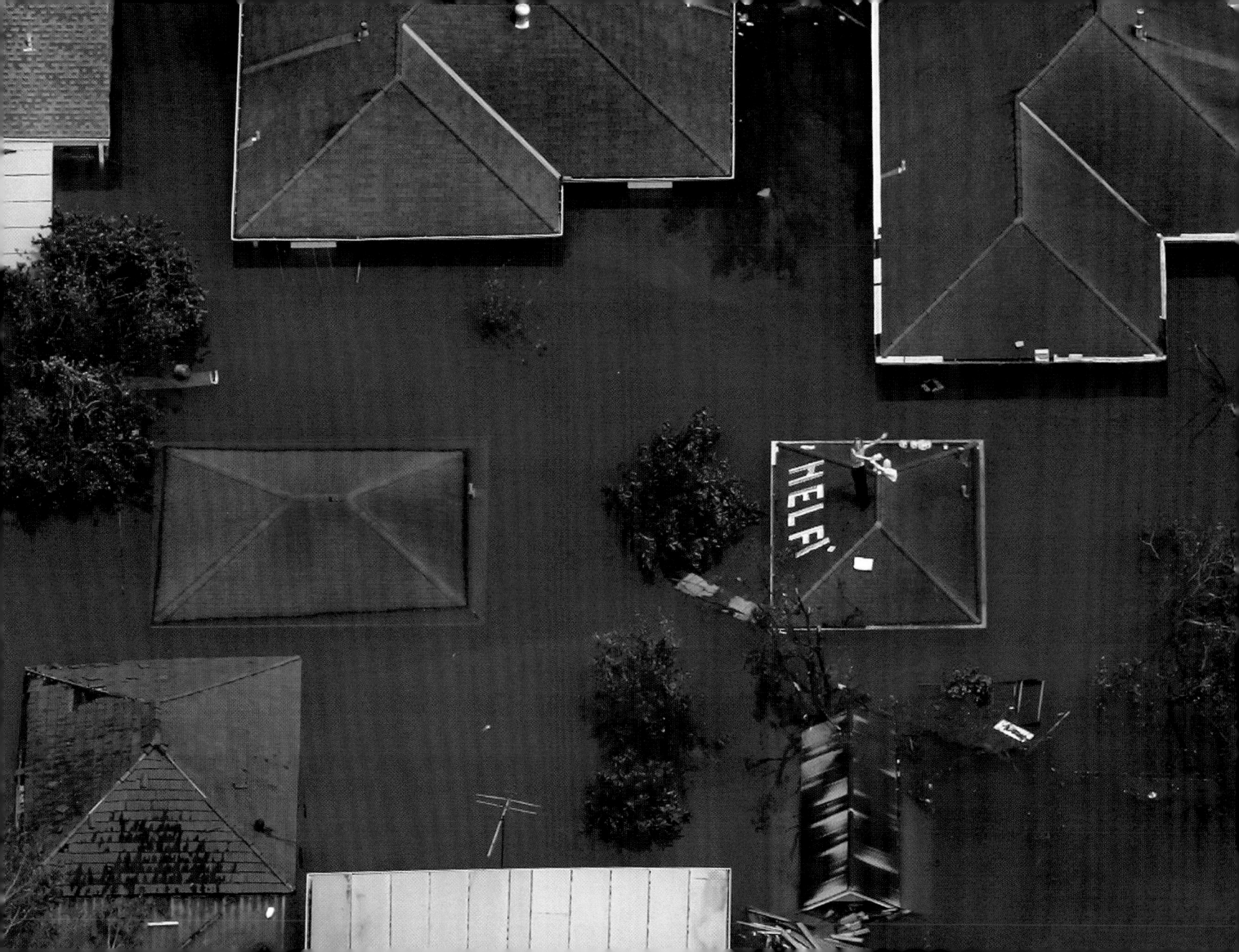

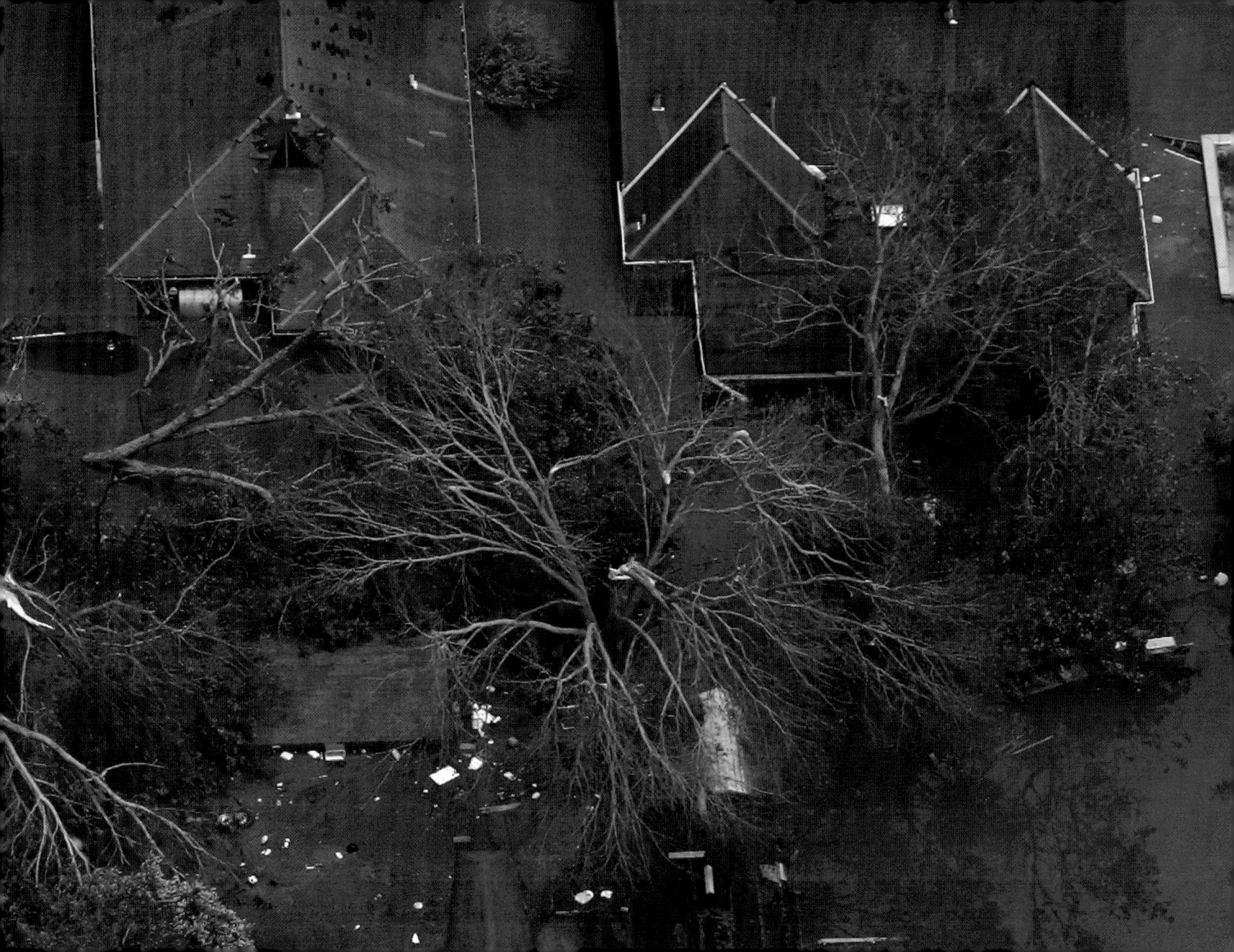

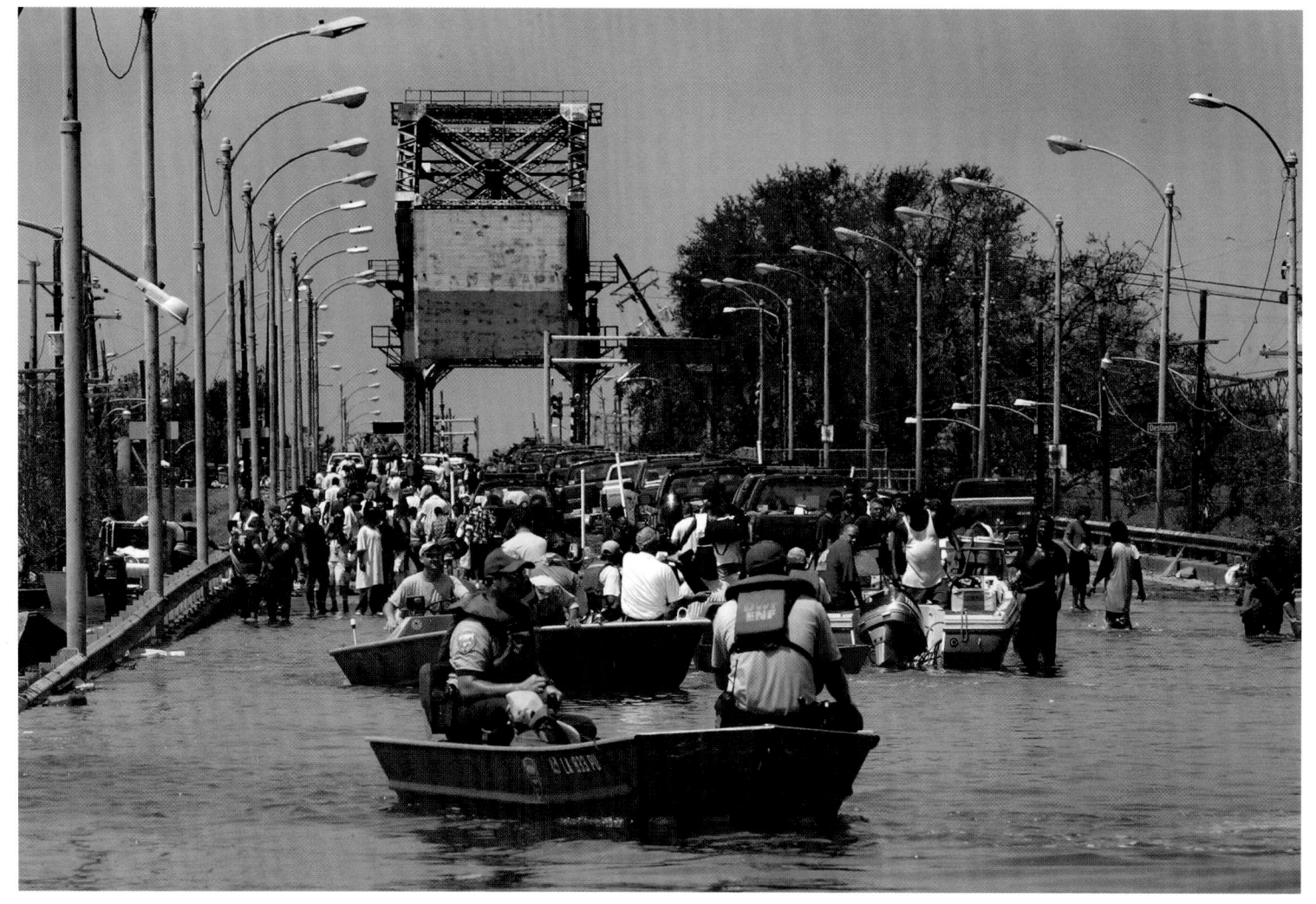

08.30.05 - New Orleans, LA - Rescue crews at the St. Claude bridge helped transport people from the Ninth Ward. • IRWIN THOMPSON

<small>Previous Page</small>

08.30.05 - New Orleans, LA - A man trapped on his roof tried to get the attention of a helicopter by sending out a call for help in giant letters. • MICHAEL AINSWORTH

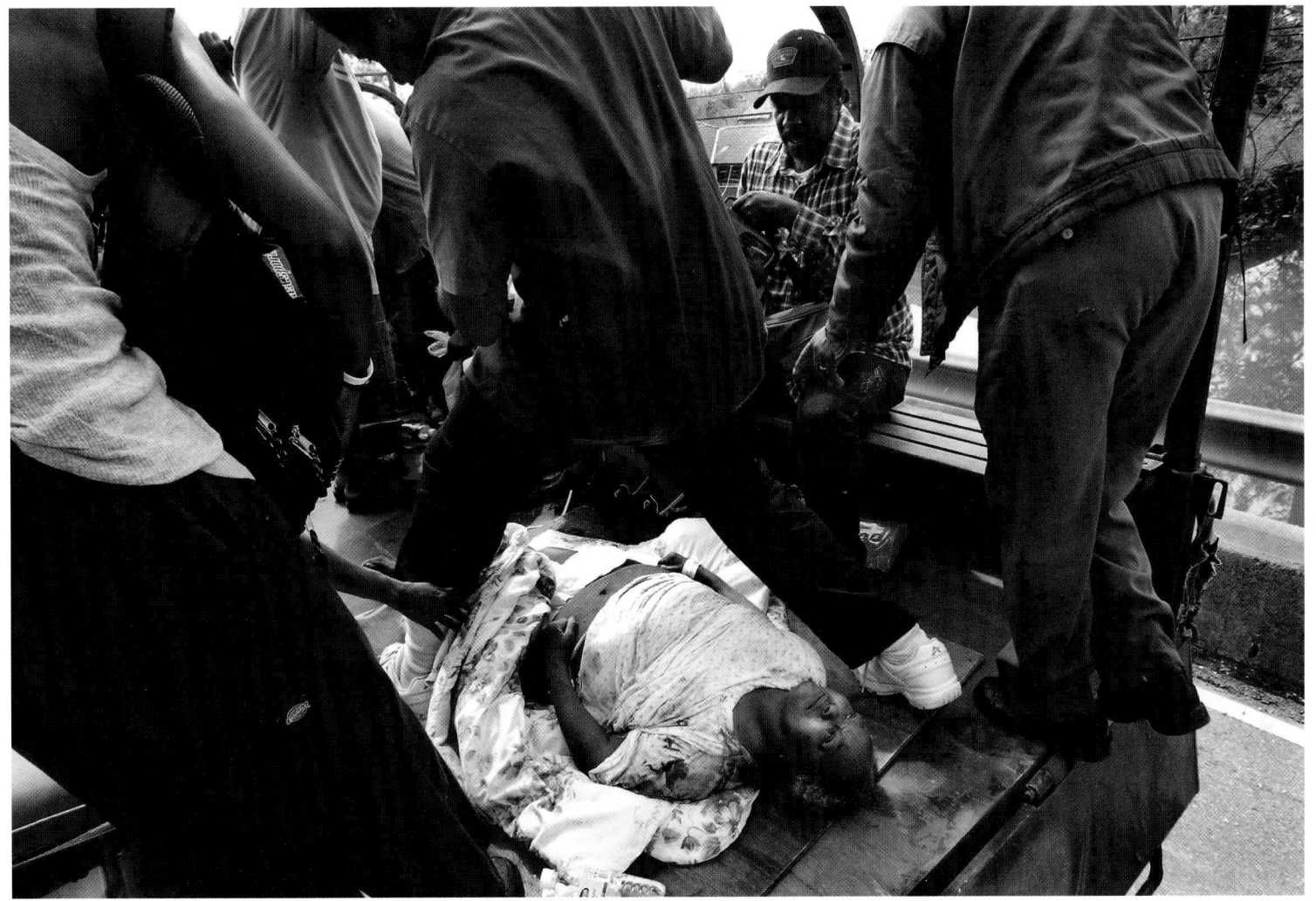

08.30.05 - New Orleans, LA - After being rescued in the Ninth Ward, evacuees walked around 70-year-old Ida Walker to get on a National Guard truck headed for the Superdome. Mrs. Walker has diabetes and a feeding tube. • IRWIN THOMPSON

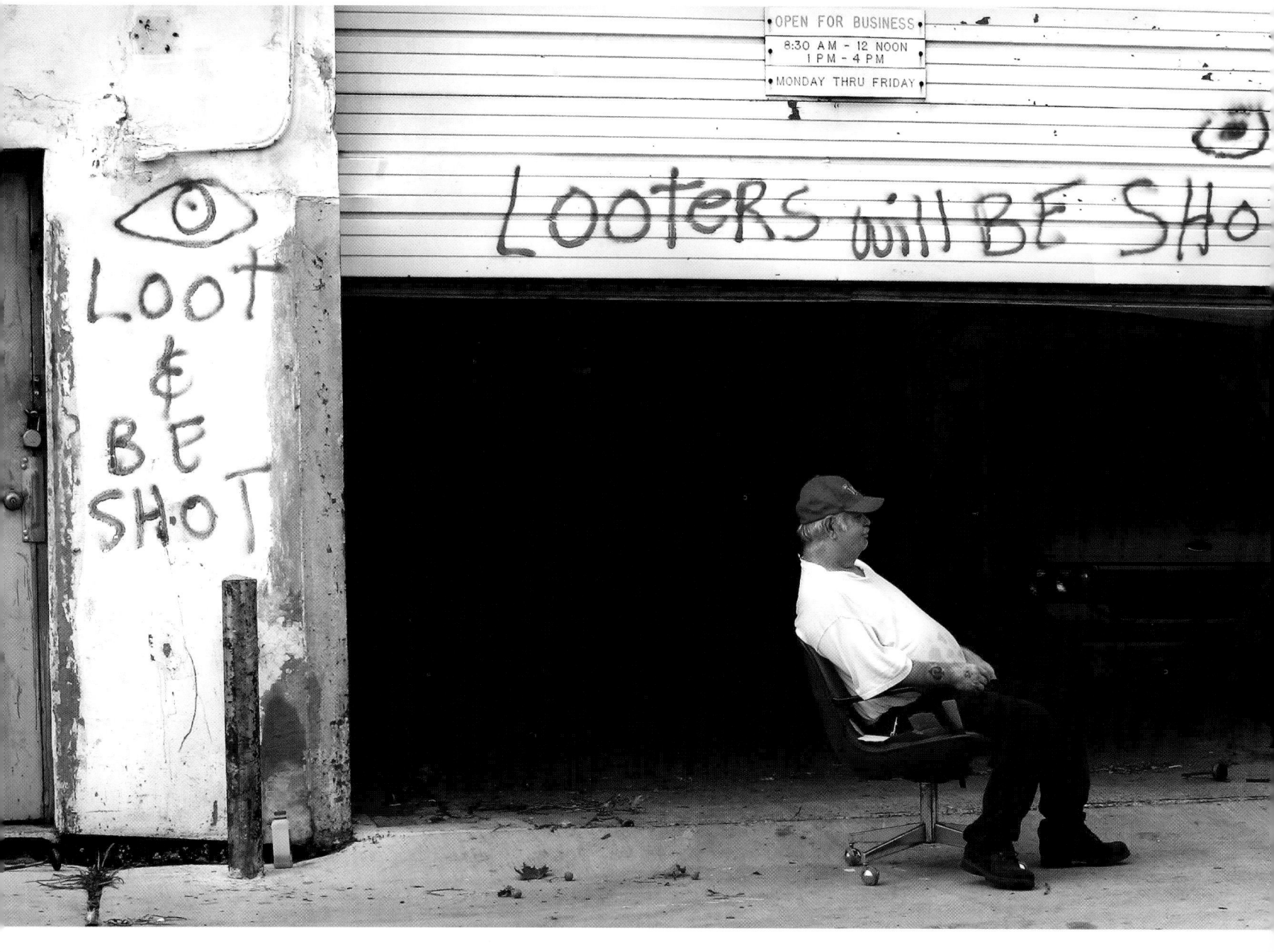

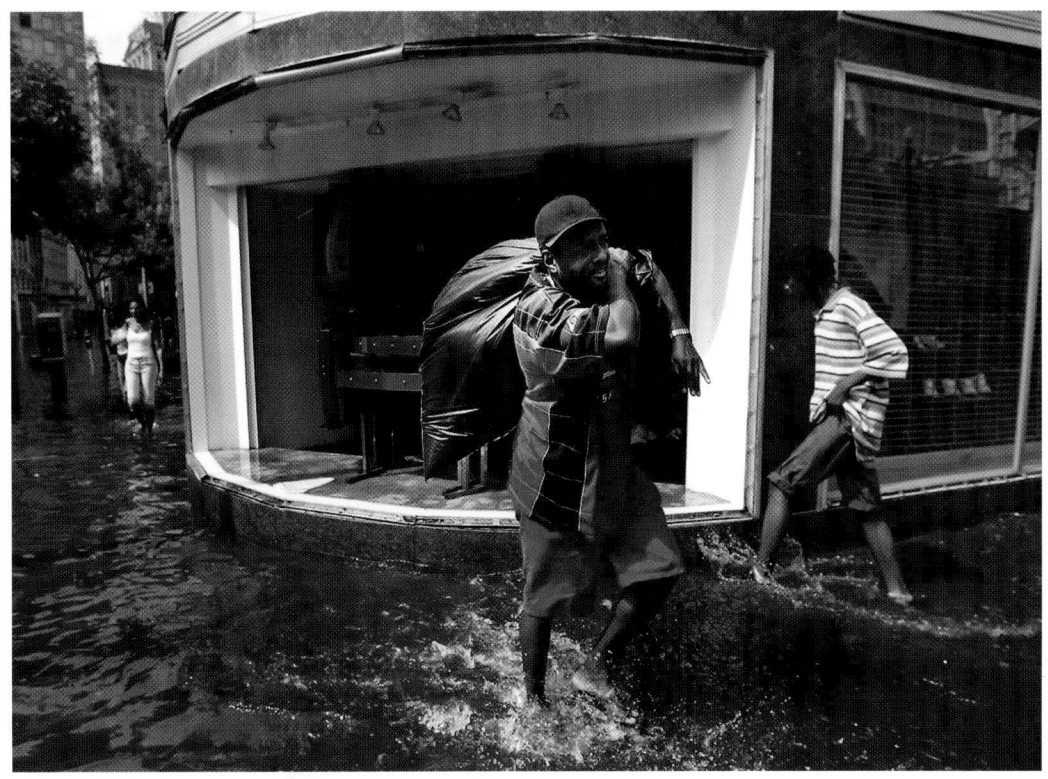

08.30.05 - New Orleans, LA - Brazen looters took items from a Foot Action store at Bourbon and Canal streets, adding insult to injury in the battered Big Easy. Saying they needed to sustain families, many began to plunder stores in full view of police officers and the National Guard. • MICHAEL AINSWORTH

LEFT
08.30.05 - New Orleans, LA - John Allen guarded A.J. Produce from looters, and his message was clear. Police said they could do little to stop the thefts. "It's like downtown Baghdad," tourist Denise Bollinger said. • IRWIN THOMPSON

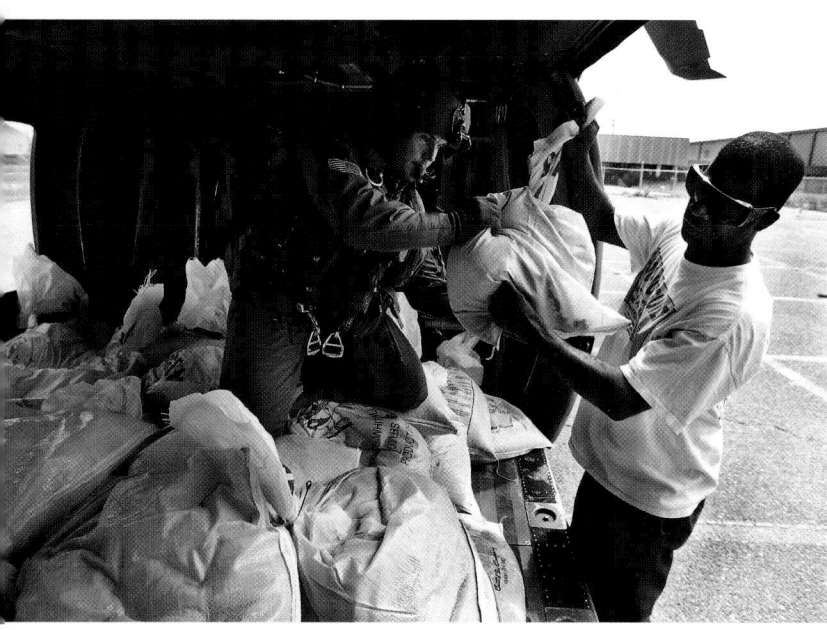

08.30.05 - New Orleans, LA - Army Sgt. 1st Class Charles Robertson grabbed sandbags from an unidentified volunteer to reinforce the Superdome from floodwaters. • MICHAEL AINSWORTH

CENTER
08.30.05 - New Orleans, LA - Volunteer LeRoy Crawford helped 80-year-old Emelda Jenkins out onto the roof of her flooded Ninth Ward home as Ricky Yeldell (left) and Randy Lively lifted her into a boat. • IRWIN THOMPSON

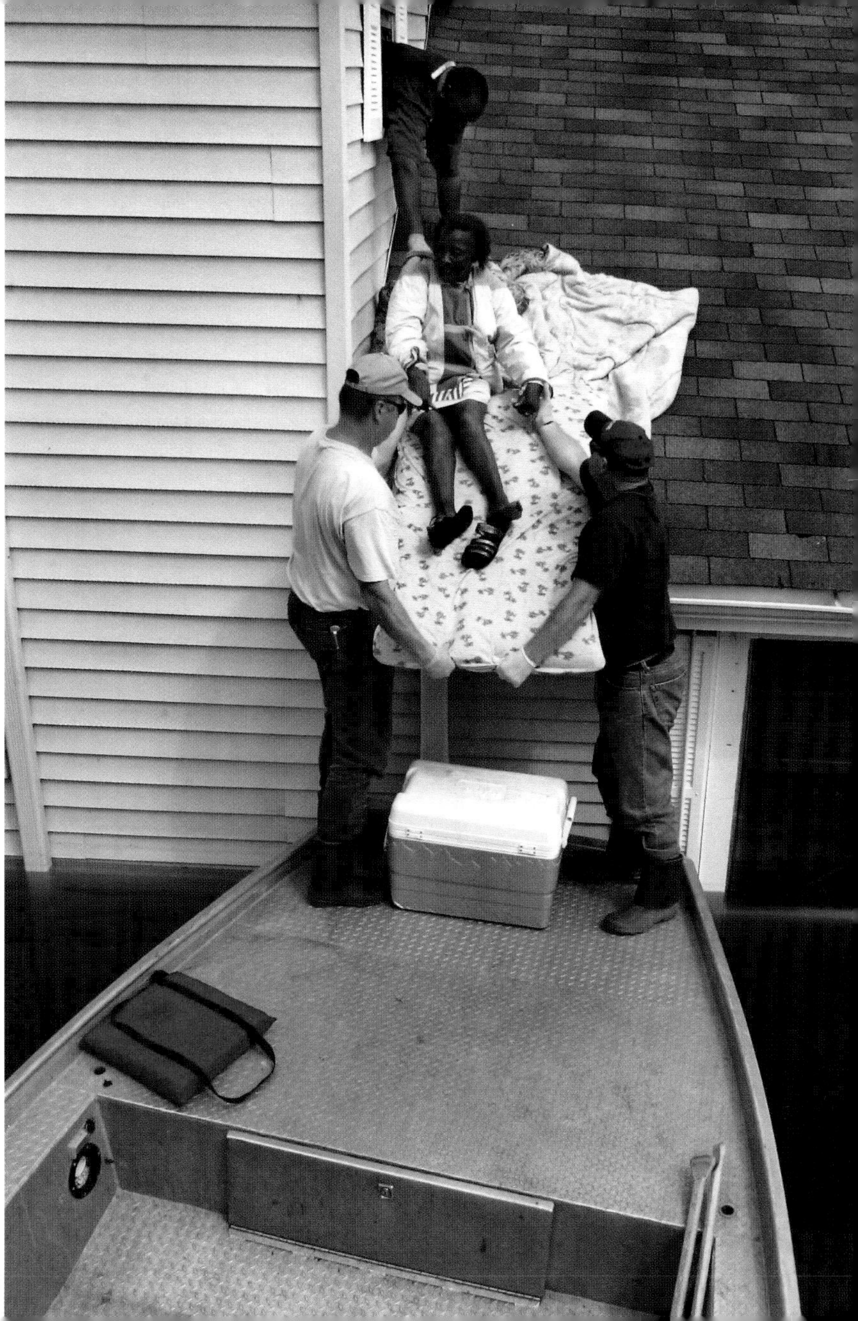

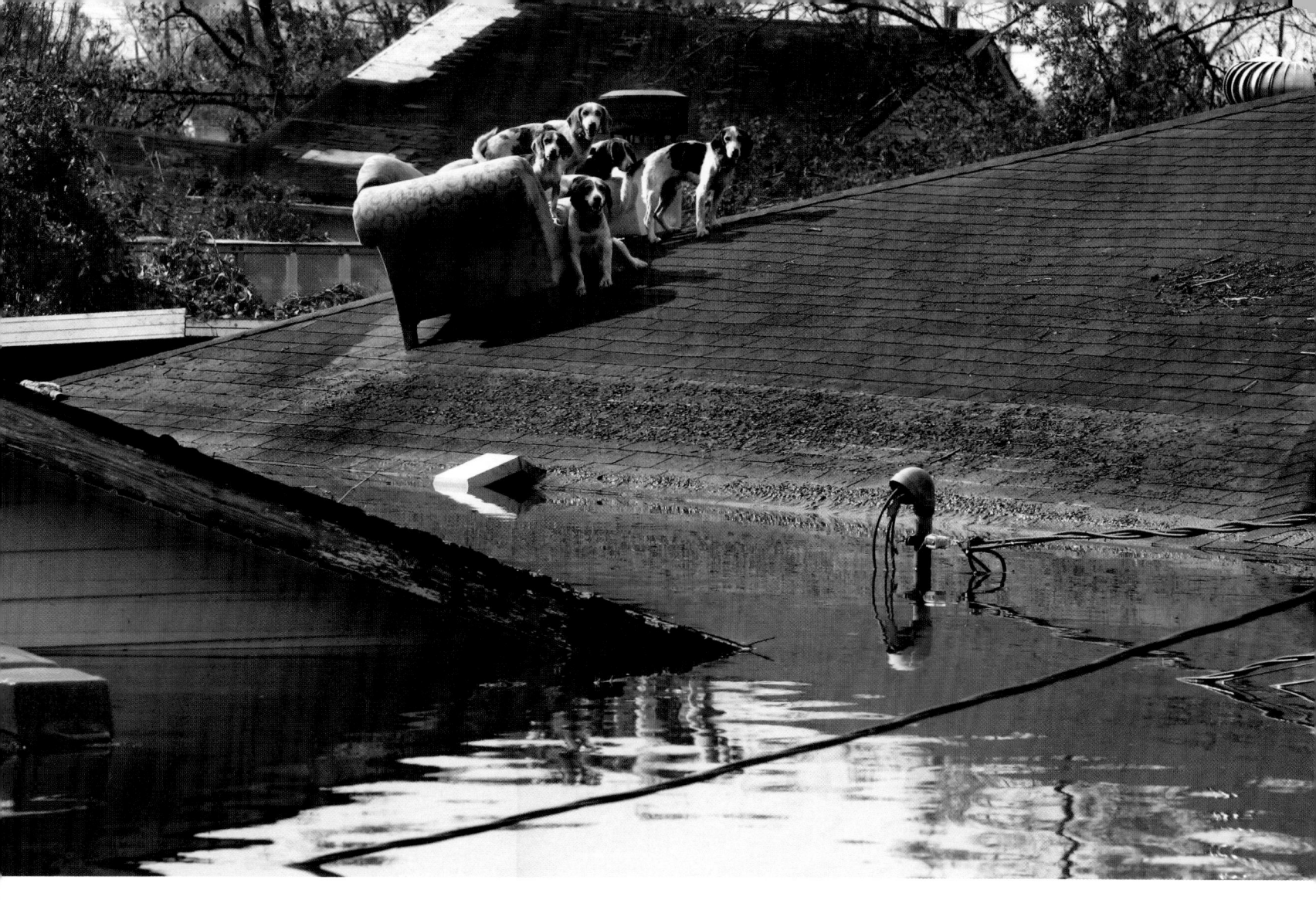

08.30.05 - New Orleans, LA - Dogs stuck together on a roof to stay dry in the Ninth Ward. Thousands of animals were stranded by the storm, trapped in homes or roaming empty streets, prompting complaints by the head of the Humane Society that state and federal officials had ignored pleas to set a policy for animal rescues. • IRWIN THOMPSON

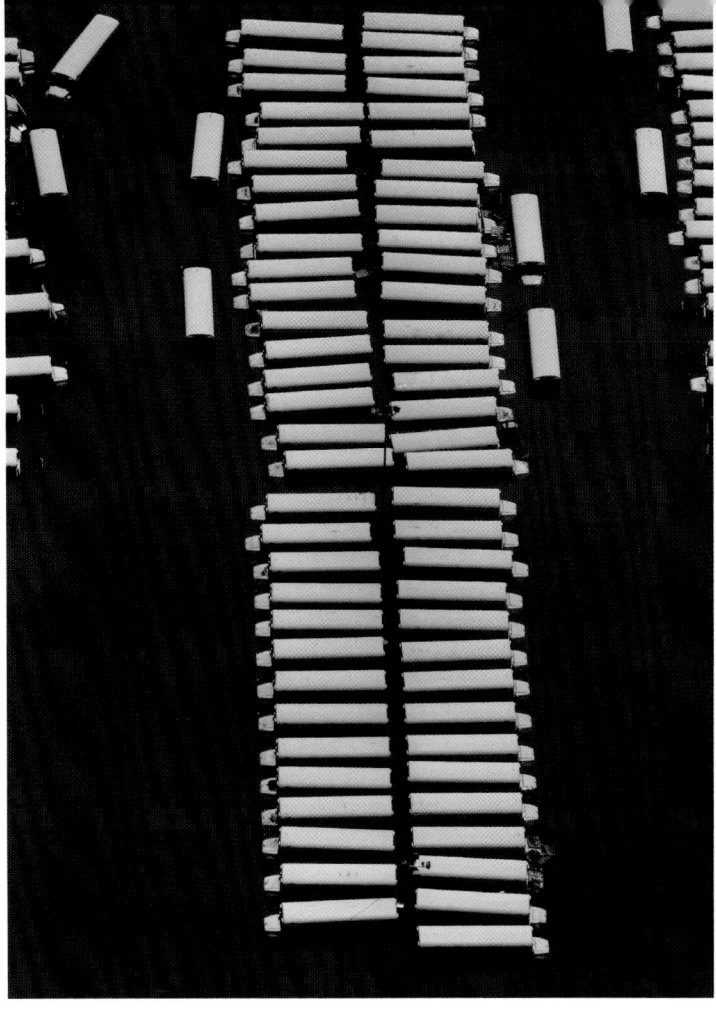

08.30.05 - New Orleans, LA - Flooded school buses resemble pencils from above.
• SMILEY N. POOL

RIGHT
08.30.05 - New Orleans, LA - Storm survivors waded as they waited for a National Guard truck to take them to the Superdome after they were rescued in the Ninth Ward. • IRWIN THOMPSON

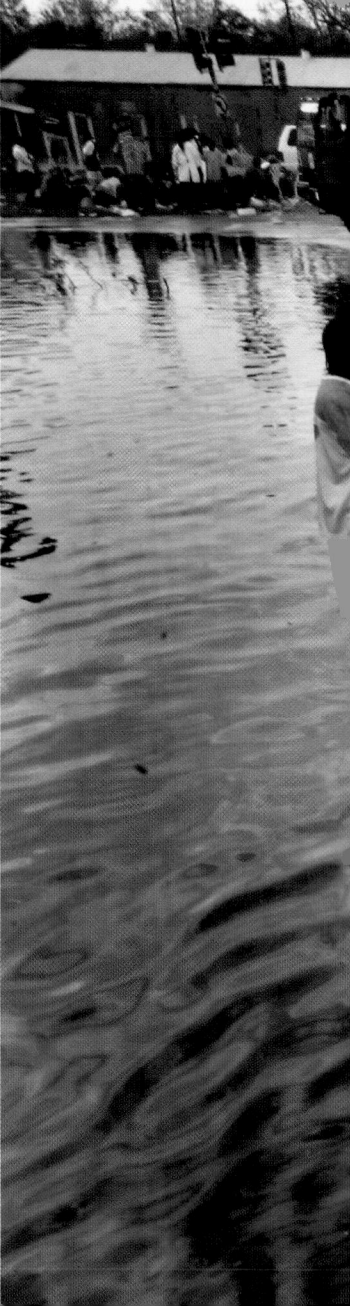

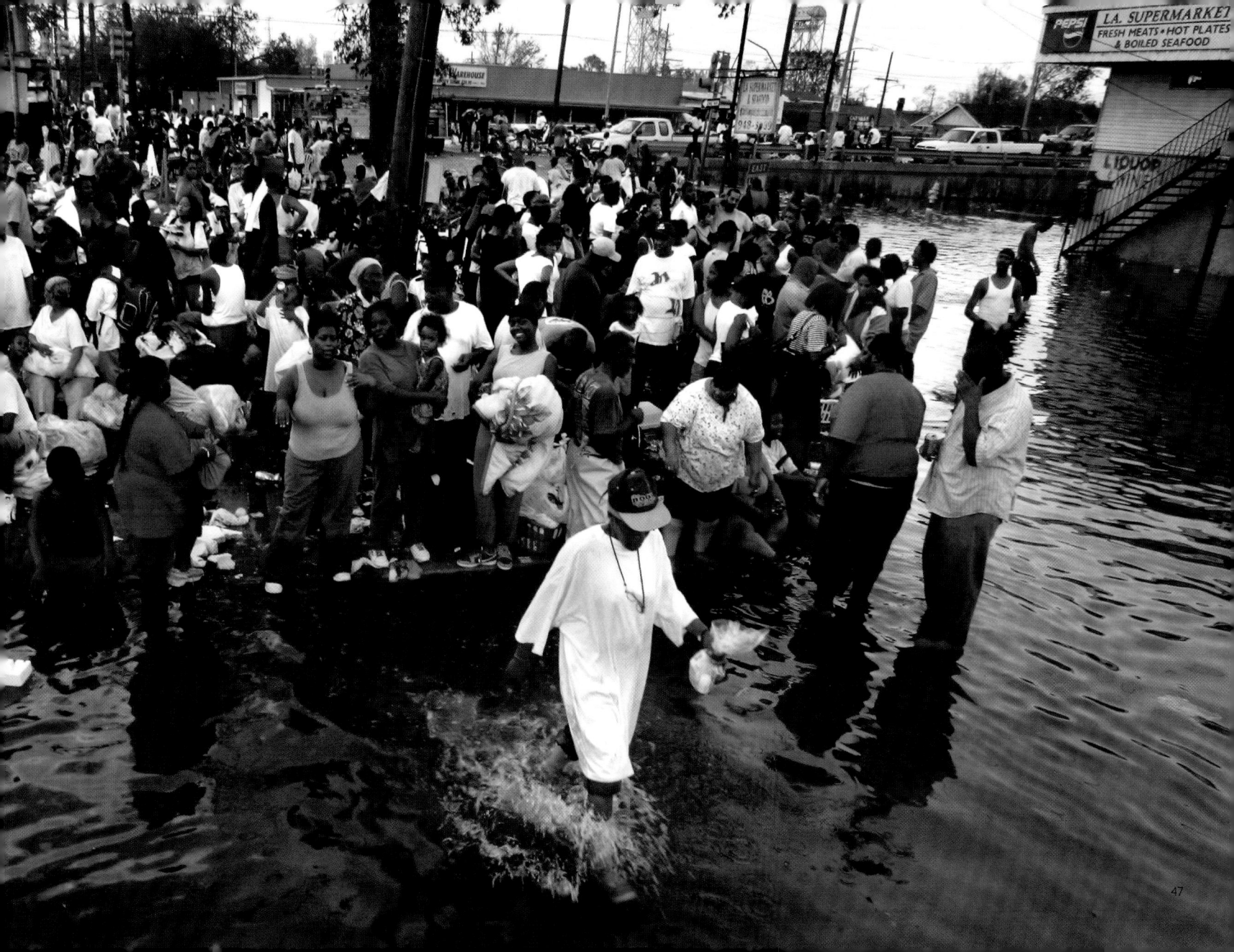

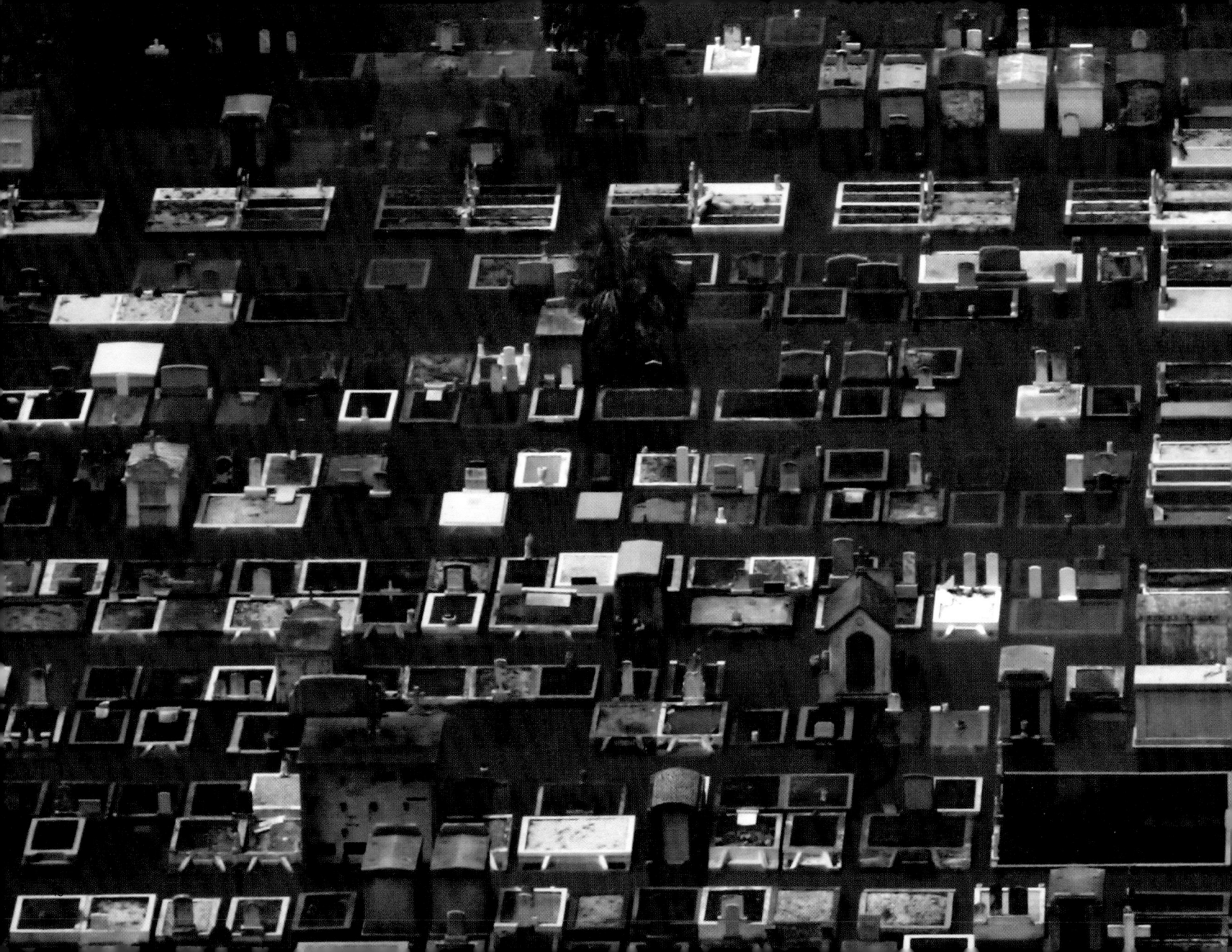

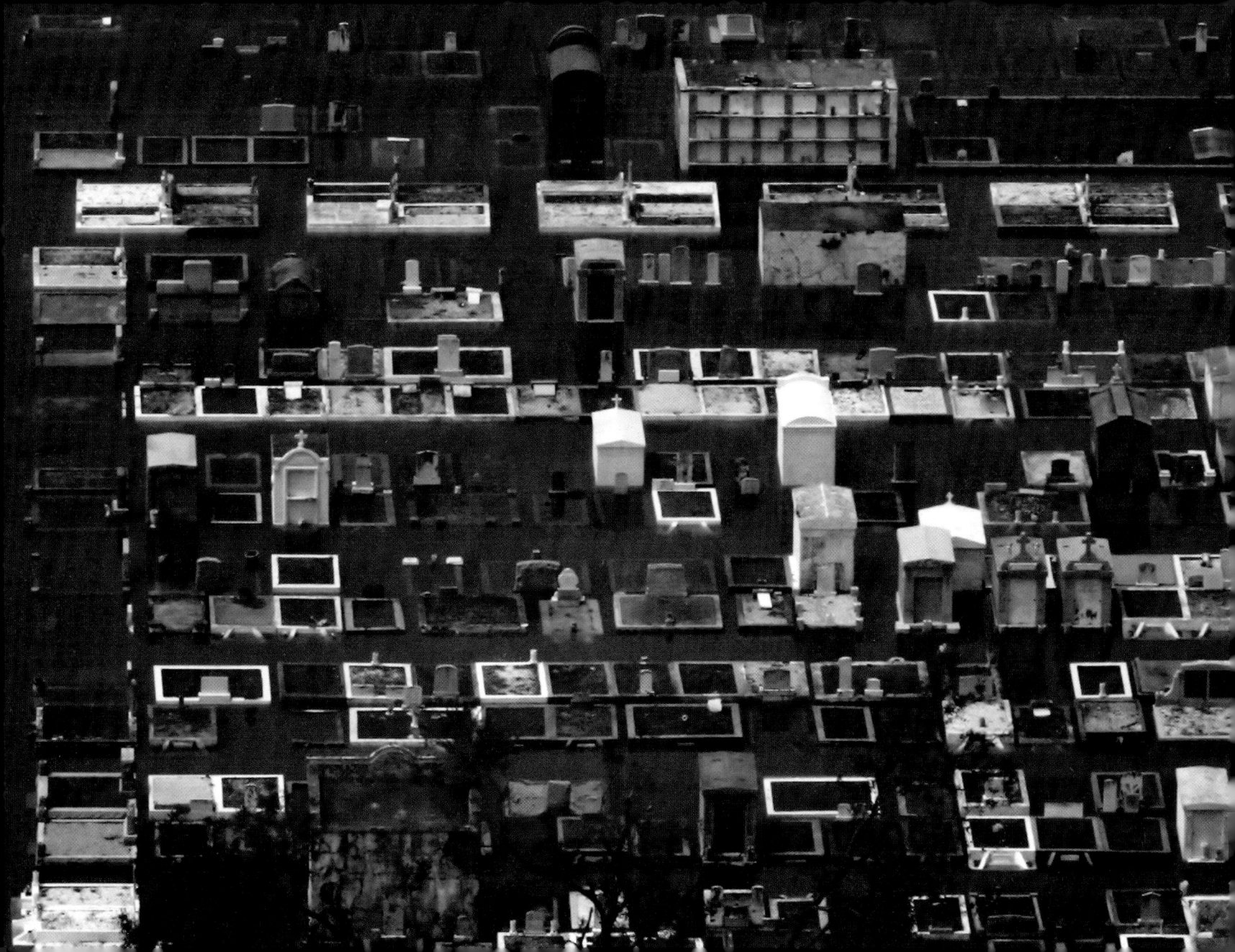

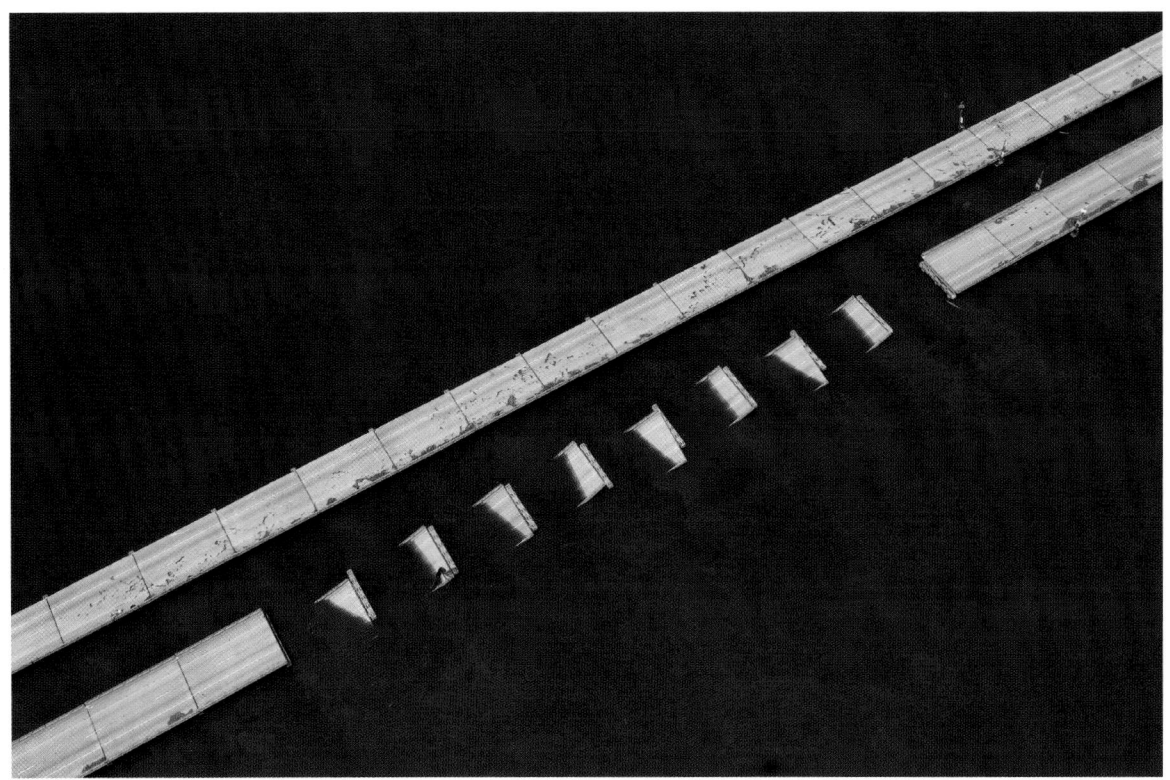

08.30.05 - New Orleans, LA - Hurricane Katrina battered the Interstate 10 bridge across Lake Pontchartrain linking Slidell and New Orleans. Officials estimated that 85 percent of Slidell homes and businesses were damaged or destroyed. • SMILEY N. POOL

PREVIOUS PAGE
08.30.05 - New Orleans, LA - Legendary New Orleans cemeteries, known as "cities of the dead," were turned into watery brown muck by the floodwaters of Hurricane Katrina. • MICHAEL AINSWORTH

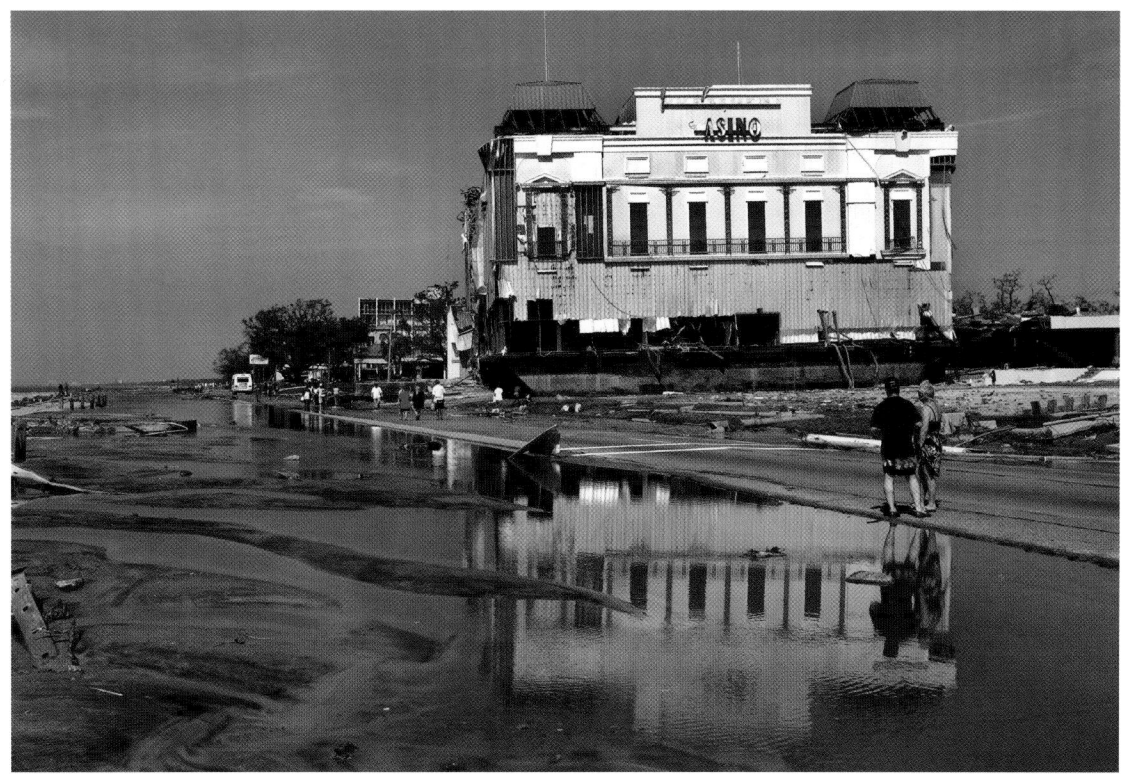

08.30.05 - Gulfport, MS - Katrina silenced the slots and stopped the card games in the flashy casinos that dot the Gulf Coast. The massive President Casino off U.S. Highway 90 was tossed from its moorings and flung almost a mile by the hurricane. The gambling houses are built on barges anchored just off the beach. • LOUIS DELUCA

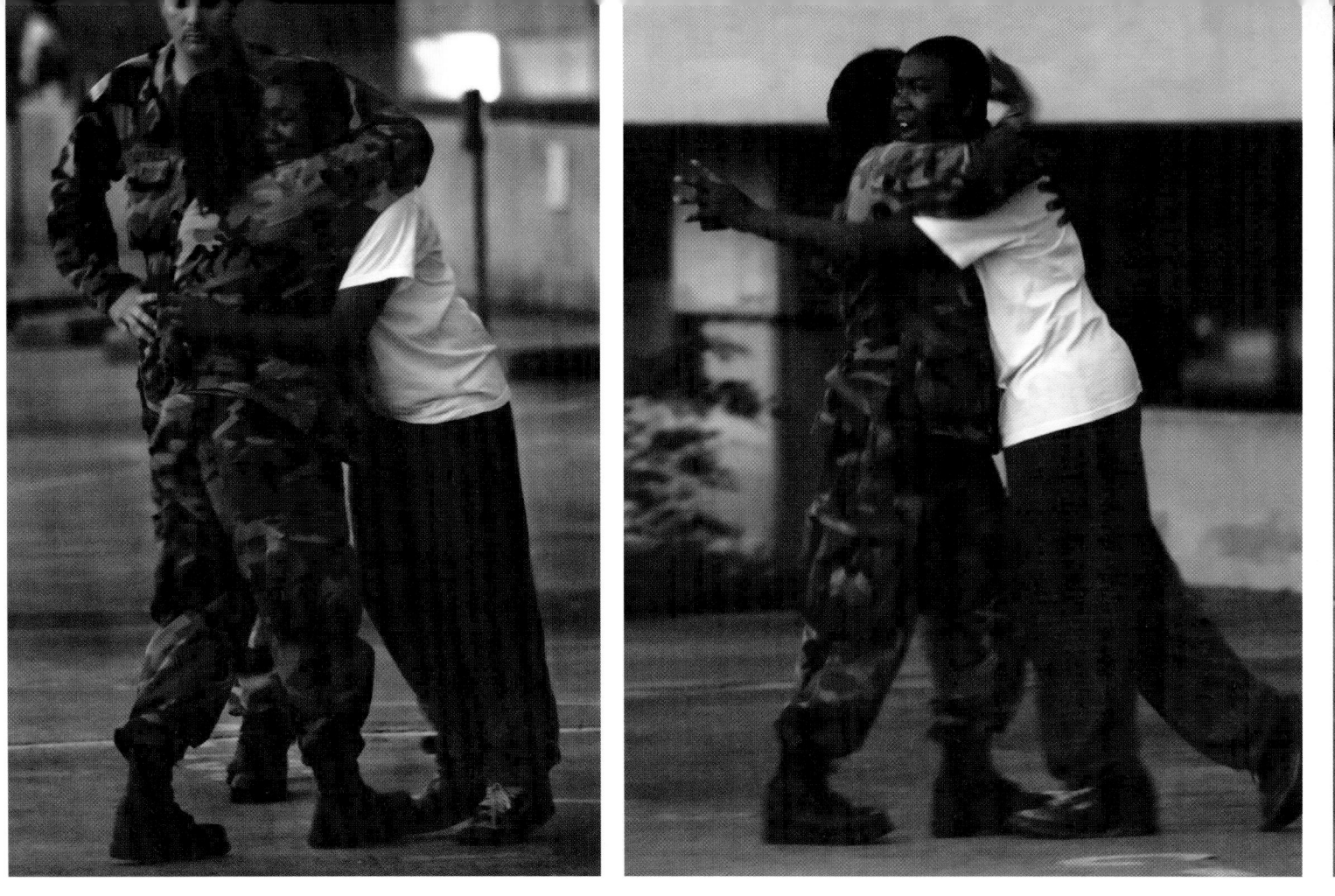

08.30.05 - New Orleans, LA - A National Guard member tried to calm a young man on the helipad at the Superdome after one of his relatives was taken to a hospital. • MICHAEL AINSWORTH

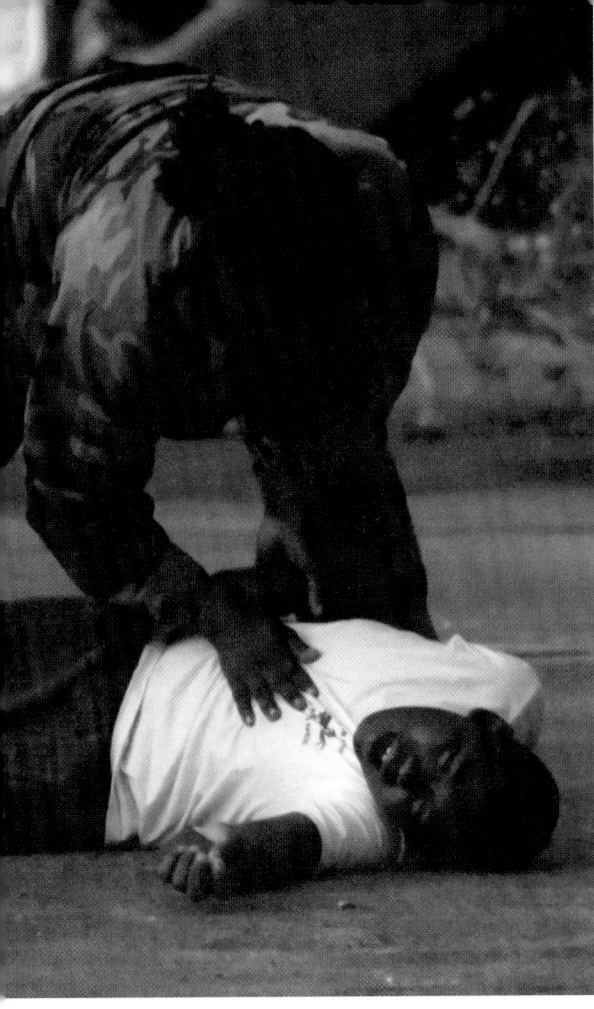

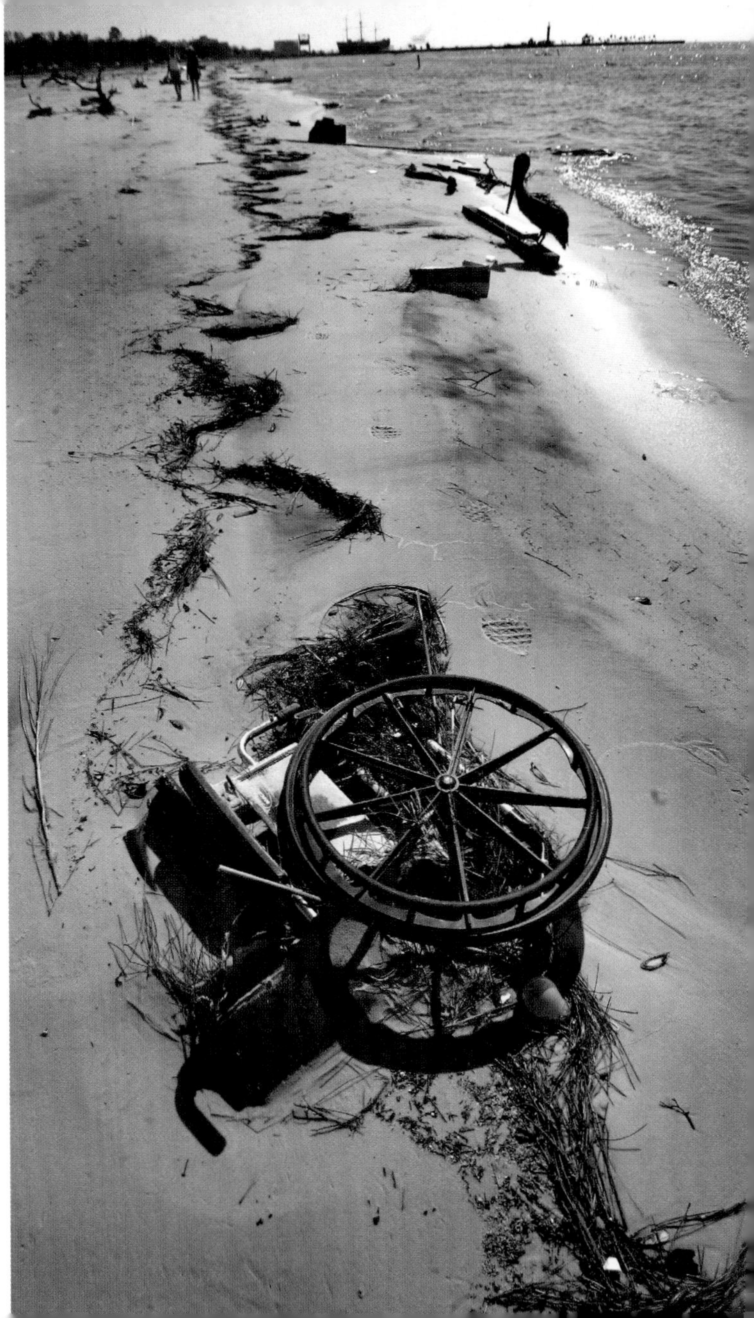

08.30.05 - Gulfport MS - A wheelchair washed up on the beach off U.S. Highway 90.
• LOUIS DELUCA

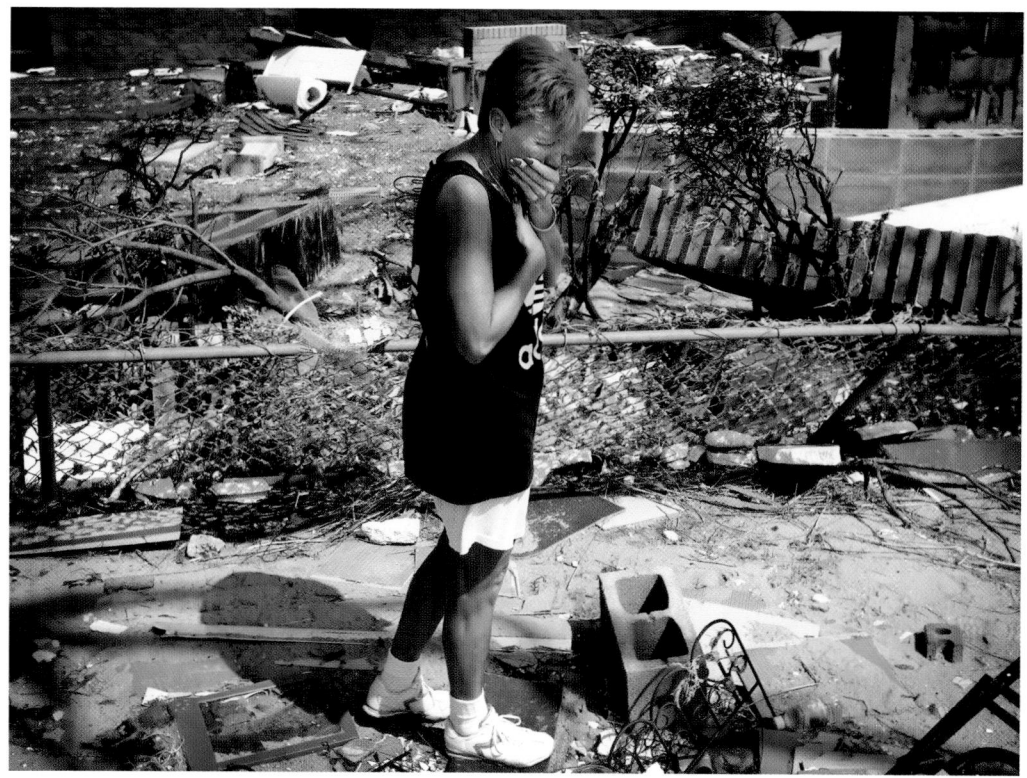

08.31.05 - Biloxi, MS - Laurie Miller was overcome by the devastation of her home as she saw it for the first time after the storm. • BARBARA DAVIDSON

RIGHT
08.31.05 - Long Beach, MS - A swimming pool and rubble were all that remained of an apartment complex obliterated by Hurricane Katrina. • SMILEY N. POOL

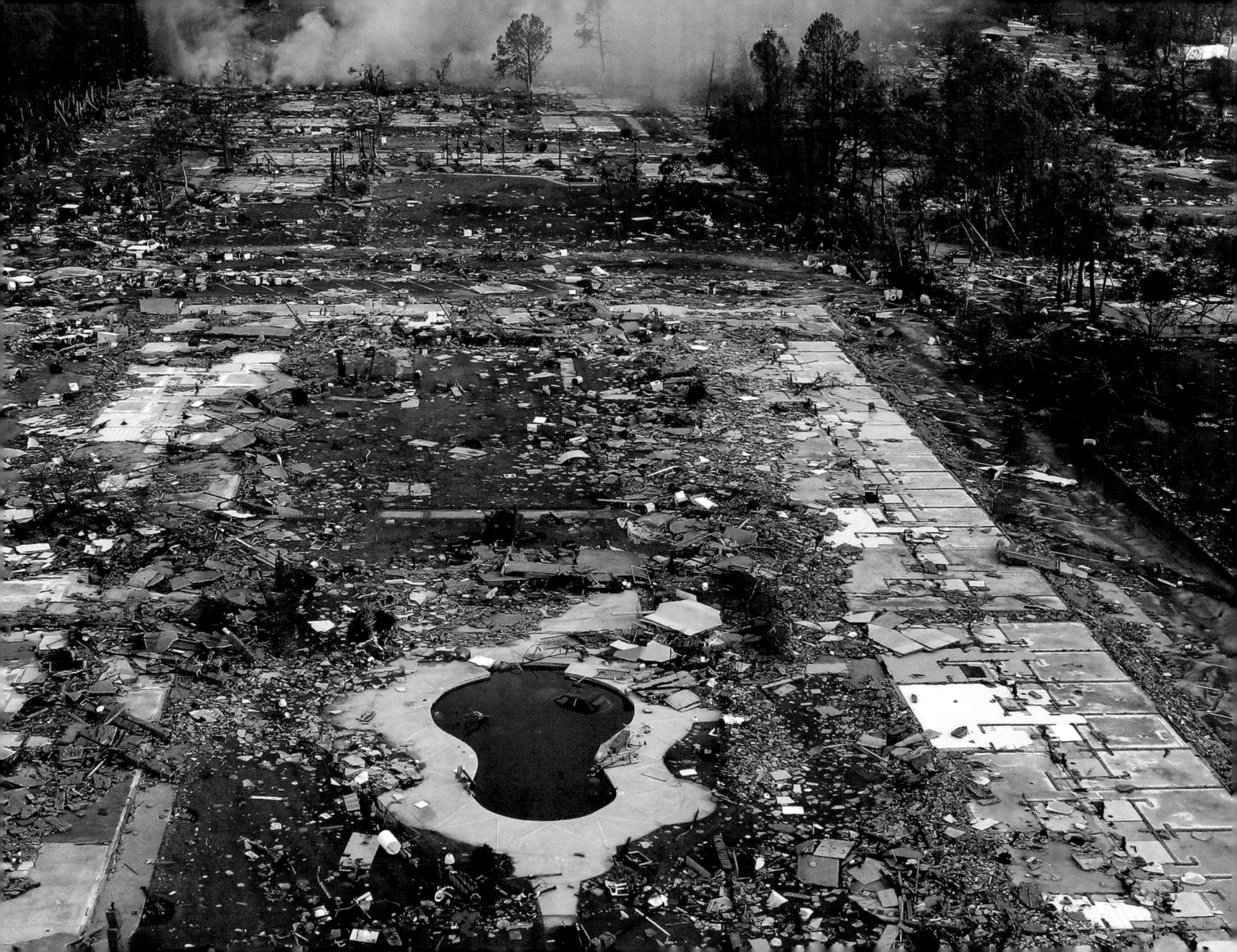

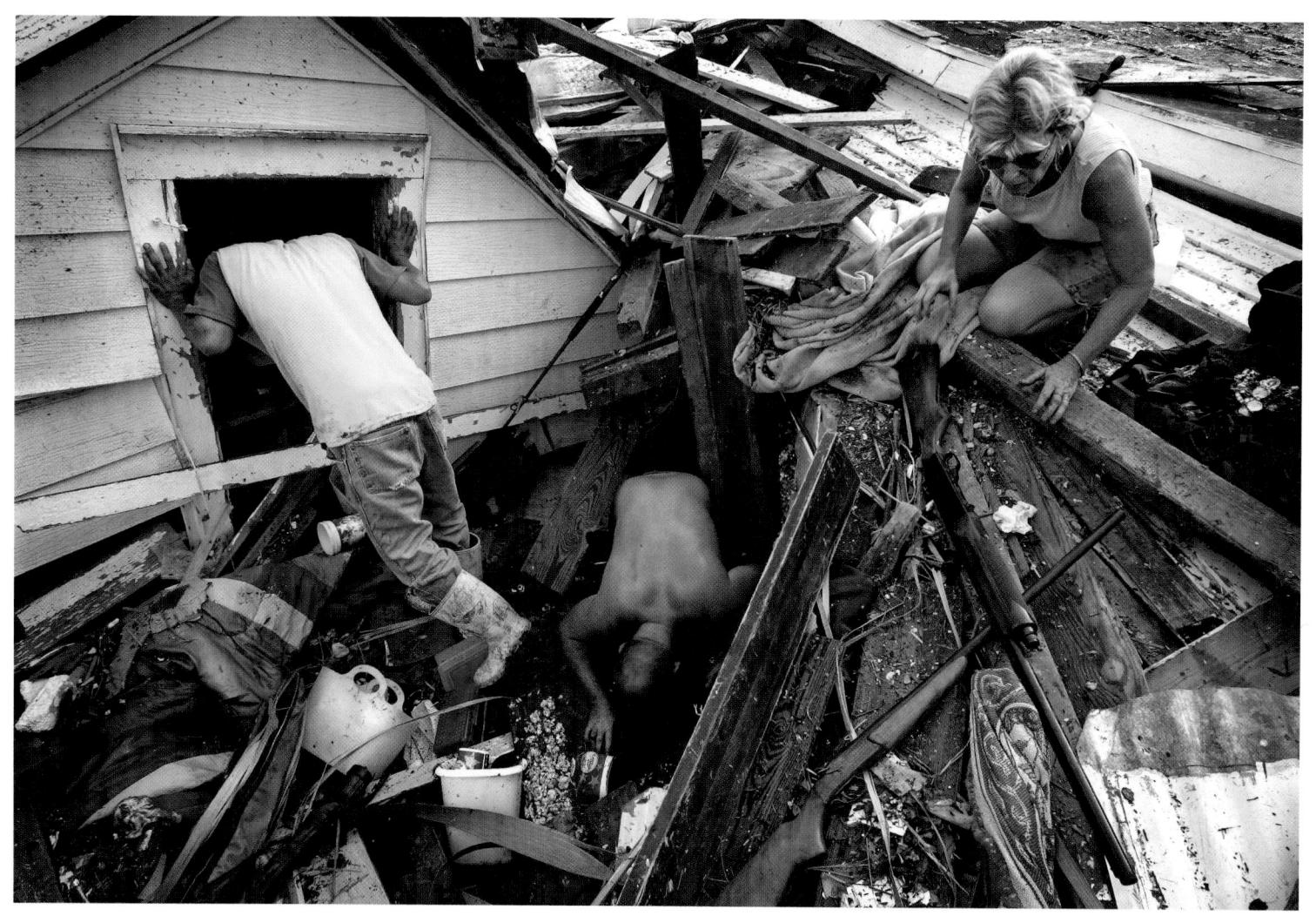

08.31.05 - Biloxi, MS - Tam Cu, Jason Jackson and Linda Bryant looked for belongings from Ms. Bryant's home, which was destroyed by the storm. • BARBARA DAVIDSON

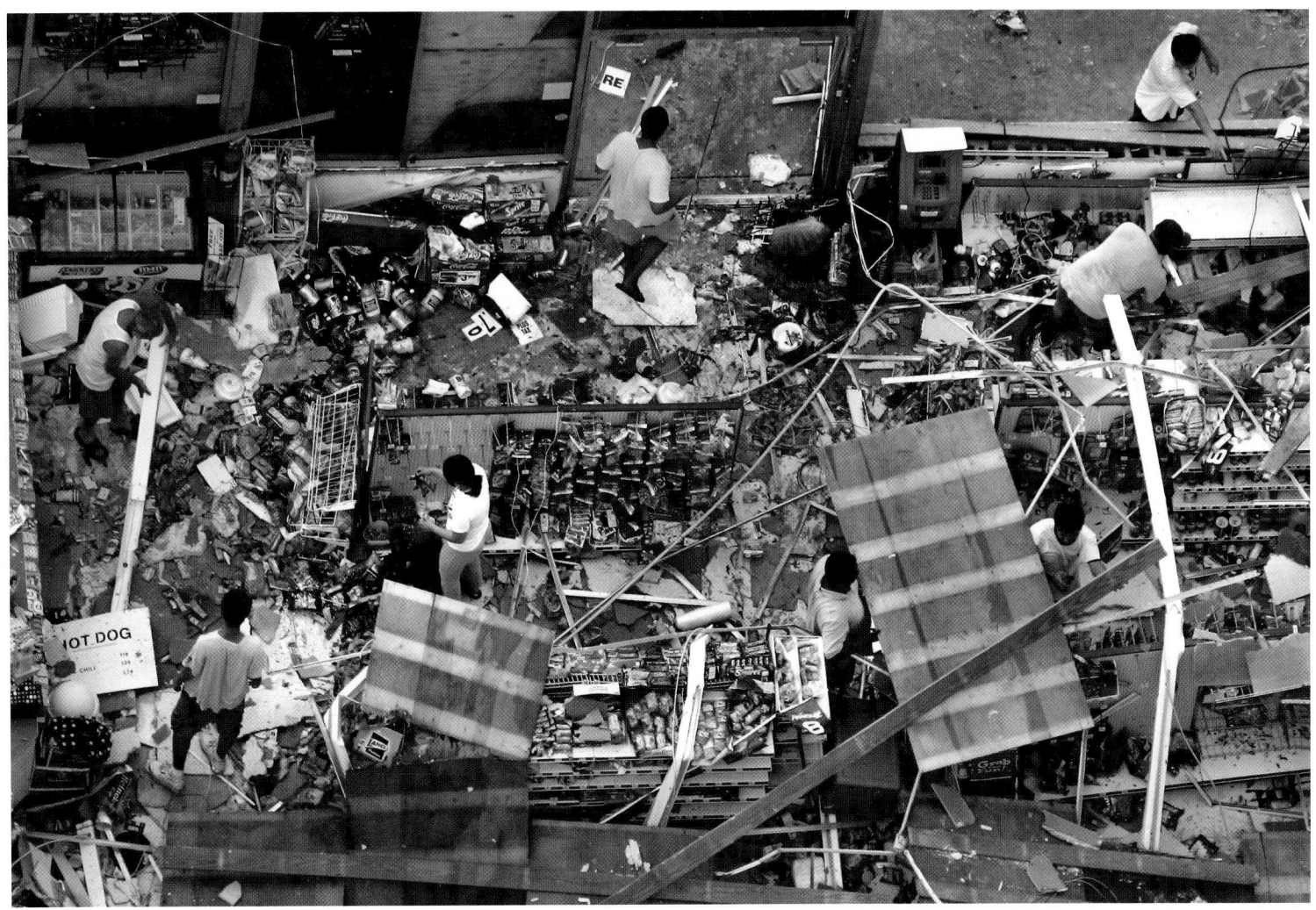

08.31.05 - Long Beach, MS - People salvaged what they could from the rubble of a convenience store. Katrina spared almost nothing along Mississippi's 90 miles of coastline, devastated in such a way that it will take years, if not decades, to recover. • SMILEY N. POOL

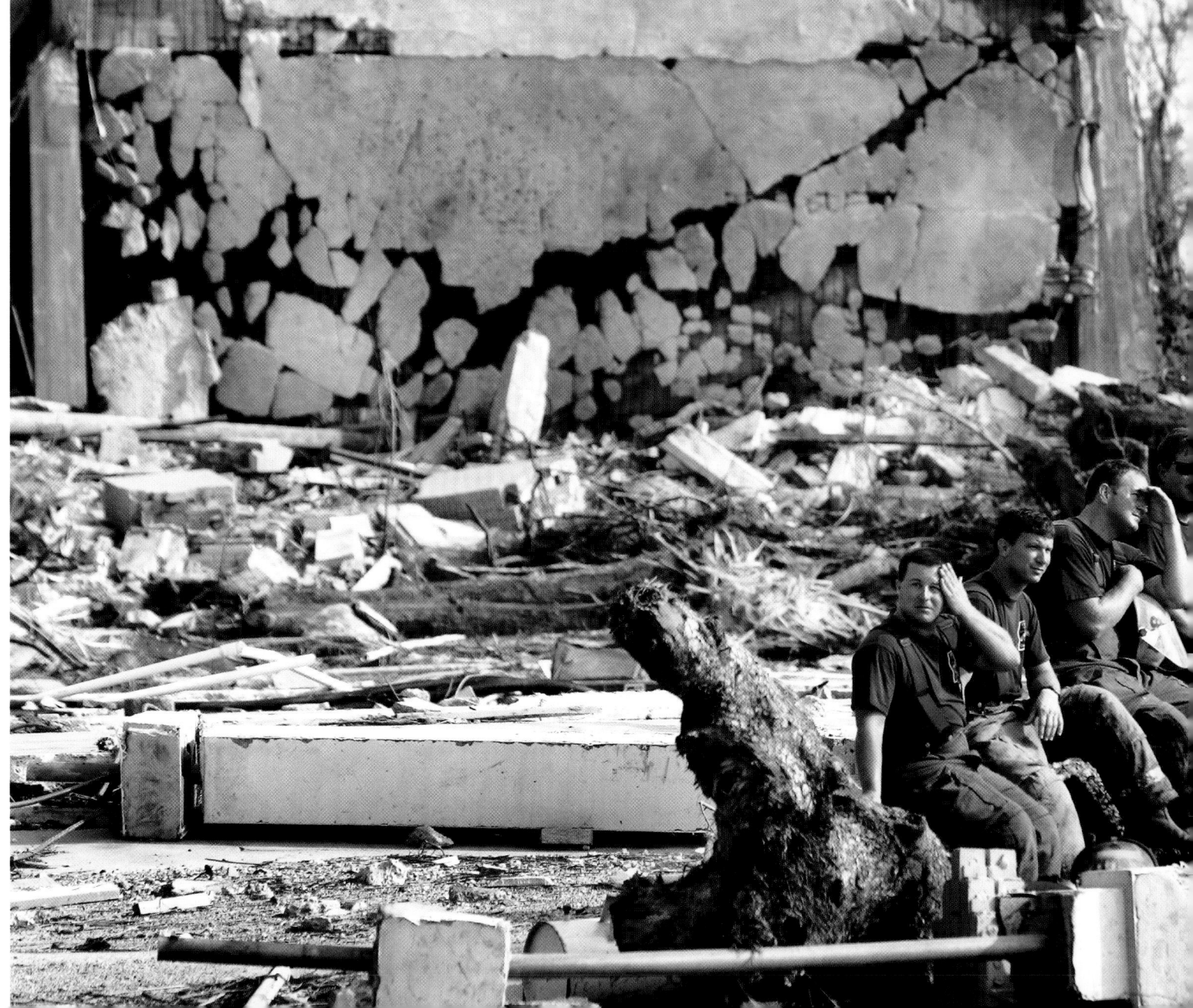

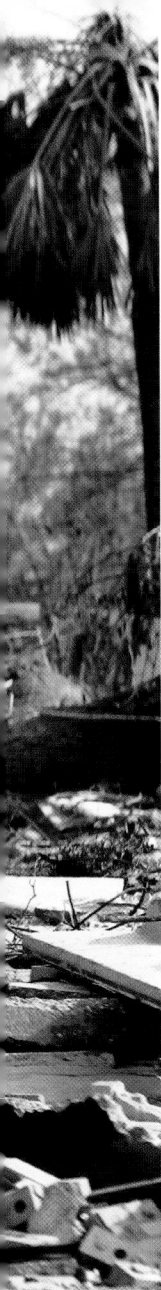

08.31.05 - Biloxi, MS - City of Biloxi fire-fighters took a break as they waited for law enforcement search teams to look for bodies or survivors at what was left of the Tivoli Hotel off U.S. Highway 90. Three bodies were later discovered at the site. • LOUIS DELUCA

RIGHT
08.31.05 - Long Beach, MS - A helicopter worked to douse a fire amid the rubble. • SMILEY N. POOL

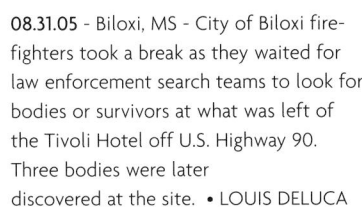

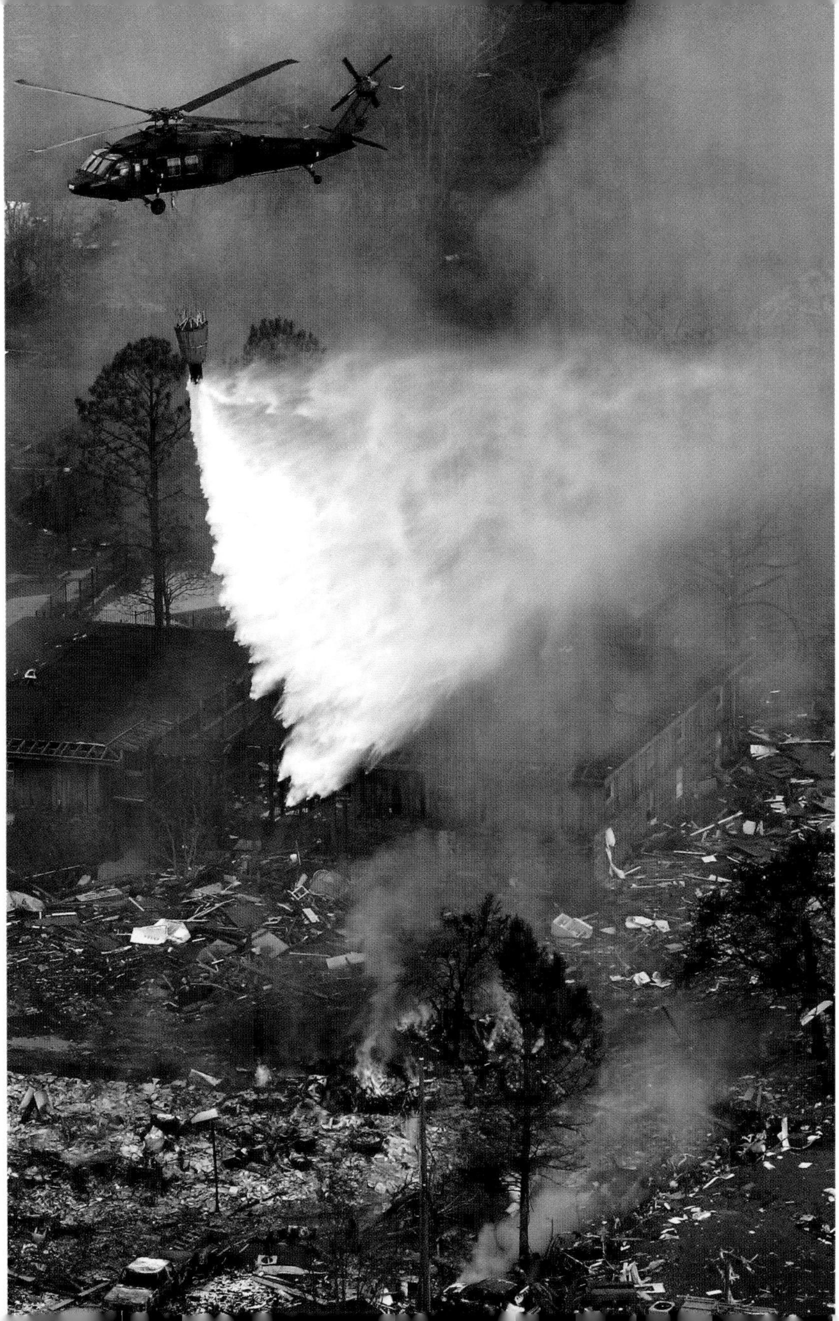

08.31.05 - New Orleans, LA - People wandered along Interstate 10 near the Superdome. Amid dire predictions, authorities decided to try to empty the city and move residents from the Superdome to shelters in Dallas and Houston in a two-day caravan of buses. • IRWIN THOMPSON

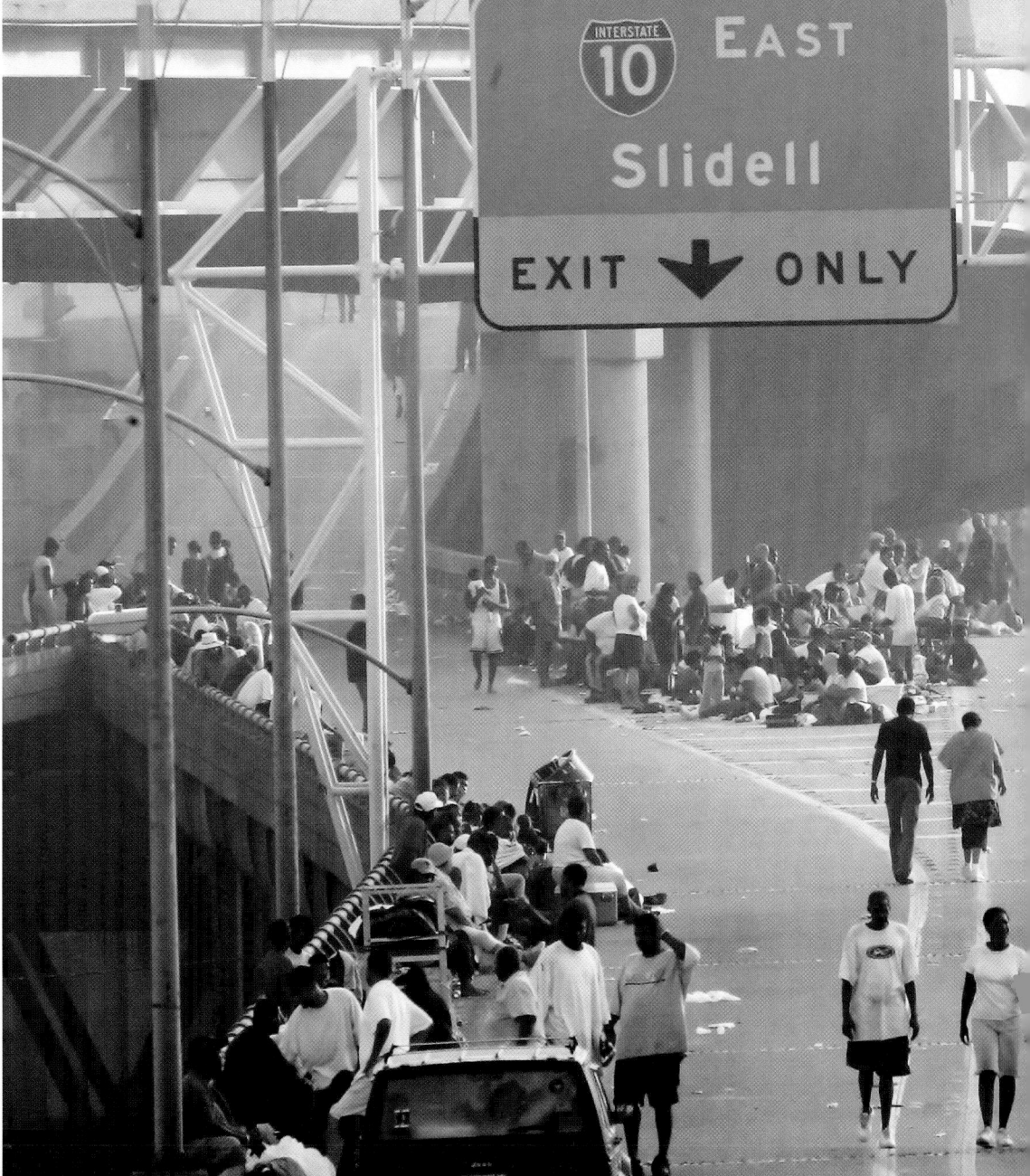

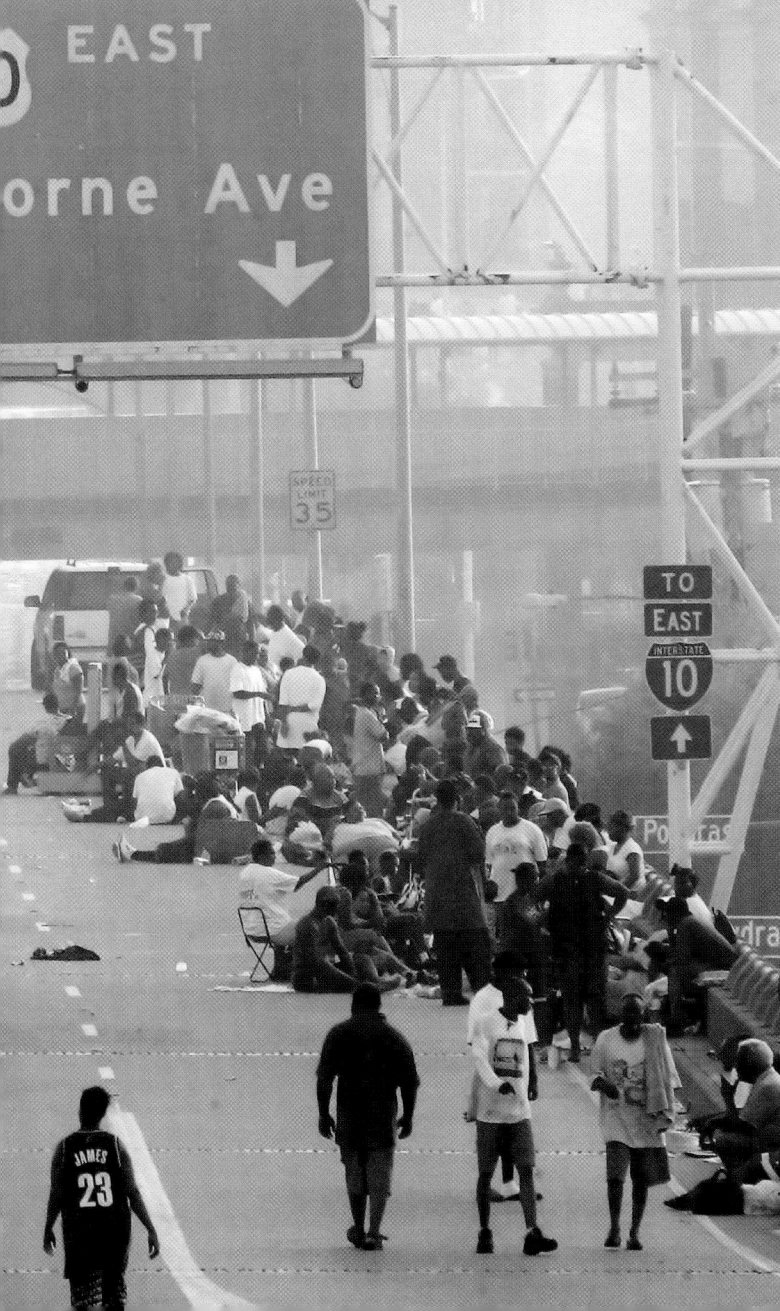

DESPERATE FOR HELP

Dead bodies lay untended at midday. Fires raged unchecked, and the sick begged for help in vain. And a massive exodus of the dispossessed was still under way as much of the city slipped toward anarchy.

"This is a desperate SOS," New Orleans Mayor Ray Nagin said.

Three days after Hurricane Katrina barreled through, despair and frustration mounted across the ruined city. Many voiced resentment - and, in some cases, bitter anger - about state and federal relief efforts, which they believe were slow in coming.

Violence repulsed some rescue and relief efforts, and Gov. Kathleen Blanco said she had ordered 300 National Guard troops, fresh from duty in Iraq, to shoot any looters who threatened police officers, evacuees or anyone helping the rescue effort.

"I have one message for these criminals: These troopers know how to shoot to kill, and they are more than willing to do so if necessary," she said.

In New Orleans, thousands waited, hungry and exhausted, for buses to take them away to Houston, where officials took more than 11,000 into the Astrodome before declaring it full and sending buses to other shelters.

Hundreds of others wandered over sections of elevated highway, their best way to escape the foul waters that drowned their neighborhoods. On one stretch of Interstate 10, the uncovered corpse of an elderly man sprawled near an abandoned fire truck.

• LEE HANCOCK and MICHAEL GRABELL

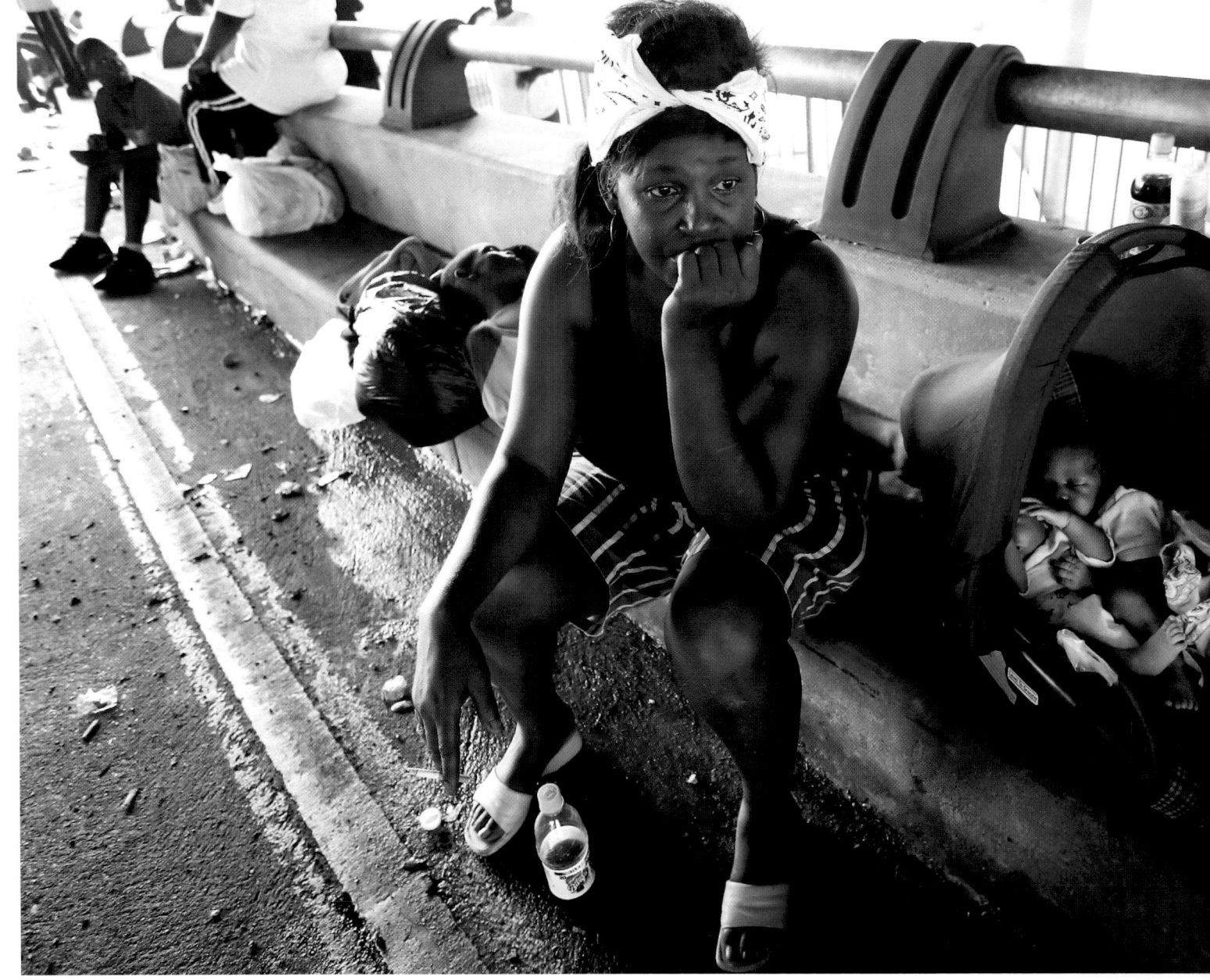

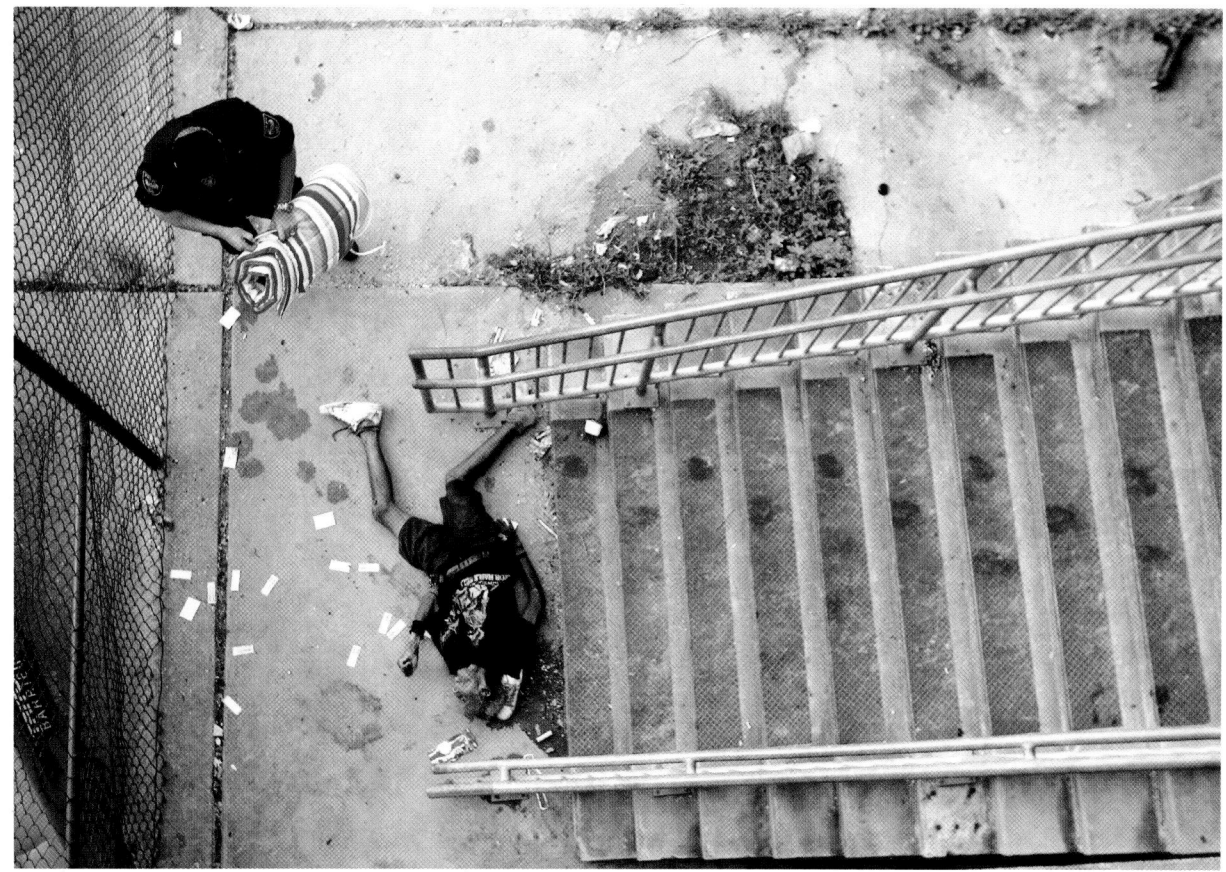

08.31.05 - New Orleans, LA - A police officer covered the body of an 80-year-old man who fell from the overpass next to the Superdome.
• MICHAEL AINSWORTH

Left

08.31.05 - New Orleans, LA - A frustrated Cynthia Scott waited under an overpass next to the Superdome with grandchildren Dwayne Alphonse (left) and 3-month-old twins Eric and Erin Alphonse. She and thousands of others were forced to sleep on the overpass. "A whole city in ruins and no one doing nothing," she said. People had been without water and food for days while sweltering on the bridges.
• MICHAEL AINSWORTH

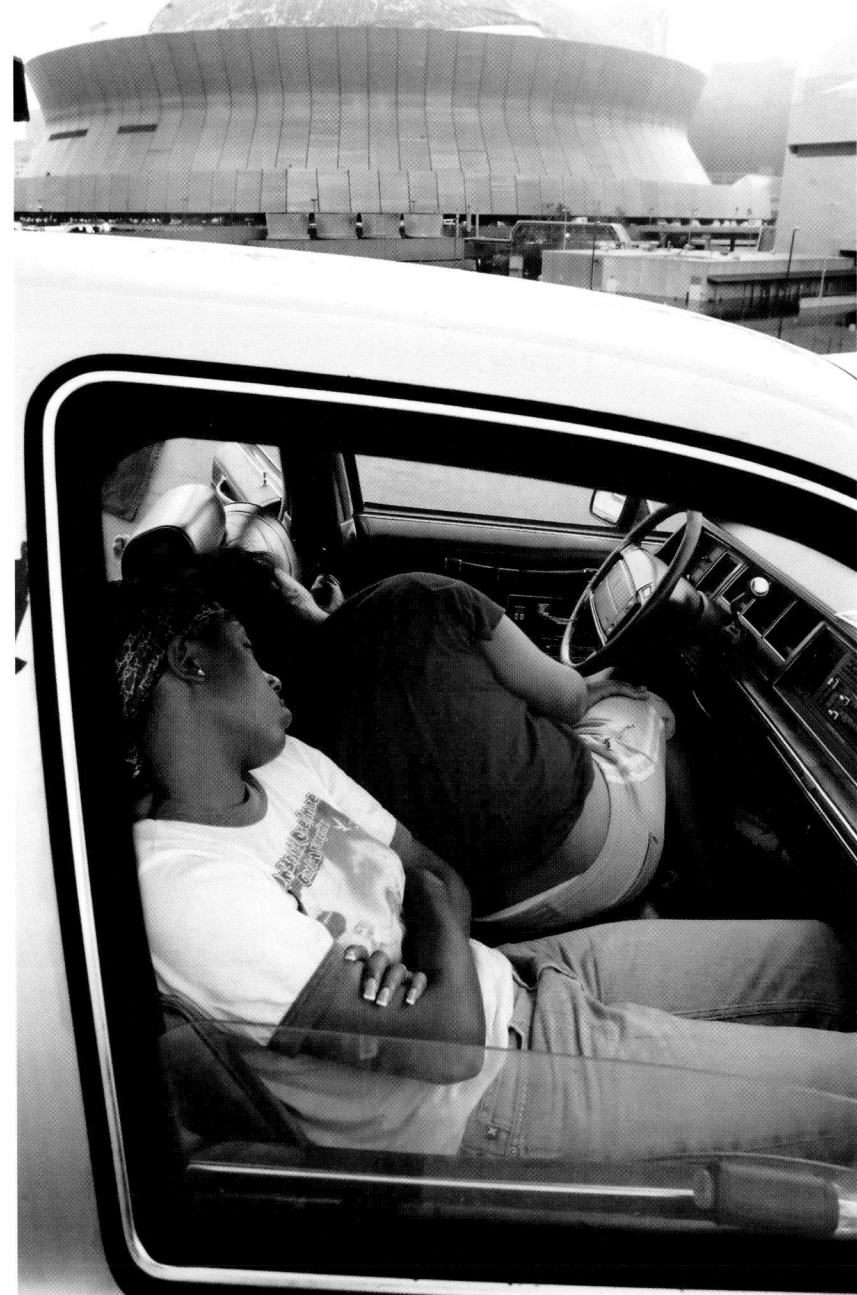

08.31.05 - New Orleans, LA - Twenty-year-old Sada Badon (left) and Brione Mitchell, 11, slept in their car along Interstate 10 near the Superdome.
• IRWIN THOMPSON

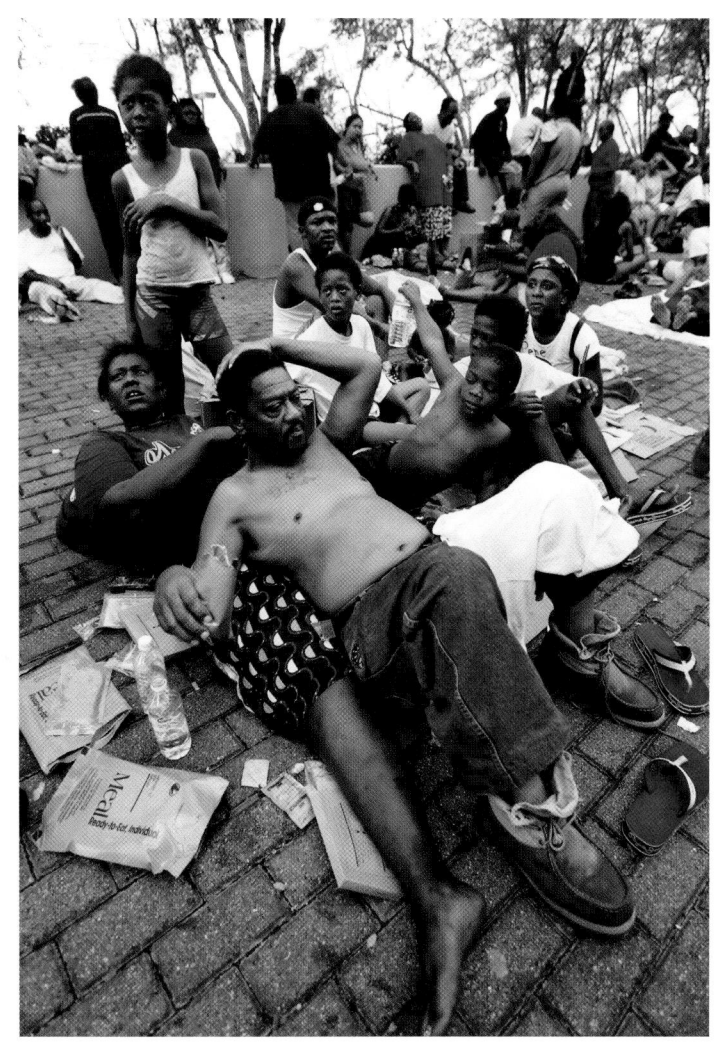

08.31.05 - New Orleans, LA - "All I can say is pray for us, because we've got a long way to go," said New Orleans resident Phyllis Lewis (left), who waited to be evacuated from the Superdome with husband James Lewis and other family members. Thousands of people set up makeshift camps on the sidewalk. Listless children watched the crowds, and stunned adults fanned themselves in the rising heat.
• MICHAEL AINSWORTH

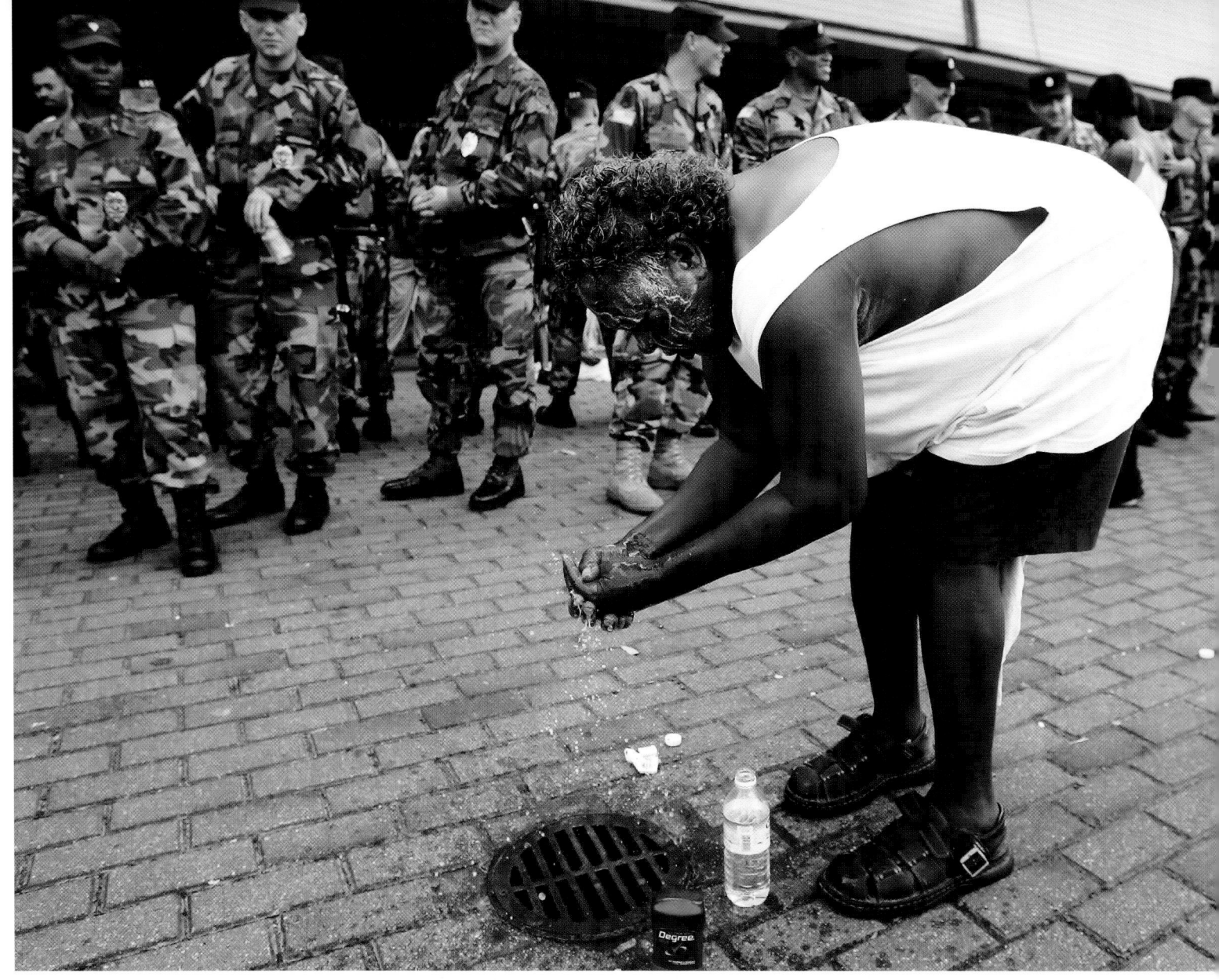

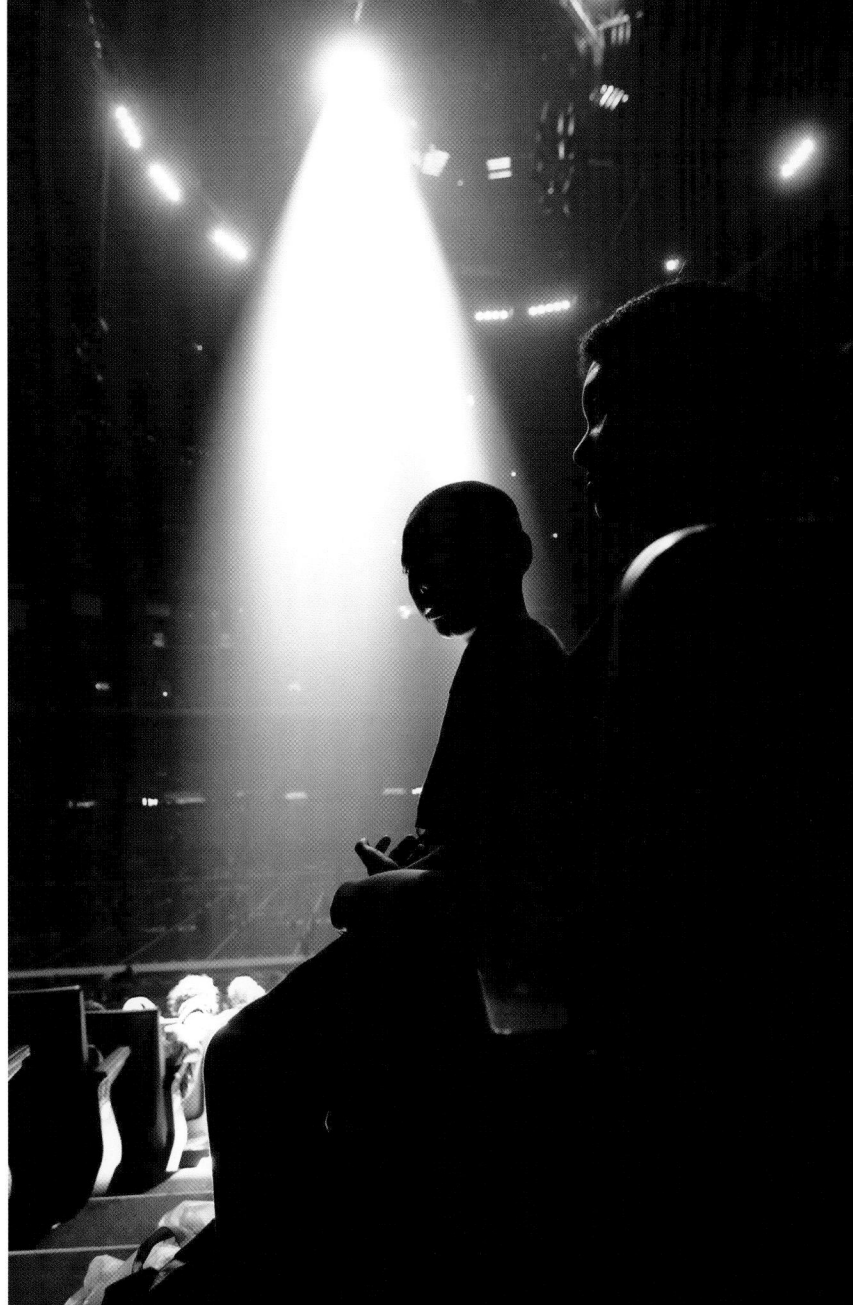

08.31.05 - New Orleans, LA - Melody Robinson and son Timothy Williams, 6, were among those enduring the heat and gloom of the Superdome. Light poured in from a hole in the roof.
• MICHAEL AINSWORTH

<small>OPPOSITE PAGE</small>
08.31.05 - New Orleans, LA - National Guard members watched as Hussein Mead of New Orleans washed with soap and bottled water at the Superdome. Floodwaters forced the Louisiana Guard's north New Orleans headquarters to the arena.
• MICHAEL AINSWORTH

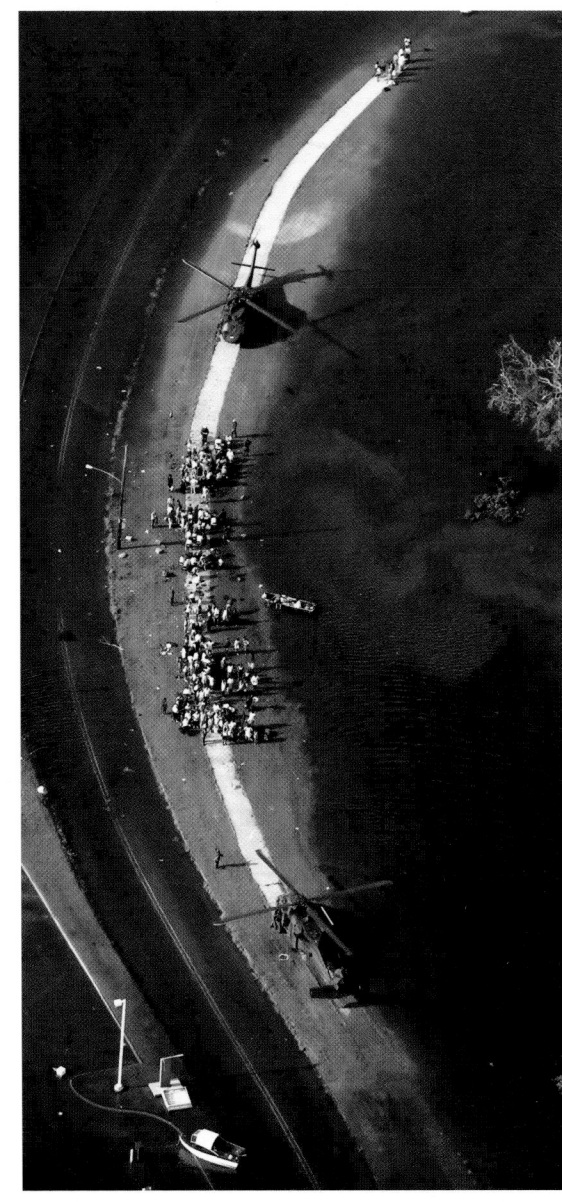

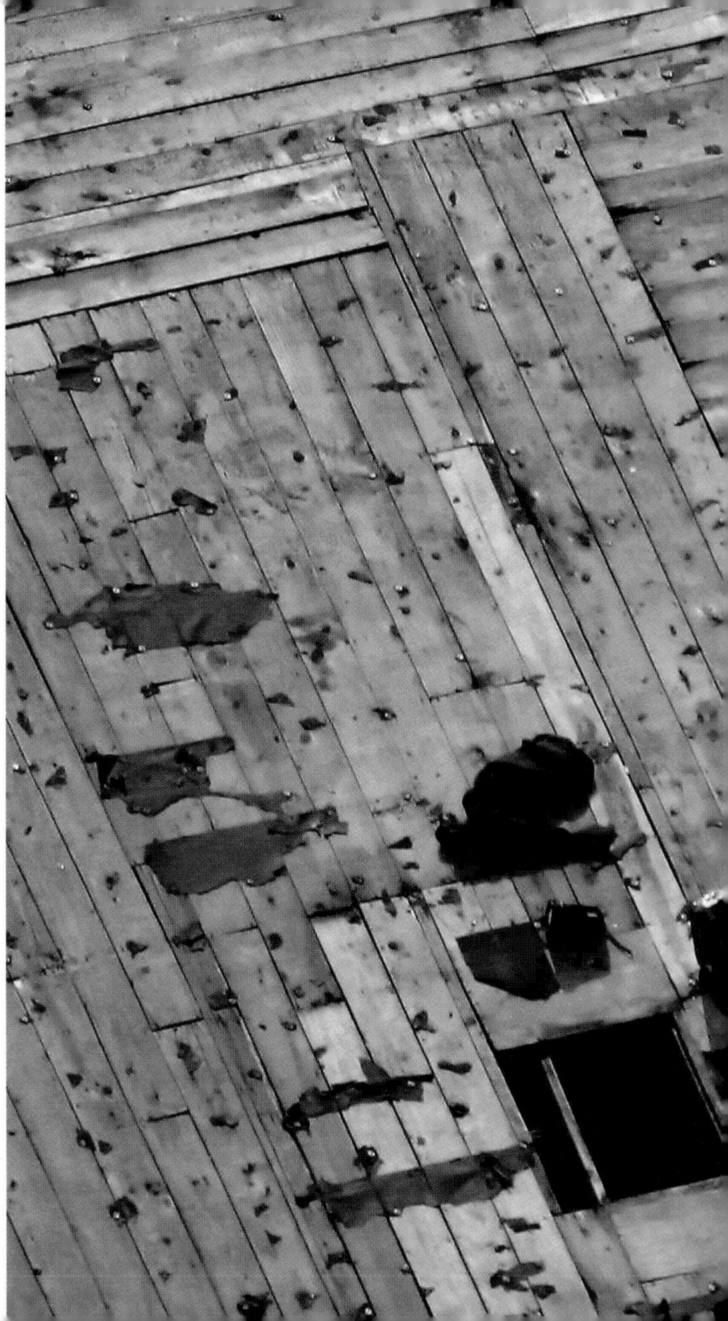

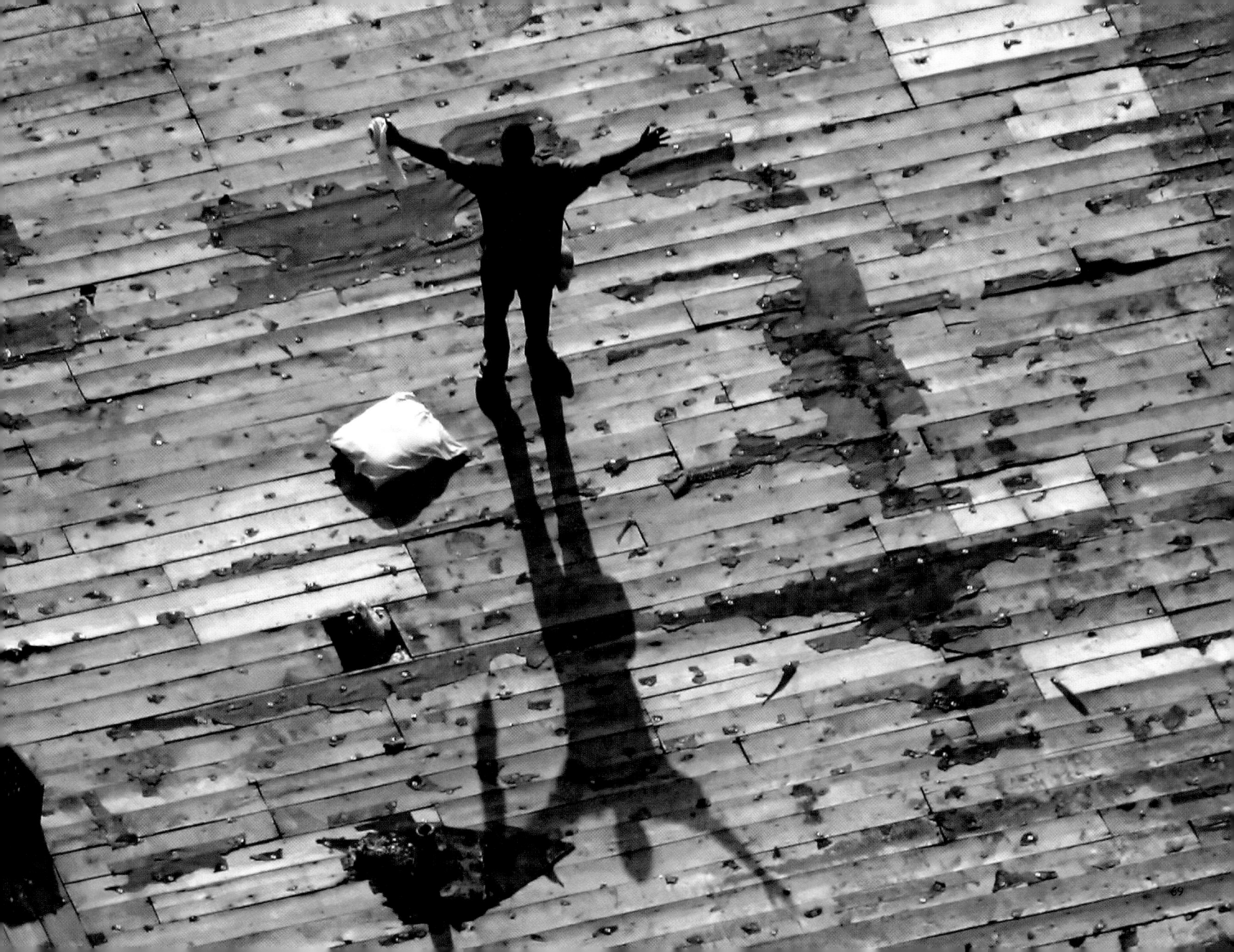

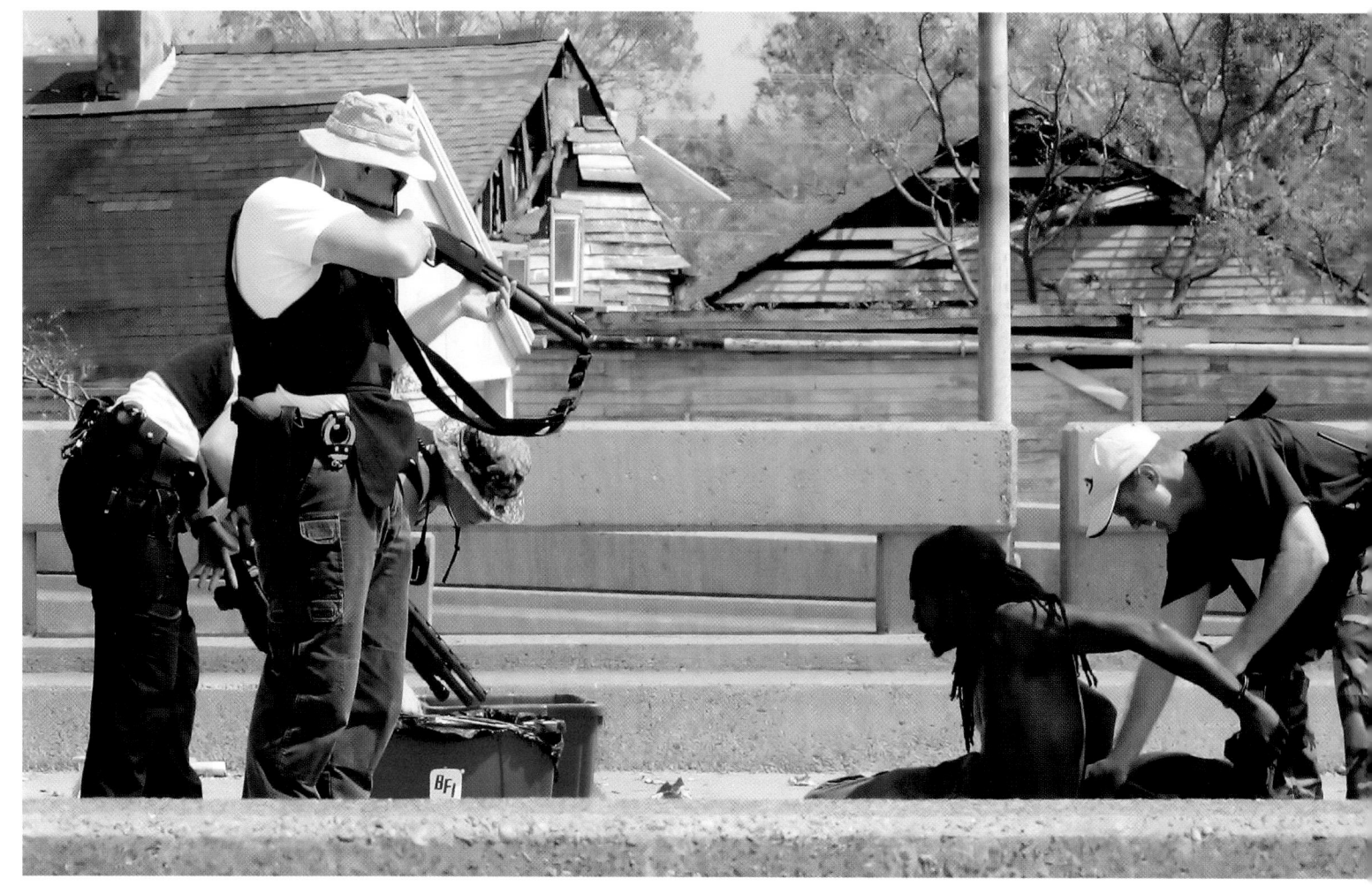

08.31.05 - New Orleans, LA - Police searched a man accused of looting on Interstate 10. They found beer in his bags. • IRWIN THOMPSON

PREVIOUS PAGE
08.31.05 - New Orleans, LA - Residents signaled to helicopters and waited to be rescued from the floodwaters. Some lived on their roofs for days to avoid the dangerous waters in the home. • SMILEY N. POOL

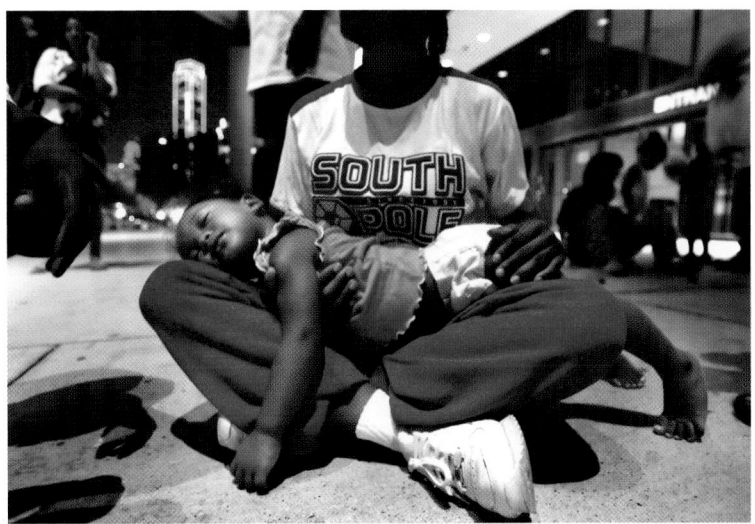

08.31.05 - Dallas, TX - Dallas officials and the American Red Cross opened Reunion Arena to hundreds of evacuees. Benita Prout of Boothville, La., and her granddaughter Essence Turner, 1, sat outside the arena. Ms. Prout was finally able to locate her daughter, Denita Prout, who was staying with a member of New Friendship Missionary Baptist Church in DeSoto. • MELANIE BURFORD

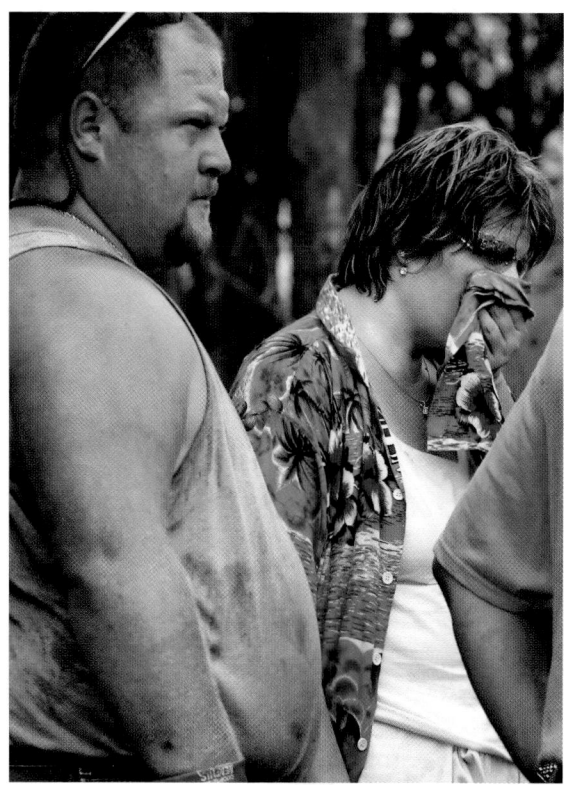

09.01.05 - Biloxi, MS - Surrounded by rescue workers, a woman was asked to identify the body of one of her neighbors, who was found dead in the rubble of his home. • BARBARA DAVIDSON

Right
09.01.05 - Biloxi, MS - Fire Department members, funeral employees and volunteers carried the body of a man killed when his Biloxi home collapsed. Urban search-and-rescue teams were seeking both bodies and people who might still be alive in the rubble. • BARBARA DAVIDSON

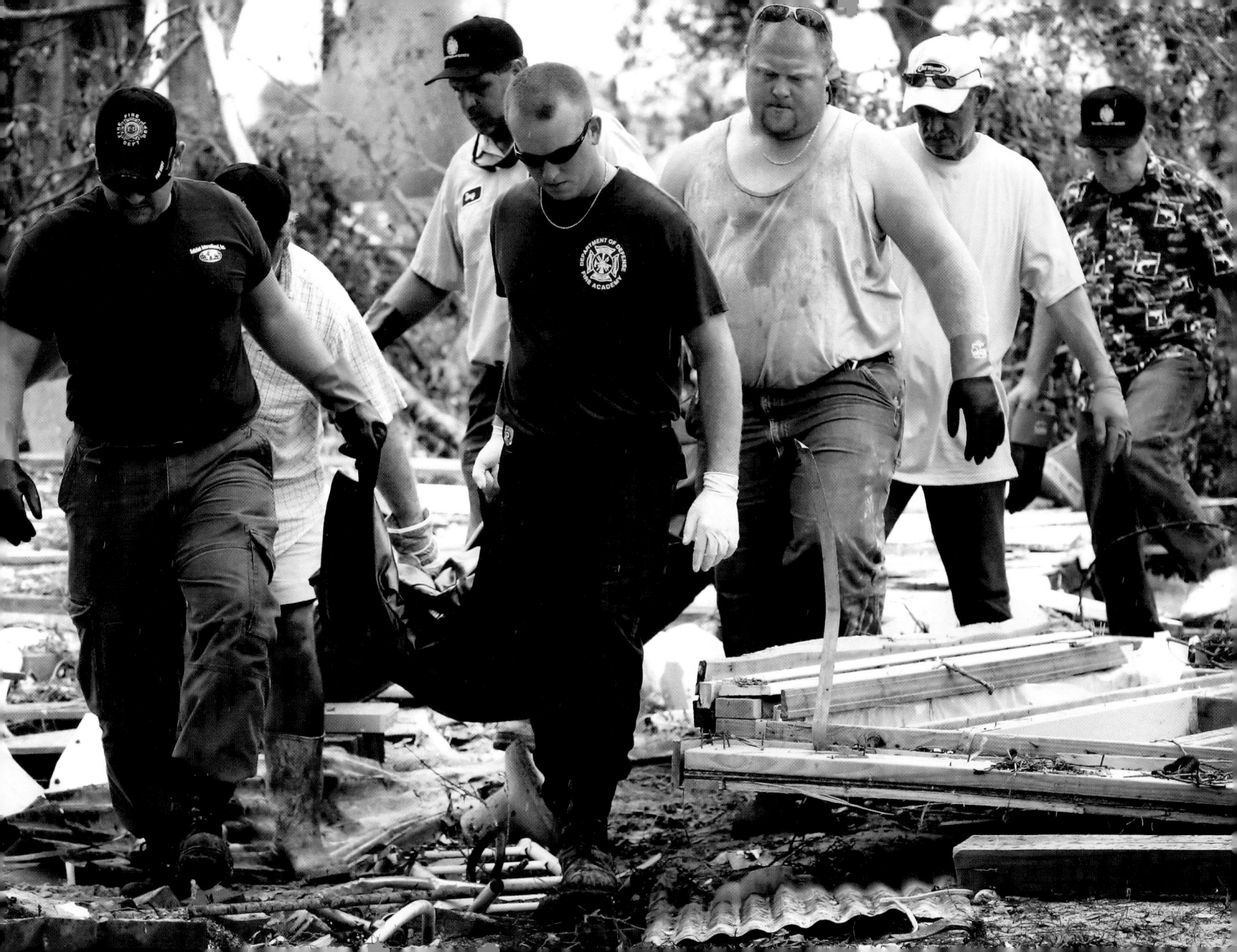

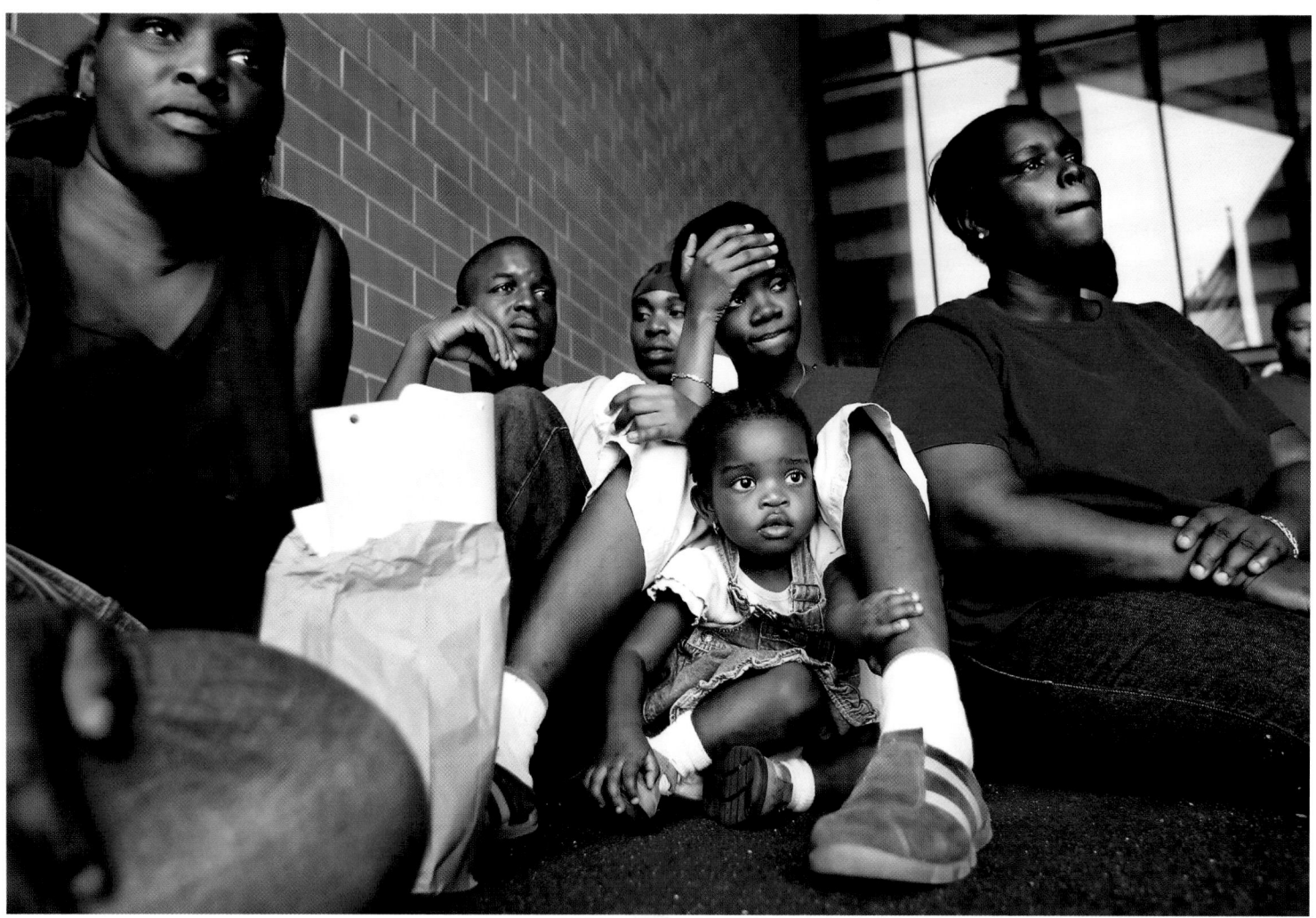

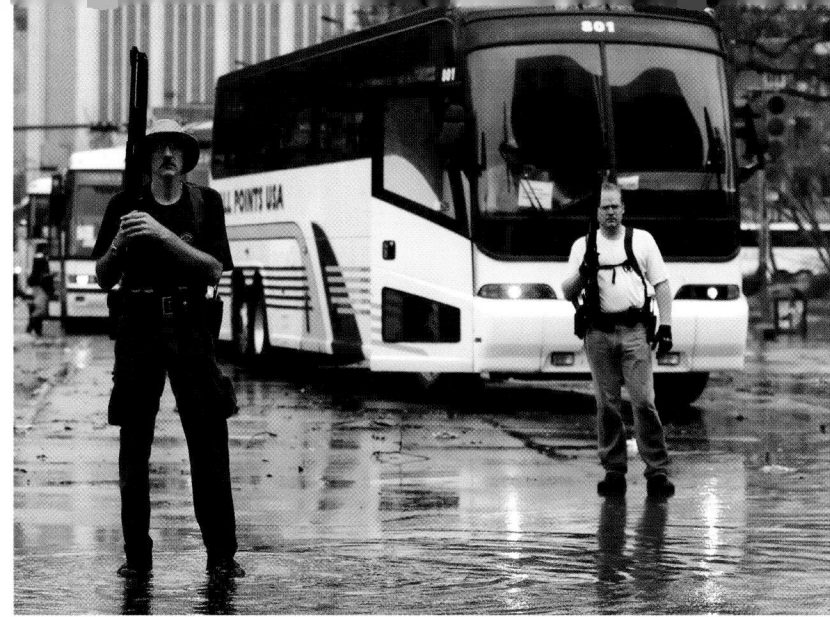

09.01.05 - New Orleans, LA - Police officers guarded the buses used to transport people from the Superdome to the Houston Astrodome, three days after Hurricane Katrina flooded the city.
• MICHAEL AINSWORTH

BELOW
09.01.05 - Houston, TX - Patients from the Veterans Affairs Hospital in New Orleans arrived at Ellington Field in Houston. An emergency triage center was set up inside a hangar at Ellington and was staffed by doctors, nurses and other personnel from Houston's VA Medical Center. • ERICH SCHLEGEL

LEFT
09.01.05 - Dallas, TX - Tyrone Jackson (from left), Alfred Glenn Hayes, Janell Cormier with daughter Taylor Cormier, 1, and Jeanette Cormier, all of New Orleans, rested outside Reunion Arena. Dallas organizations were there to provide medical care, information and counseling.
• MELANIE BURFORD

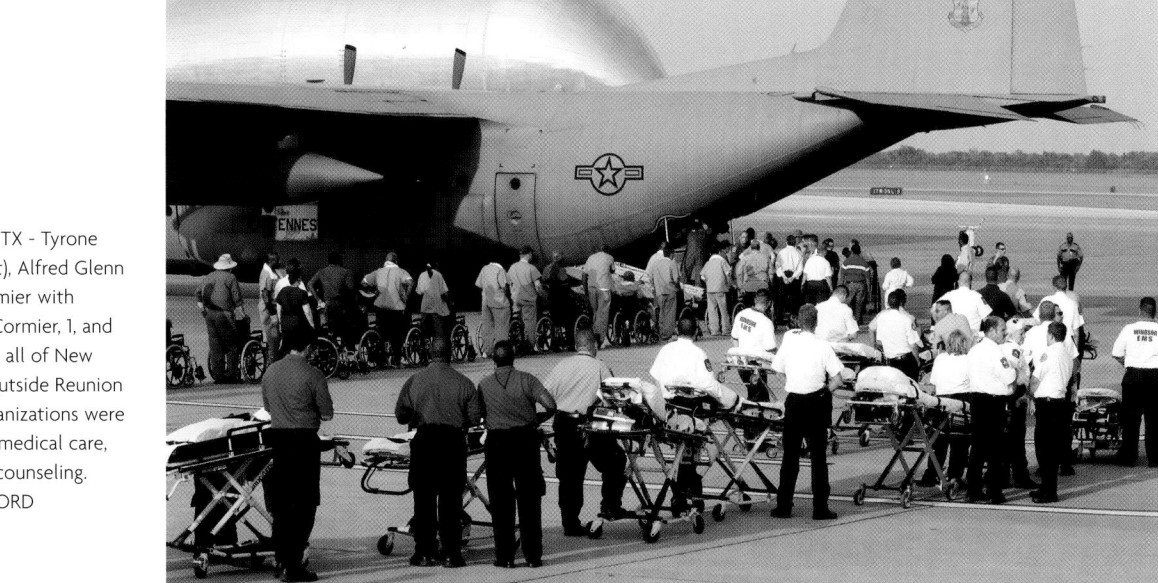

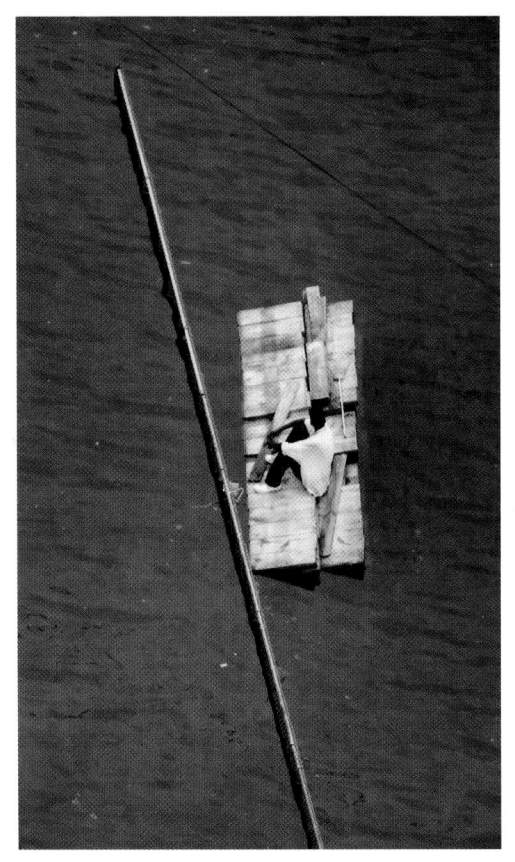

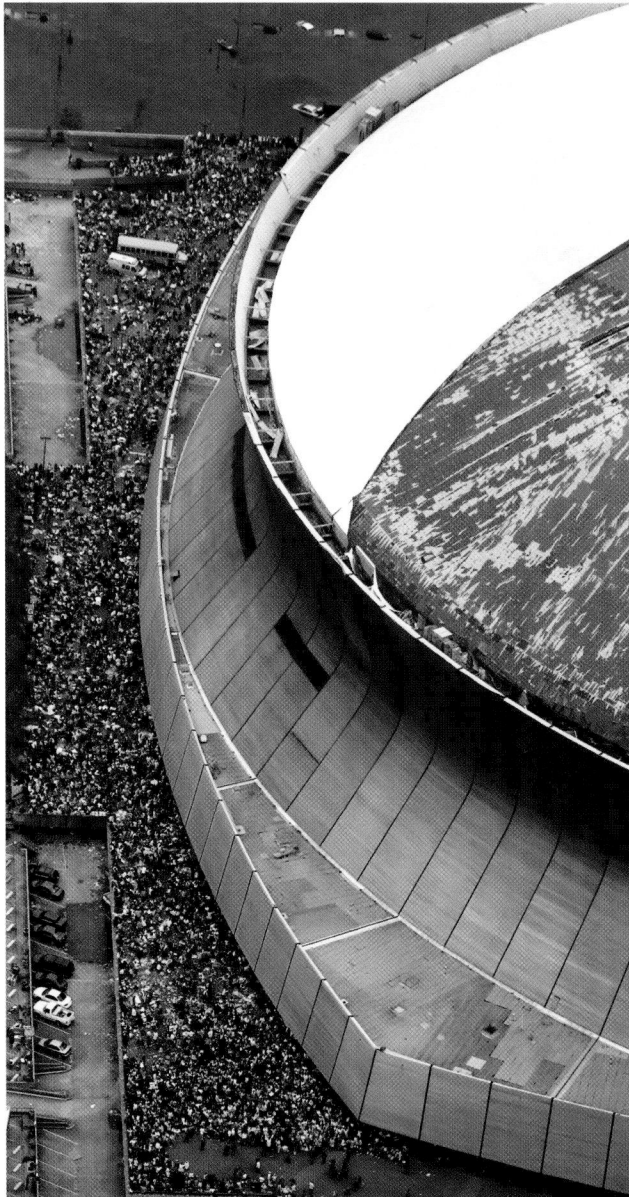

09.01.05 - New Orleans, LA - A throng of people waited to be evacuated outside the Superdome.
• SMILEY N. POOL

LEFT
09.01.05 - New Orleans, LA - A man floated on lumber in the floodwaters of the city. • SMILEY N. POOL

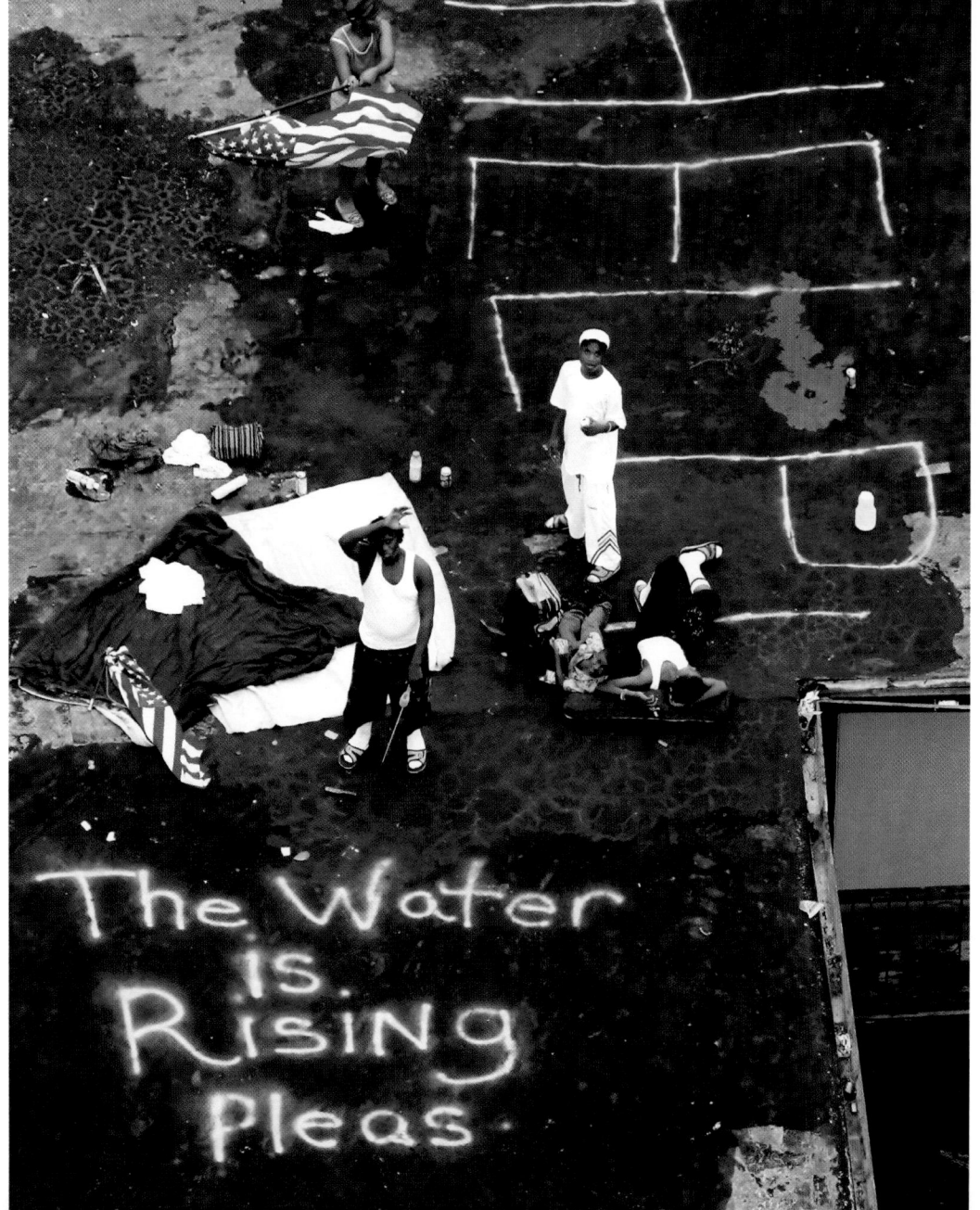

09.01.05 - New Orleans, LA - Residents sent out a desperate plea for help as they waited to be rescued from the roof of an apartment complex.
• SMILEY N. POOL

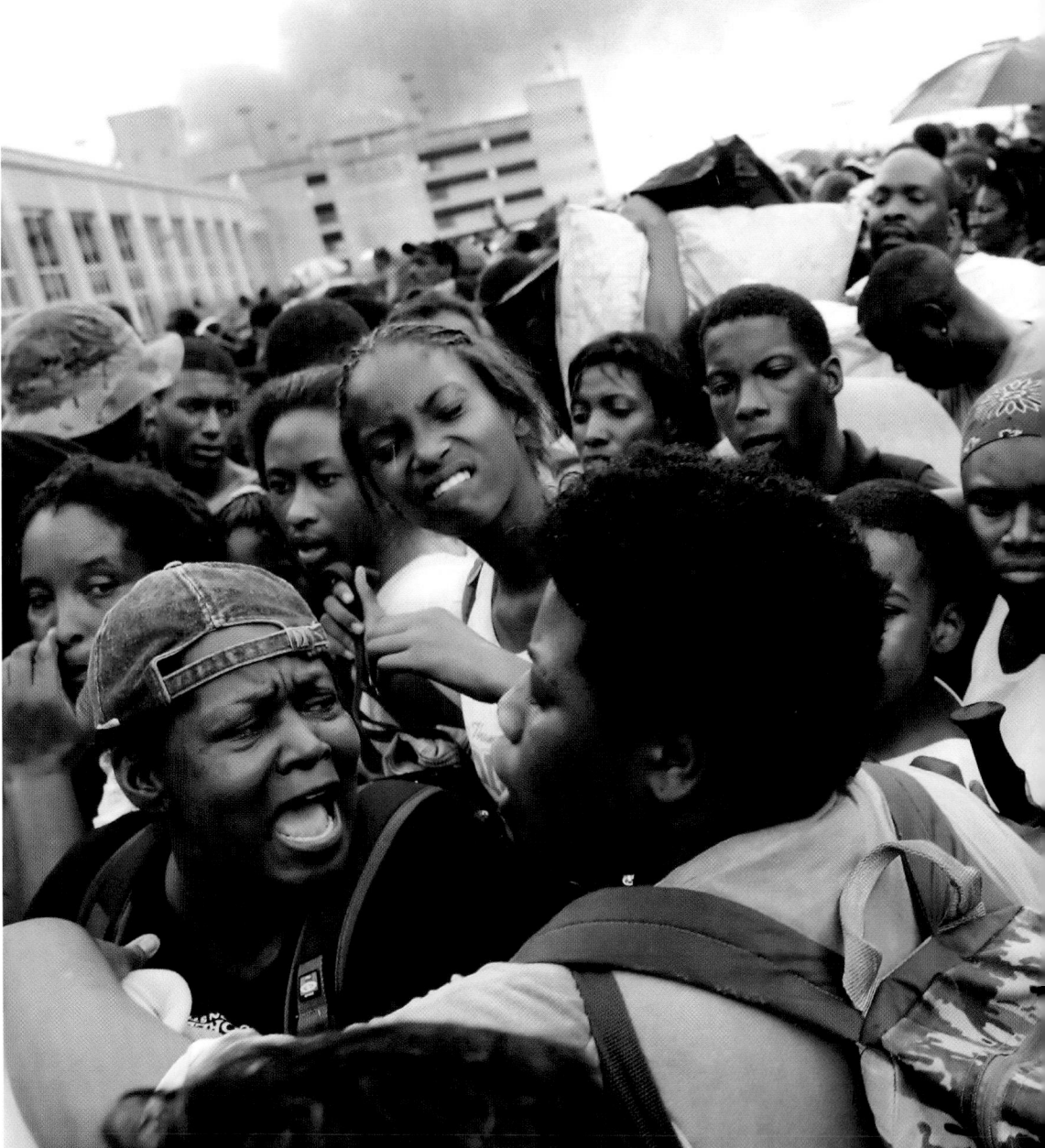

09.01.05 - New Orleans, LA - Evacuees at the Superdome argued in the tangled line for a bus trip to the Houston Astrodome. All over New Orleans, tempers flared as thousands waited for a way out of town.
• MICHAEL AINSWORTH

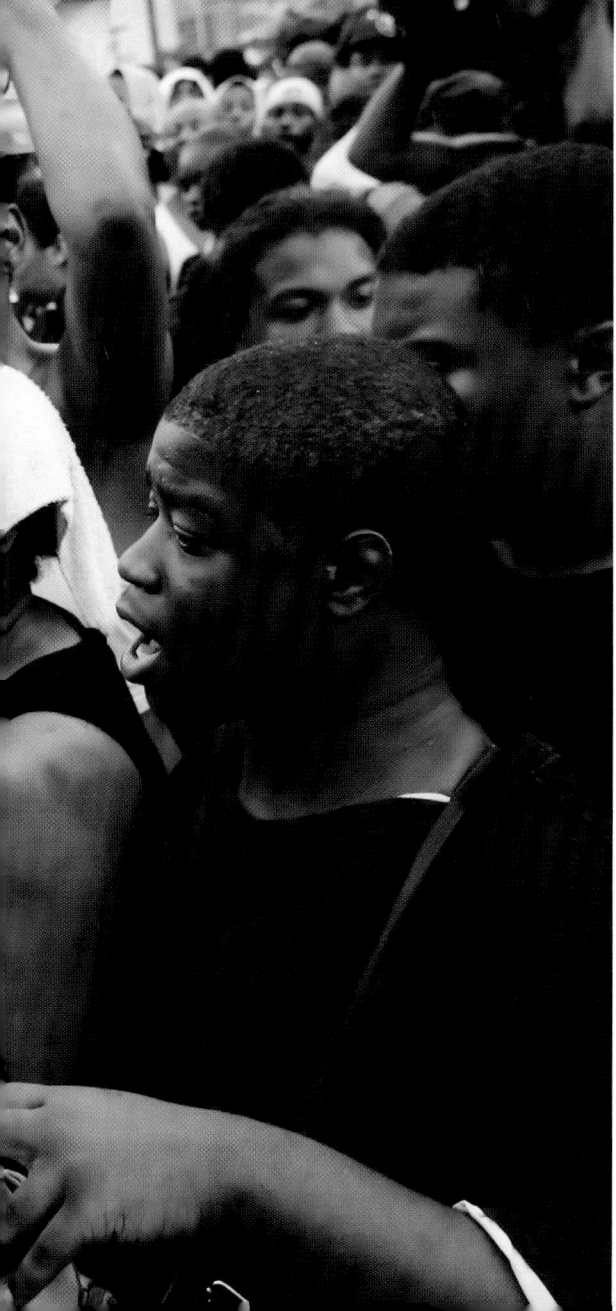

"This is a desperate SOS."

- **Ray Nagin,** Mayor of New Orleans

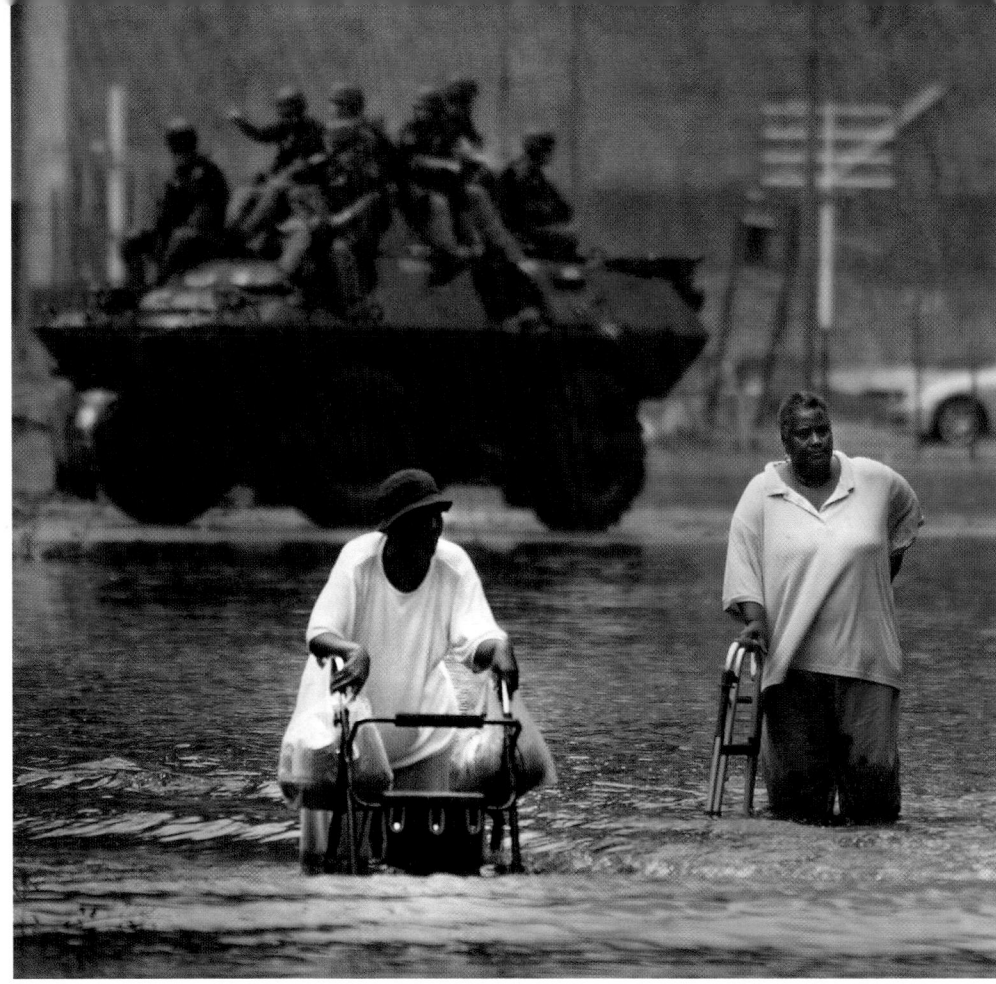

09.01.05 - New Orleans, LA - Tossed together by crisis, 81-year-old Louis Jones (left) and 62-year-old Catherine McZeal joined forces to navigate Poydras Street in their trek to the Superdome and a chance at evacuation. Both said their children couldn't get through barricades to help them out. • MICHAEL AINSWORTH

RIGHT
09.01.05 - New Orleans, LA - Not as refreshing as a cold bottle of water, but they were on their way: Evacuees sqeezed into a water truck as they left New Orleans and headed toward Baton Rouge. • MICHAEL AINSWORTH

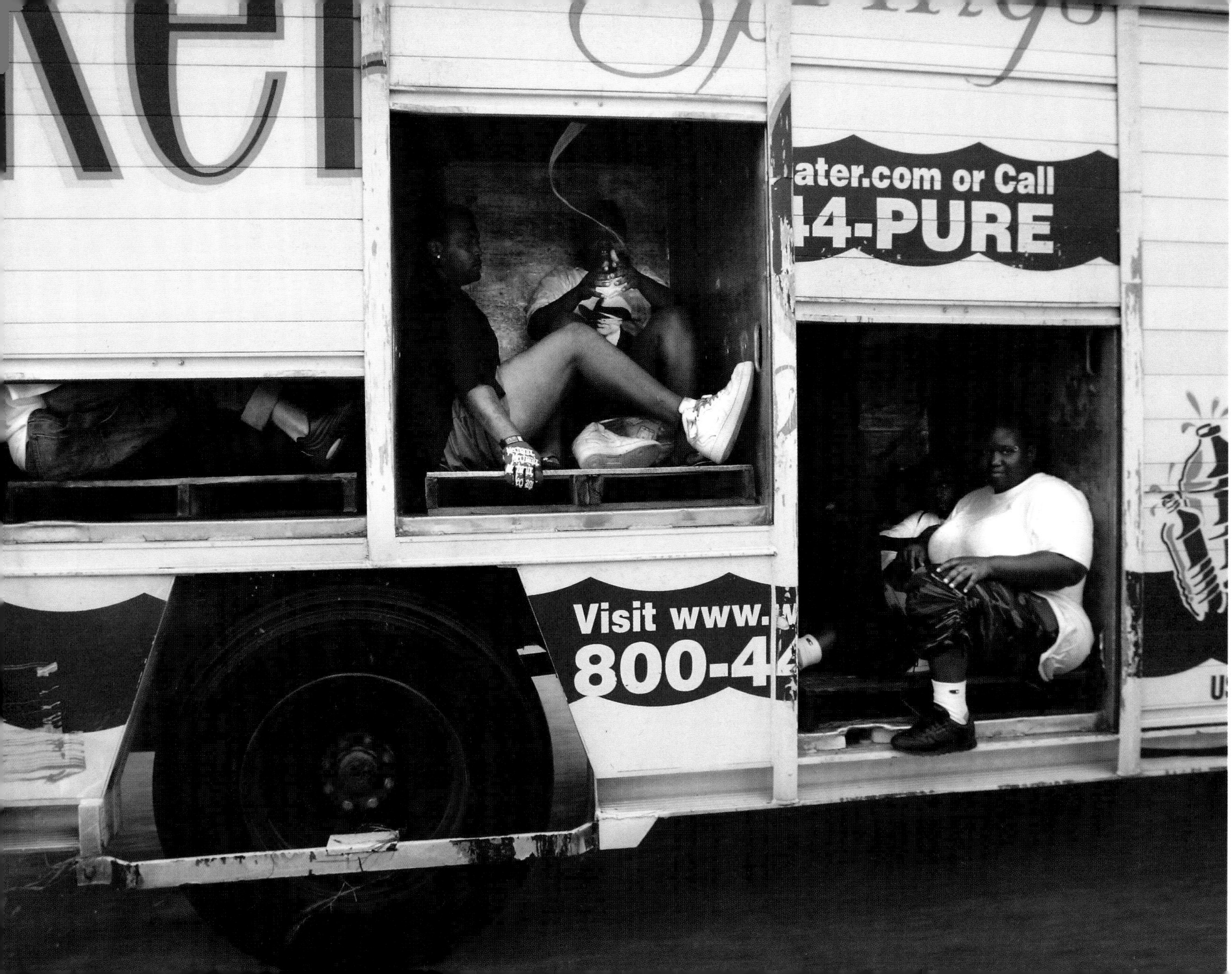
ater.com or Call
44-PURE
Visit www.
800-44

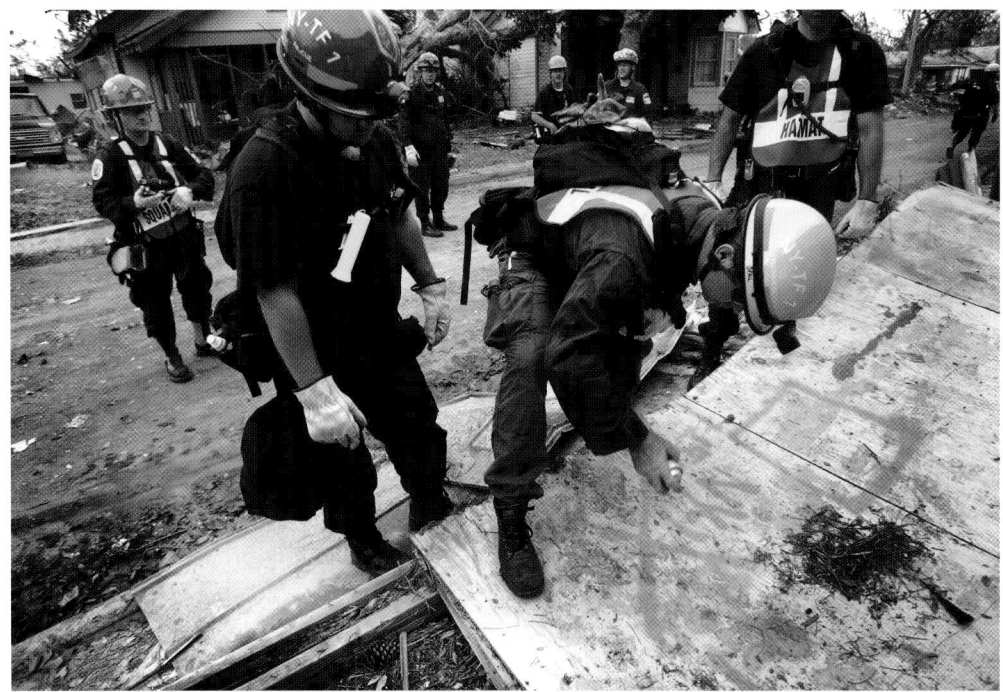

09.01.05 - Biloxi, MS - New York search and rescue team members marked a house, indicating that no bodies were found and that it had been checked. In Biloxi, local law enforcement patrolled the streets as search teams from Tampa, Fla., Indianapolis and New York City helped local rescue workers search buildings, cars and trailers for survivors and bodies. • BARBARA DAVIDSON

RIGHT
09.01.05 - Pascagoula, MS - Charles Quave (second from left), Nakita Chisholm and Greg Dufault saved gas and pushed their vehicles while waiting to fill up. • LOUIS DELUCA

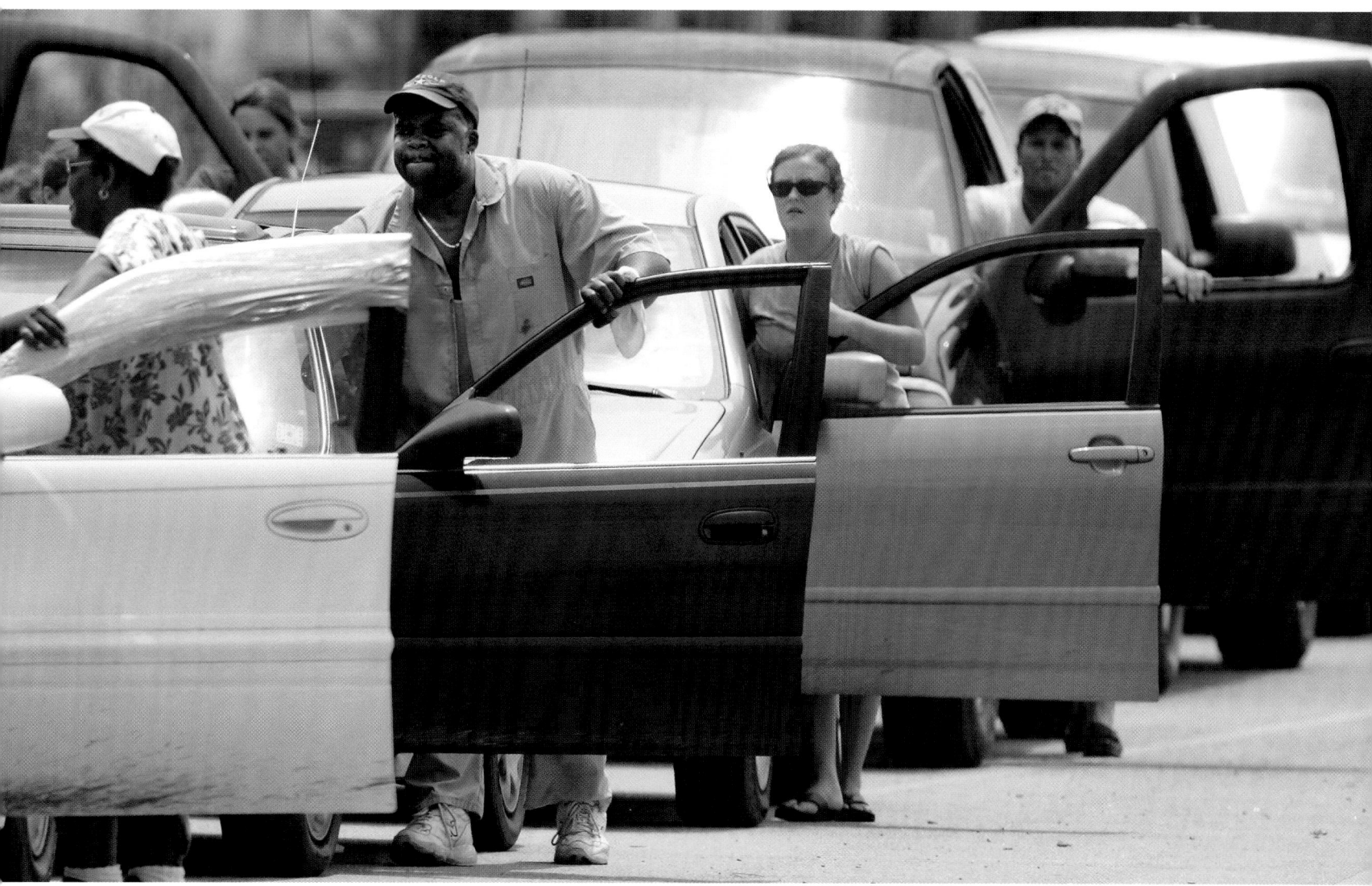

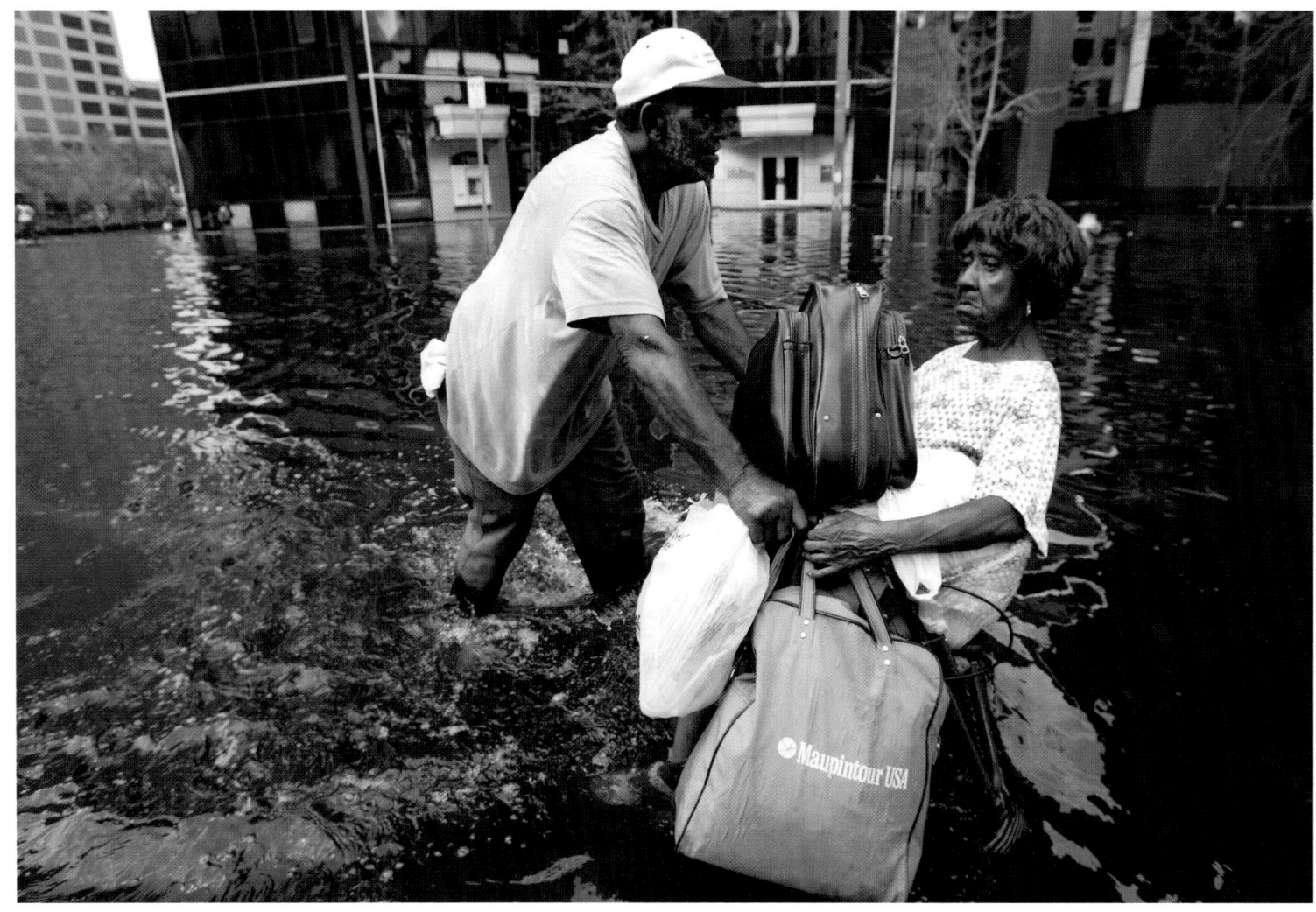

09.01.05 - New Orleans, LA - Miller Scott Jr., 66, helped his aunt Elouise Joseph, 75, make her way down flooded Poydras Street heading toward the Superdome. "No one else would help her," Mr. Scott said. • MICHAEL AINSWORTH

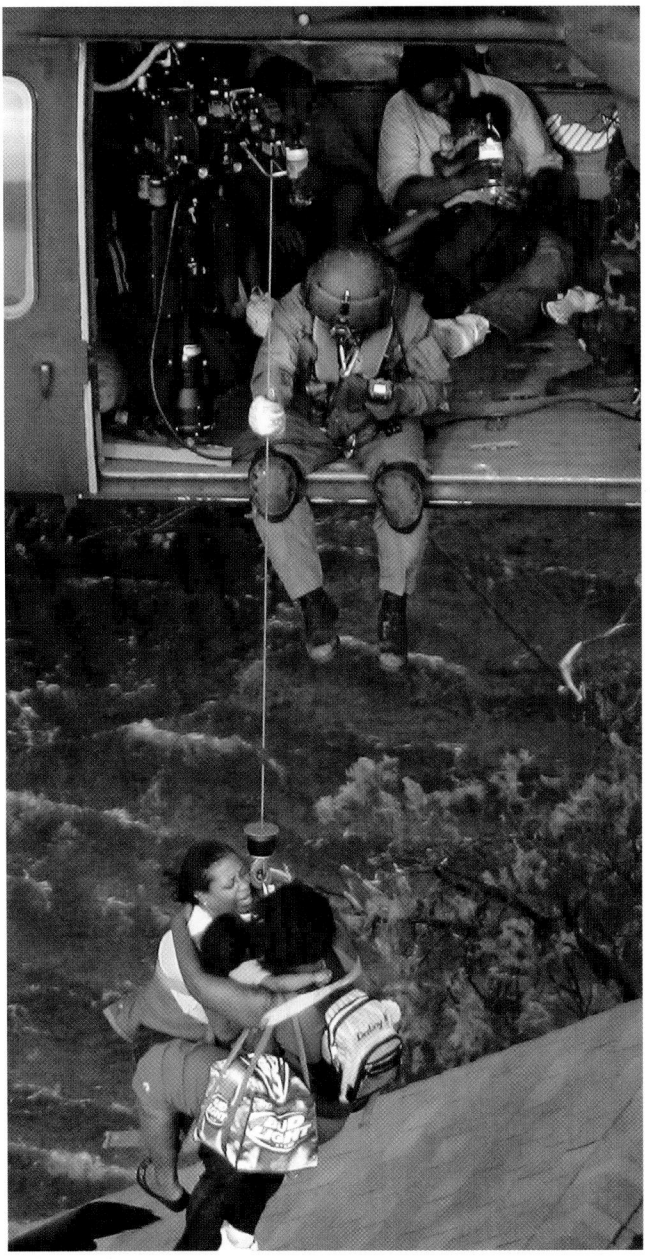

09.01.05 - New Orleans, LA - Two women clutched a baby as they were lifted by a helicopter from the roof of a house surrounded by floodwaters.
• SMILEY N. POOL

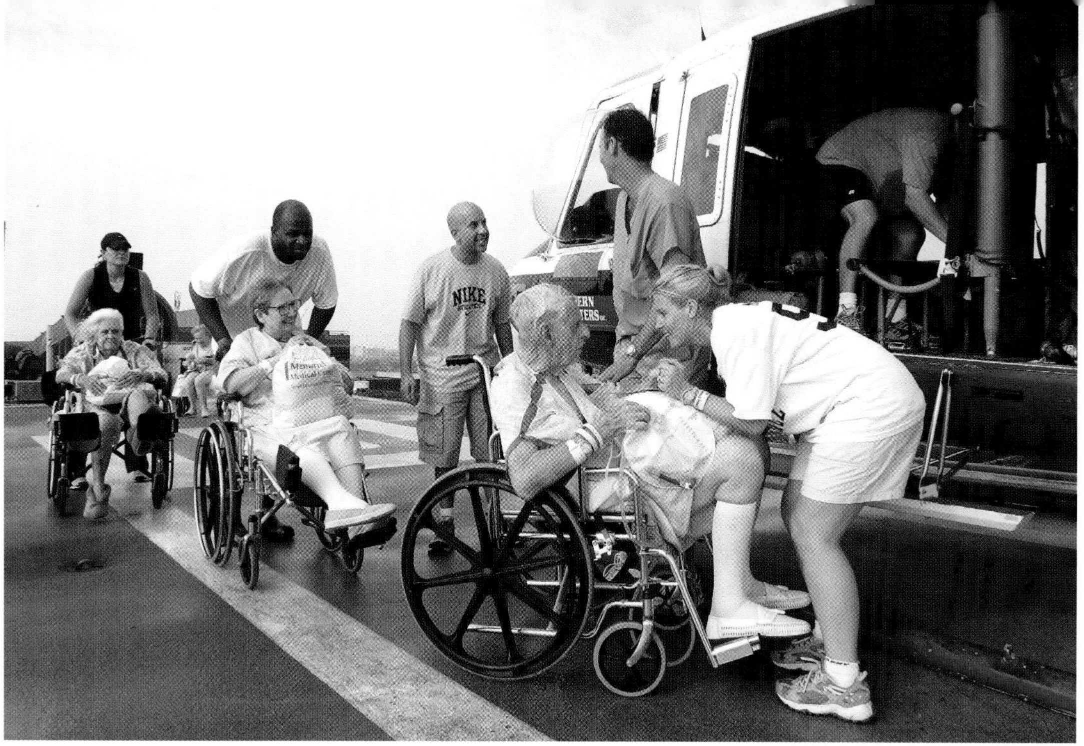

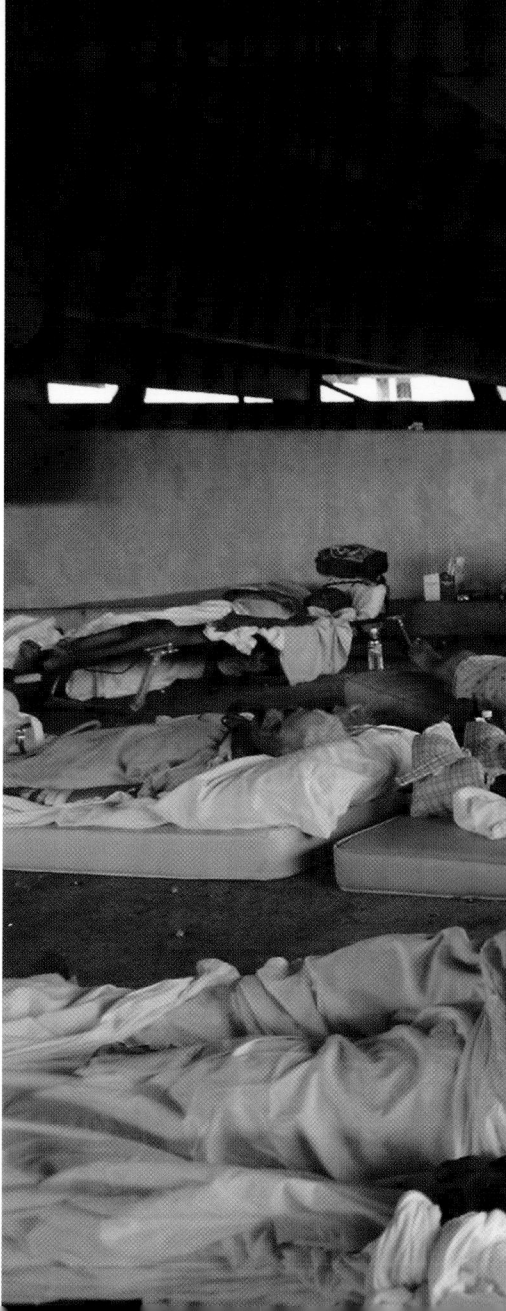

09.01.05 - New Orleans, LA - Nurse Ashley Uffman (right) bid farewell to a patient preparing to be evacuated by helicopter from Memorial Medical Center. • BRAD LOPER

CENTER
09.01.05 - New Orleans, LA - Memorial Medical Center nurse Mary Jo D'Amico fanned a patient waiting in the hospital's parking garage for helicopter transport from New Orleans.
• BRAD LOPER

RIGHT
09.02.05 - New Orleans, LA - Staff members at Memorial Medical Center waved to co-workers being airlifted while they waited their turn for a ride. • BRAD LOPER

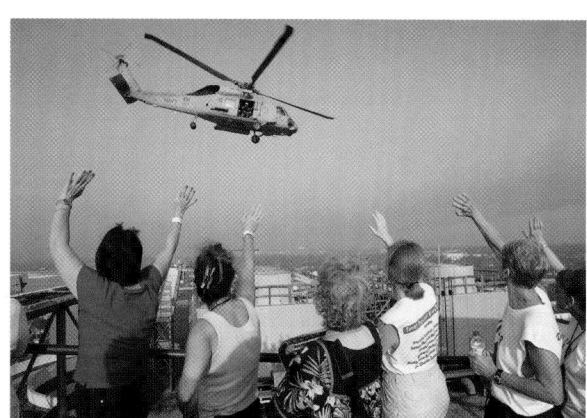

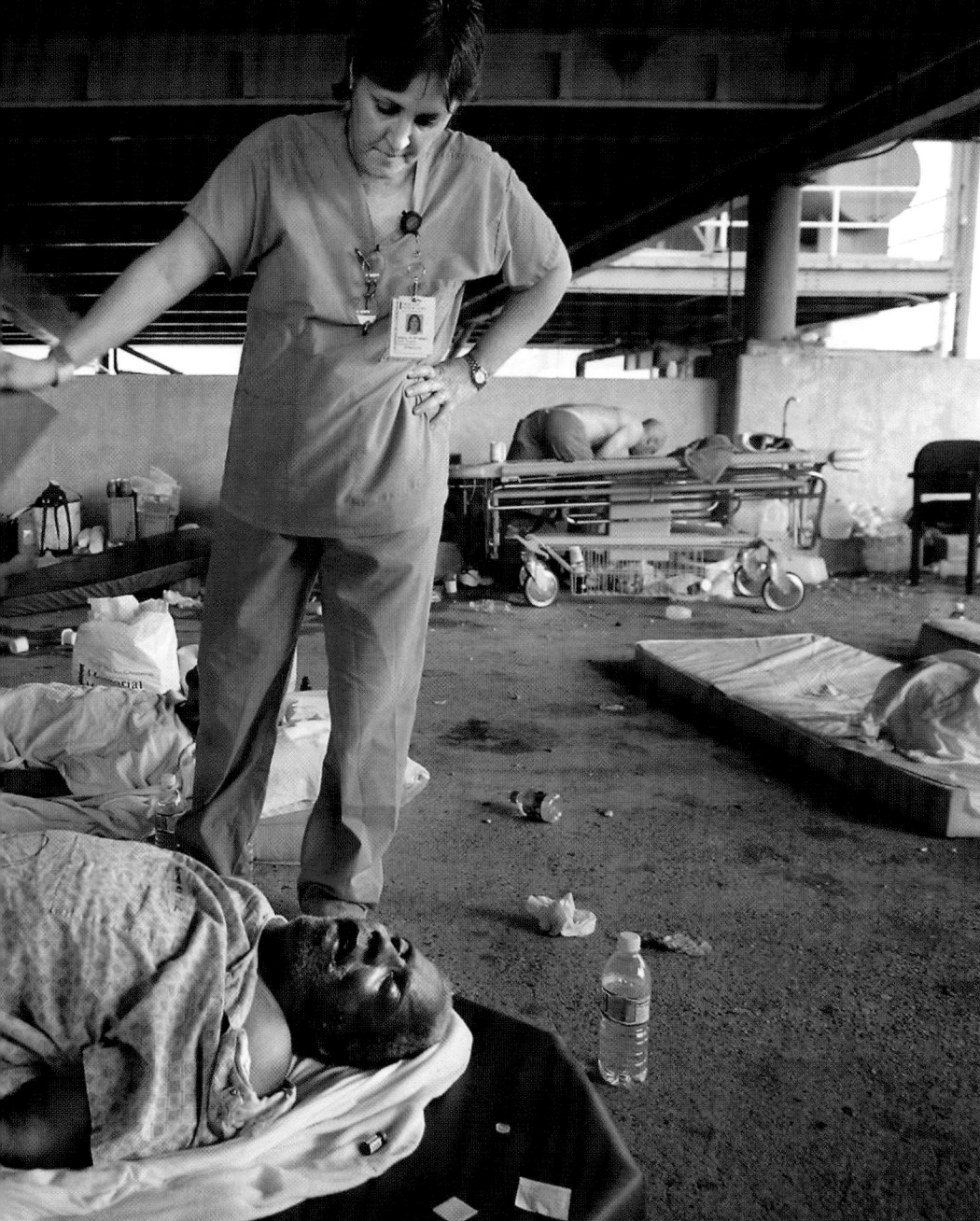

ON THEIR OWN

All along, Tenet Healthcare Corp. officials expected the government to take control of the situation, as it had in every other natural disaster.

That notion was shattered in the call from an official with Louisiana's Office of Emergency Preparedness to Bob Smith, senior vice president of Tenet's Texas-Gulf Coast region.

That official asked whether Tenet had arranged "private assets" to evacuate its facilities, including Memorial Medical Center.

"Are you telling me we have to use private assets to evacuate?" Mr. Smith asked.

"I'm telling you, you need to use private assets if you want it done quickly," she replied.

"Private assets" meant that Tenet would have to create its own rescue airlift.

That 9 a.m. phone call, 48 hours after Katrina slammed New Orleans, would set in motion a military-strength effort to save thousands of Tenet employees and patients from a flooded, paralyzed city that was plummeting toward anarchy.

By the time Tenet finally evacuated its stricken Gulf Coast hospitals, it had mobilized a fleet of helicopters and private jets, tapped the military connections of Ross Perot Sr. and Ross Perot Jr., and relied on ham radio operators to bypass downed phone lines and dead cell networks.

• SUDEEP REDDY

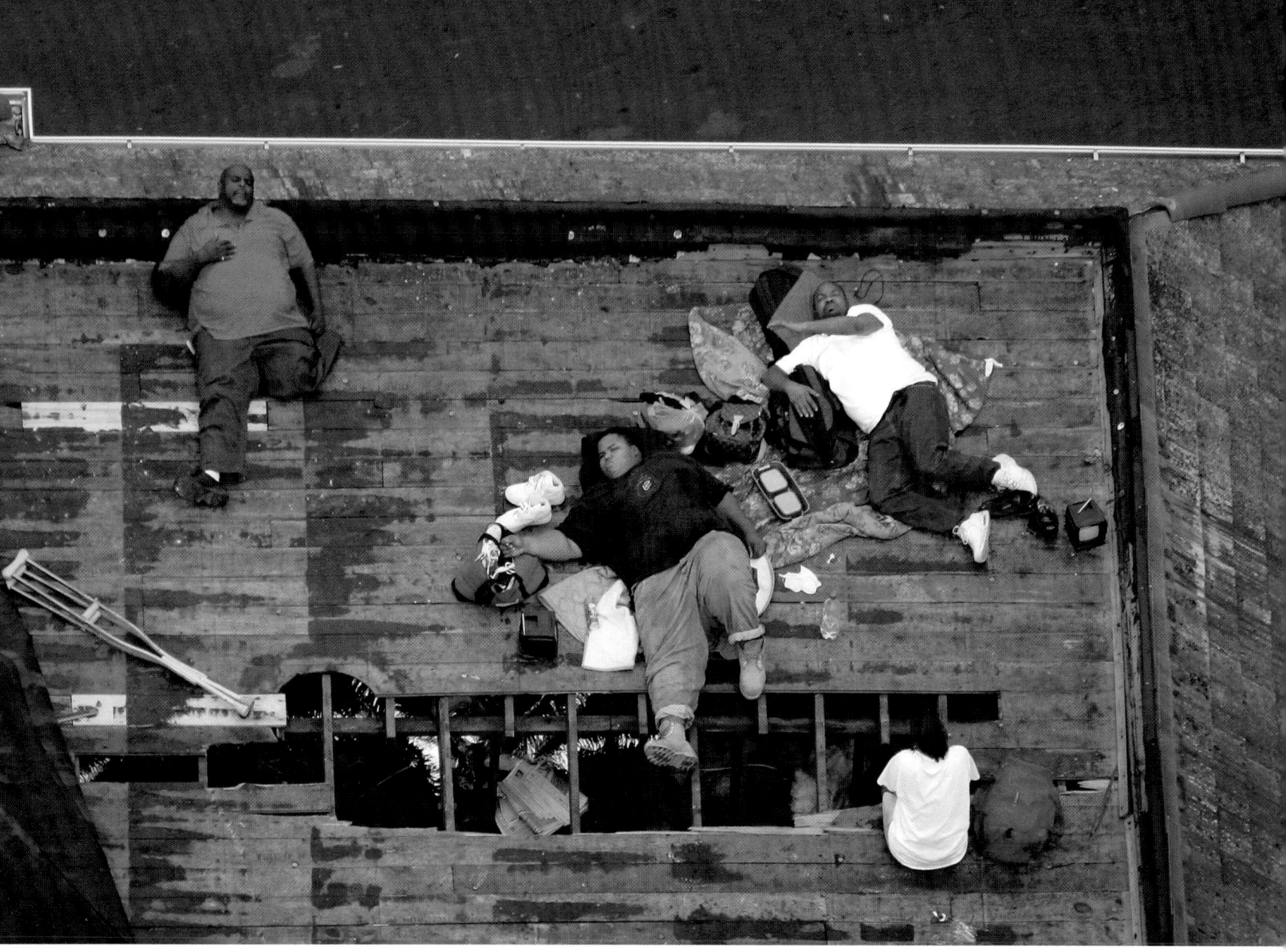

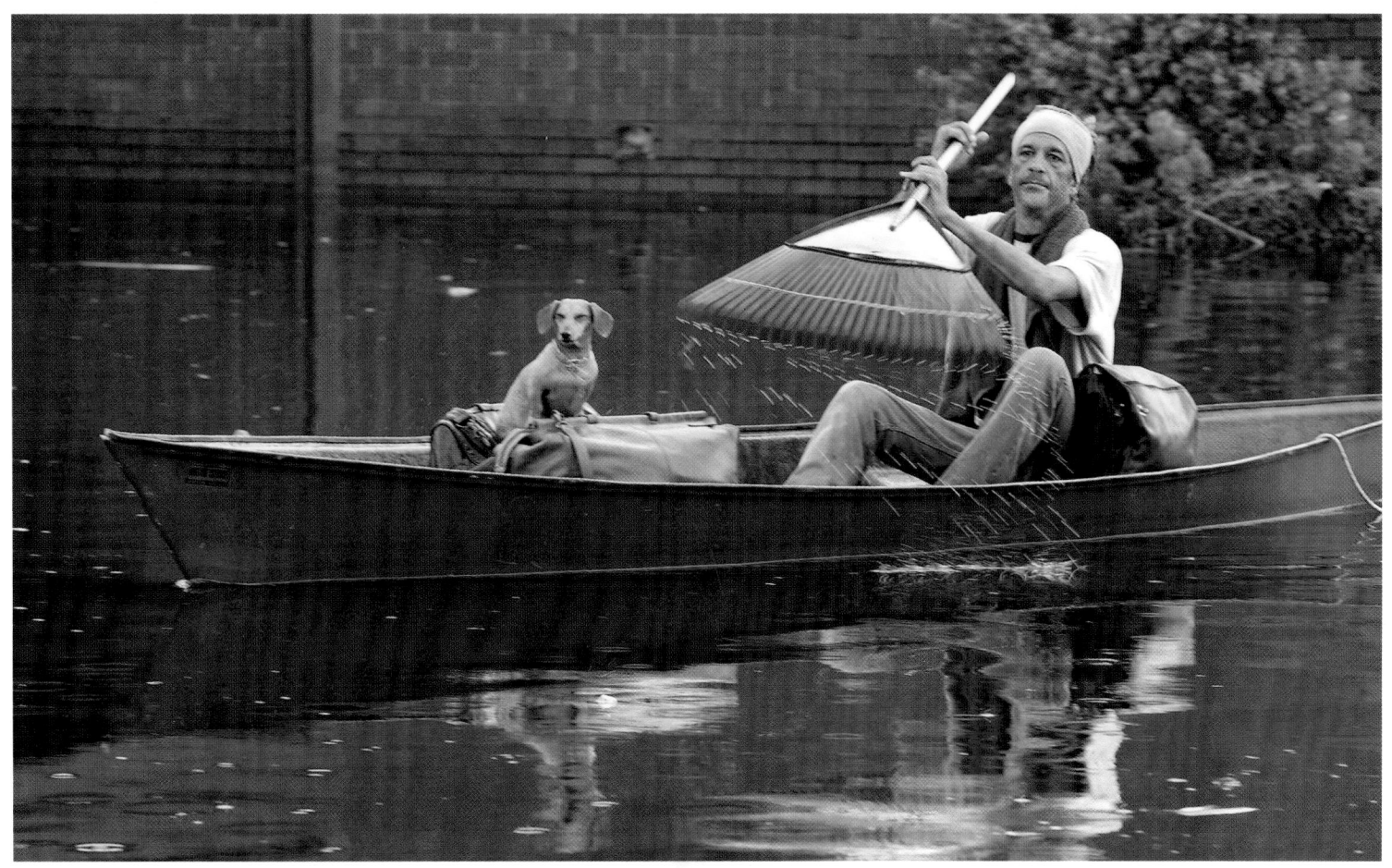

09.01.05 - New Orleans, LA - A man made do with a rake as a paddle as he headed down St. Bernard Avenue with his dog. • IRWIN THOMPSON

LEFT
09.01.05 - New Orleans, LA - No doubt weak and hungry, residents languished while waiting to be rescued. • SMILEY N. POOL

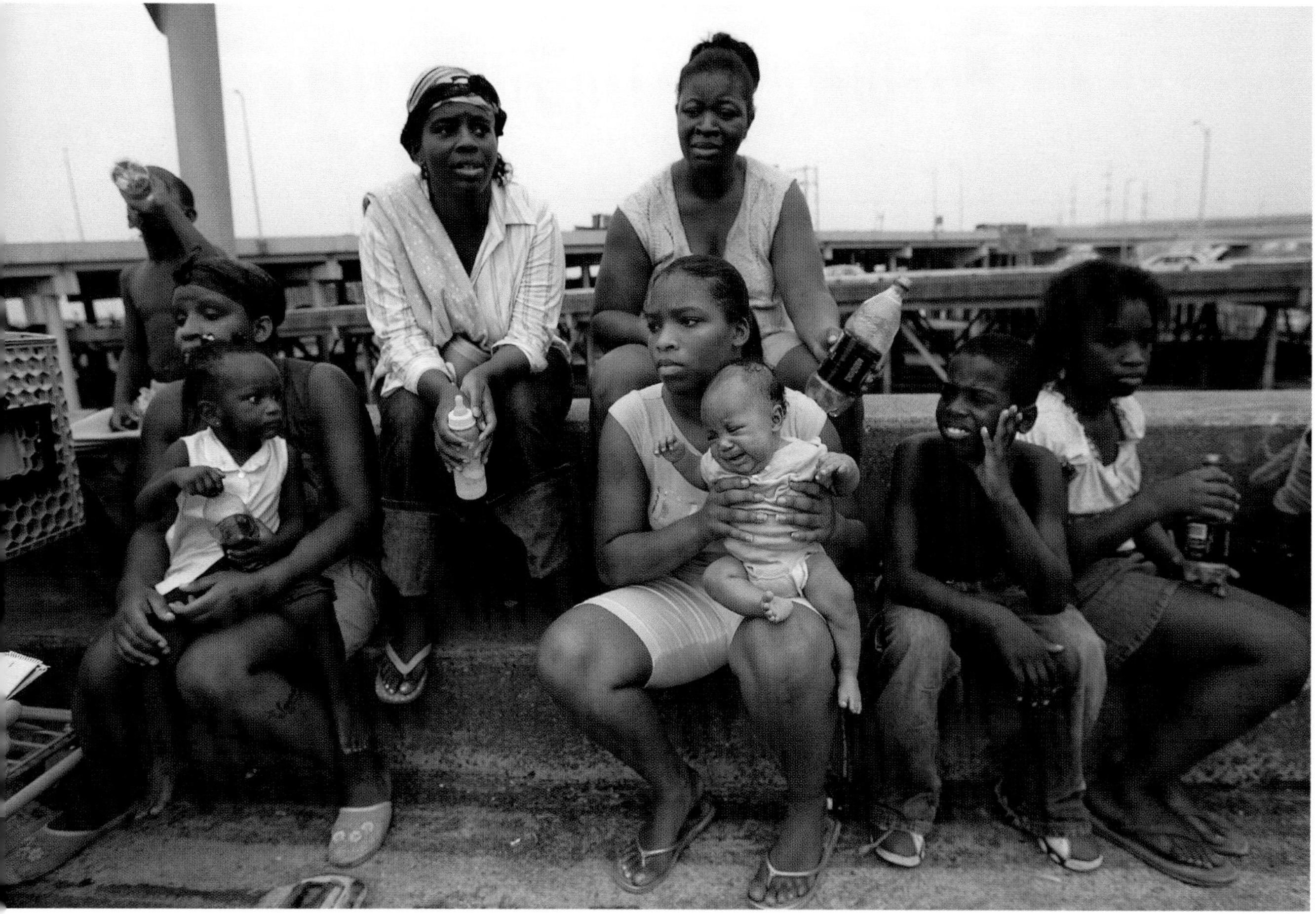

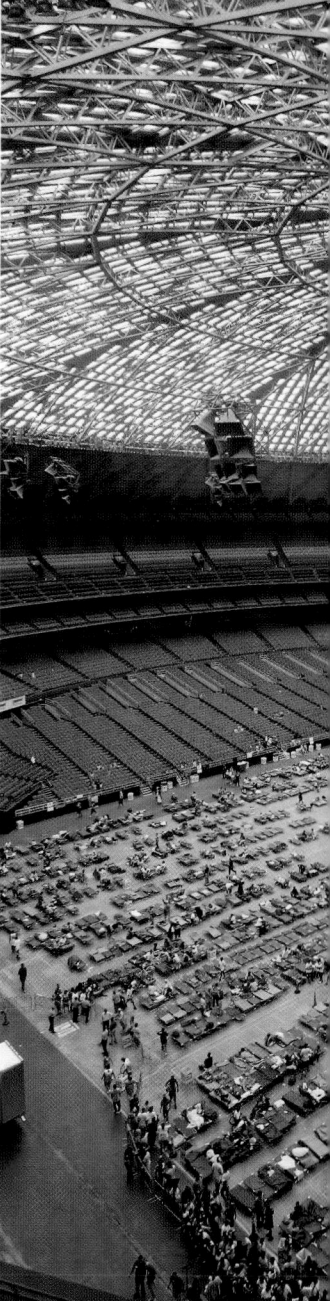

09.01.05 - New Orleans, LA - Brenda Smith (top center) kept her family and friends together on the Interstate 10 overpass near the Superdome, three days after Katrina hit. "I'm so thirsty and hungry," she said. "We have our babies getting sick."
• MICHAEL AINSWORTH

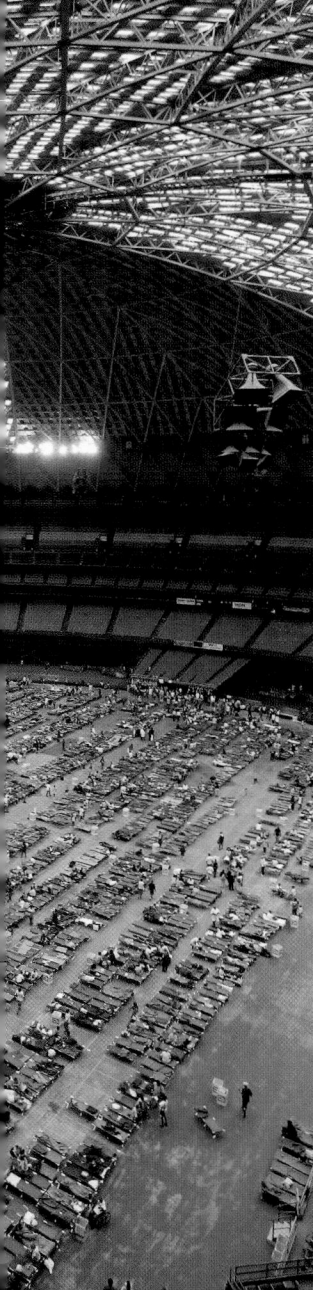

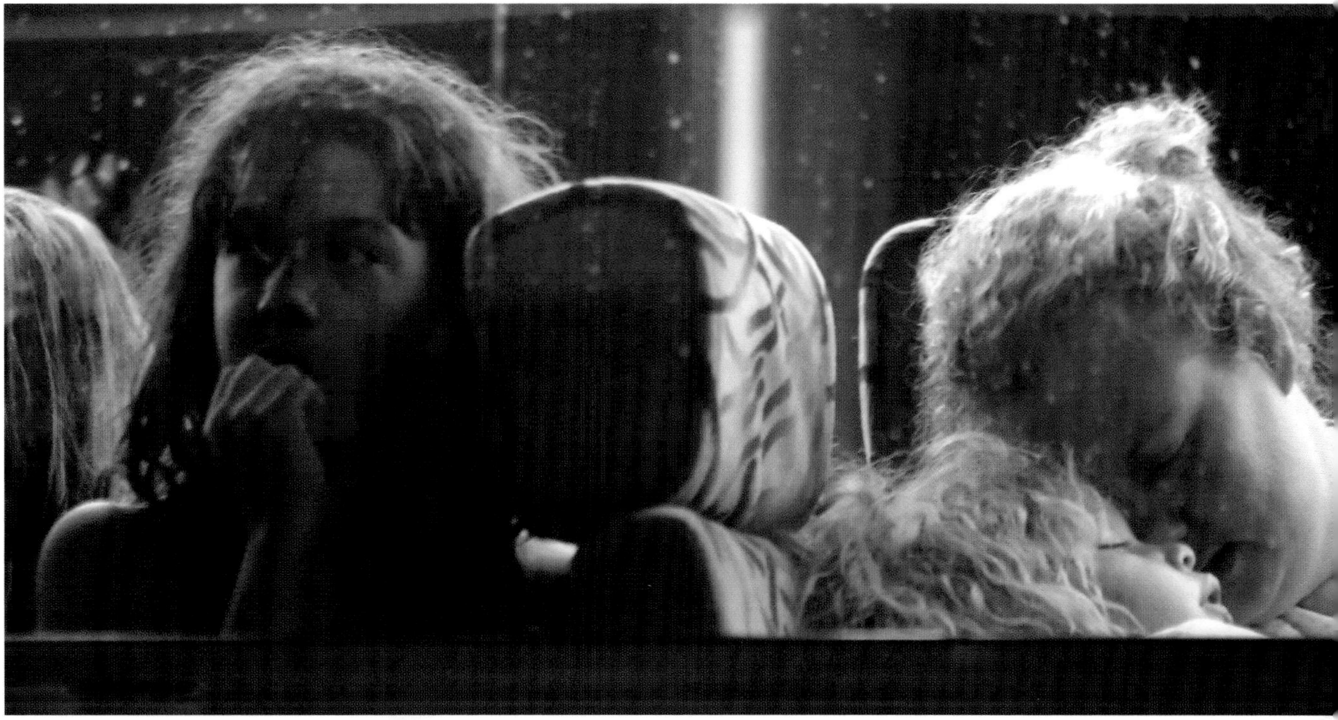

09.01.05 – Houston, TX – Buses from the Superdome began pulling into Houston's Astrodome. • ERICH SCHLEGEL

<small>CENTER</small>
09.01.05 – Houston, TX – As evacuees arrived at the Astrodome, they were given a hot meal and a chance to shower in the old athletic locker rooms – after three days without water and electricity in New Orleans. • ERICH SCHLEGEL

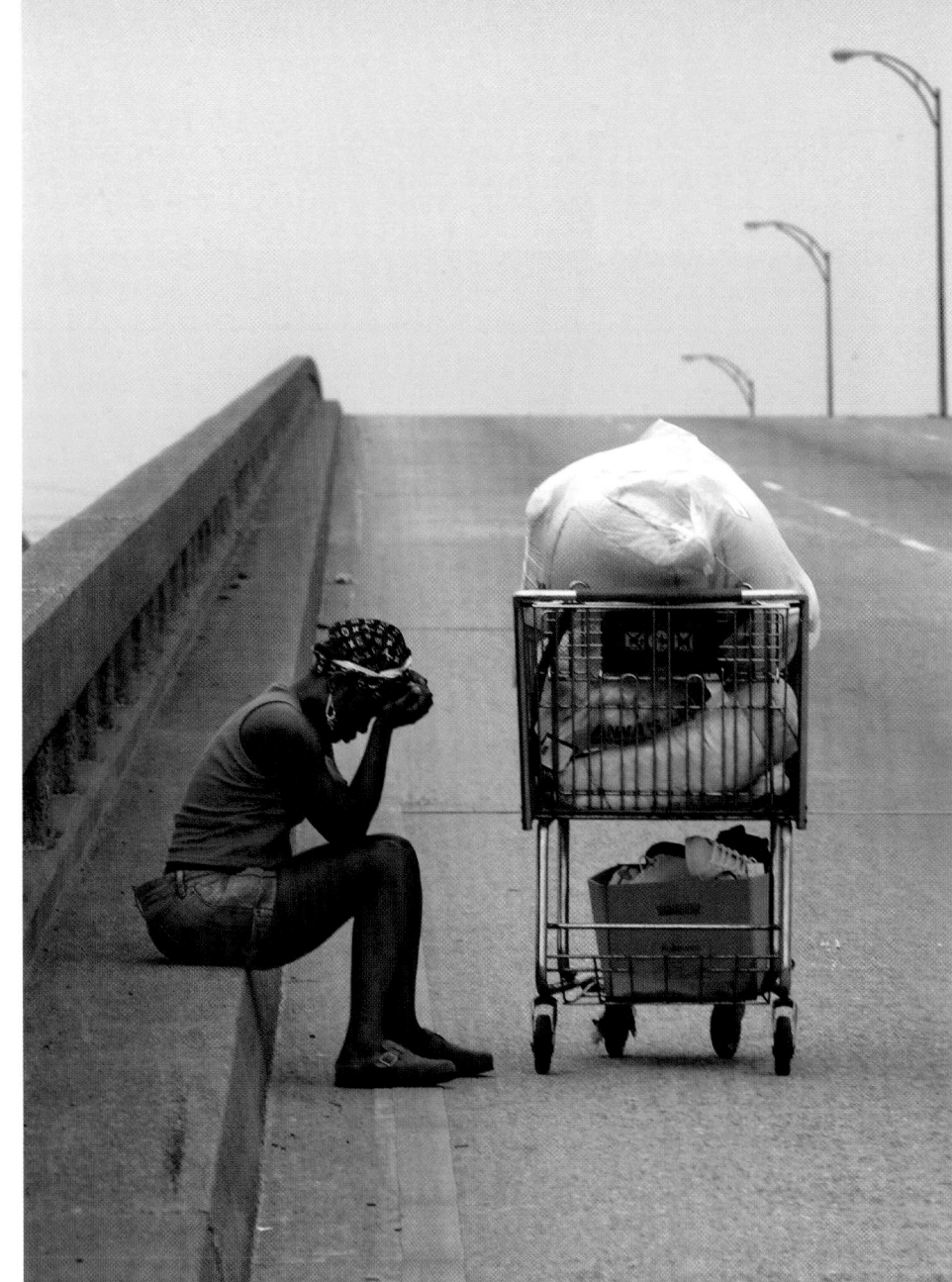

09.01.05 - New Orleans, LA - Kimi Seymour, 27, took a break from pushing her few remaining possessions along Interstate 10.
• IRWIN THOMPSON

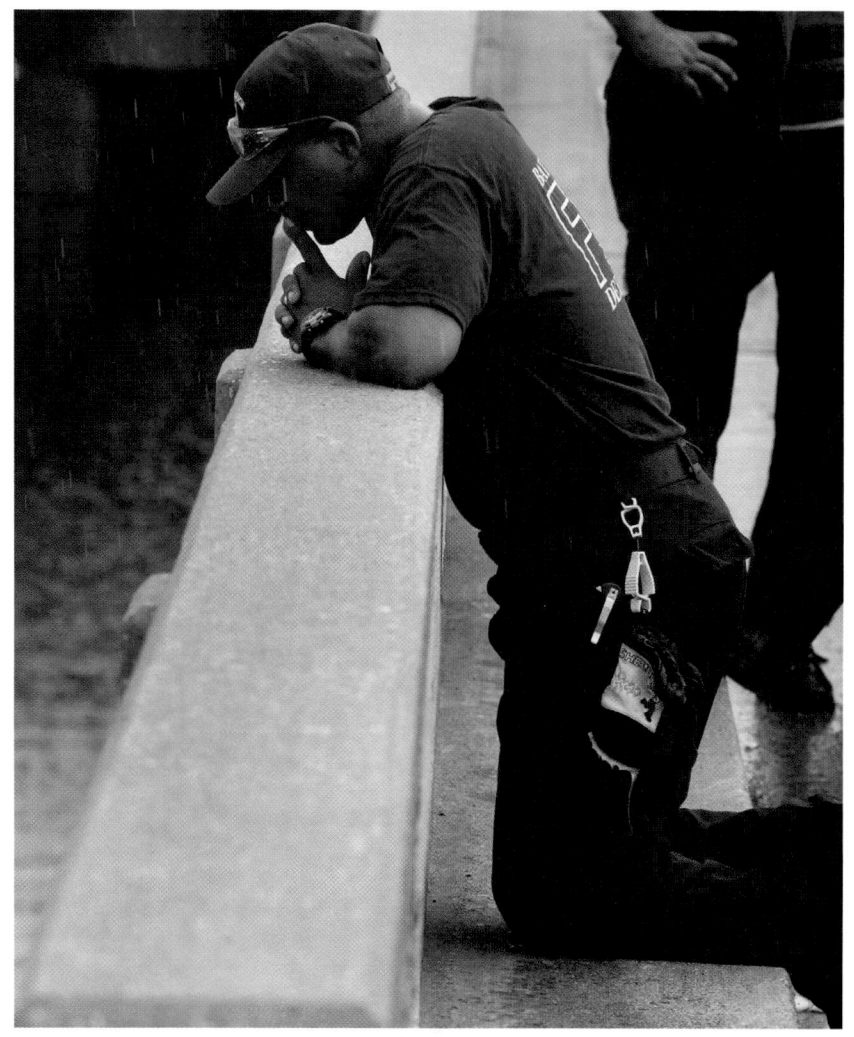

09.01.05 - New Orleans, LA - Baton Rouge firefighter Michael Adams paused to pray after search and rescue efforts ended for the day. • IRWIN THOMPSON

*"We have so many people suffering.
This is a great Louisiana tragedy."*

- Kathleen Blanco, Louisiana governor

RIGHT
09.01.05 - New Orleans, LA - Dejon Fisher, 8, waited fearfully with Cavel Fisher Clay, 33, and Alexis Fisher, 14, in a hostile line for buses to the Houston Astrodome.
• MICHAEL AINSWORTH

94

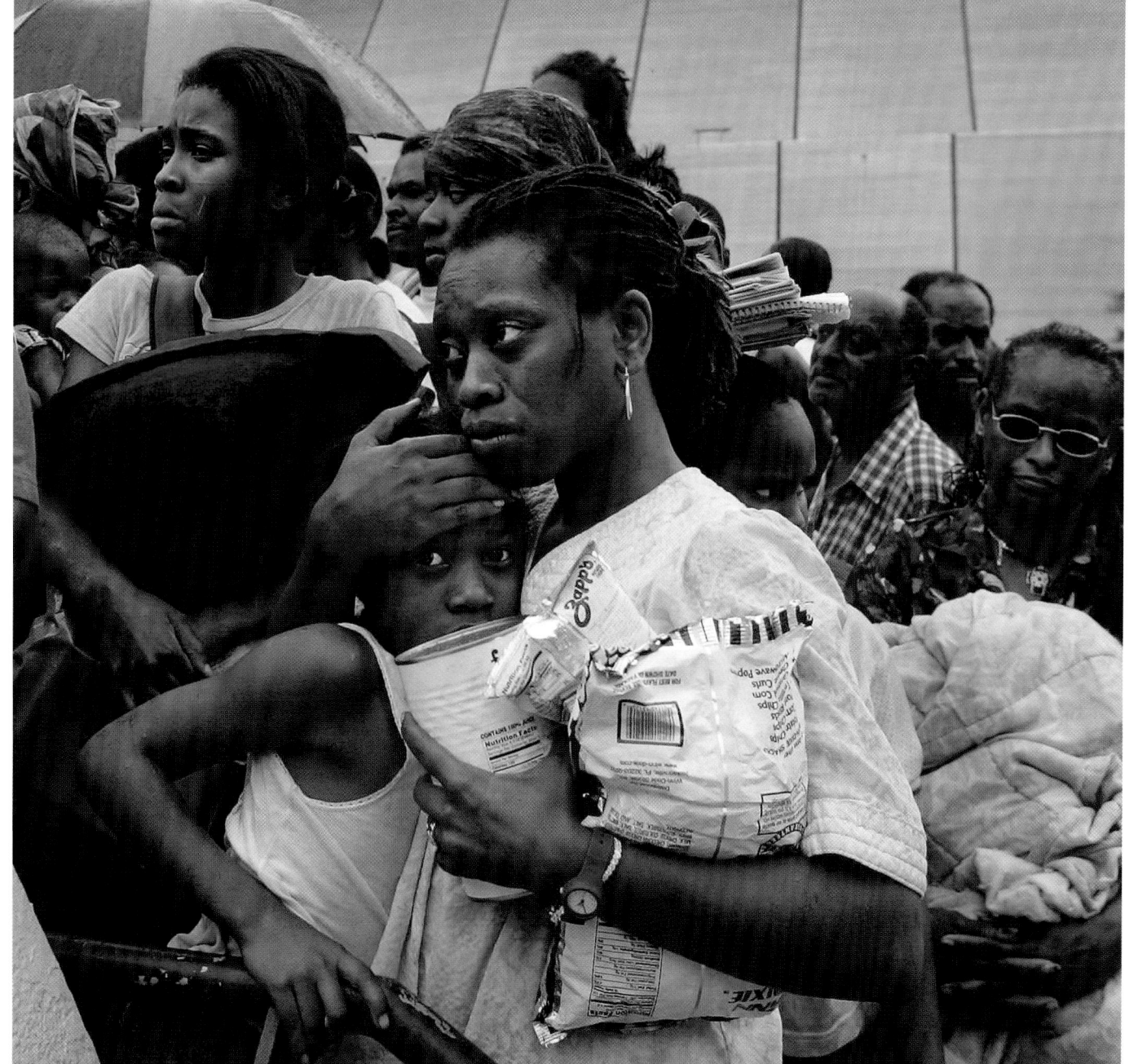

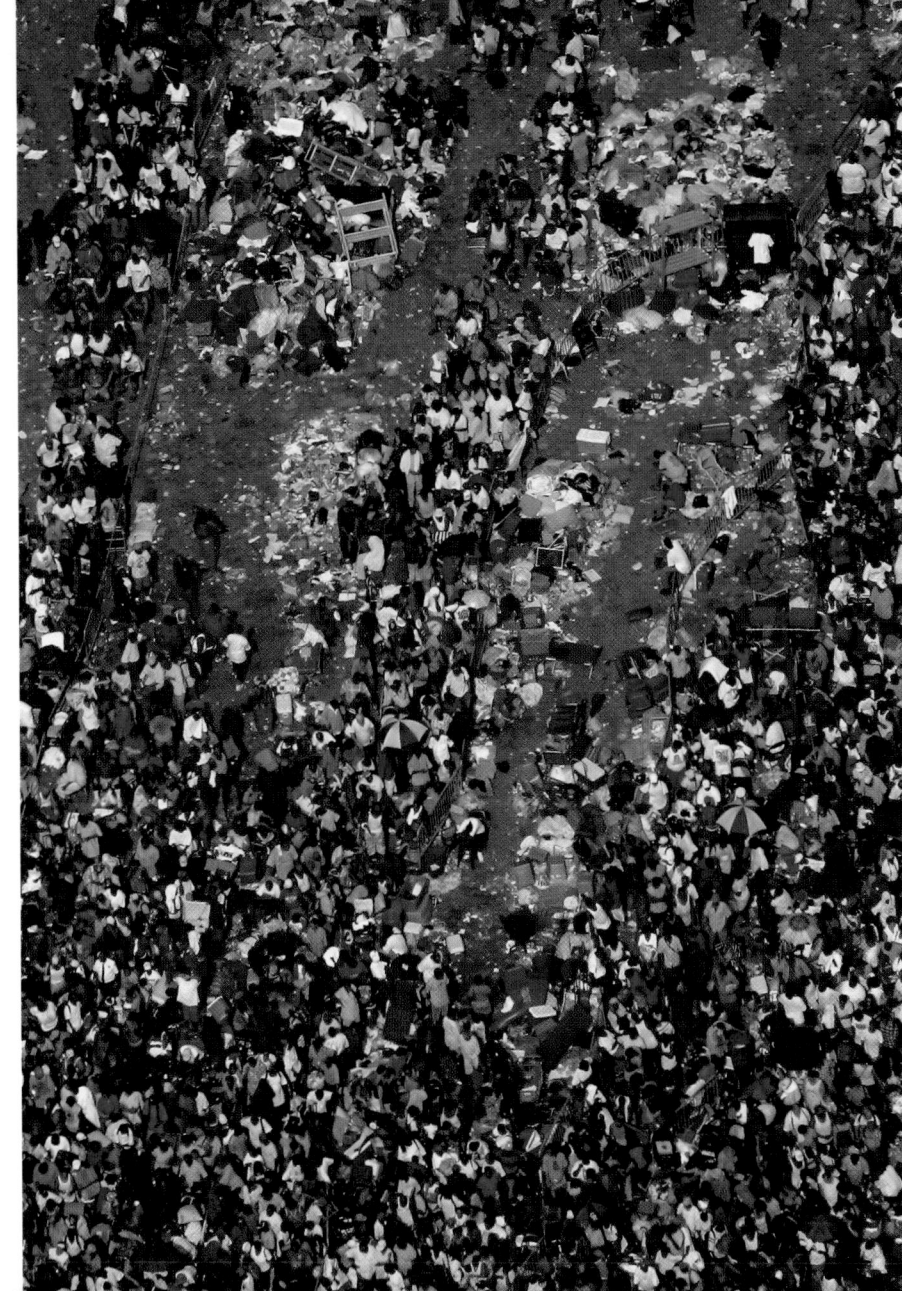

09.02.05 - New Orleans, LA -
Storm survivors waited to evacu-
ate at the Superdome.
• SMILEY N. POOL

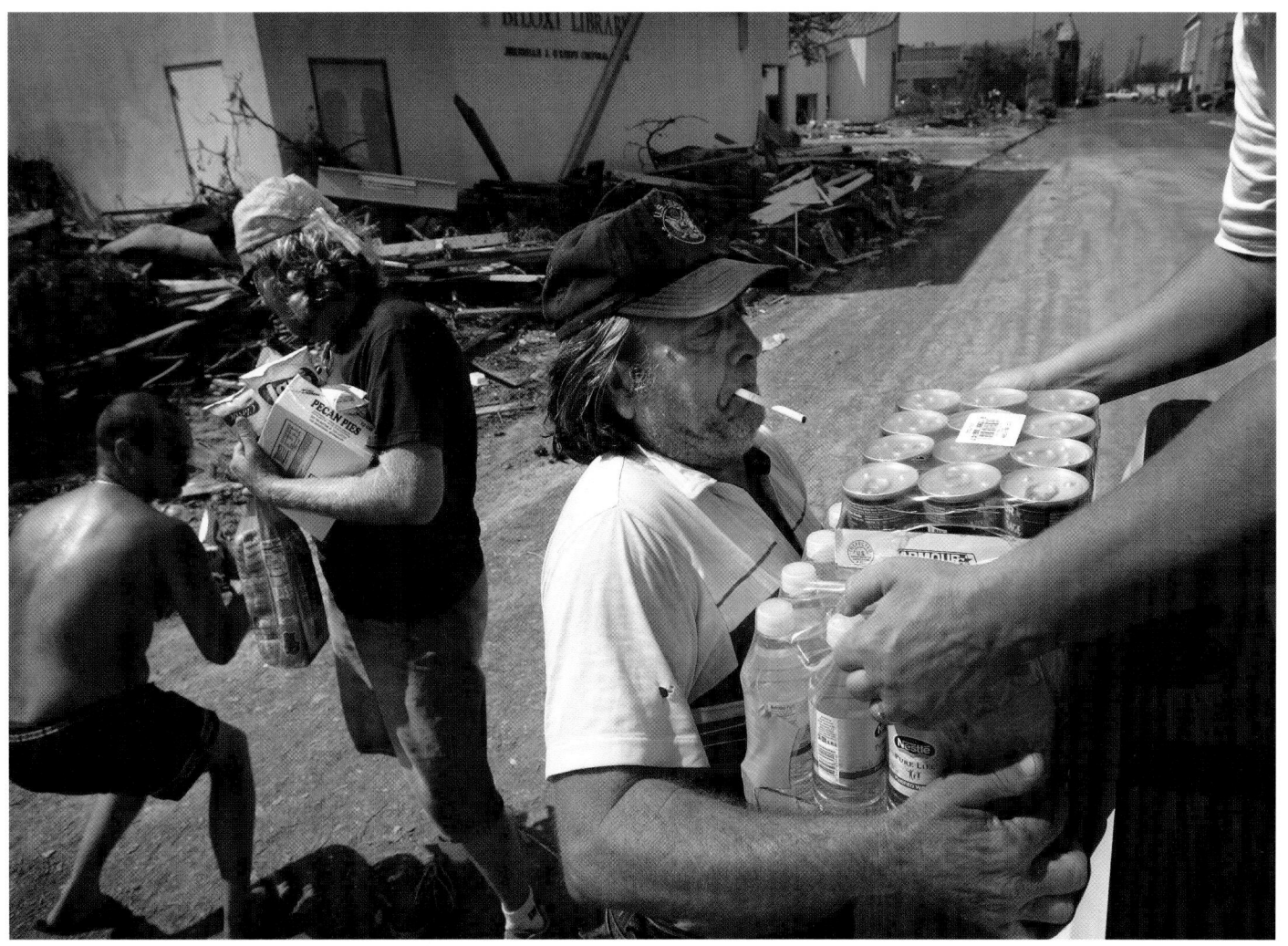

09.01.05 - Biloxi, MS - James Dean Robinson received a load of supplies from concerned citizen Tammy Young, who took it upon herself to help the people of Biloxi after she heard on the radio that residents were still waiting for aid. • BARBARA DAVIDSON

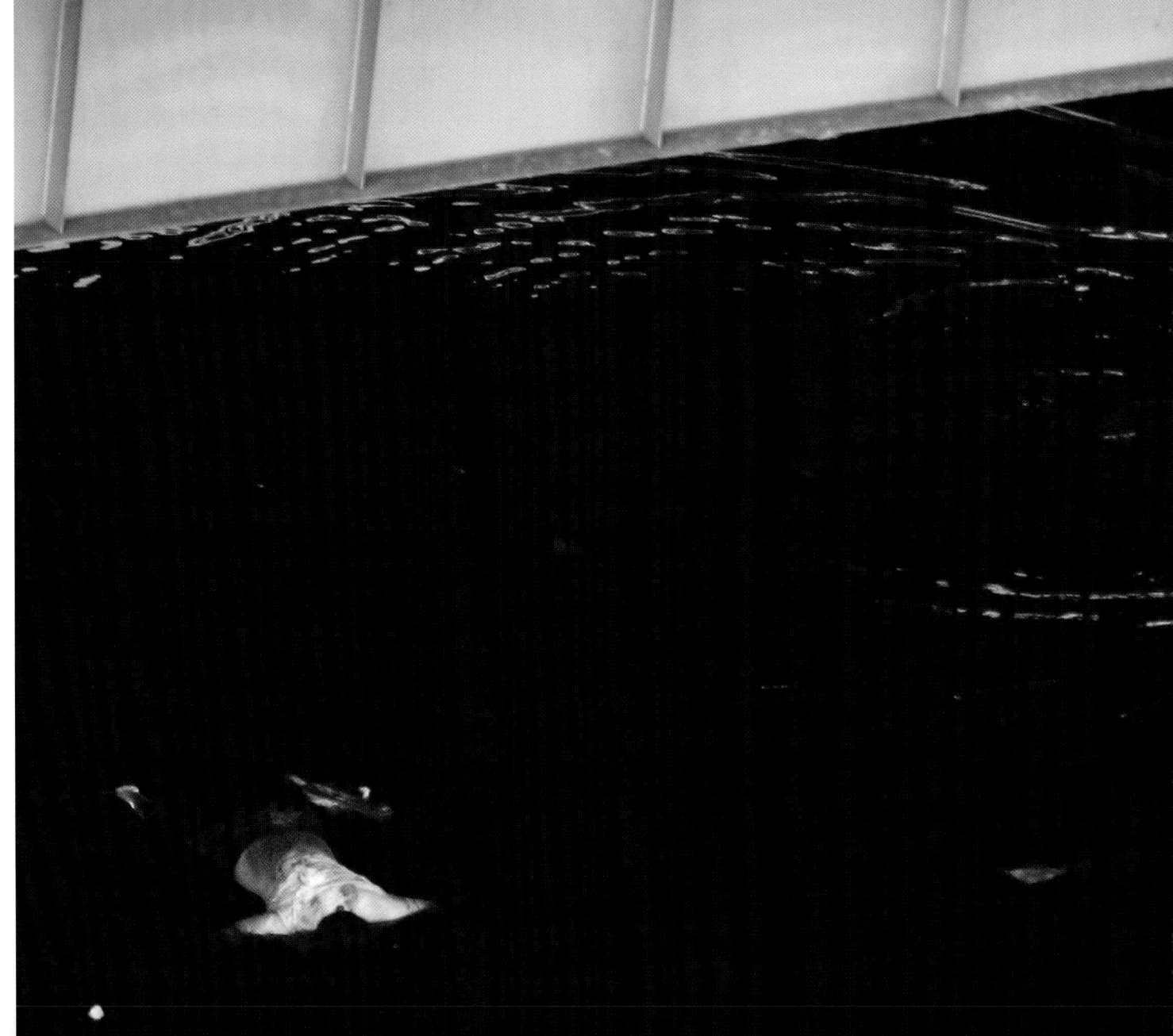

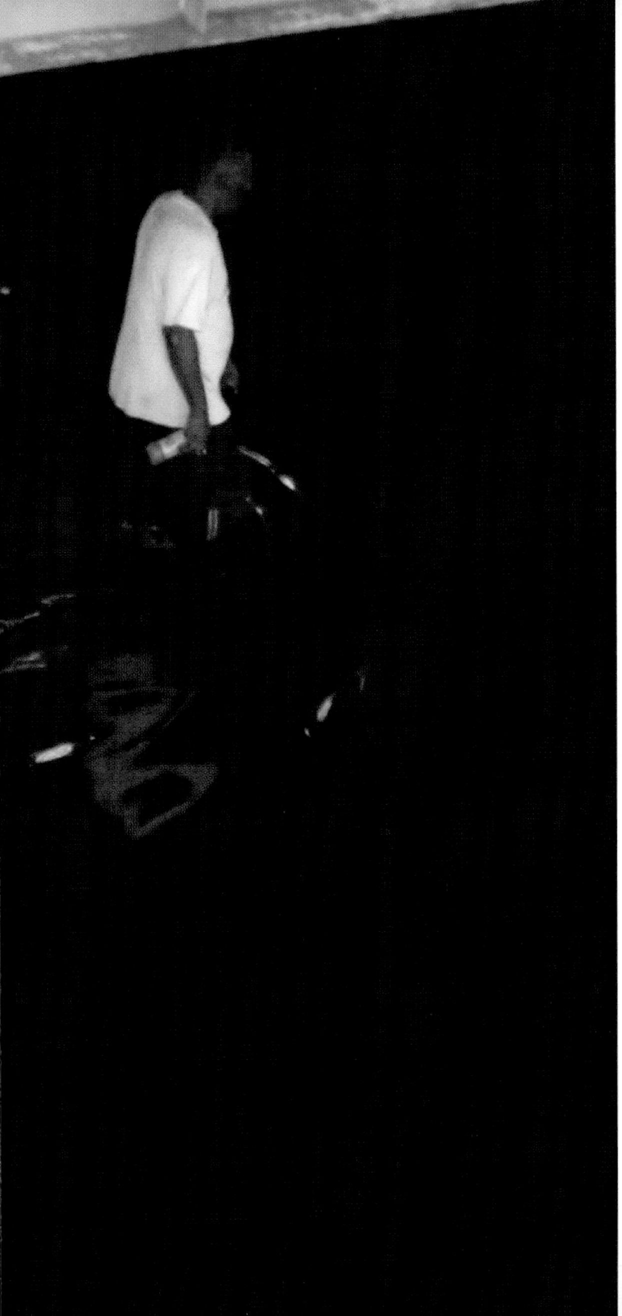

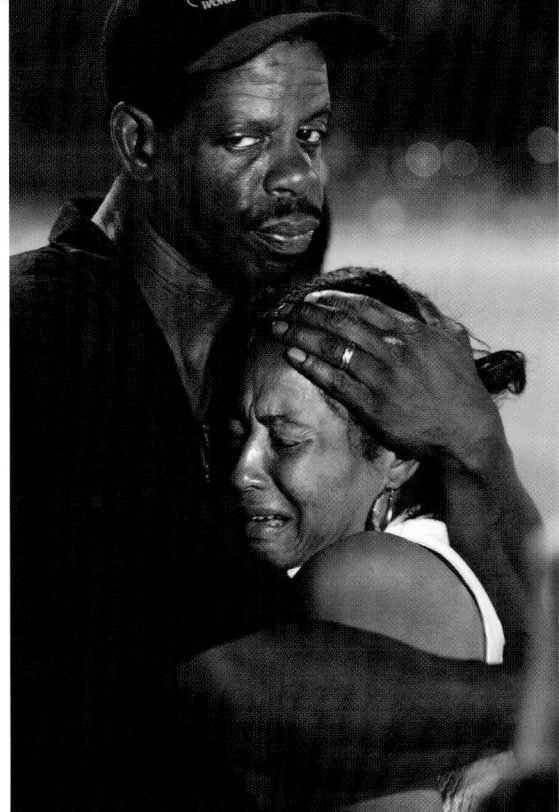

09.02.05 - Houston, TX - Charles Waxter of Slidell, La., consoled family friend Sonya Lacey of New Orleans after arriving at the Astrodome, which had been closed to any more evacuees. The Reliant Center next door was set up to temporarily receive evacuees. • ERICH SCHLEGEL

LEFT
09.02.05 - New Orleans, LA - A man waded past a floating body underneath a bridge. Four days after Hurricane Katrina barreled through, despair and frustration mounted across the ruined city.
• SMILEY N. POOL

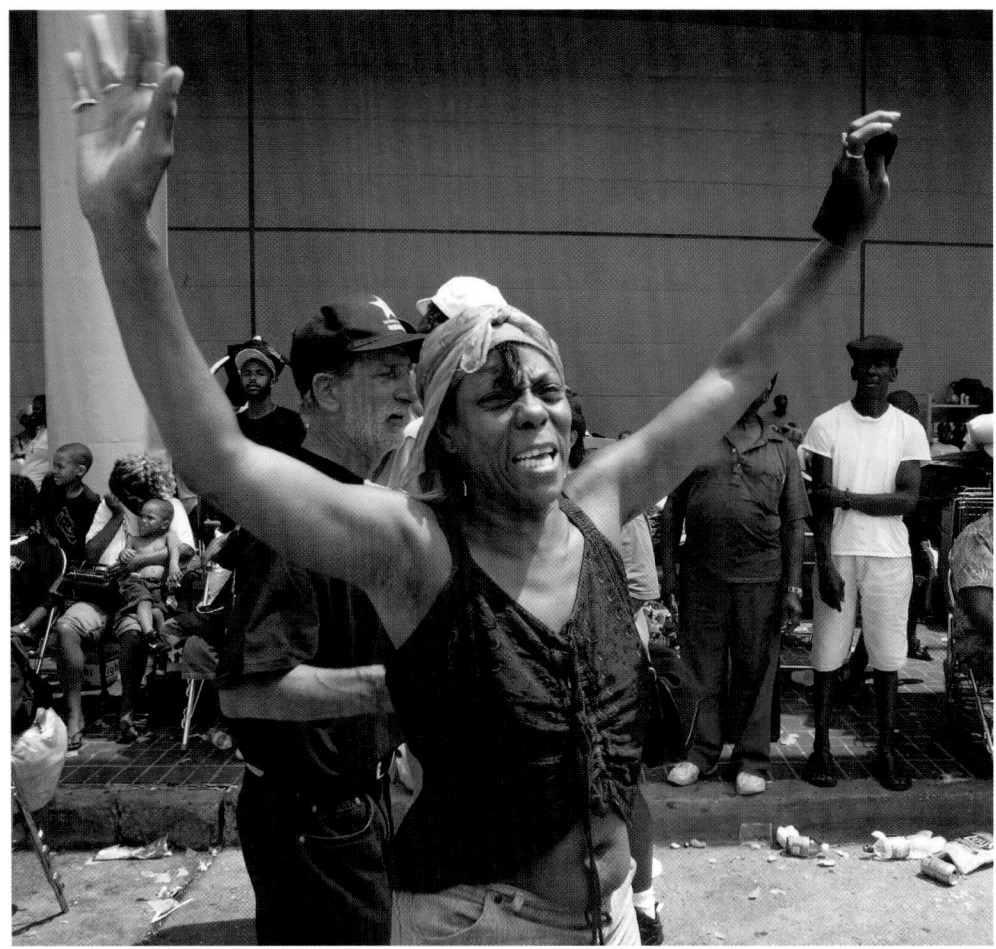

09.02.05 - New Orleans, LA - "Thank you, Jesus," proclaimed Jeannie Holmes after she heard that Meals Ready to Eat, or MREs, would be passed out in front of the Morial Convention Center. • IRWIN THOMPSON

RIGHT
09.02.05 - New Orleans, LA - Mark Smith of the French Quarter Jackson Square Band toted his tuba and other belongings near downtown as the National Guard moved equipment into the area. • IRWIN THOMPSON

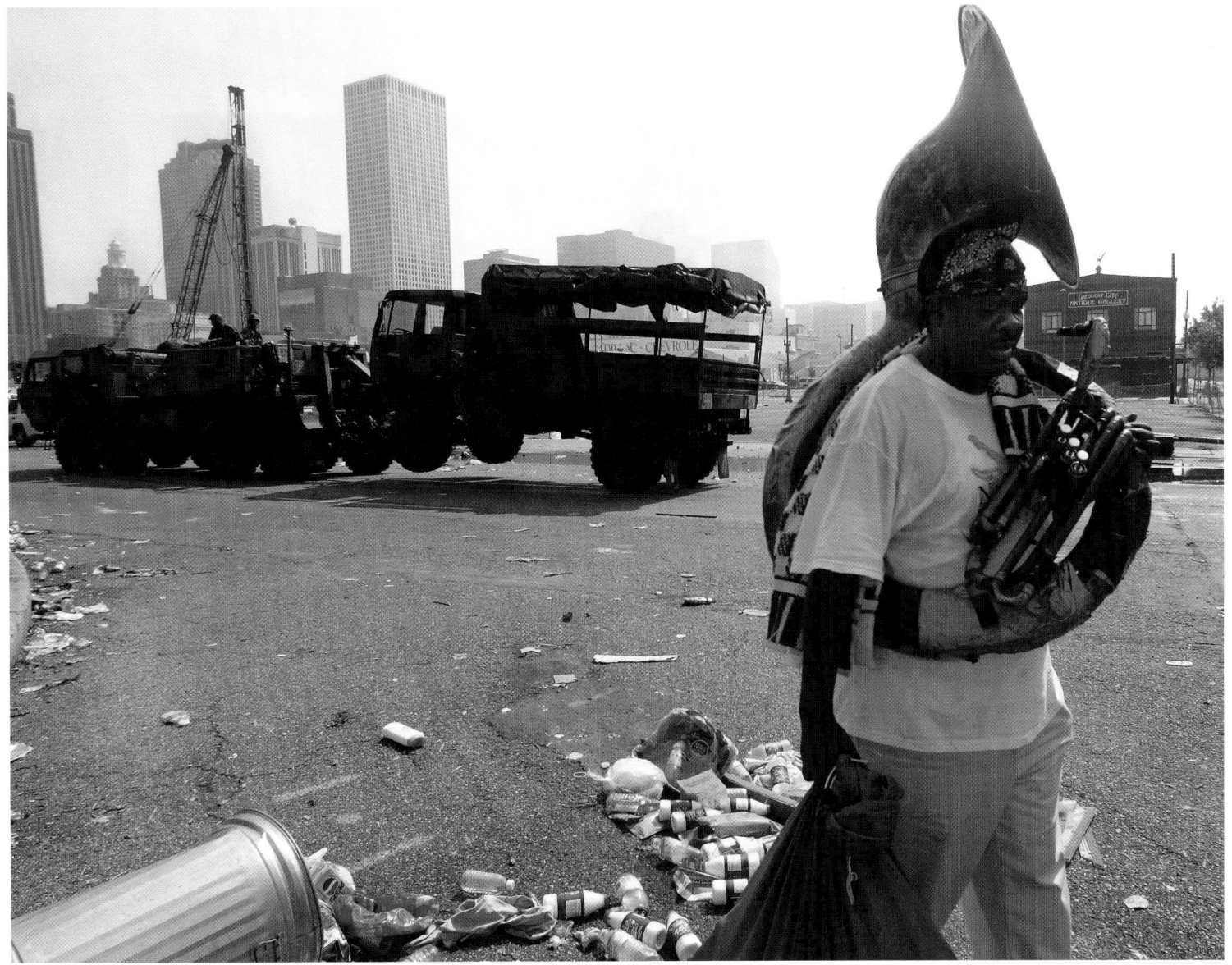

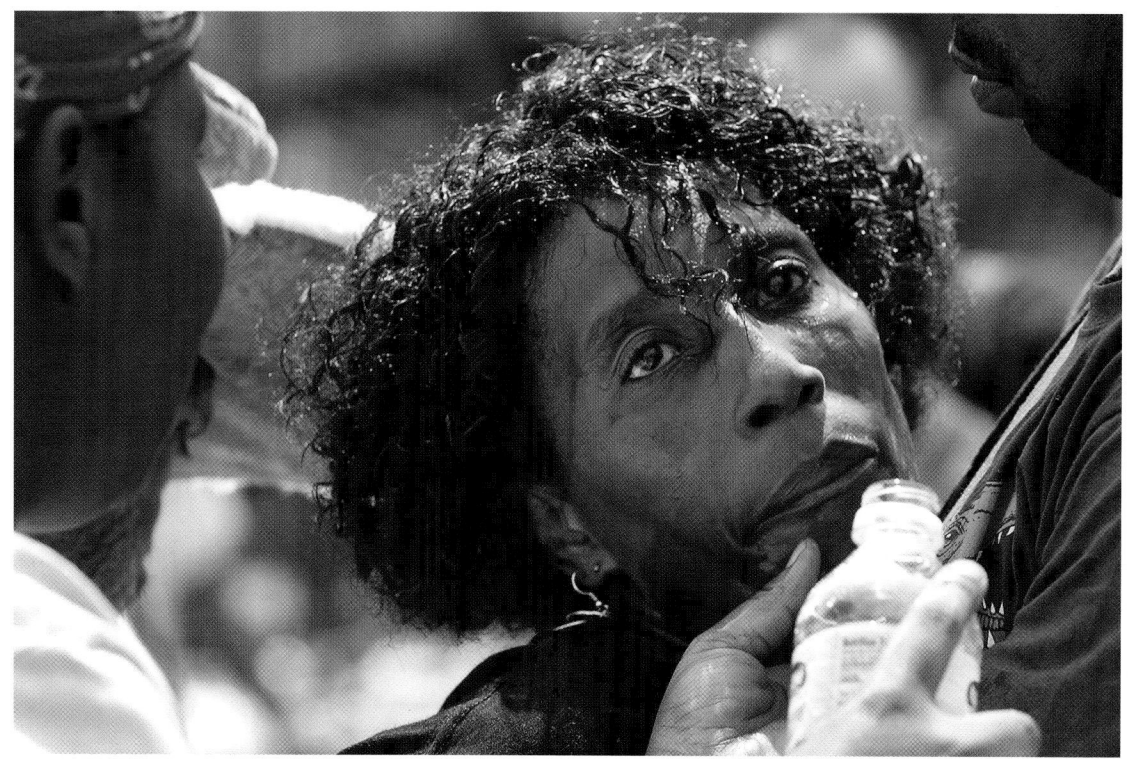

09.02.05 - New Orleans, LA - Friends moved 41-year-old Dana Clark into the shade after she fainted outside Morial Convention Center. • IRWIN THOMPSON

<small>RIGHT</small>
09.02.05 - New Orleans, LA - The National Guard handed out Meals Ready to Eat, or MREs, and water to residents left stranded at Morial Convention Center downtown. • IRWIN THOMPSON

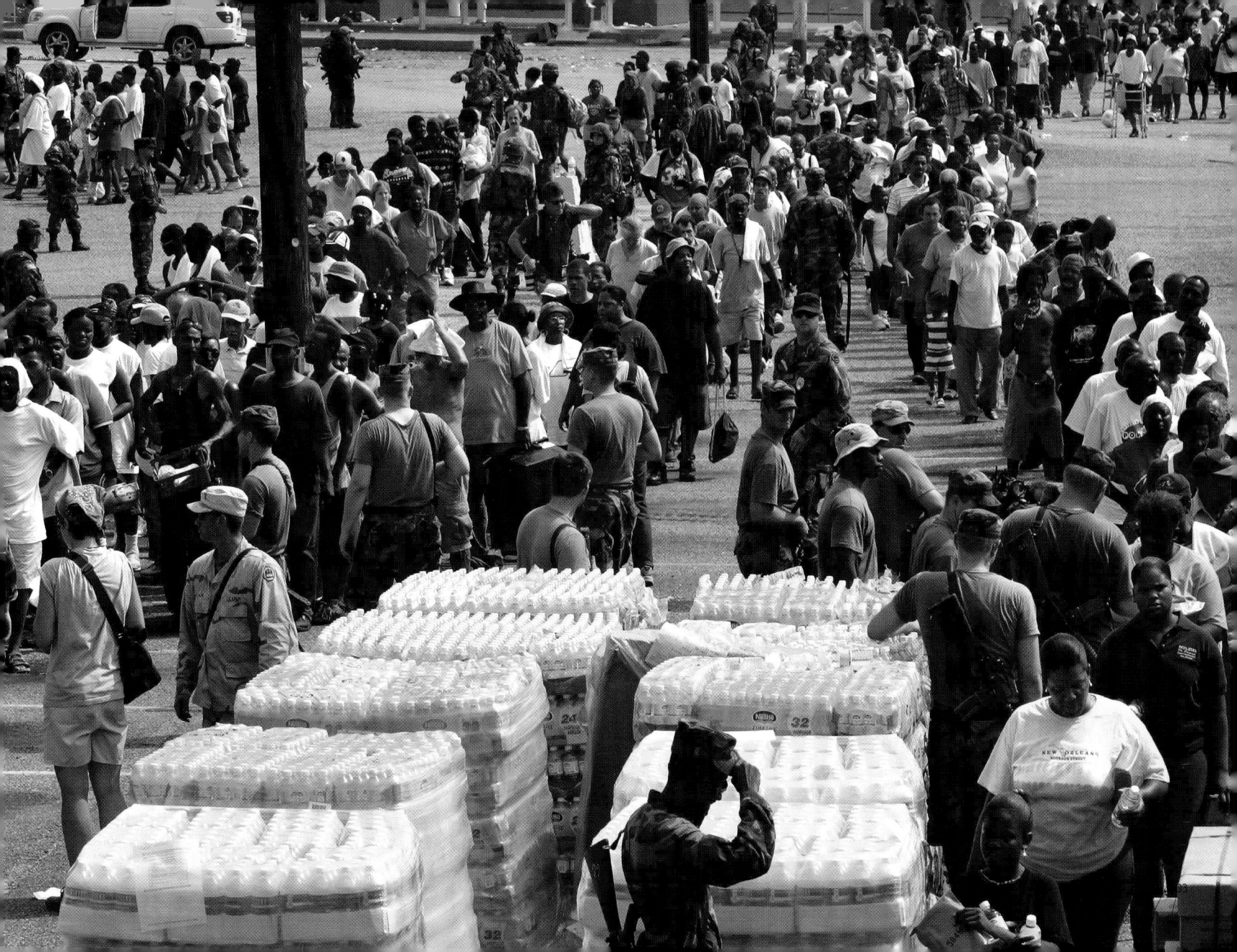

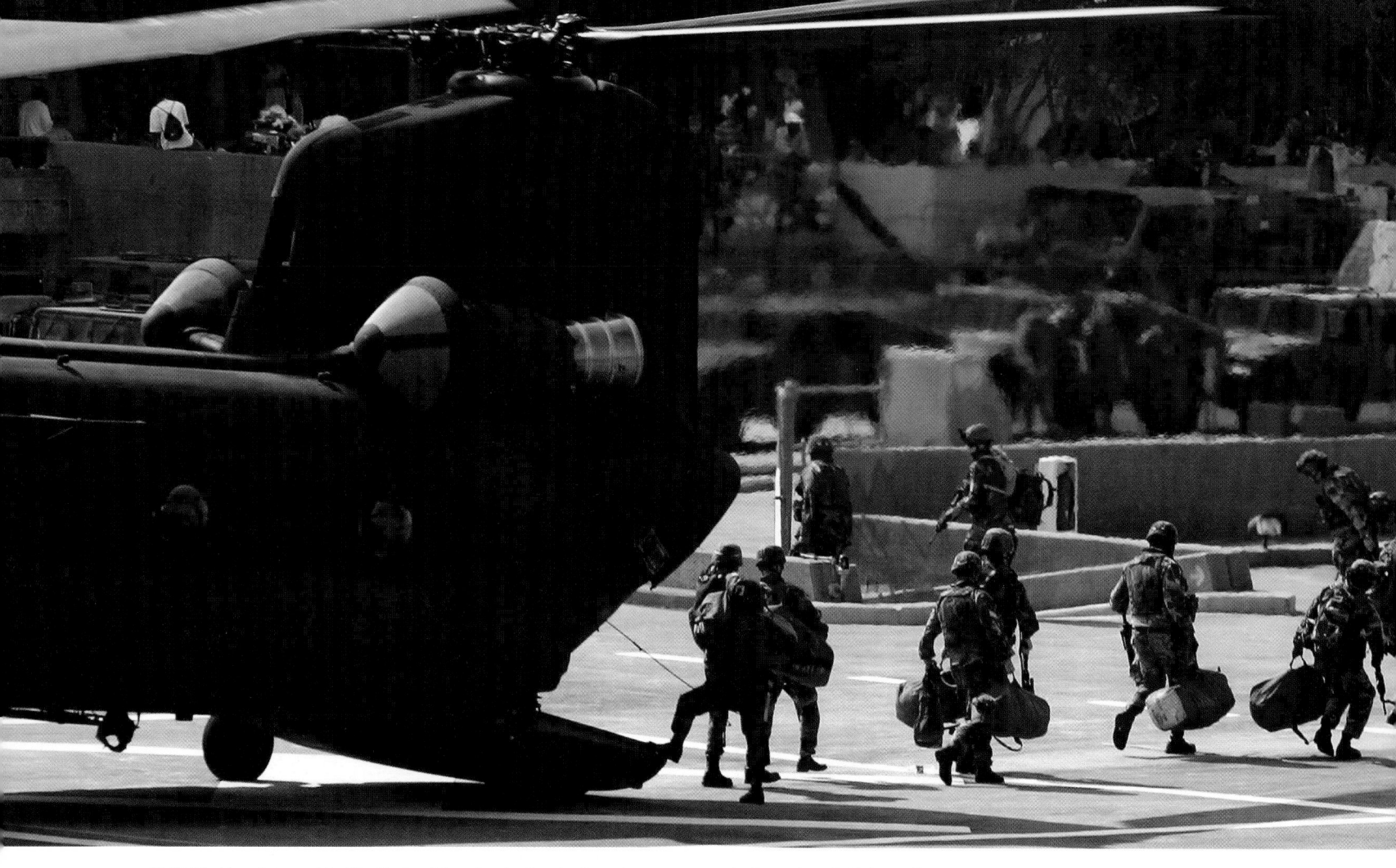

09.02.05 - New Orleans, LA - The National Guard arrived at the Superdome. Top Guard officers described their efforts to run the Dome as an operational success, especially considering its evolution from a short-term, bring-your-own-food shelter to a longer-term, ill-equipped mini-city. • IRWIN THOMPSON

RIGHT

09.02.05 - New Orleans, LA - National Guardsmen helped 87-year-old Ester Frederick leave the Superdome and board a bus for evacuation. • IRWIN THOMPSON

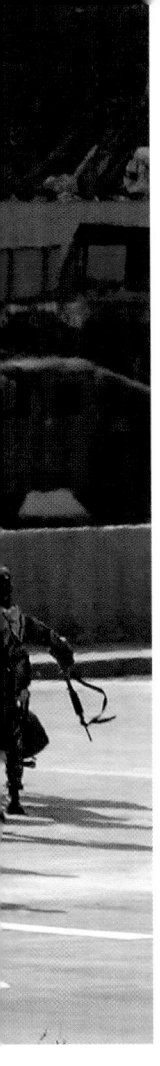

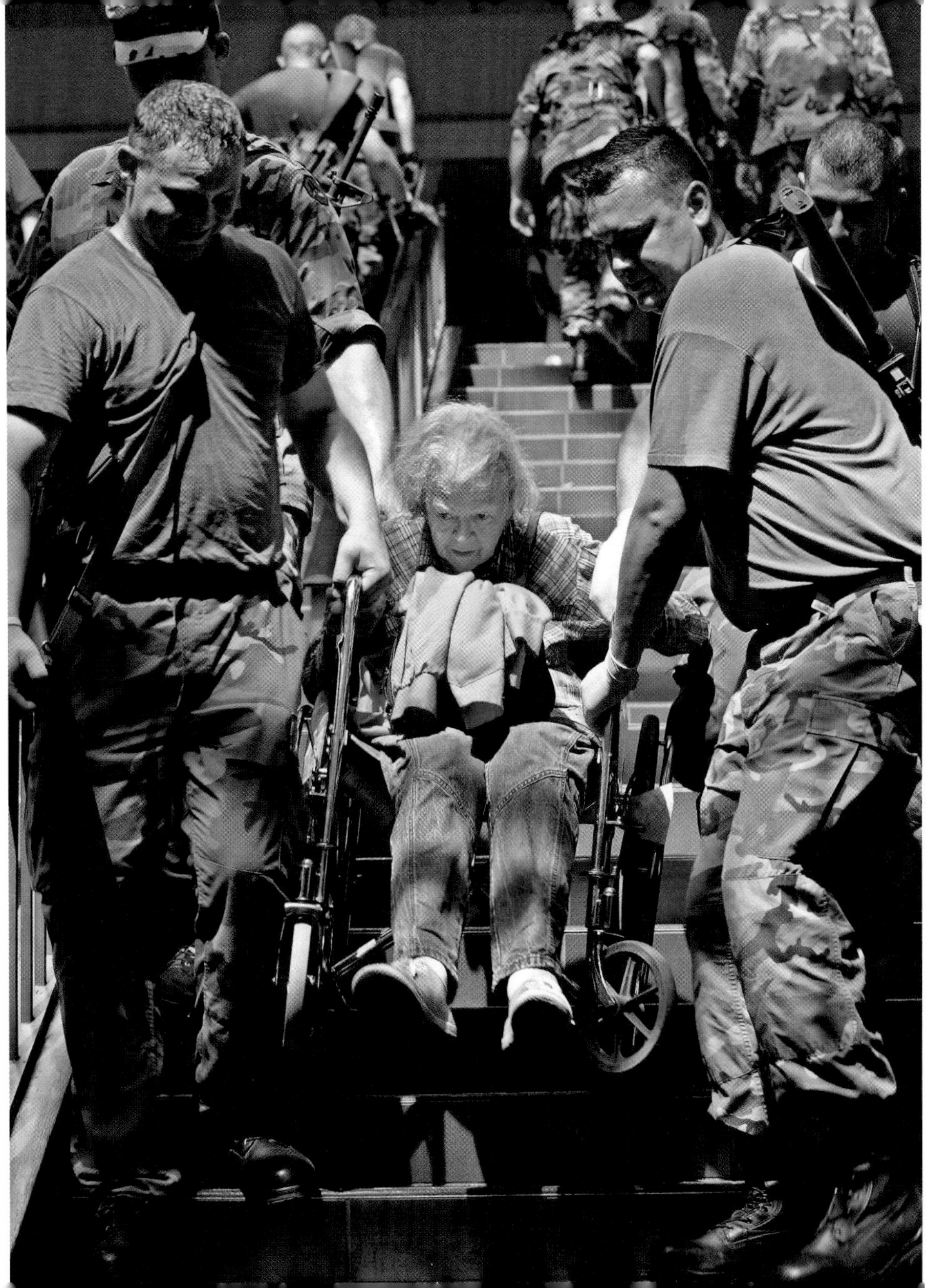

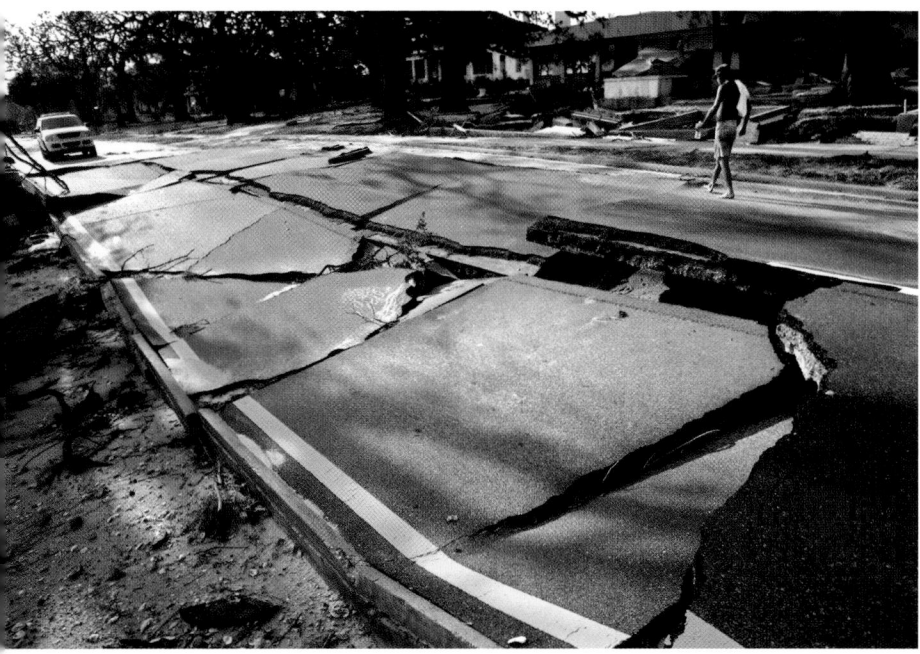

09.02.05 - Gulfport, MS - Hurricane Katrina's surge left a section of U.S. Highway 90 that runs near the beach in Gulfport broken and curled. • MICHAEL MULVEY

CENTER
09.02.05 - Slidell, LA - Boats were stacked upon one another like toys. The flood had carried cars, trucks and boats and left them strewn across parking lots and up against railroad tracks. About 85 percent of houses and businesses in Slidell had been damaged. • BRAD LOPER

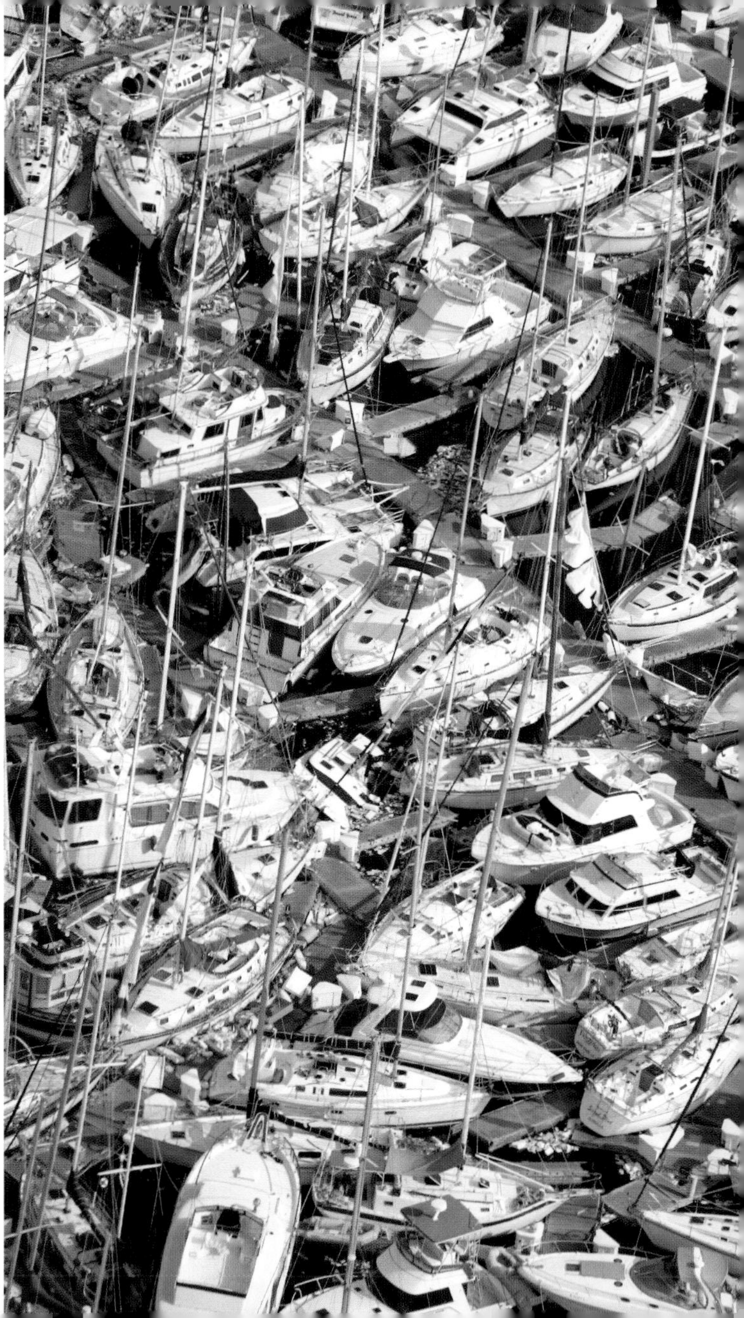

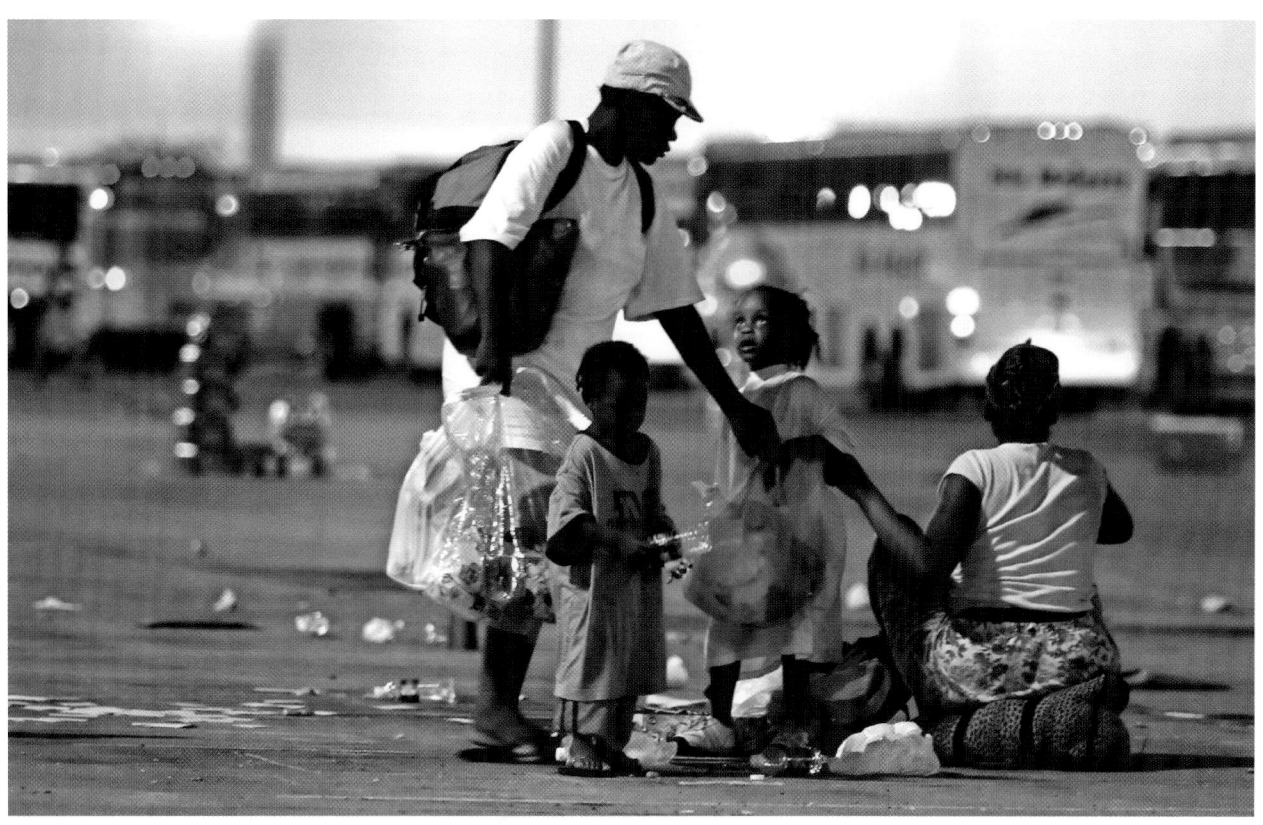

09.02.05 - Houston, TX - A family gathered its belongings and tried to figure out its next move after arriving at the Astrodome from New Orleans.
• ERICH SCHLEGEL

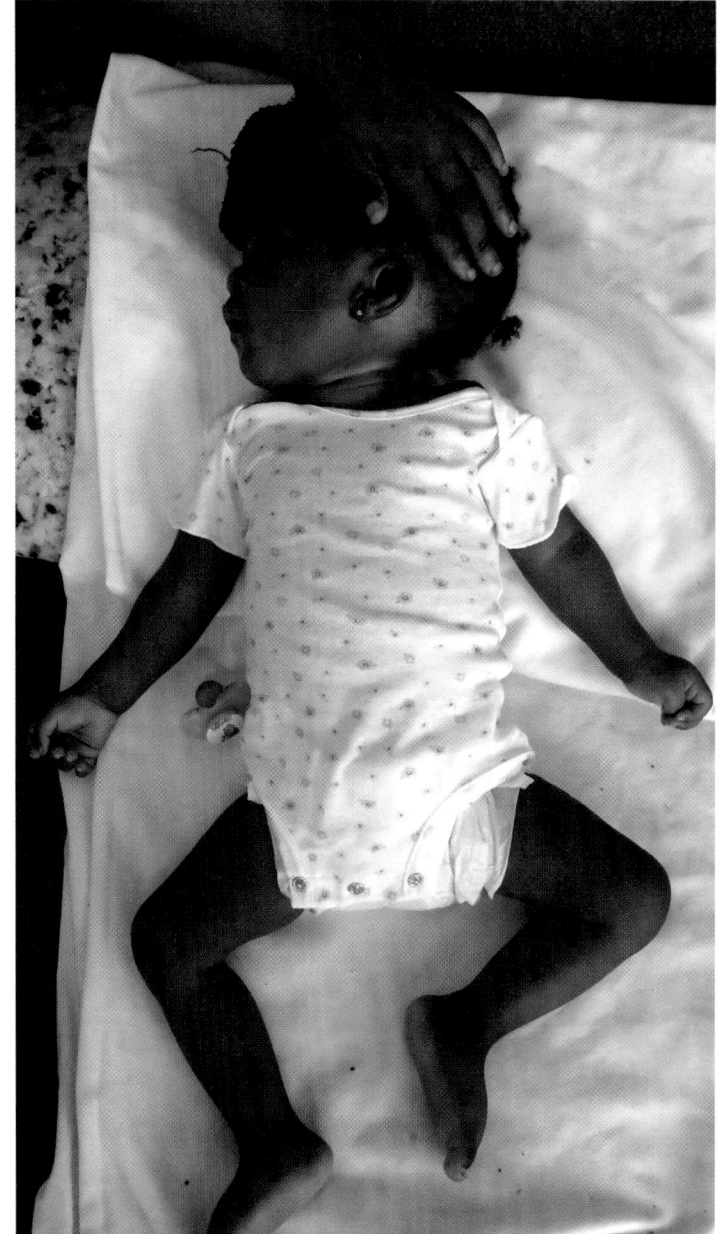

09.02.05 - New Orleans, LA - Felicia Brown caressed 19-month-old niece Cahmyri Thomas at Morial Convention Center downtown. No one has been able to say how many people died inside the convention center. Nor has there been any official documentation of the number of assaults, robberies and rapes that witnesses reported seeing between the time the first people broke into the center seeking shelter on the afternoon of Aug. 29, and when units of the Arkansas National Guard moved in four days later.
• IRWIN THOMPSON

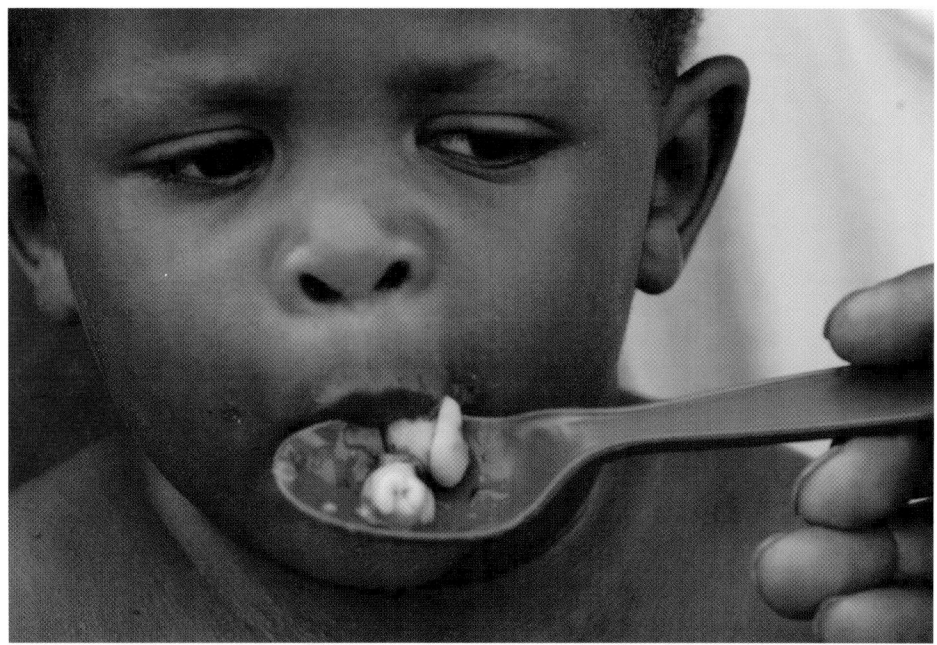

09.02.05 - New Orleans, LA - Fifteen-month-old Jaquan Pugh gets a little something to eat from his dad, Percy Pugh, at Morial Convention Center. • IRWIN THOMPSON

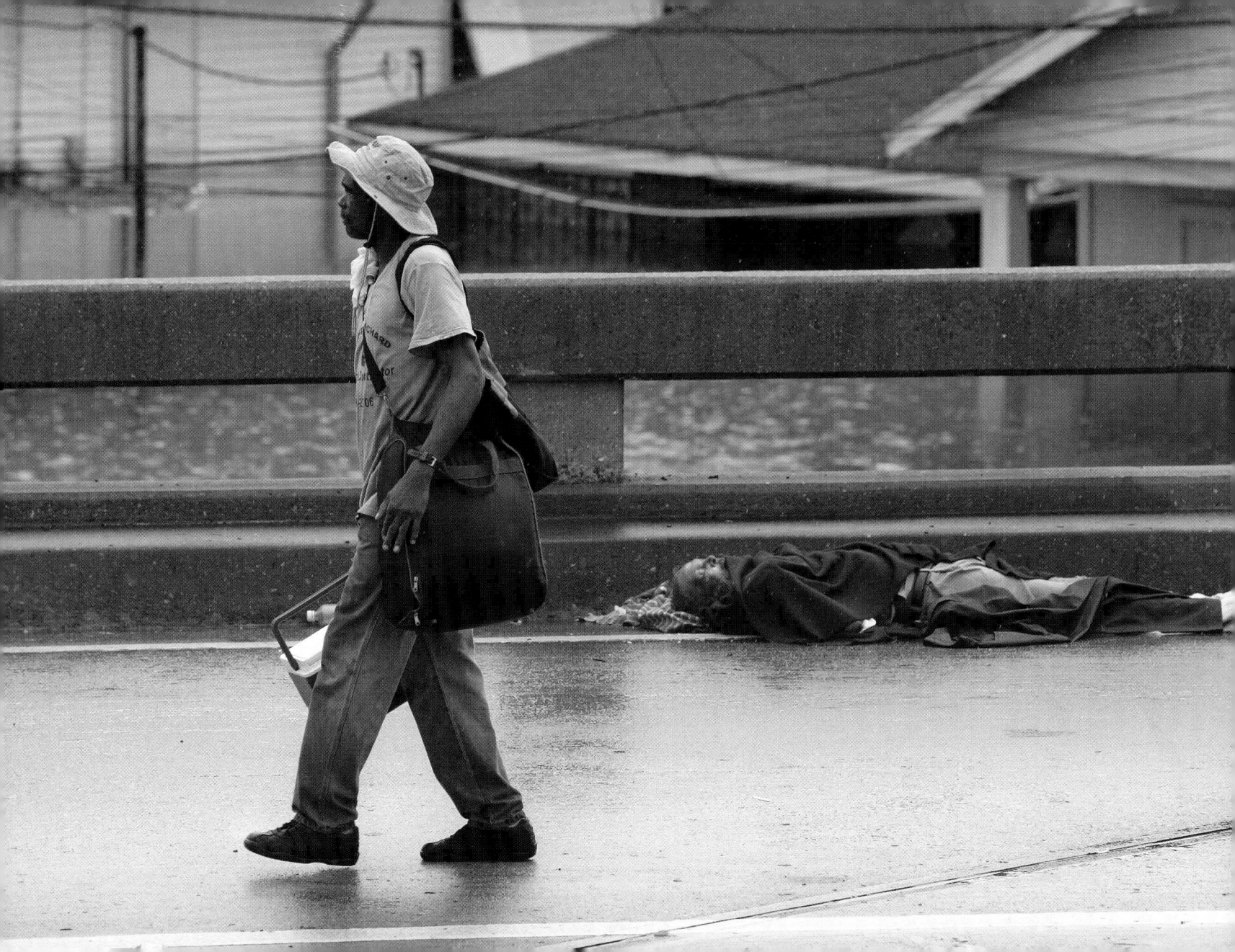

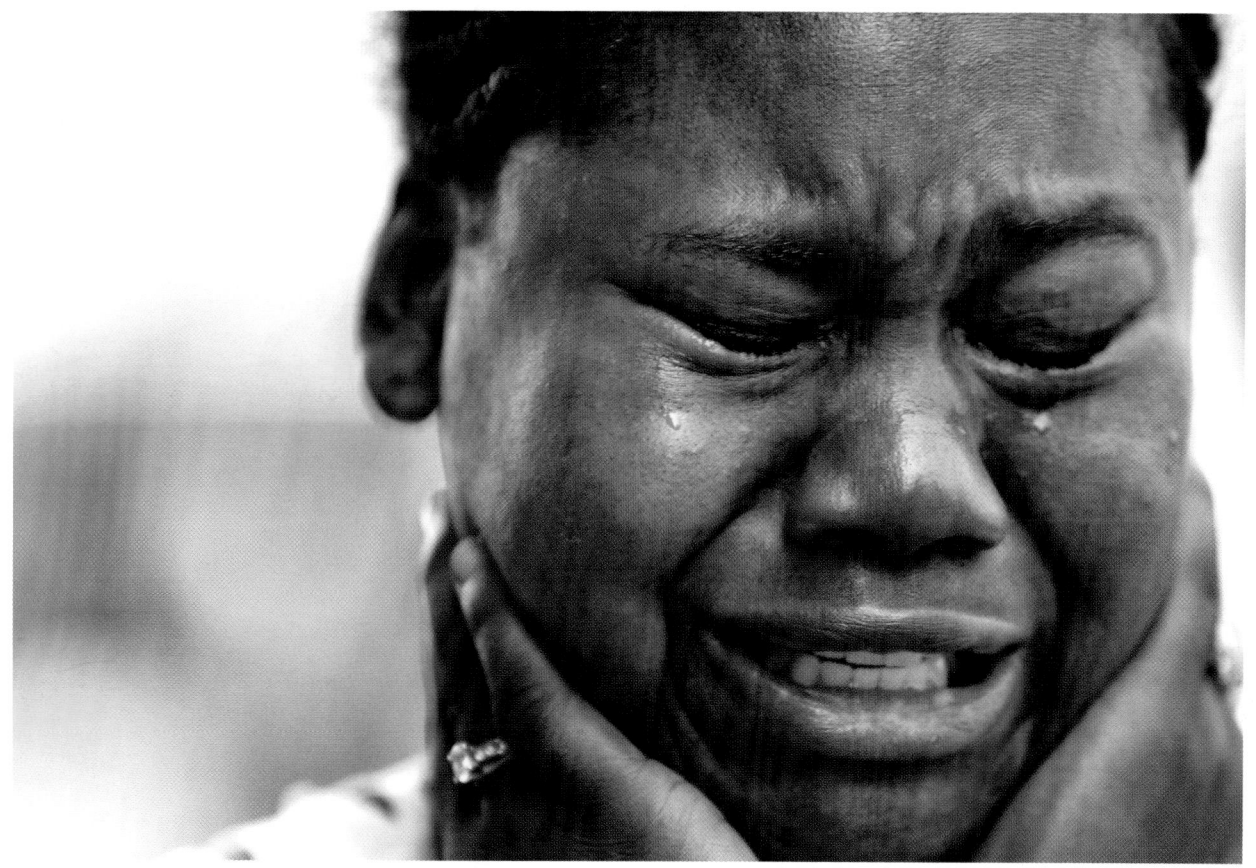

09.02.05 - Dallas, TX - Stacy Nolan lost track of her 7-month-old son, A'Mahd MaGee, when she was forced to leave for Dallas. A'Mahd had been visiting with a family friend when the storm hit New Orleans, and floodwaters prevented Ms. Nolan from reaching her child before she had to be evacuated by helicopter on Aug. 30. But it was a happy ending for both. They were reunited four days later in Dallas with the help of Prestonwood Baptist Church. • MELANIE BURFORD

LEFT
09.01.05 - New Orleans, LA - A man passed a body as he walked down Interstate 10. • IRWIN THOMPSON

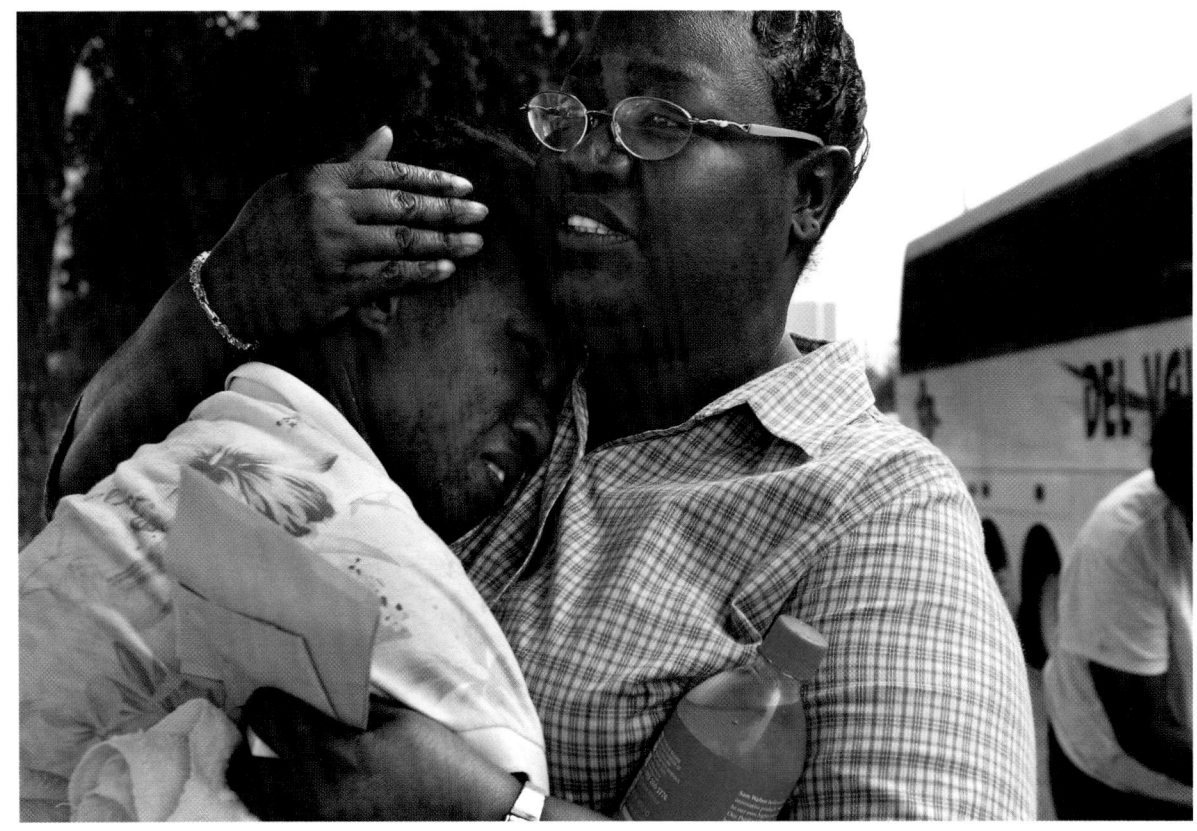

09.02.05 - Dallas, TX - Laura Oates of Dallas (center) was unexpectedly reunited with her friend Brenda Reynolds after Ms. Reynolds stepped off a bus from New Orleans at Reunion Arena. • MELANIE BURFORD

RIGHT
09.02.05 - Long Beach, MS - Carol Cuevas, 71, clutched her Our Lady of Sorrows statue as she transported her remaining belongings to a relative's house after hers was destroyed by Katrina. Ms. Cuevas has lived in Long Beach since 1962. • LOUIS DELUCA

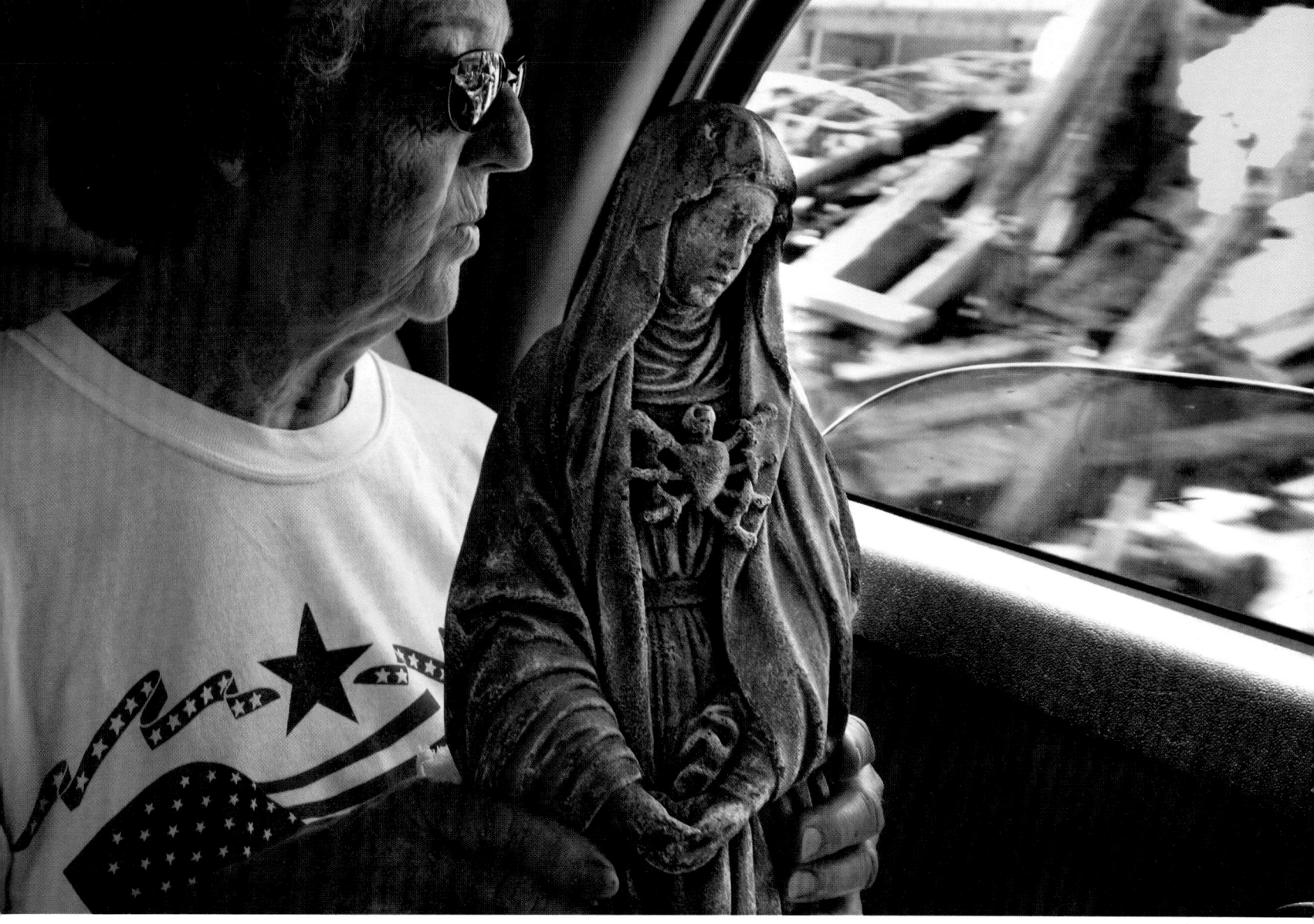

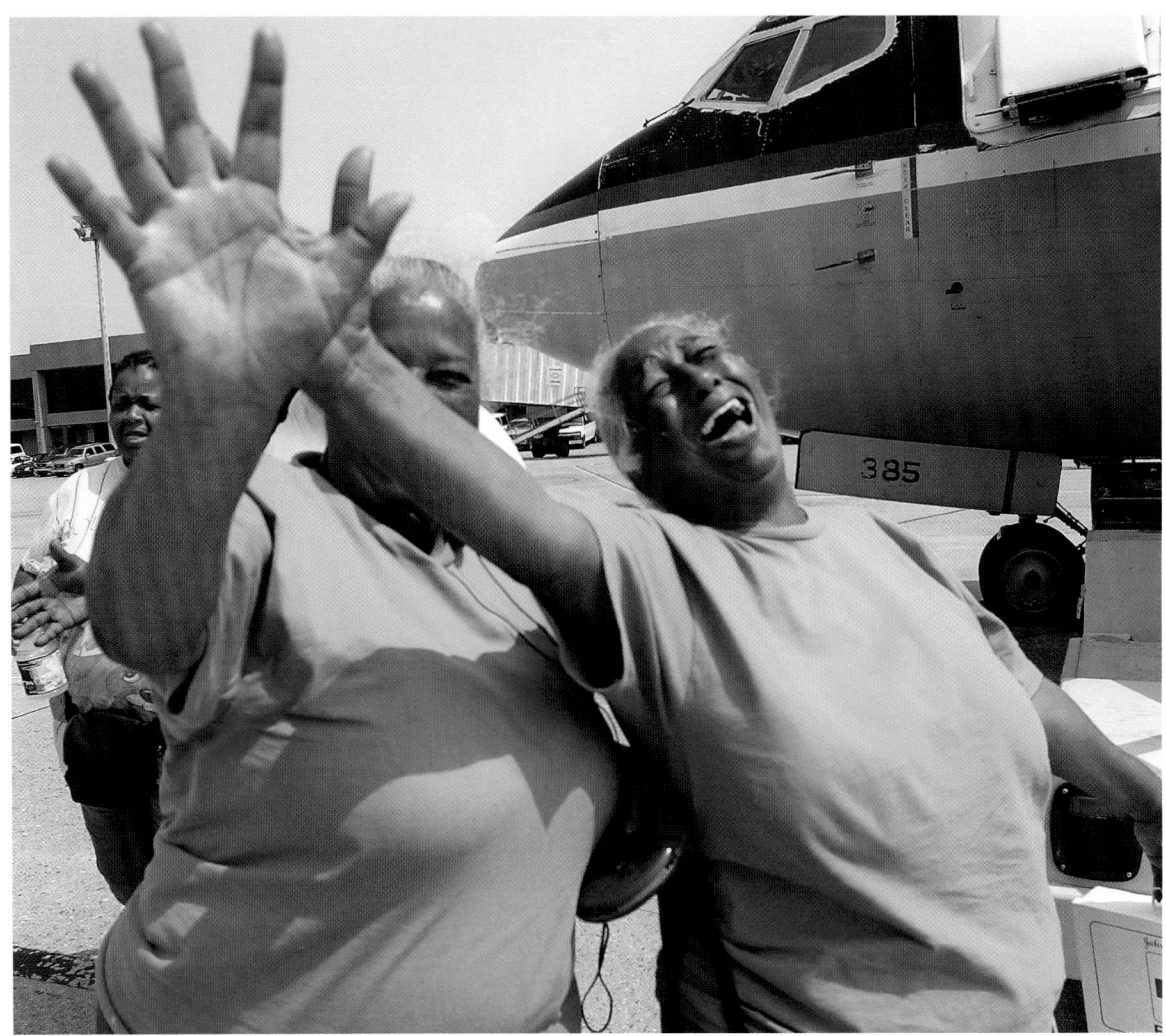

09.03.05 - New Orleans, LA - Brenda Leonard (left) and her twin, Linda Herbert, rejoiced as they boarded a plane bound for San Antonio at the New Orleans airport. They had been stuck at Morial Convention Center downtown. • IRWIN THOMPSON

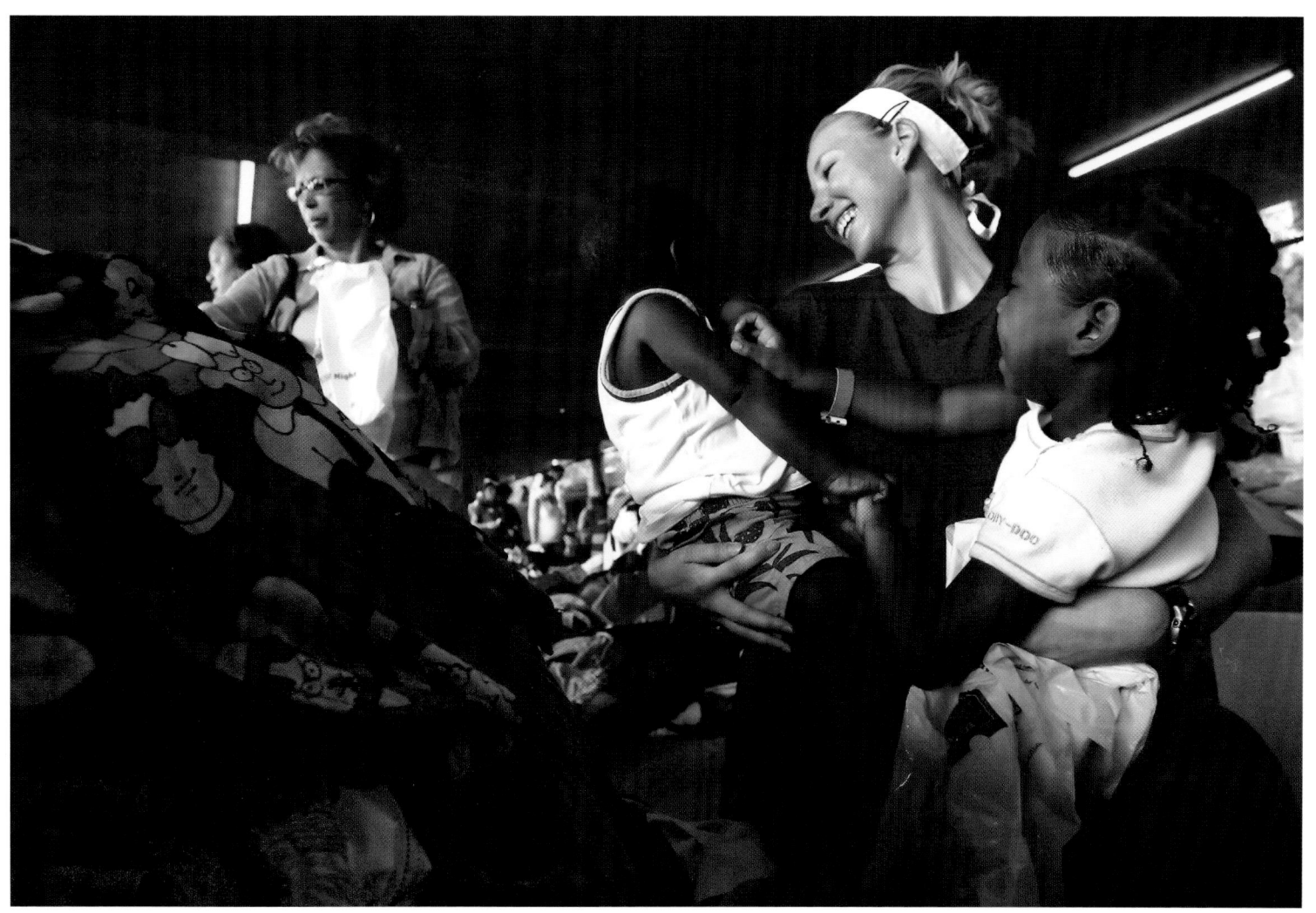

09.03.05 - Dallas, TX - Red Cross volunteer and Dallas Theological Seminary student Mary Lowery played with young evacuees Ryan Chambers, 2, and Wysheka Nicholson, 4, while they collected clothing from a market area near Reunion Arena. • MELANIE BURFORD

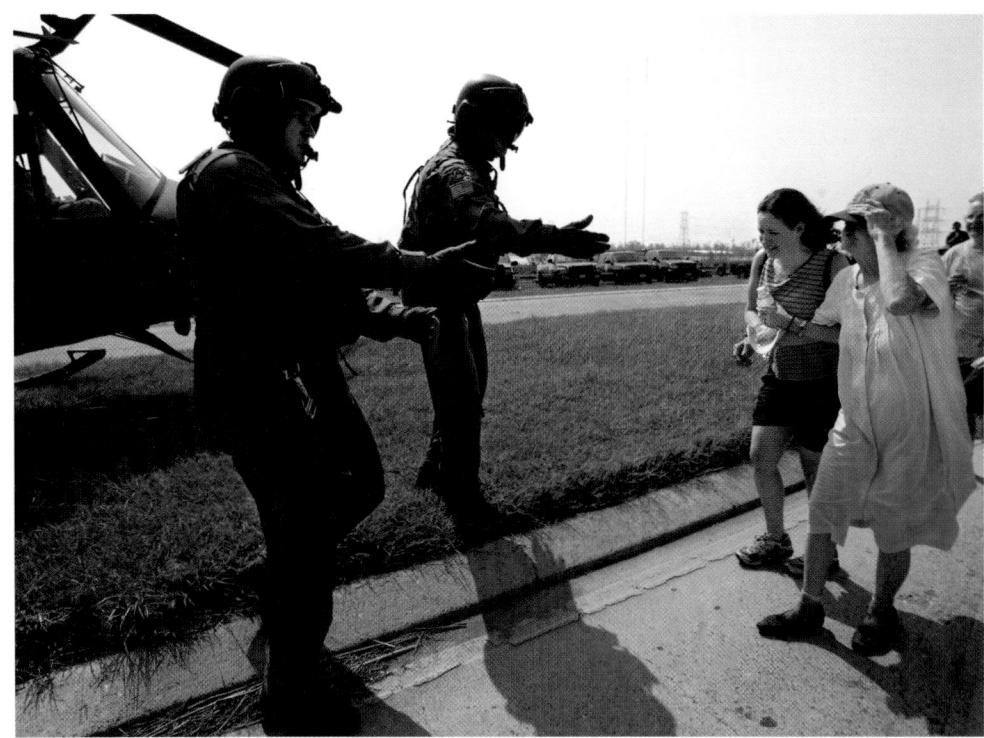

09.03.05 - Chalmette, LA - Army helicopter pilots offered helping hands to Sherron Downs and her mother-in-law, 79-year-old Trudy Hendricksen, as they evacuated. • MICHAEL AINSWORTH

RIGHT
09.03.05 - Chalmette, LA - Evacuees rode out of Chalmette on a dump truck. Local agencies were racing to rescue residents from attics and rooftops, but dozens were found dead. • MICHAEL AINSWORTH

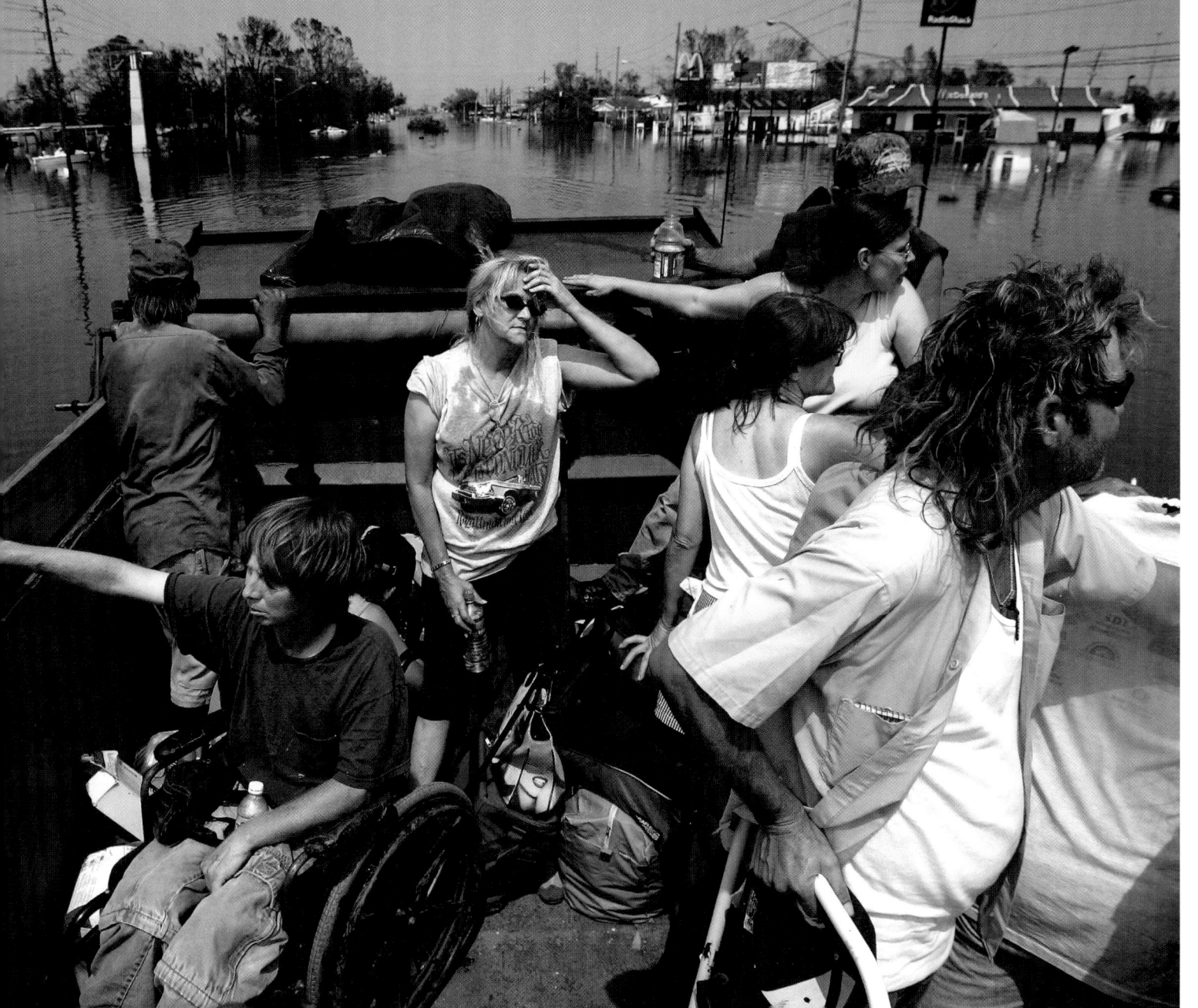

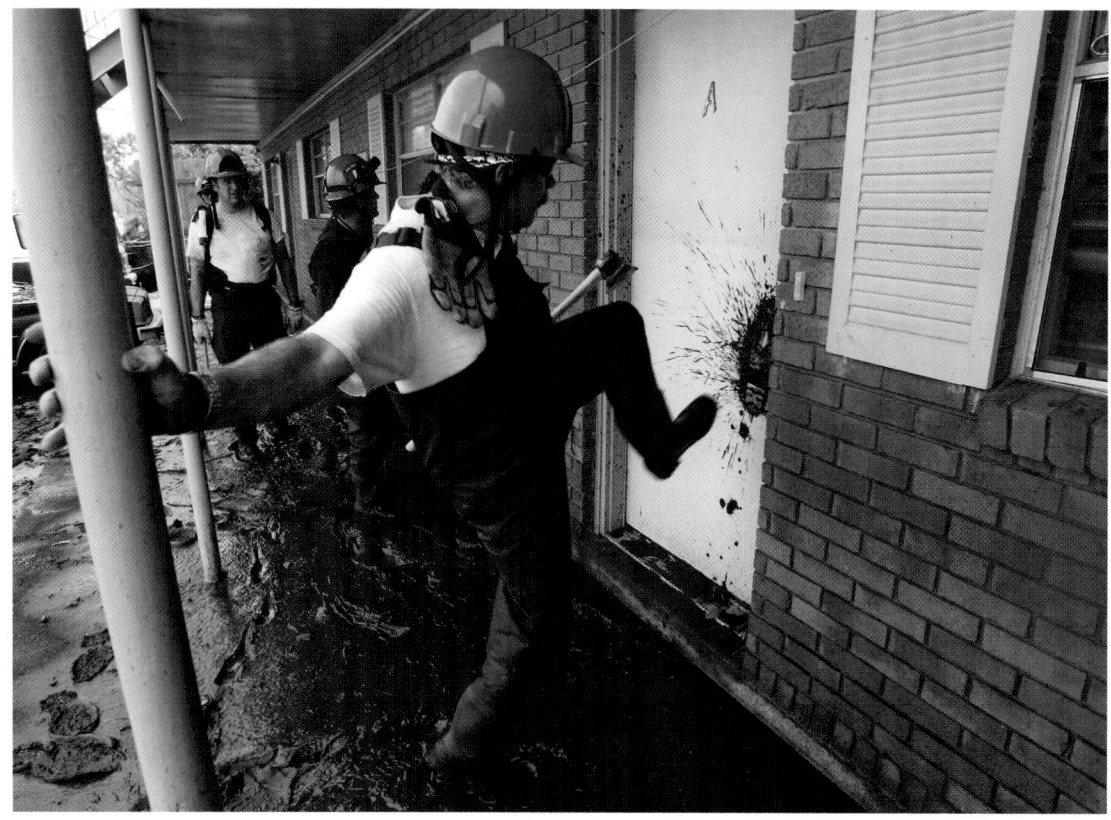

09.03.05 - Chalmette, LA - Rob Weddess of the Vancouver, Canada, fire and rescue team kicked down a door as the crew searched house-to-house for anyone needing to be evacuated. • MICHAEL AINSWORTH

<small>RIGHT</small>
09.03.05 - Chalmette, LA - Fire and rescue team members from Vancouver, Canada, carried an elderly woman to a medical tent after she was evacuated. Katrina's vicious winds and water left Chalmette and surrounding St. Bernard Parish towns wastelands of toxic mud, downed trees, splintered homes and wrecked cars. • MICHAEL AINSWORTH

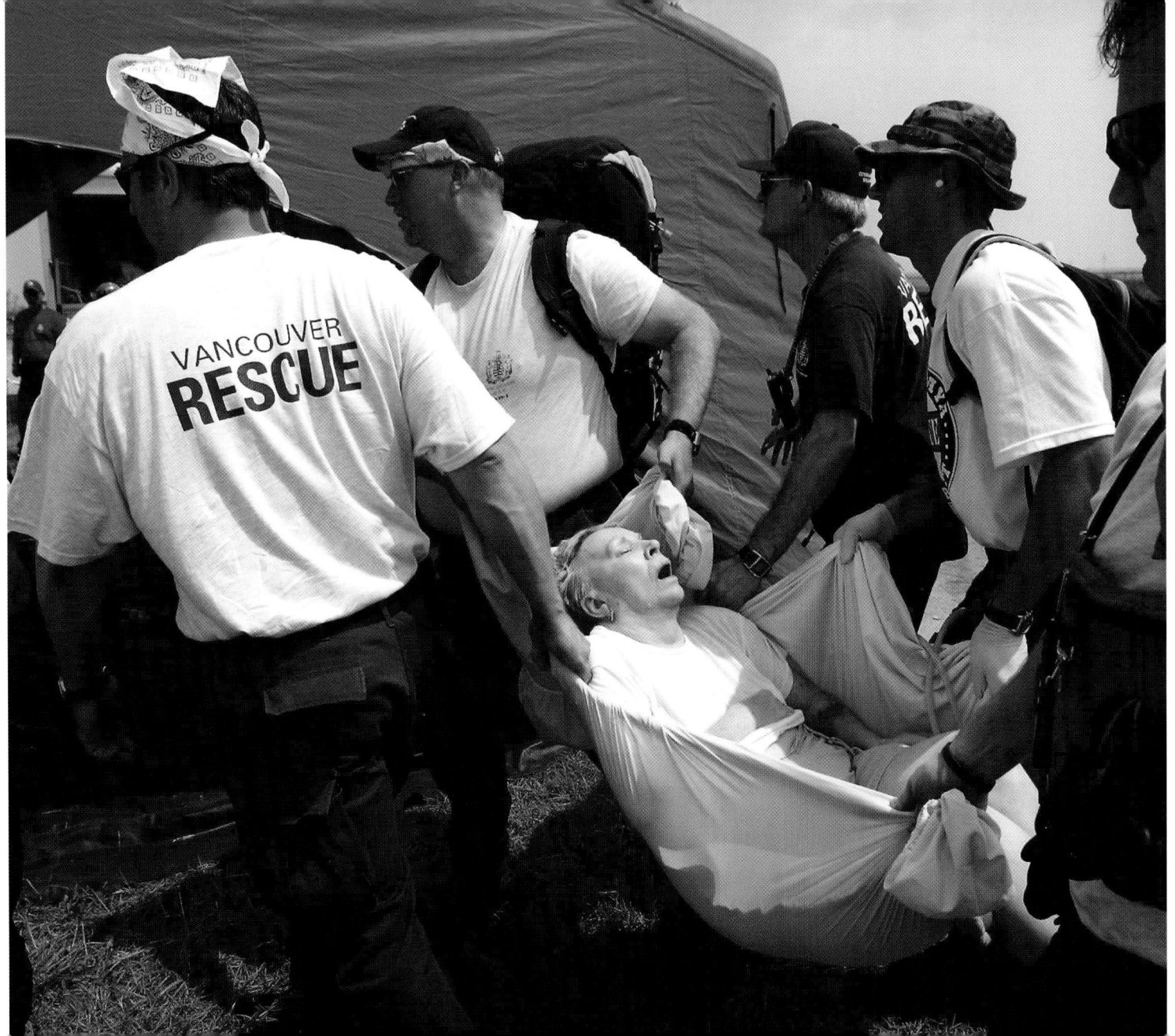

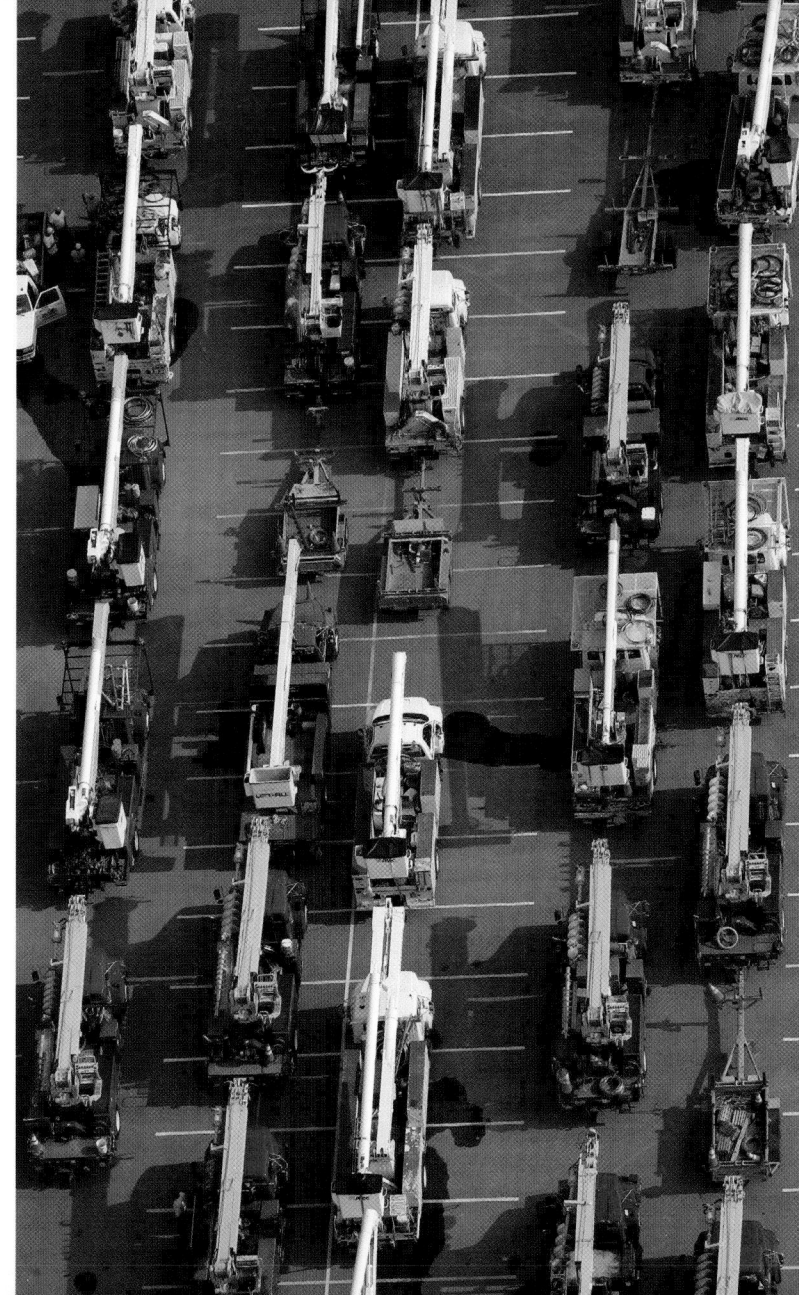

09.03.05 - Kenner, LA - Rows of power company trucks were staged in a parking lot in Kenner. Crews from around the country came to Louisiana to help restore power.
• SMILEY N. POOL

RIGHT
09.03.05 - Waveland, MS - Charles Gray wept after finding his partner's ashes in the rubble as friend Ecker Frank took them to a safe spot. Mr. Gray and his partner were together for 30 years.
• MICHAEL MULVEY

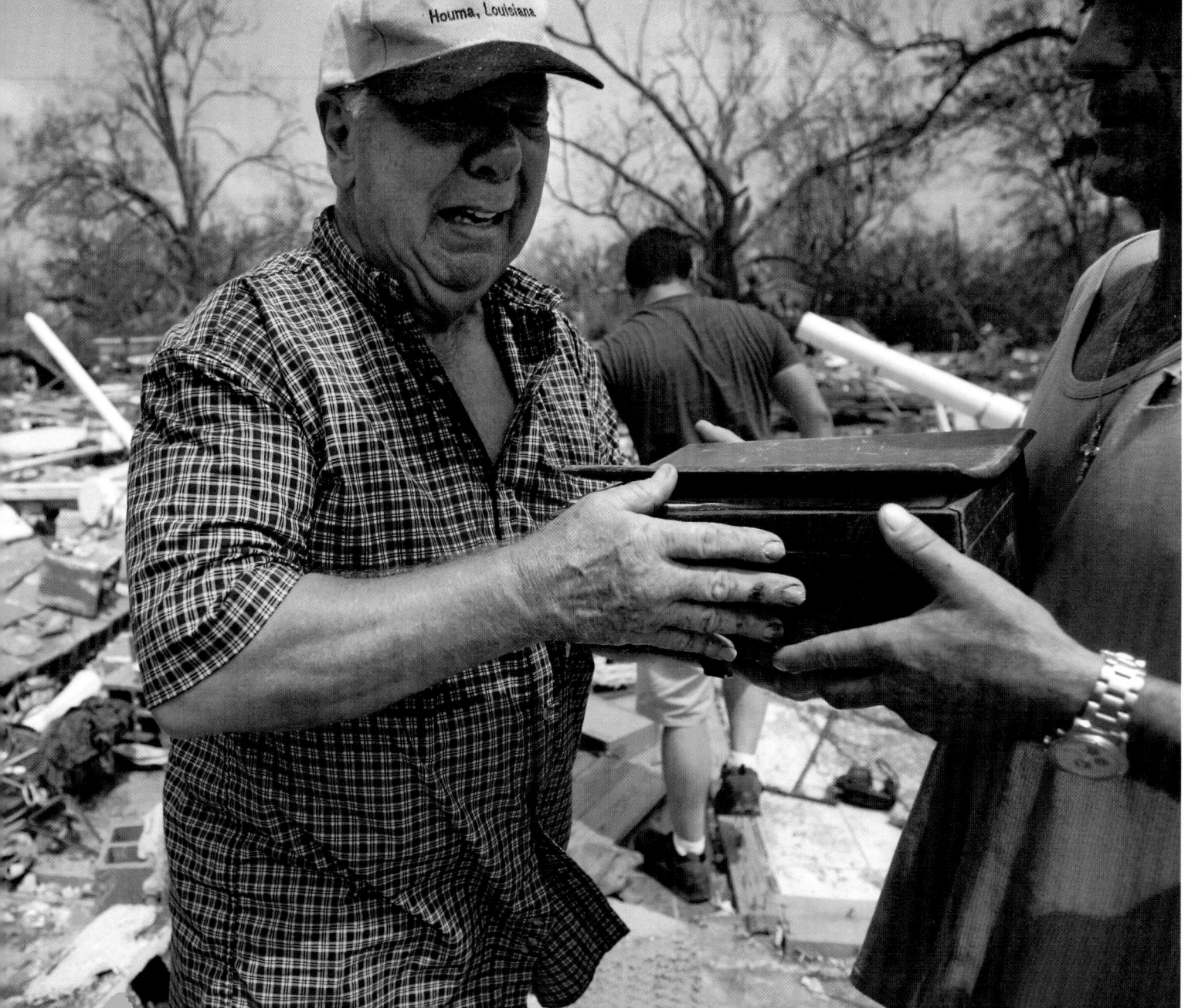

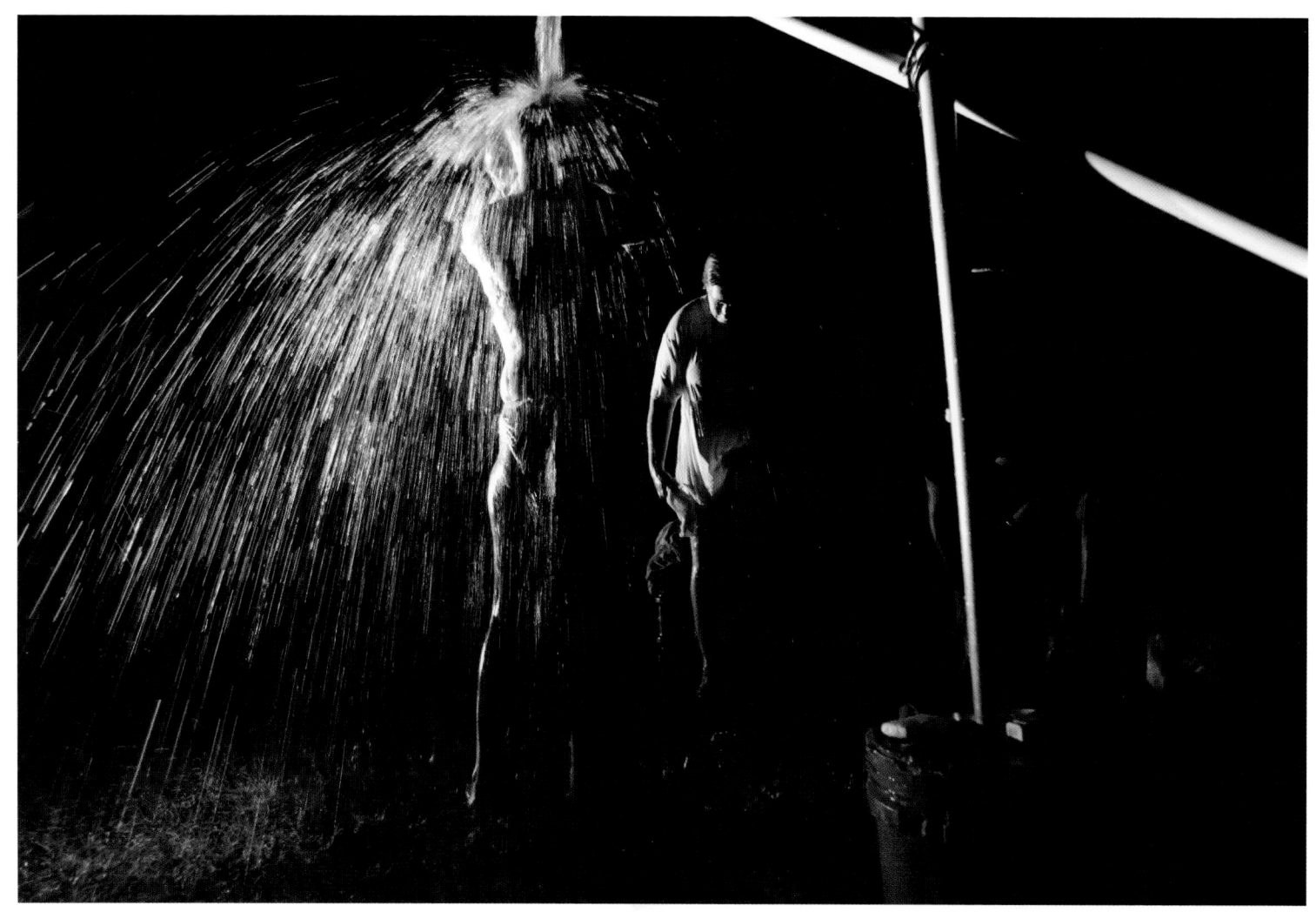

09.03.05 - Waveland, MS - Darlene Jordan showered in an artesian spring by car light. Residents near Long Beach flocked there to take showers and get water.
• MICHAEL MULVEY

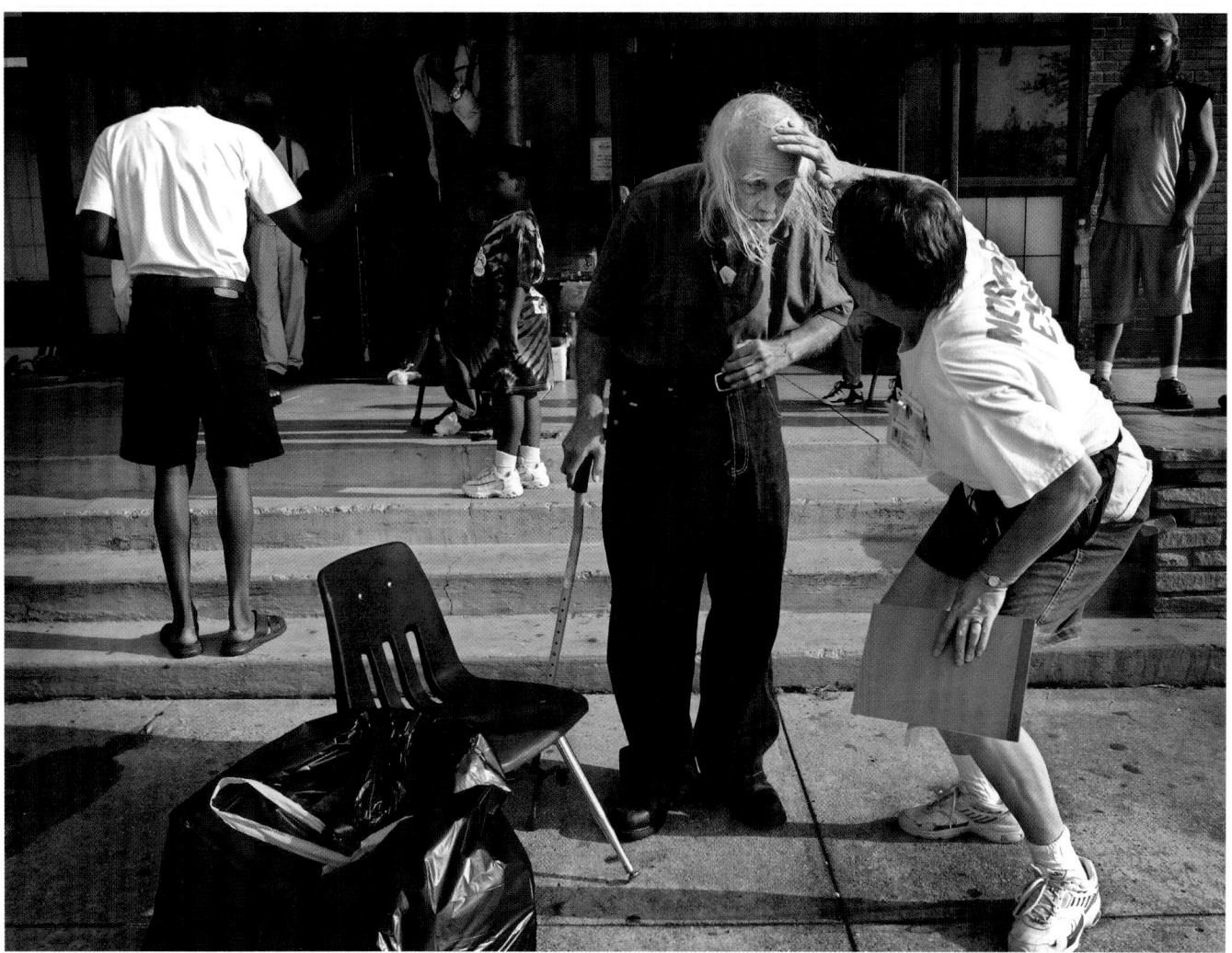

09.03.05 - Biloxi, MS - Red Cross aid worker Barbara Collison checked Paul Lunberg for fever. The man was waiting to be taken to a hospital to be treated for symptoms of dysentery, a disease that was beginning to spread among the approximately 400 hurricane evacuees at the Biloxi shelter. • BARBARA DAVIDSON

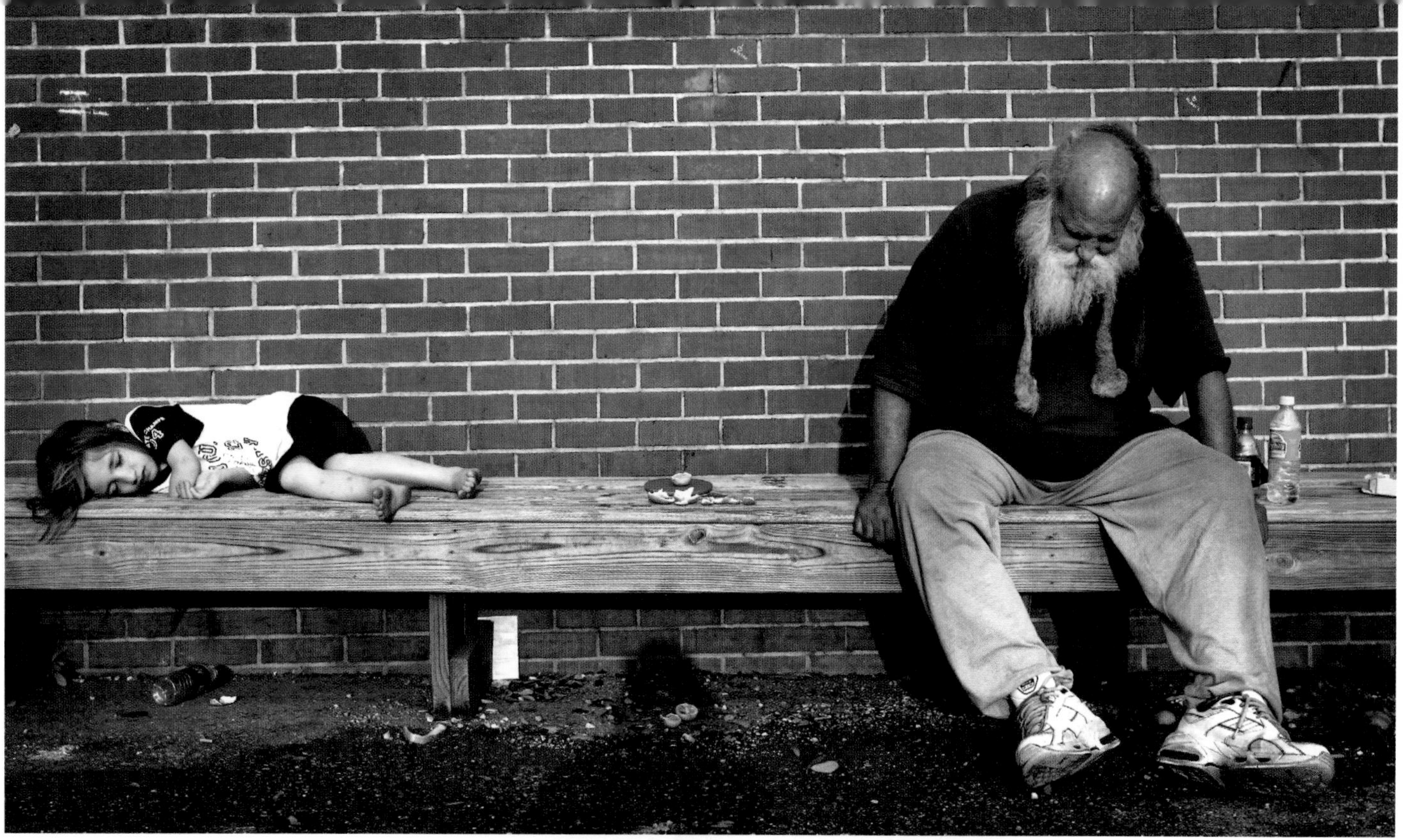

09.03.05 - Biloxi, MS - Molly Weems, 6, and Larry Devone rested outside Mary J. Michel Seventh Grade School, which was being used as a shelter. Many inside had no cots or mattresses to sleep on. • BARBARA DAVIDSON

09.03.05 - Biloxi, MS - Berttan Antwon, 4, waits with his mother and others in a food line at Biloxi Regional Hospital after being taken from the school shelter. The boy's mother said her son was sick and needed antibiotics. • BARBARA DAVIDSON

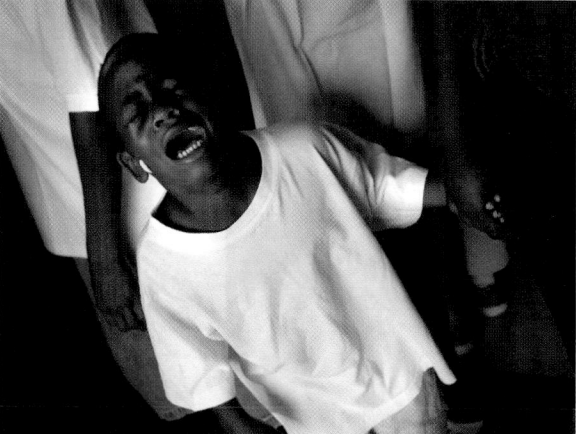

09.03.05 - Biloxi, MS - Faces of misery: Sheila Wright, Paul Lunberg (background) and Charles Carlborne waited in a police van to be taken to the hospital after officials closed the shelter where they were staying because more than 20 people fell ill. Doctors believe the patients may have contracted dysentery from tainted water. Another 20 people in the area also were treated for vomiting and diarrhea. • BARBARA DAVIDSON

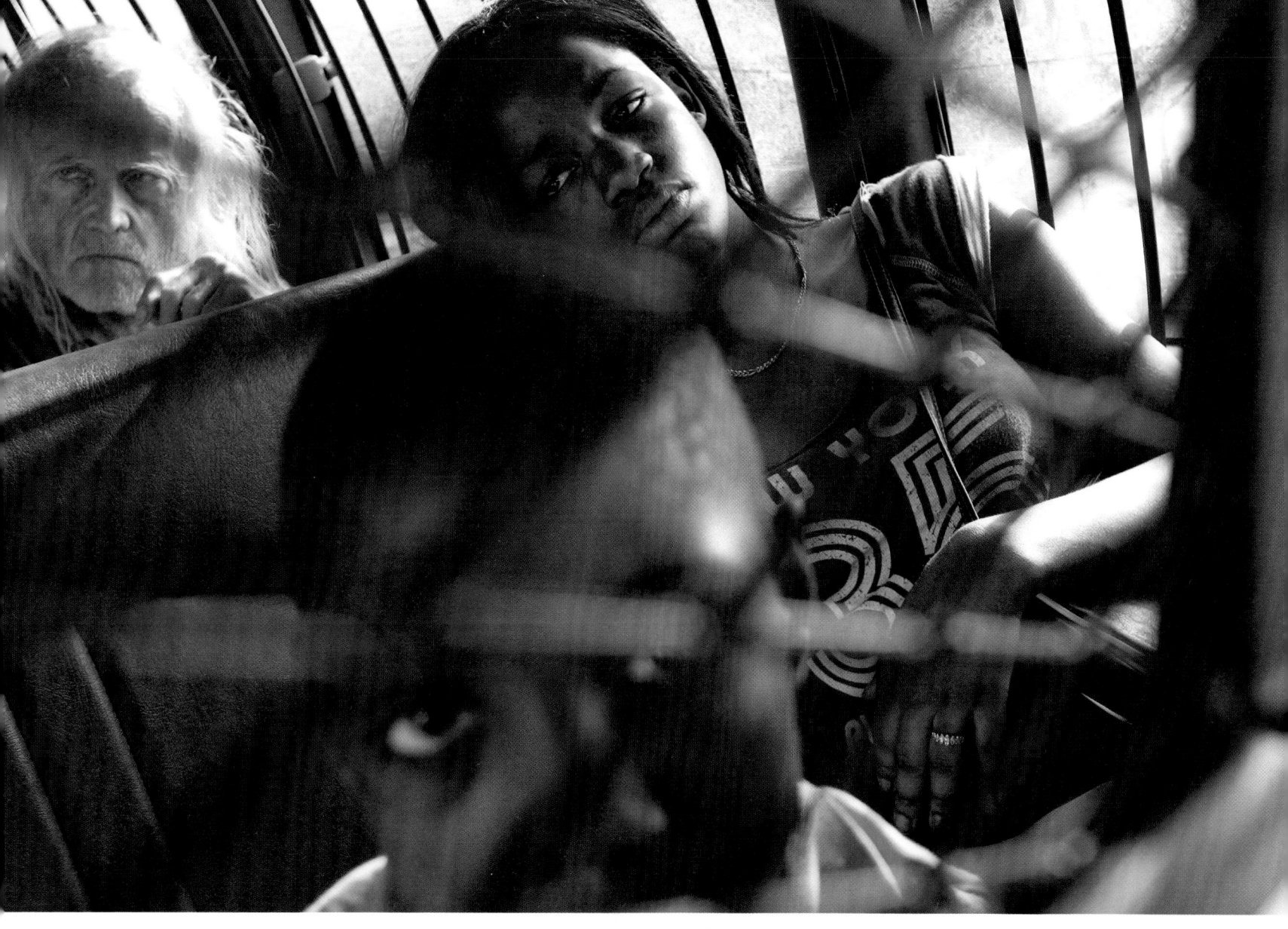

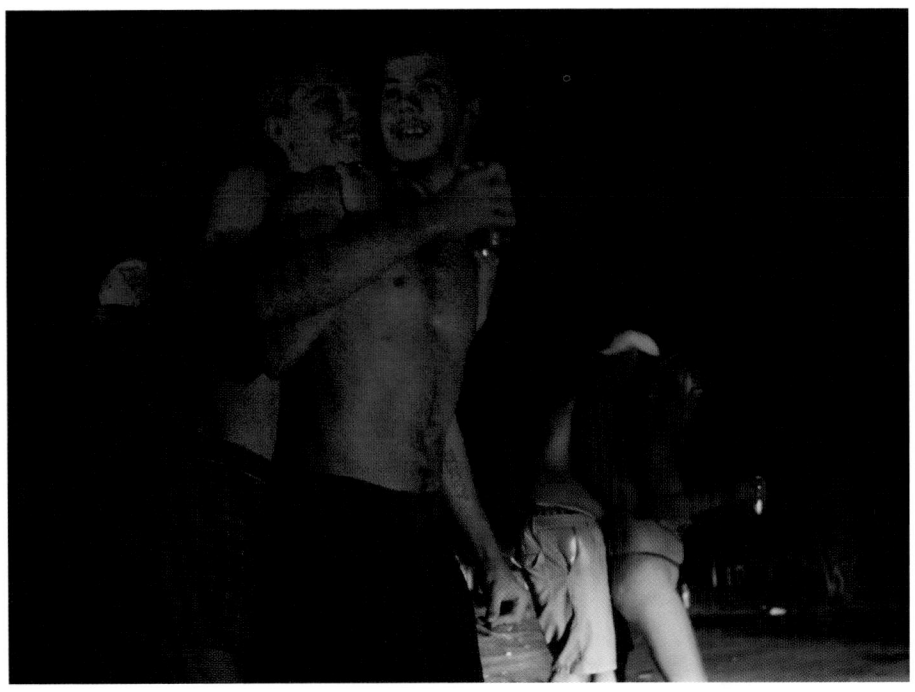

09.04.05 - Long Beach, MS - A group of young adults decided to make the best of a bad situation as they danced to music by car light near an artesian spring. • MICHAEL MULVEY

RIGHT
09.04.05 - Biloxi, MS - Rodrick Wiggins (far left) and Lois Bolton clasped hands in worship with others under an oak tree outside Our Mother of Sorrows Catholic Church. The church was in need of repair and cleaning after Katrina. • MICHAEL MULVEY

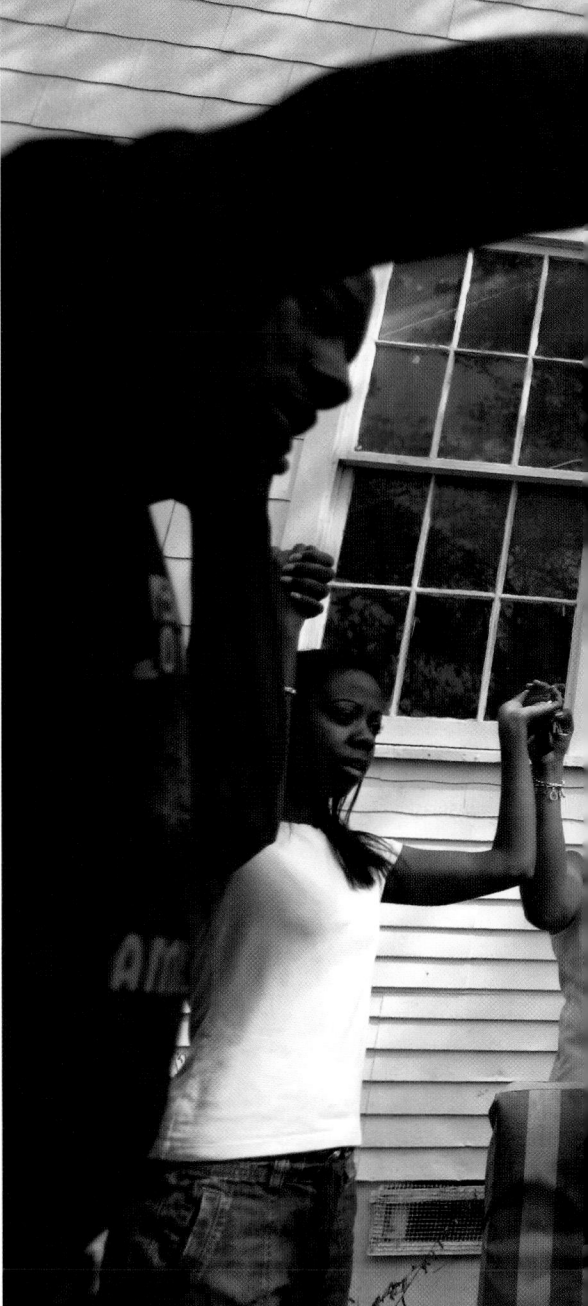

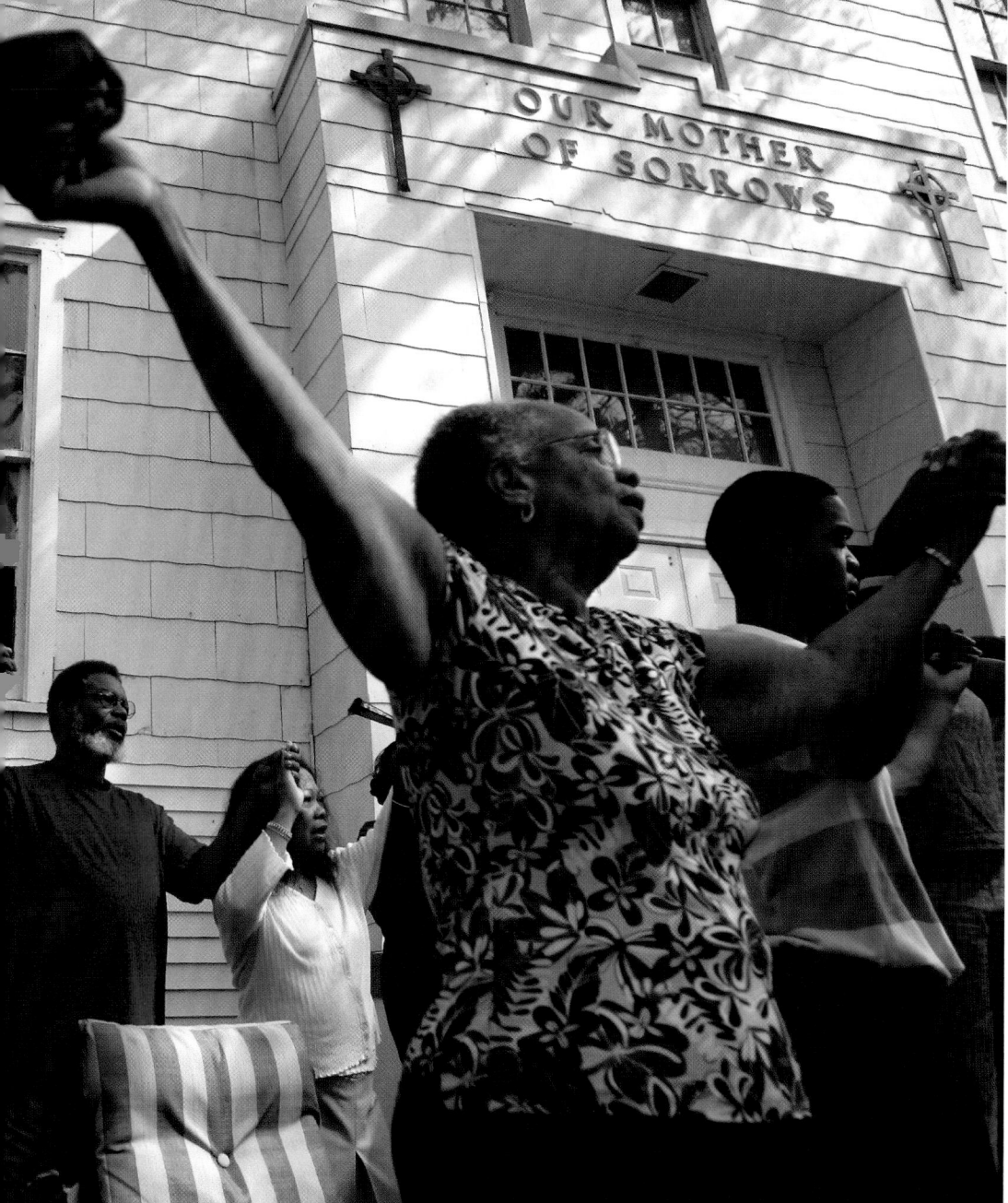

127

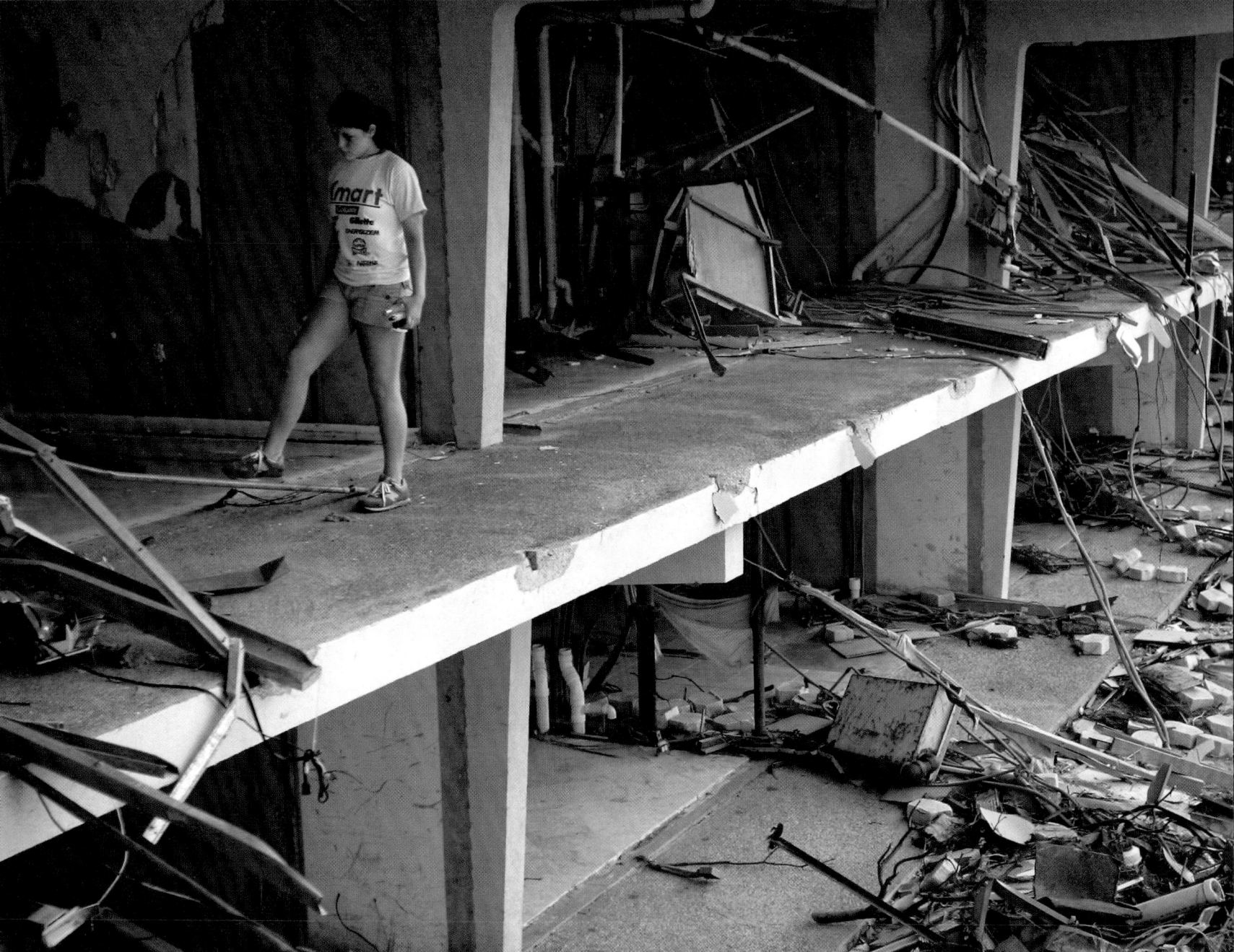

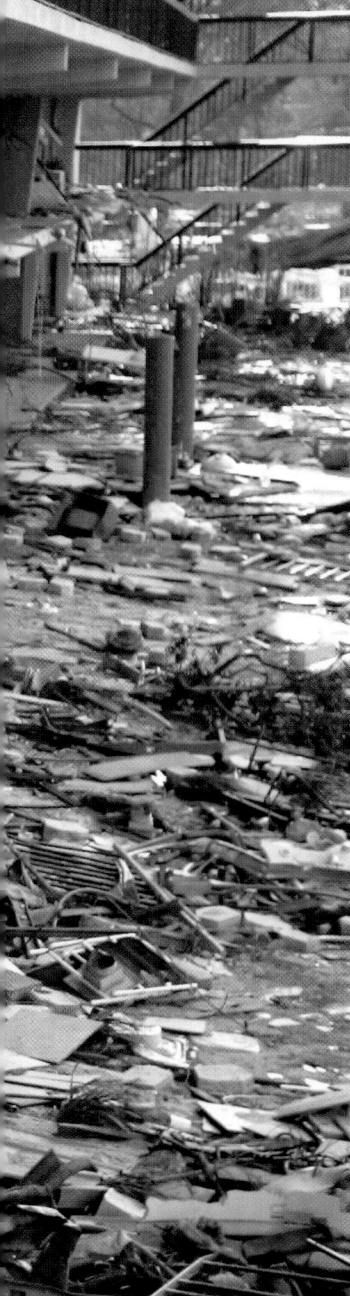

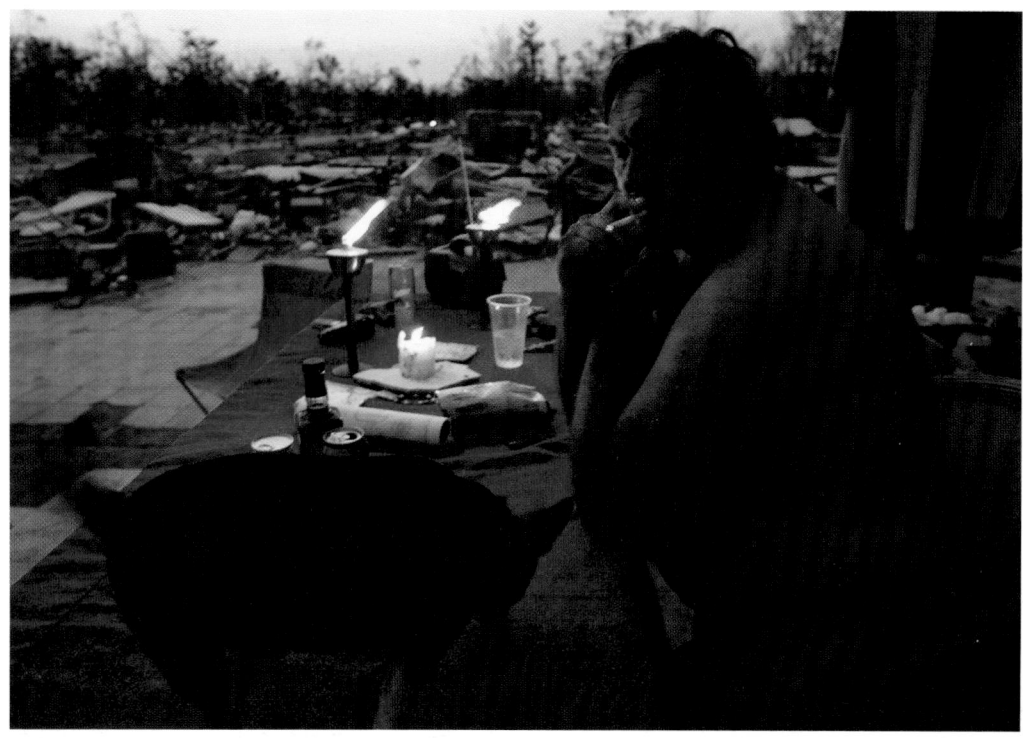

09.03.05 - Waveland, MS - Storm survivor Brian Mollere took a smoke break while sitting with his dog Rocky where his home once stood. He made a valiant effort to deal with the destruction: lighting candles, listening to the radio, having a drink. • MICHAEL MULVEY

LEFT
09.04.05 - Biloxi, MS - C.J. Higdon roamed around the destroyed second-floor apartment that her father lived in on the beachfront. • MICHAEL MULVEY

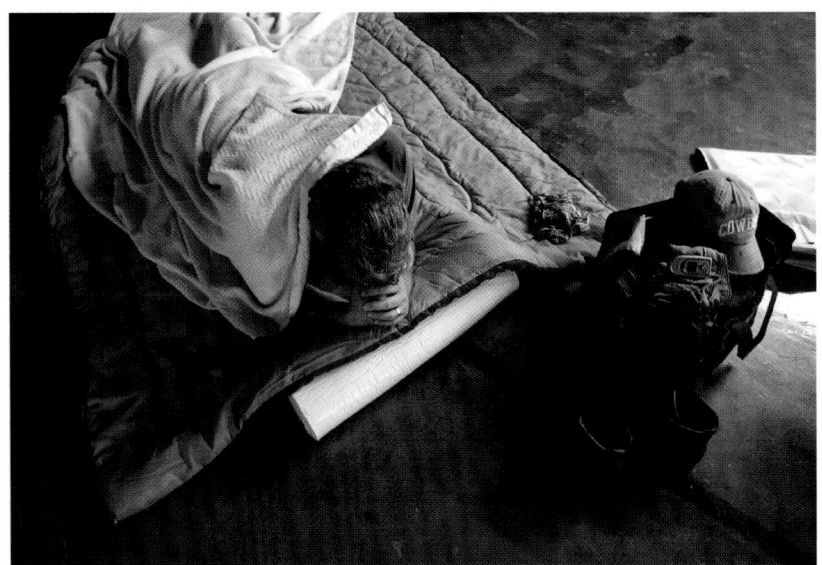

09.02.05 - Alexandria, LA - Joey Stevens, of Lewisville, Texas, takes a moment to pray before bedding down for the night on the floor at Air Base Baptist Church, en route to Slidell, La., with a church group offering aid to affected residents. • LARA SOLT

RIGHT
09.04.05 - New Orleans, LA - Mona Tucker's despair lifted for a moment with a visit from Sachse, Texas, church members (from left) Joey Stevens, Jillian Schoelen, Jenny Davis and Savannah Davis. They provided her with food, water, money and lots of hugs. • LARA SOLT

SMALL ACTS OF KINDNESS

SLIDELL, La. — The blisters on her feet stung, but she removed her shoes and walked through the black mud. She showed the Texas church group what had happened to her house and her back yard.

The waters from Lake Pontchartrain had risen high and fast and slammed all her furniture against the doors and through a wall. The winds uprooted the oak tree that she had planted a dozen years ago. Her parents' ashes, which she kept in an urn, were swept away. She had no flood insurance. All she had were the clothes in the back seat of her car.

"Can I get a hug?" she asked.

One by one, the church members embraced her. Then someone gave her a bag of food. Nothing fancy - just granola bars, cheese and crackers. But inside the bag, the woman came upon a $100 bill. "Oh, no," she said. She put her hands to her face and sobbed. The church members began to cry too.

When the disaster is immense and the loss is great, there's only so much ordinary folks can do to help.

But sometimes you have to try.

And even though they had received no training, assignment or sponsorship from any disaster relief organization, the people of Park Lake Church in Sachse, Texas, had decided to try.

It didn't make a whole lot of sense. Anything they could accomplish in the disaster zone would be a drop in the bucket. But sometimes, with faith and determination, you can end up exactly where you're meant to serve.

They joined dozens, if not hundreds, of grass-roots humanitarian groups that journeyed to the Gulf Coast immediately after the devastation of Hurricane Katrina to deliver not only aid but also hope.

• THOMAS HUANG

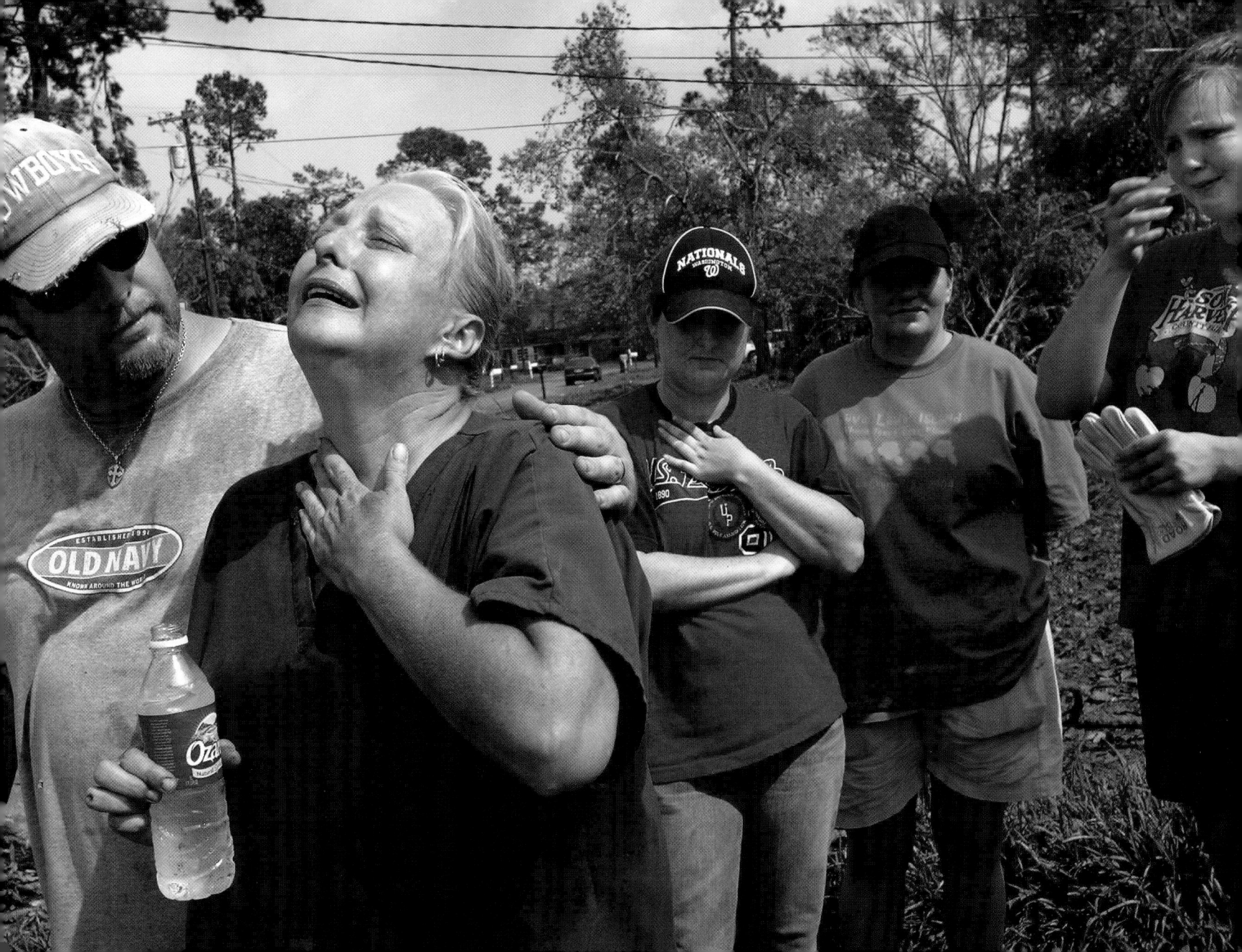

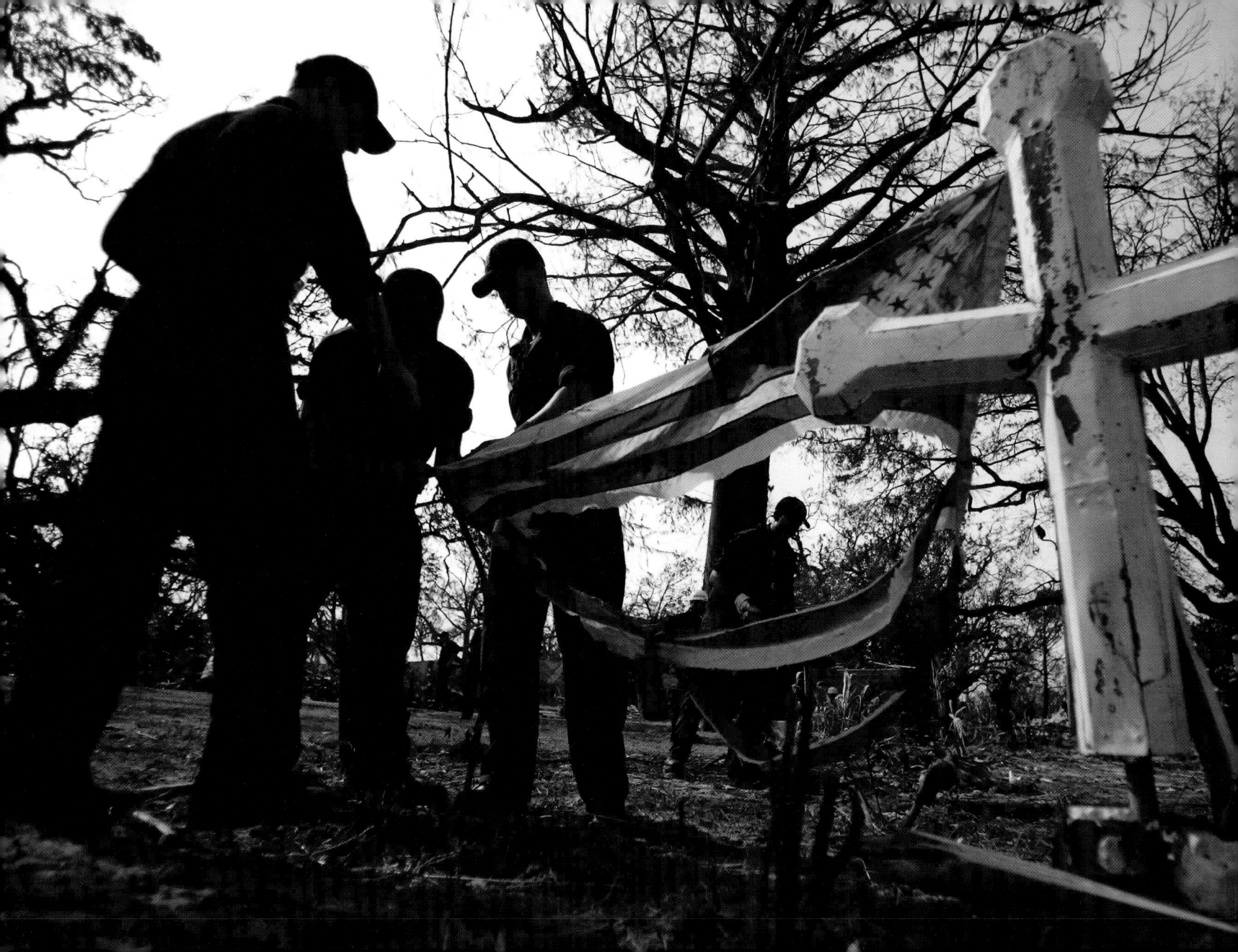

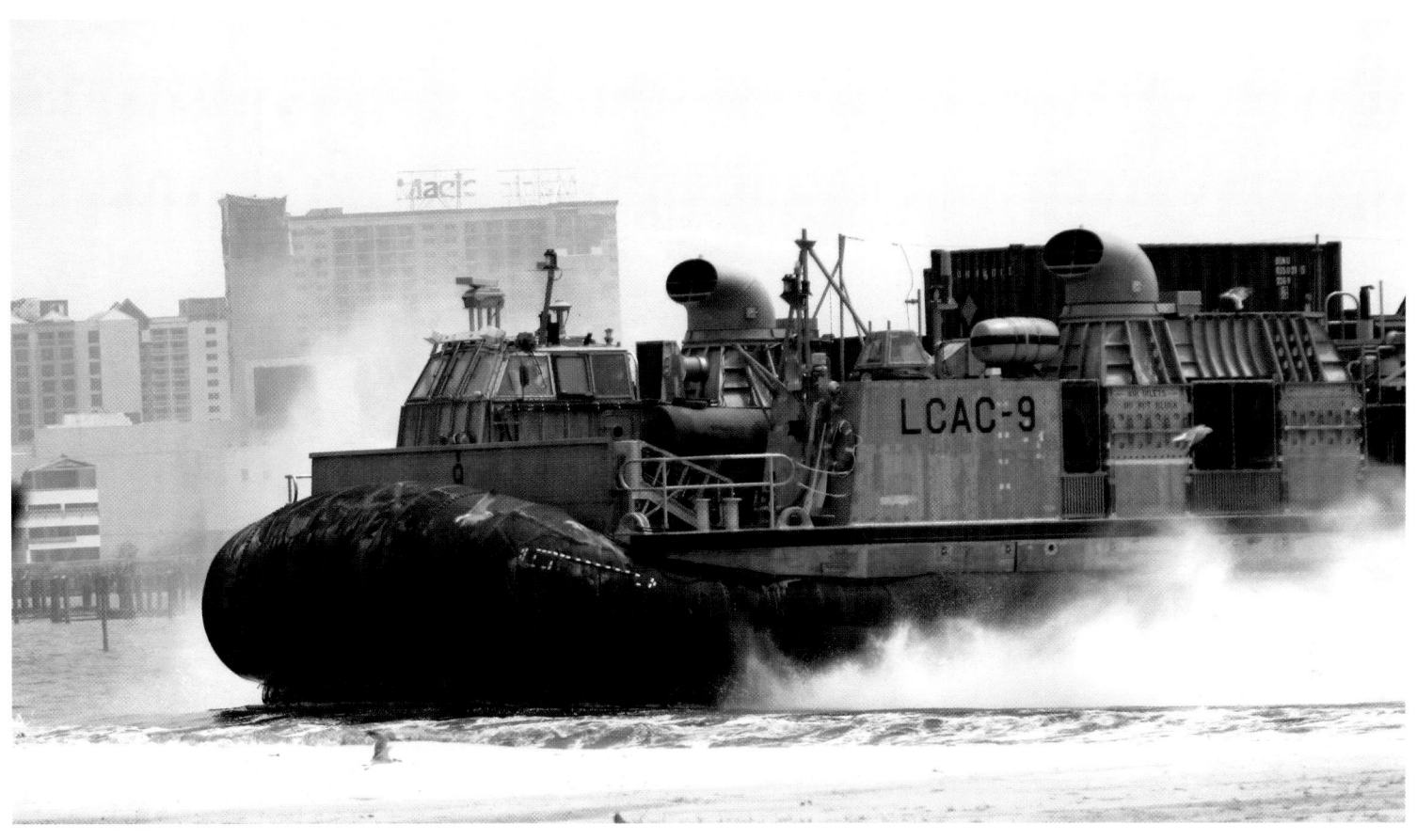

09.04.05 - Biloxi, MS - A Navy LCAC (landing craft air cushion) or hovercraft landed near casinos with equipment and personnel. • MICHAEL MULVEY

LEFT
09.04.05 - Biloxi, MS - Navy sailors fixed a tattered American flag tied to a cross as sailors from the USS Iwo Jima came ashore and cleaned up the site of Episcopal Redeemer Church near the beach. • MICHAEL MULVEY

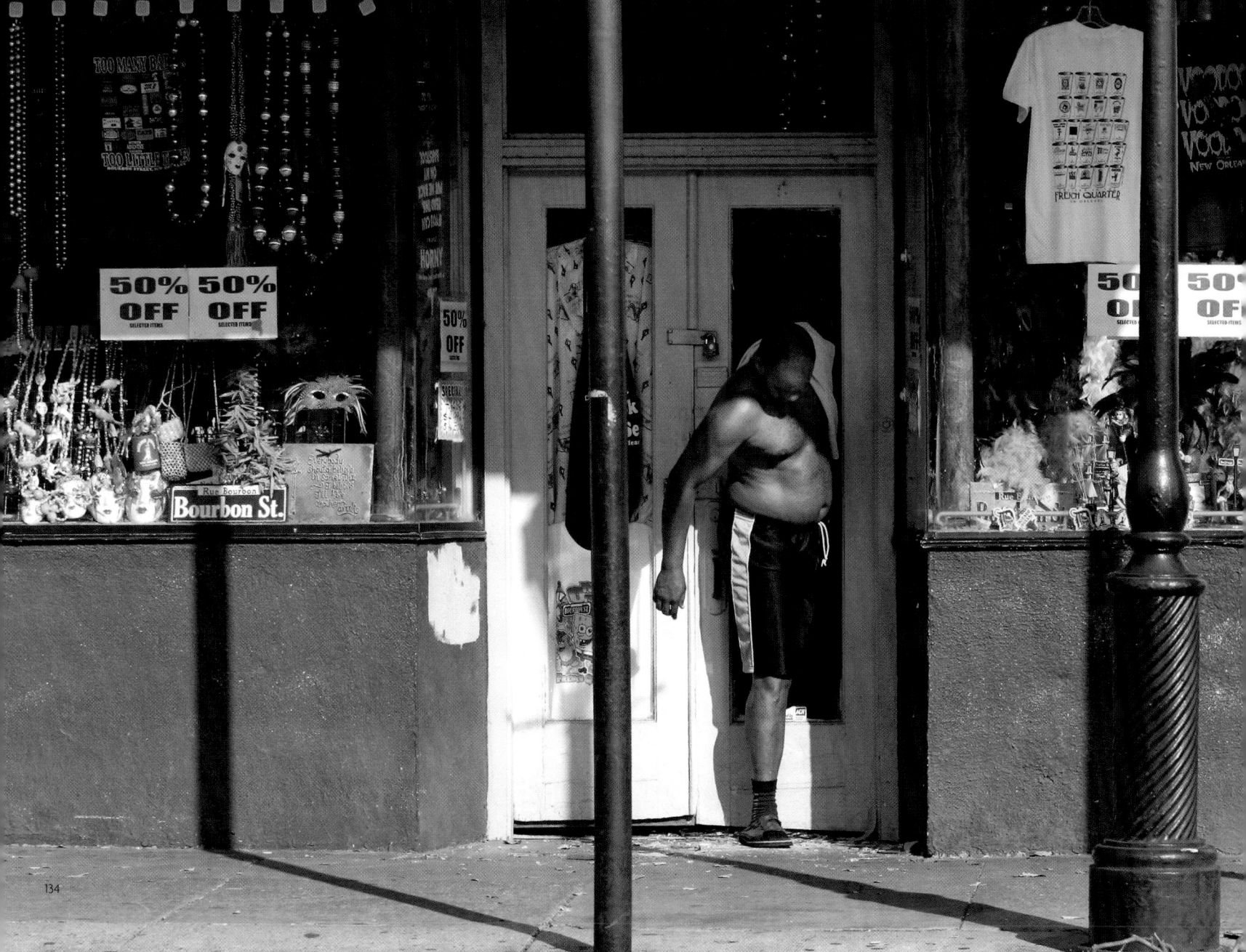

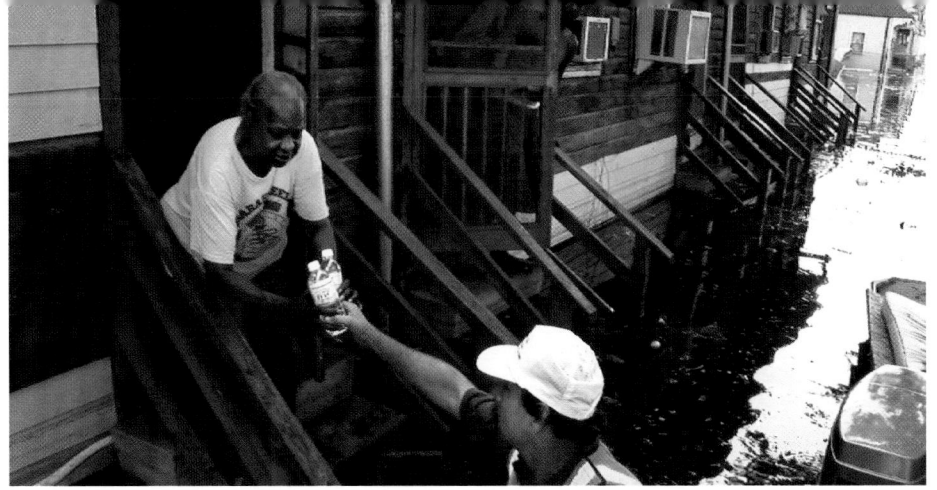

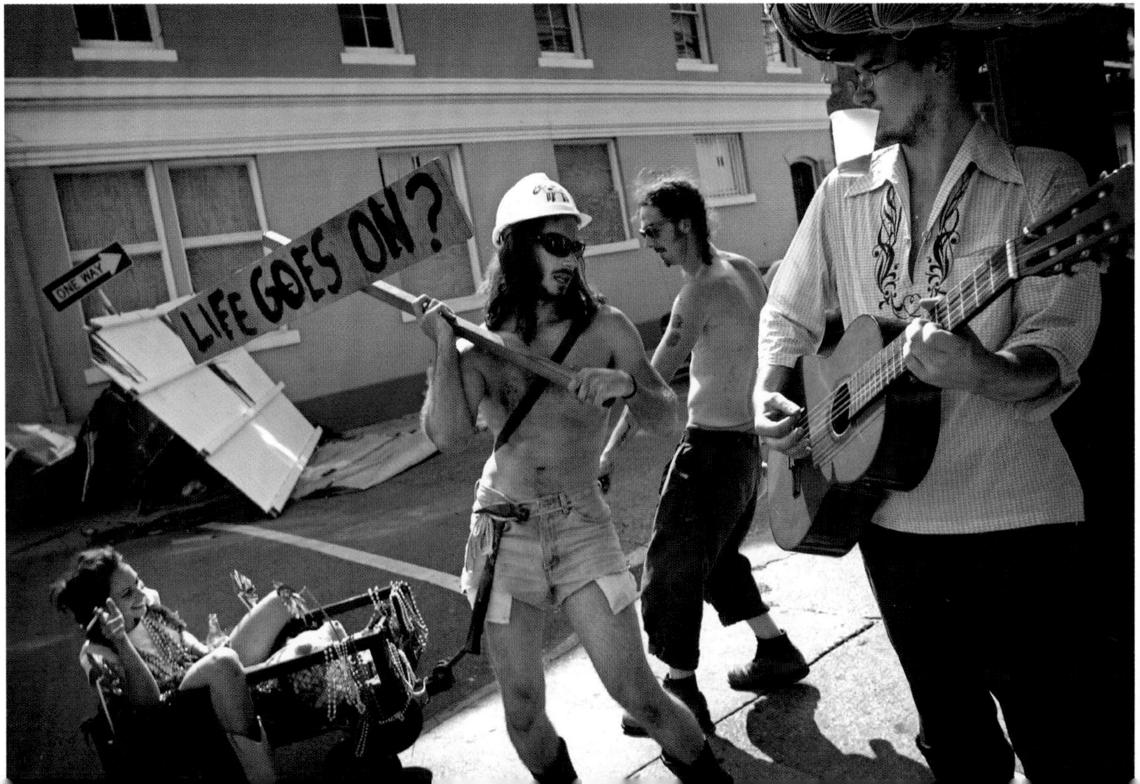

09.04.05 - New Orleans, LA - An elderly woman who had refused to leave her home is given some fresh water by a volunteer rescue worker on a boat in New Orleans. This image was taken with a high definition video camera. • DAVID LEESON

LEFT
09.04.05 - New Orleans, LA - Mat James (center) joined other revelers in drinking, dancing and singing during the Southern Decadence gay pride parade in the French Quarter. • BARBARA DAVIDSON

OPPOSITE PAGE
09.04.05 - New Orleans, LA - Herman Johnson stepped out of a broken window after taking a T-shirt from a shop on Decatur Street in the French Quarter. Police were reportedly allowing residents to take items they needed but were stopping wanton looting. • IRWIN THOMPSON

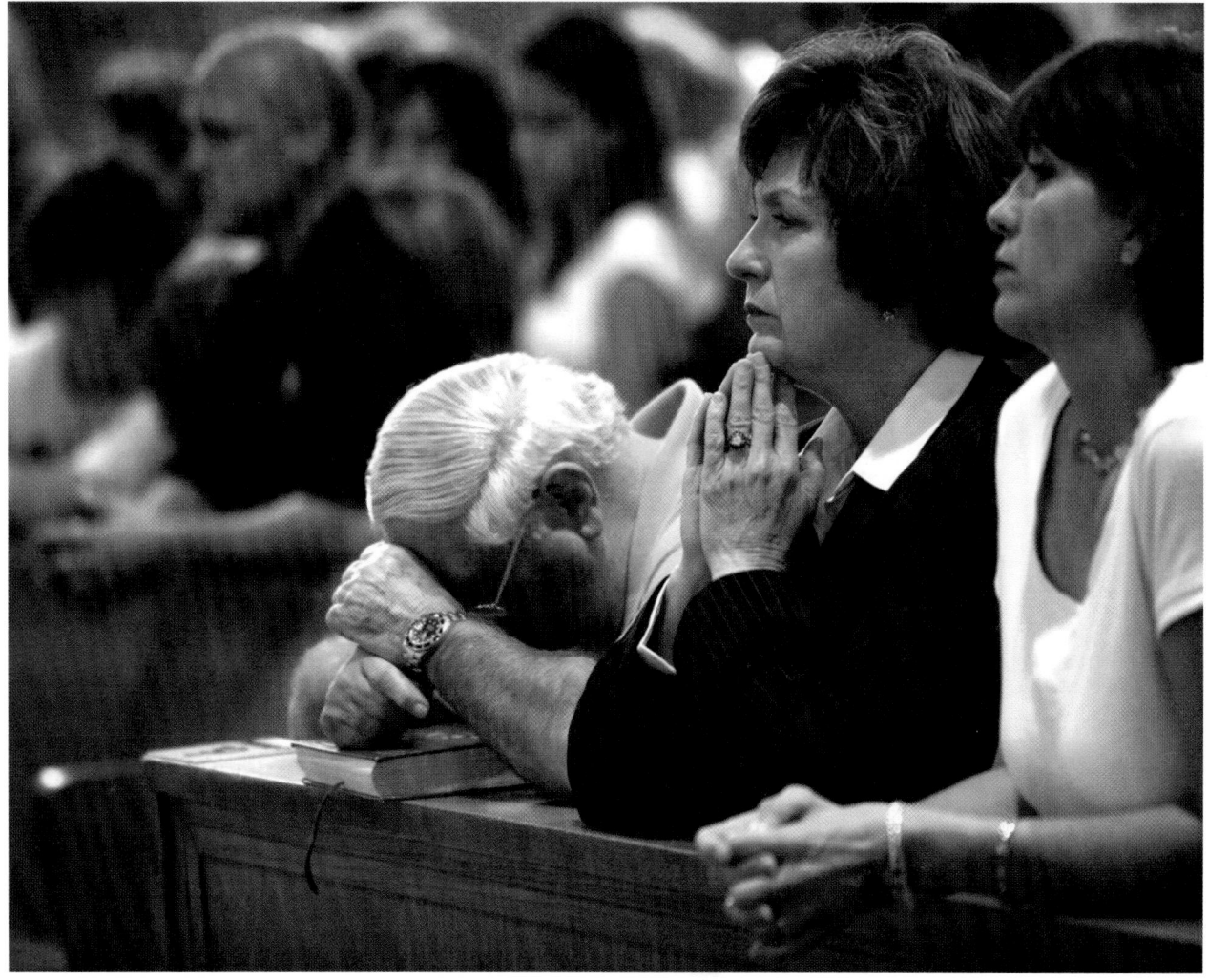

09.04.05 - Baton Rouge, LA - Gov. Kathleen Blanco (center) prayed with her husband, Raymond, and daughter Karmen Blanco during Mass at the Cathedral Church of Saint Joseph. In the wake of Hurricane Katrina, New Orleans Archbishop Alfred Hughes came to Baton Rogue to lead the community in prayer. • TOM FOX

RIGHT
09.04.05 - New Orleans, LA - A sandbag was lowered into the broken section of a levee just south of the University of New Orleans. Critics said flood-protection projects along Louisiana's coast hadn't been a White House budgeting priority for decades. • SMILEY N. POOL

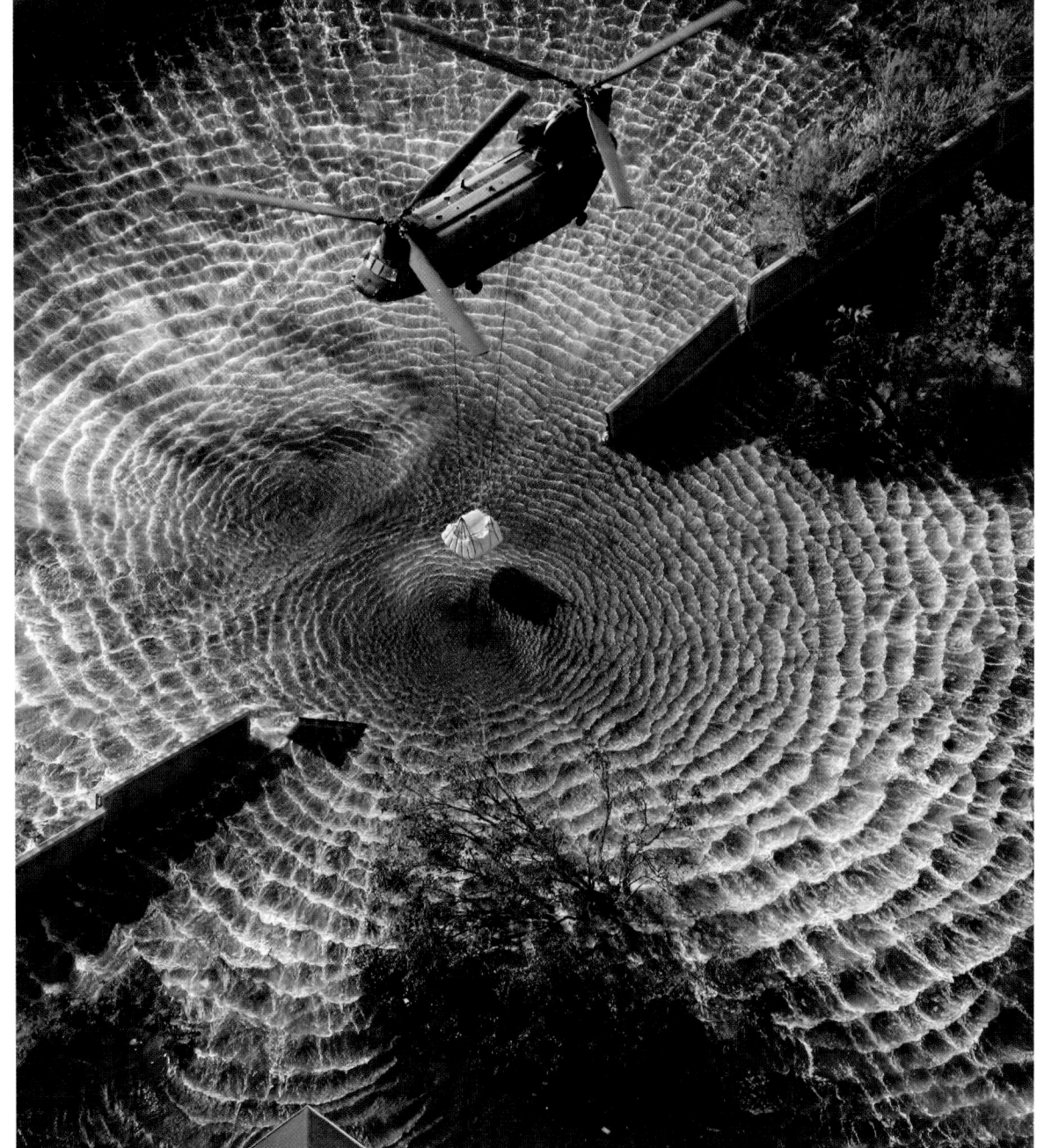

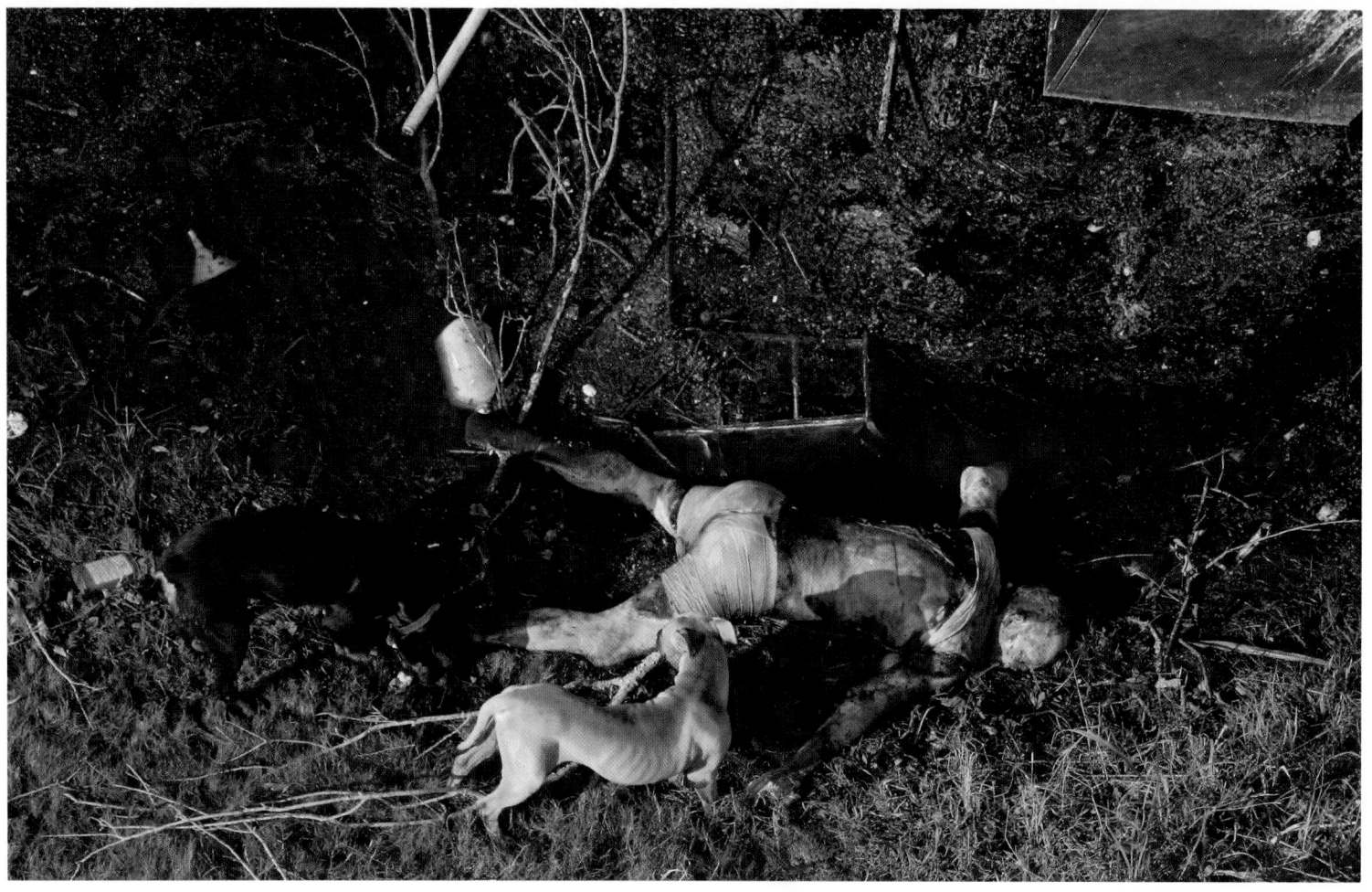

09.04.05 - New Orleans, LA - Abandoned dogs inspect a corpse washed up at the edge of receding floodwaters. • SMILEY N. POOL

RIGHT
09.04.05 - New Orleans, LA - Members of the Alabama and Florida Army National Guard evacuated thousands of people from the Ninth Ward. Many in the hard-hit neighborhood had waited nearly a week to be rescued from their flooded homes. • MONA REEDER

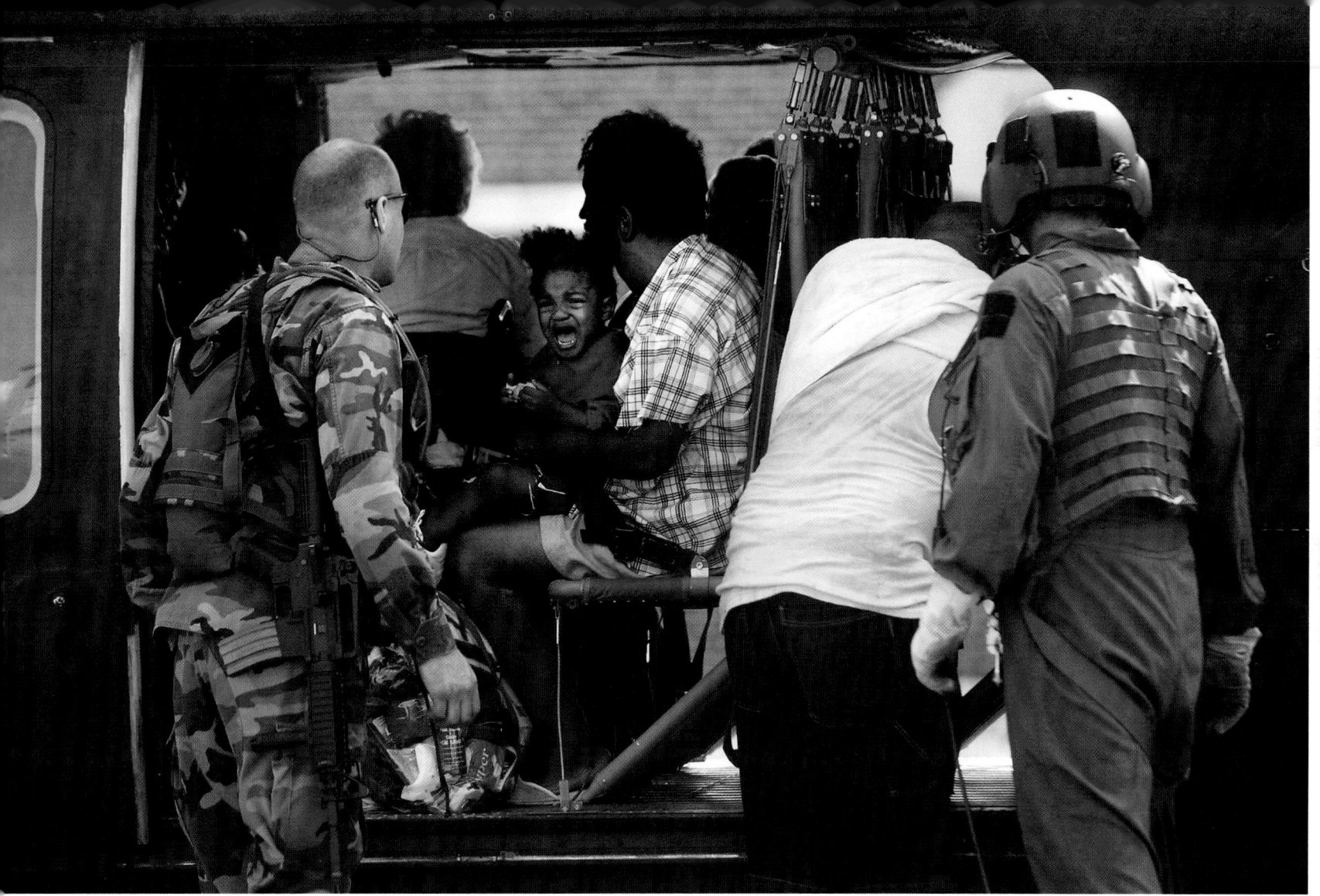

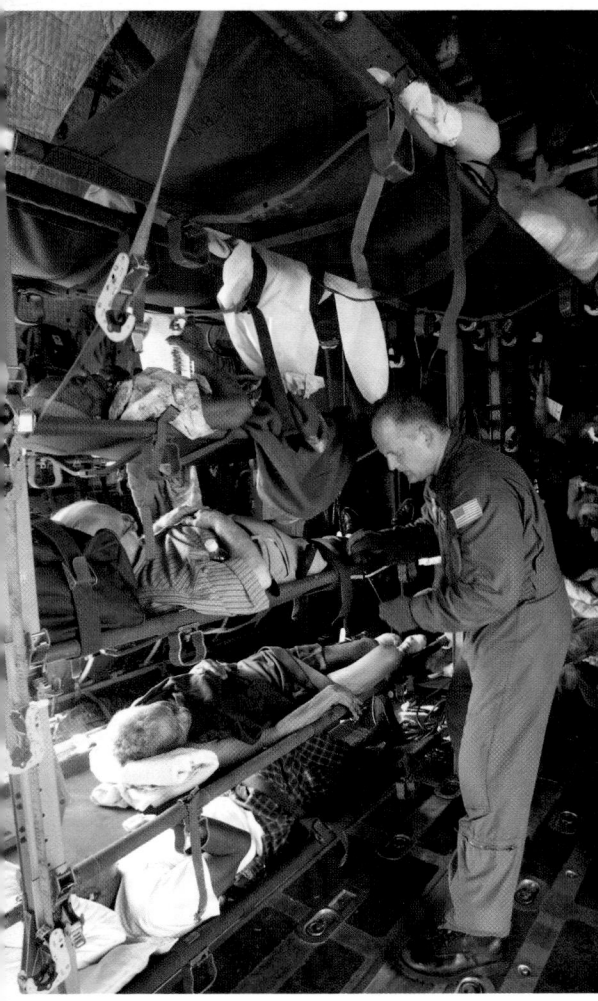

09.03.05 - Kenner, LA - Patients lay on cots in a C-130 Hercules that was about to leave New Orleans / Louis Armstrong International Airport for Lackland Air Force Base in San Antonio, Texas. • IRWIN THOMPSON

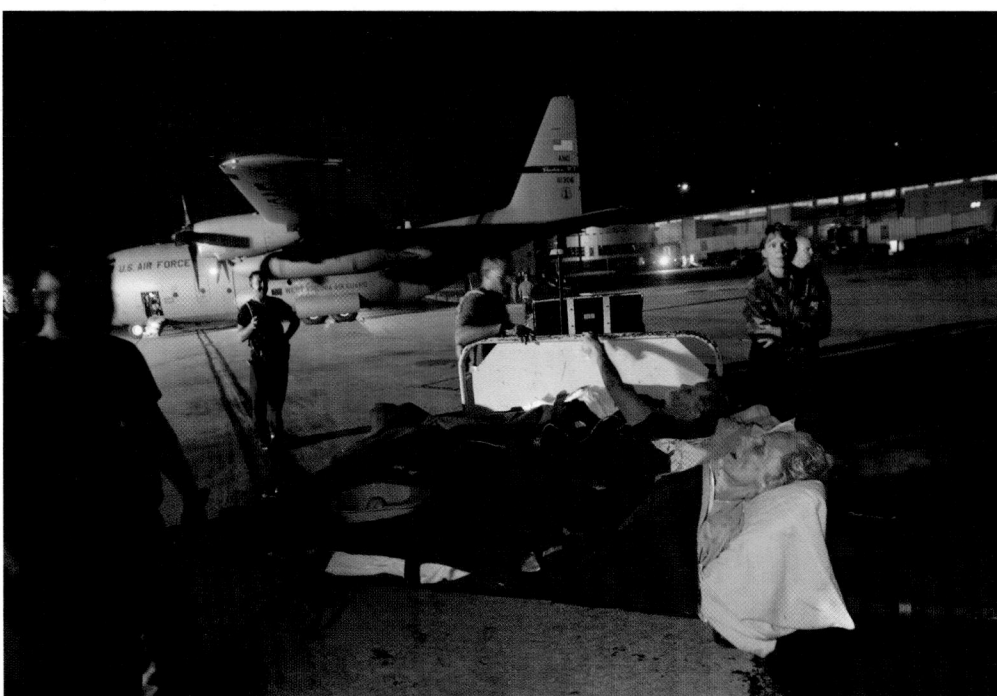

09.04.05 - Kenner, LA - Medical technicians from the 59th Medical Wing at Lackland Air Force Base in San Antonio watched as the C-130 flight crew settled elderly evacuees for transport at the New Orleans airport. • TOM FOX

09.04.05 - Dallas, TX - Demetrius Lebeau, 12, played with his nephew Corey Reed, 2, at the Dallas Convention Center. They were among the thousands who had few, if any, possessions from home • MELANIE BURFORD

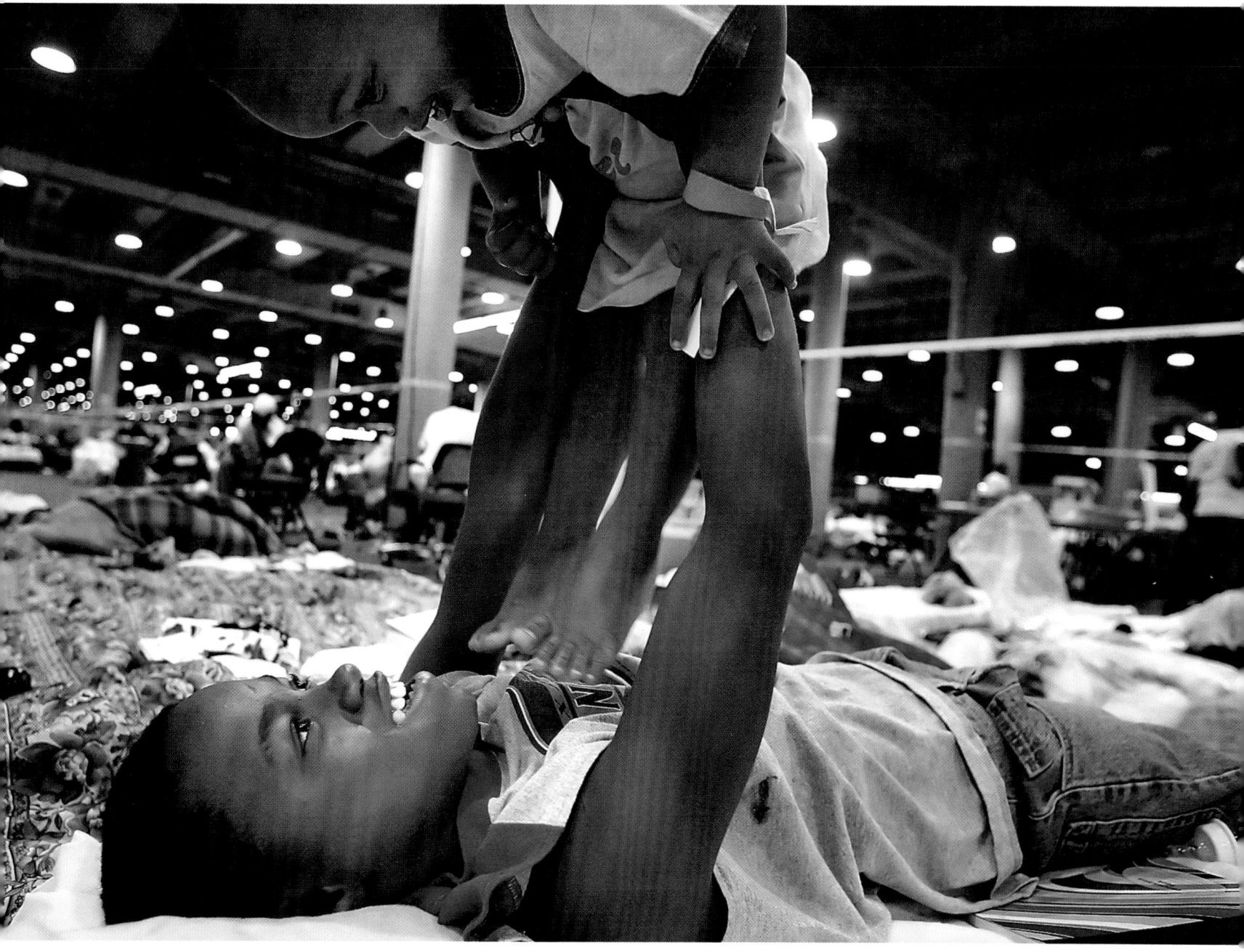

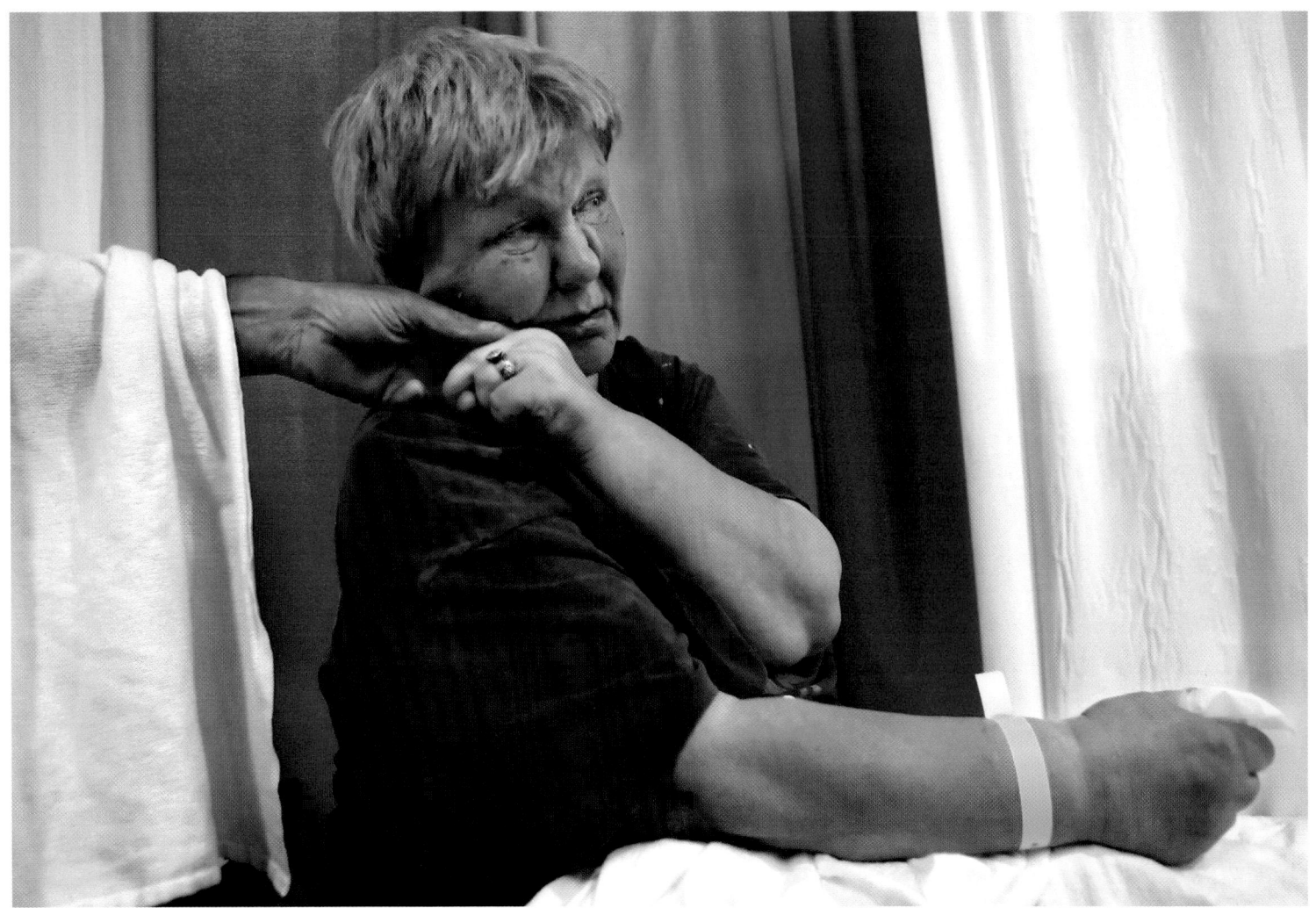

09.04.05 - Dallas, TX - Dixie Neeley of New Orleans was comforted by her husband of 20 years, David Gonzalez, while getting medical attention at the clinic in the Dallas Convention Center. The couple had been in water up to their necks, hanging onto their house's gutters, for two days. The Coast Guard took them to the Superdome. "I didn't think we'd make it. We prayed we'd make it off," Mr. Gonzalez said. "We told each other how much we loved each other. ... We lost everything we ever had. At least we didn't lose the biggest thing, our lives and each other." • MELANIE BURFORD

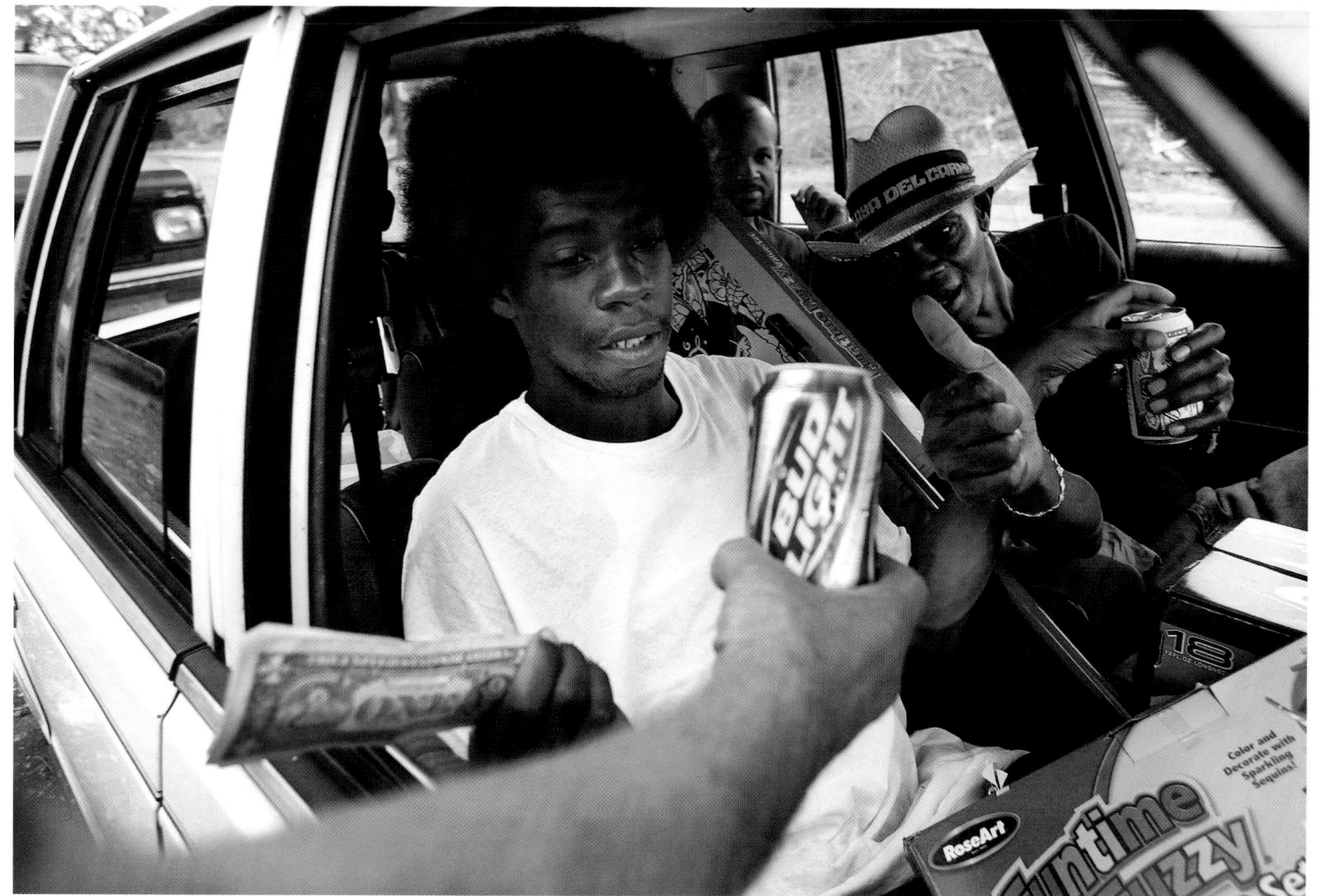

09.05.05 - Biloxi, MS - Cold comfort: A carload of residents pulled up to buy beer at J.R.'s Lounge, one of the older bars in Biloxi. The bar had some damage but was selling beer from the back porch for $2.50 a can, kept cold with donated ice. Residents were gathering there to share their stories, and some of the displaced were living in tents behind the bar. • MICHAEL MULVEY

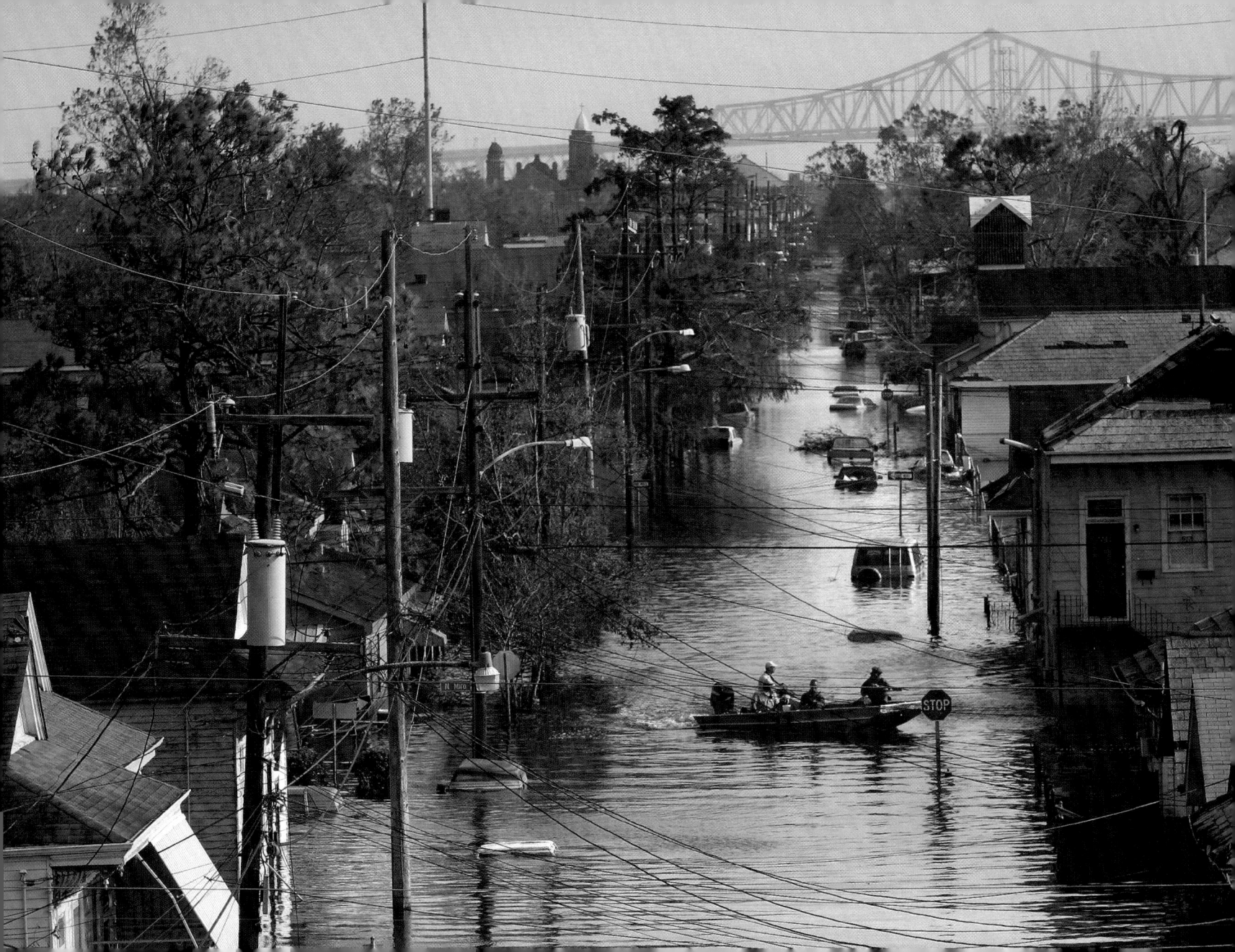

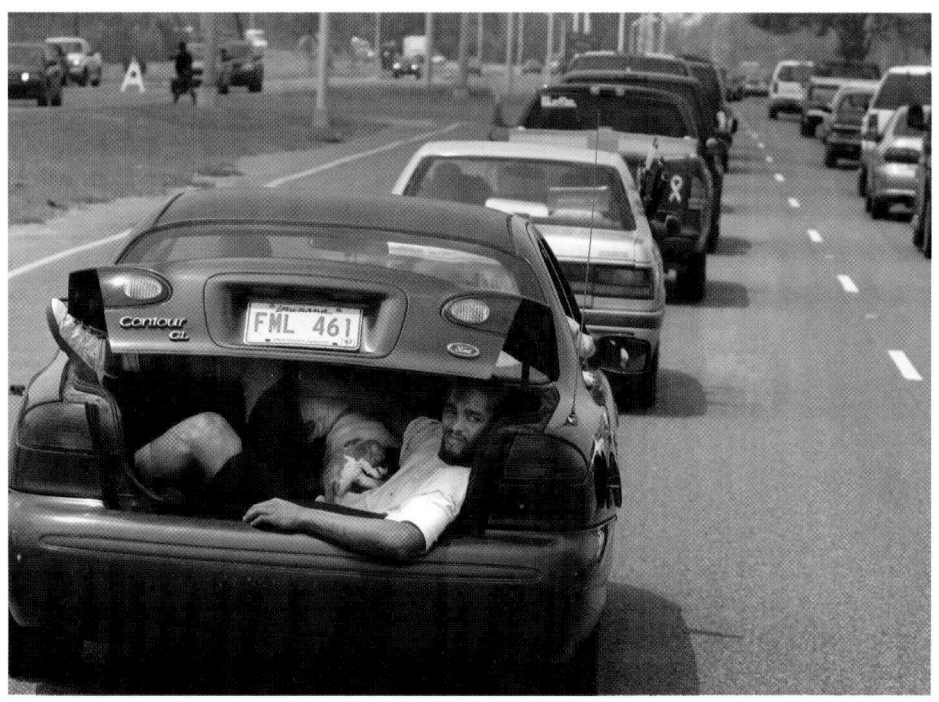

09.05.05 - Westwego, LA - Eric Mayes, 23, of New Orleans got comfortable in the trunk of his car with four of his 10 dogs while heading to Baton Rouge. He said National Guardsmen told him to leave his house in the hurricane-ravaged city and flee town. "They came by and told us we had to leave our dogs," Mr. Mayes said. "They are our family. They are the only children we've got ... I love them. I couldn't let them die." He took a seat in the trunk after he and his girlfriend picked up David Brooks, his wife and three kids, who didn't have a ride.
• IRWIN THOMPSON

LEFT
09.05.05 - New Orleans, LA - An armed search and rescue team motored down N. Miro St. near Interstate 10 looking for survivors. The Crescent City Connection (Hwy 90 toll bridge) in top background was one of the few remaining ways into New Orleans after the storm. • TOM FOX

09.05.05 - New Orleans, LA - California National Guardsmen searched Jason Zeigler's belongings for looted goods before putting him on a bus for evacuation. • BARBARA DAVIDSON

OPPOSITE PAGE
09.05.05 - Marrero, LA - Jefferson Parish resident Donna Polk tried to secure her home after authorities let her and other residents into the ravaged area to collect a few things and survey the damage. She and her daughters had lived in the home for more than 11 years. They had no insurance. • MONA REEDER

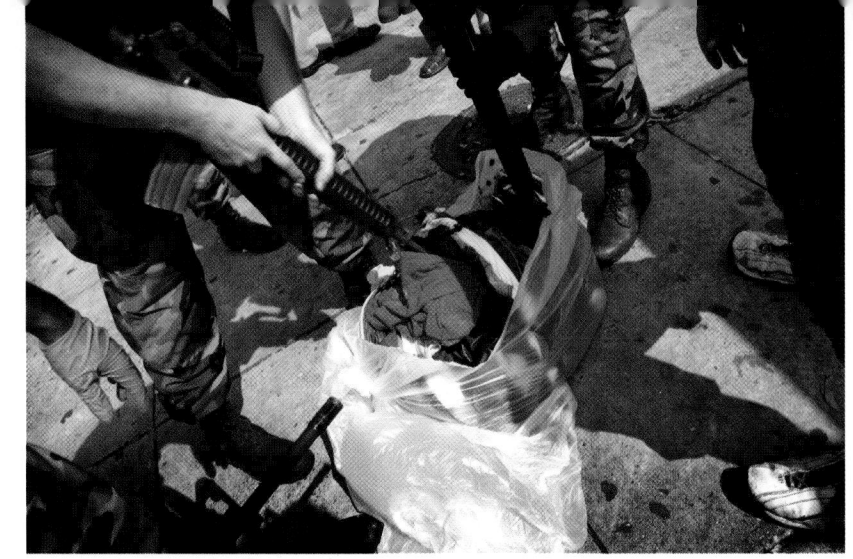

09.05.05 - Kenner, LA - Dawn Rodick fought her emotions after seeing her home for the first time since Katrina struck, while a tarp was placed on the damaged roof of her house. "I've cried already," she said. • DAVID LEESON

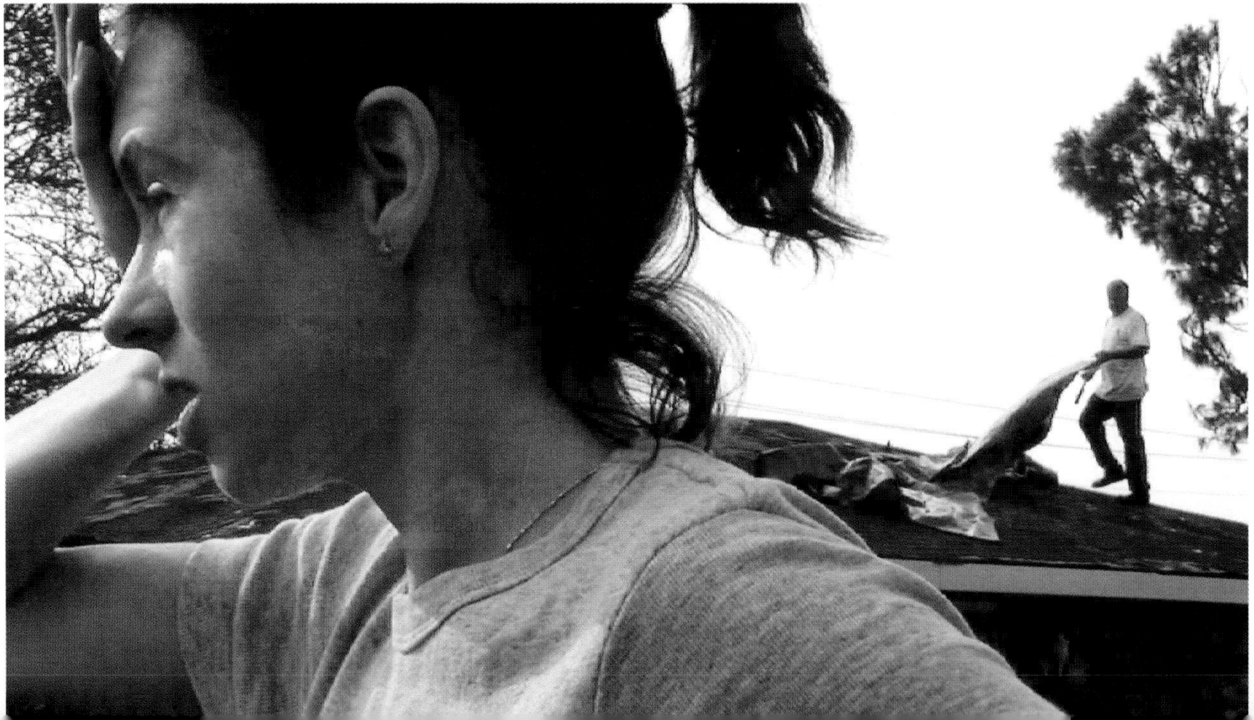

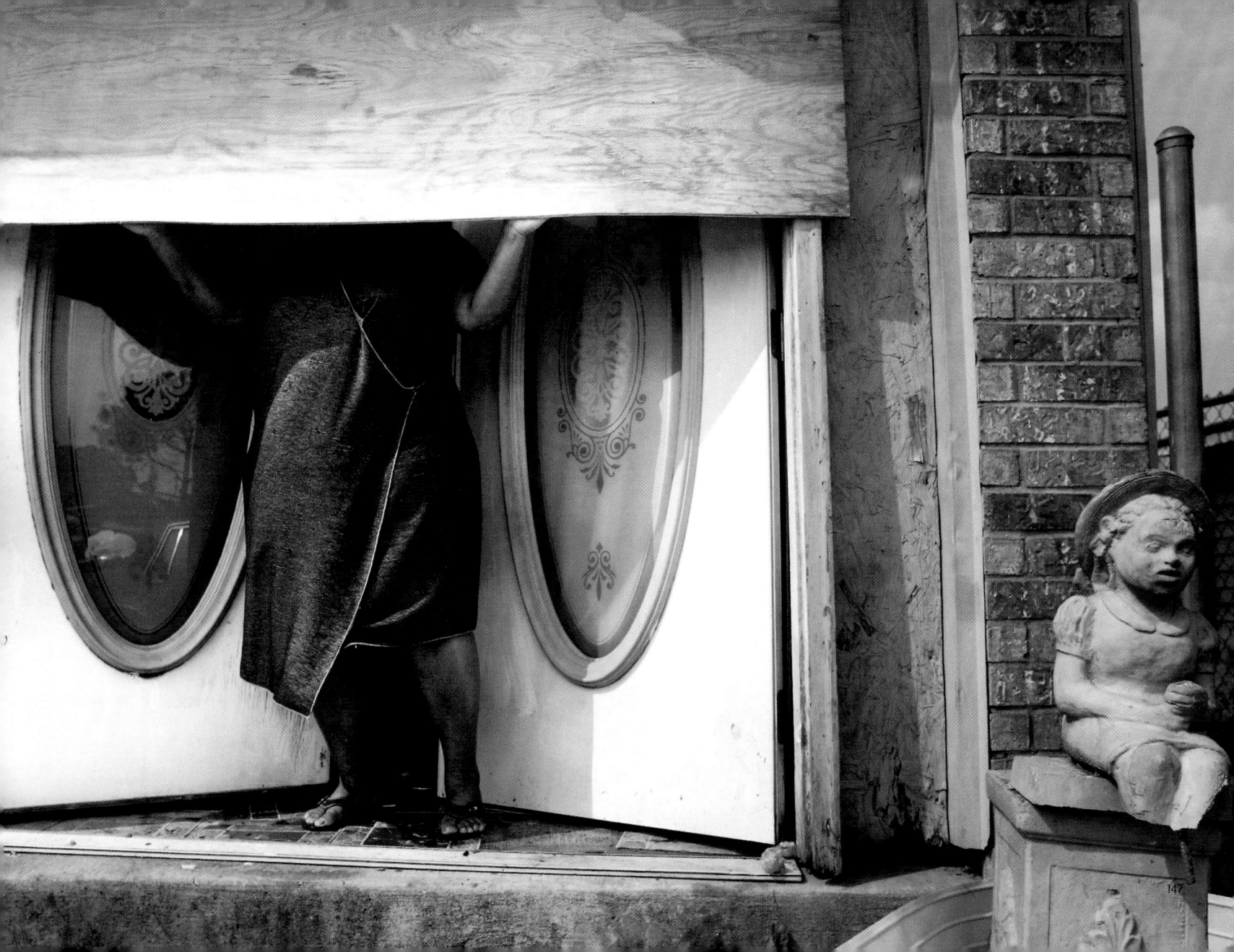

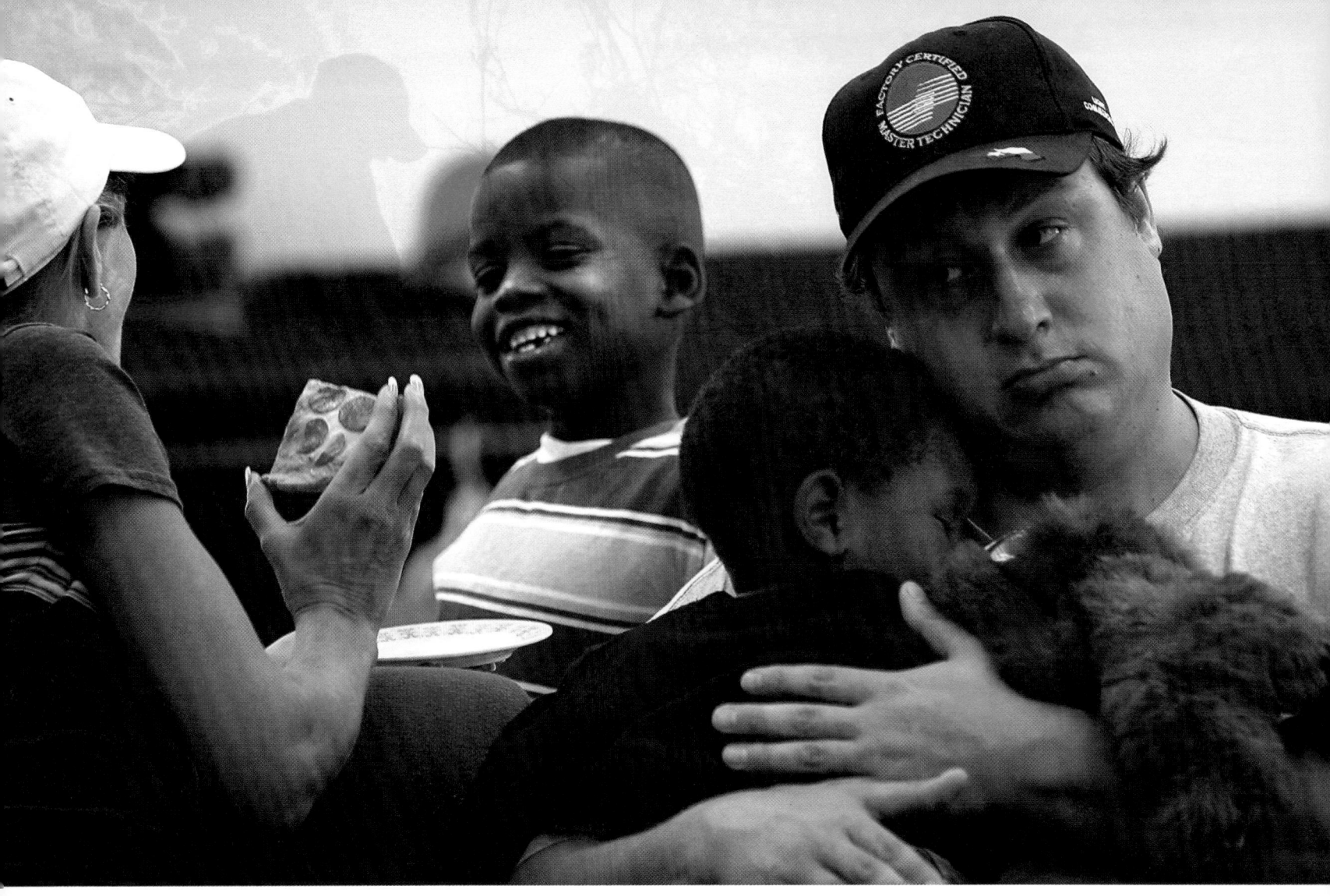

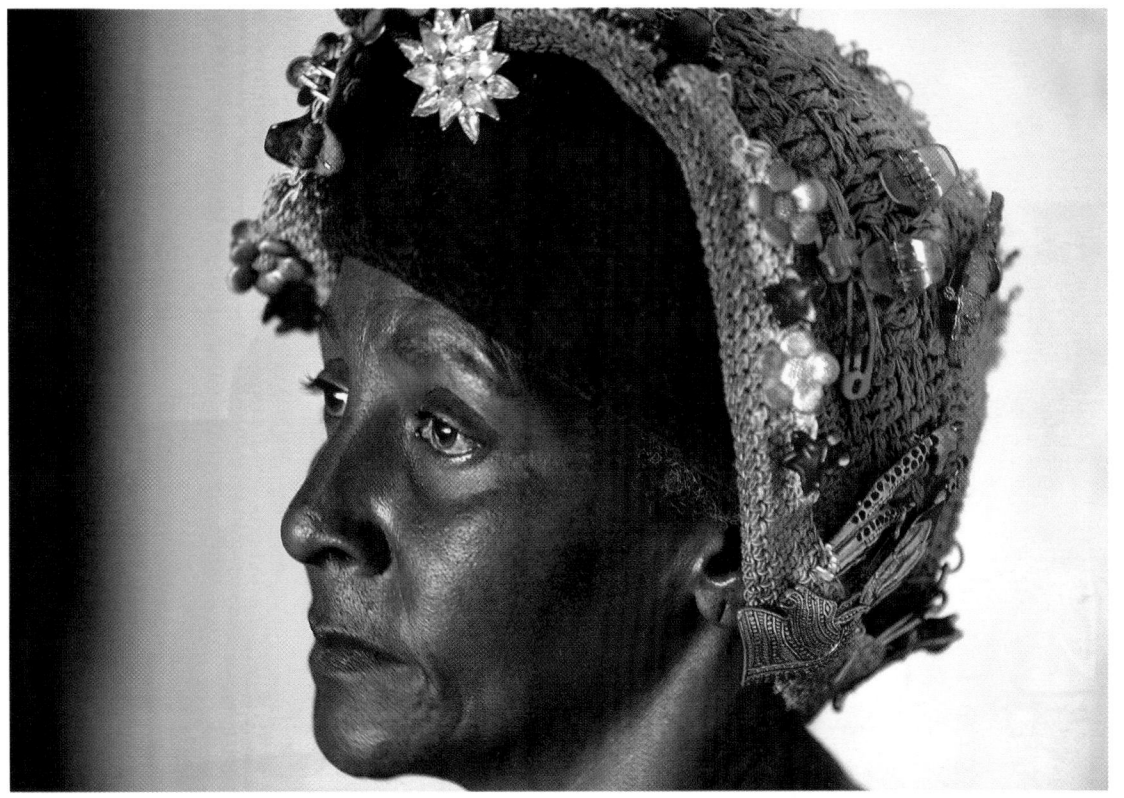

09.05.05 - Dallas, TX - Evacuee Mona Monroe of New Orleans waited outside the Dallas Convention Center for days, hoping her brother would find her. • MELANIE BURFORD

LEFT
09.04.05 - Duncanville, TX - Art Orozco helped soothe Jeremiah Pichon of New Orleans to sleep at First Baptist Church of Duncanville, where health care, food and shelter were offered to Katrina evacuees. • ERIN TREIB

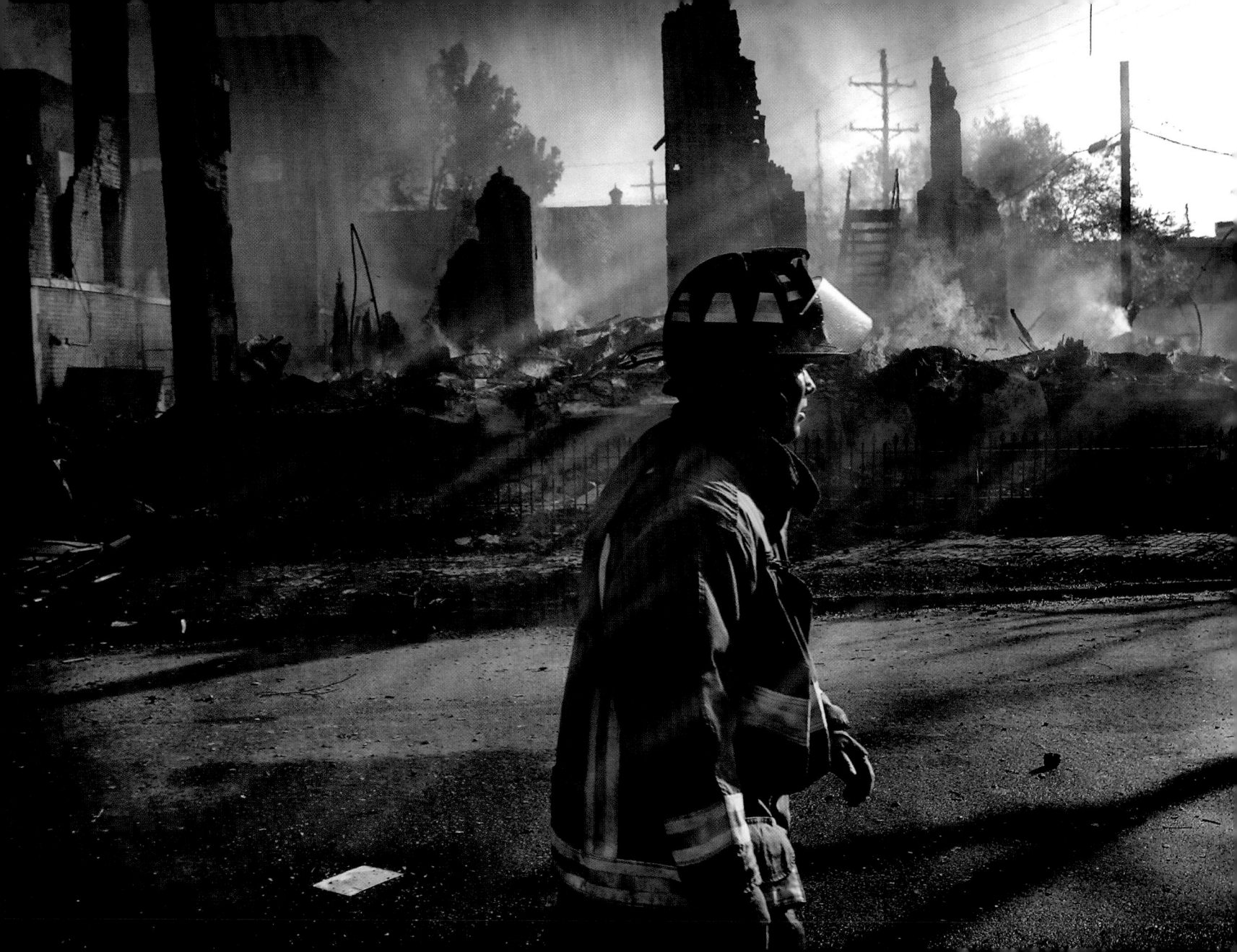

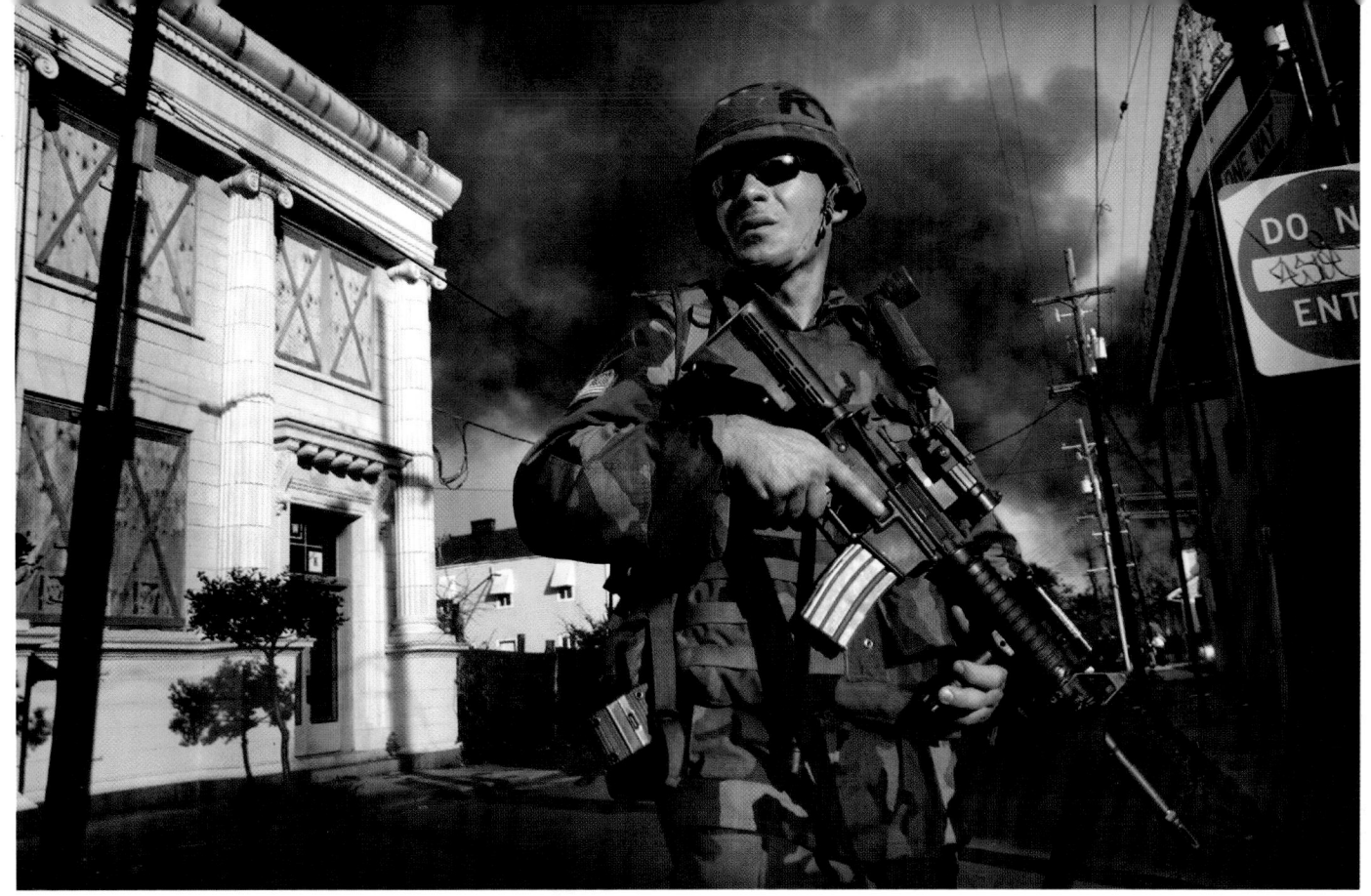

09.06.05 - New Orleans, LA - A National Guardsman blocked off the road leading to a burning 19th-century apartment building near the famed Magazine Street antique district. The city was plagued with fires after the storm. • BARBARA DAVIDSON

<small>LEFT</small>
09.06.05 - New Orleans, LA - A firefighter walked past all that was left of the historic apartment building, taken down by flames. • BARBARA DAVIDSON

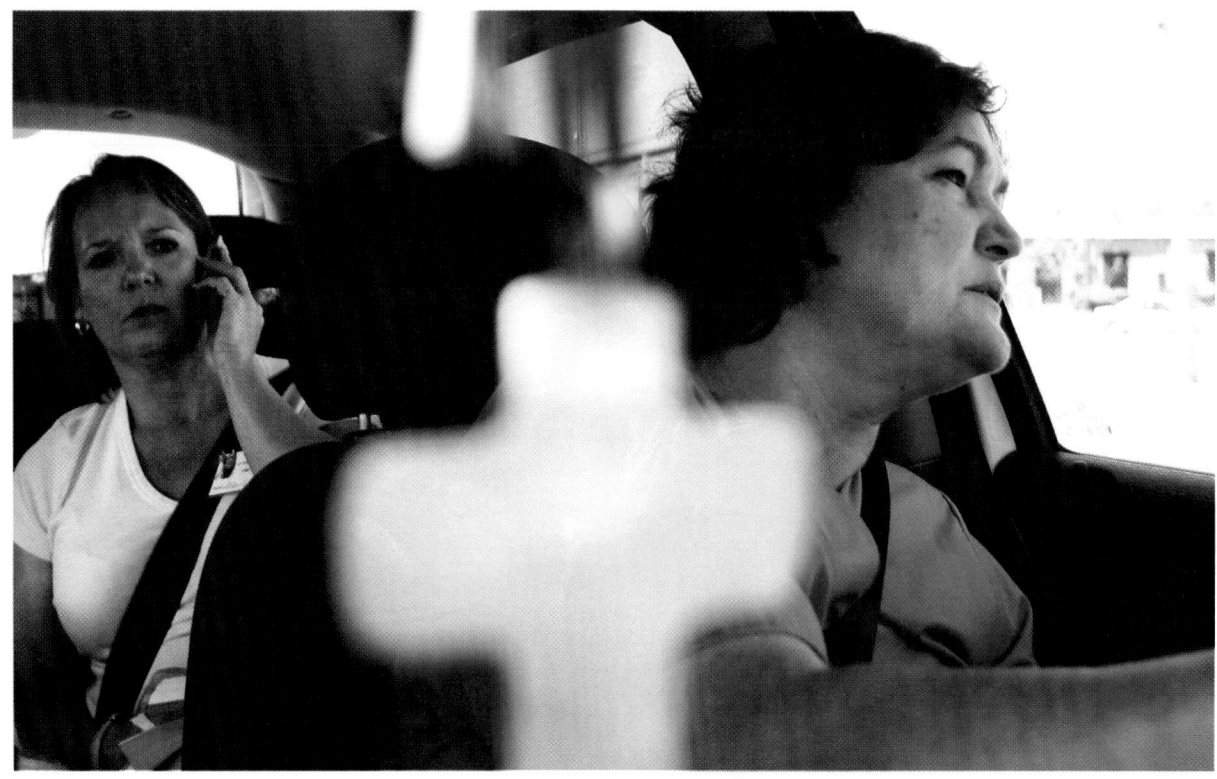

09.07.05 - Biloxi, MS - Nurse Shirley Hulgan drove as colleague Cindy Ward learned by phone that Ms. Hulgan's next scheduled hospice patient had died. In her white PT Cruiser with crosses dangling from the mirror, Ms. Hulgan spent her days driving back roads, dodging traffic jams, looking for patients. When she did find a patient, she performed her routine examinations and provided whatever medicine she had.
• MICHAEL MULVEY

RIGHT
09.06.05 - Biloxi, MS - Joey Thompson (left) was reunited with daughter Josette Clements and son Lil' Joe Thompson at J.R.'s Lounge after losing communication after the hurricane. • MICHAEL MULVEY

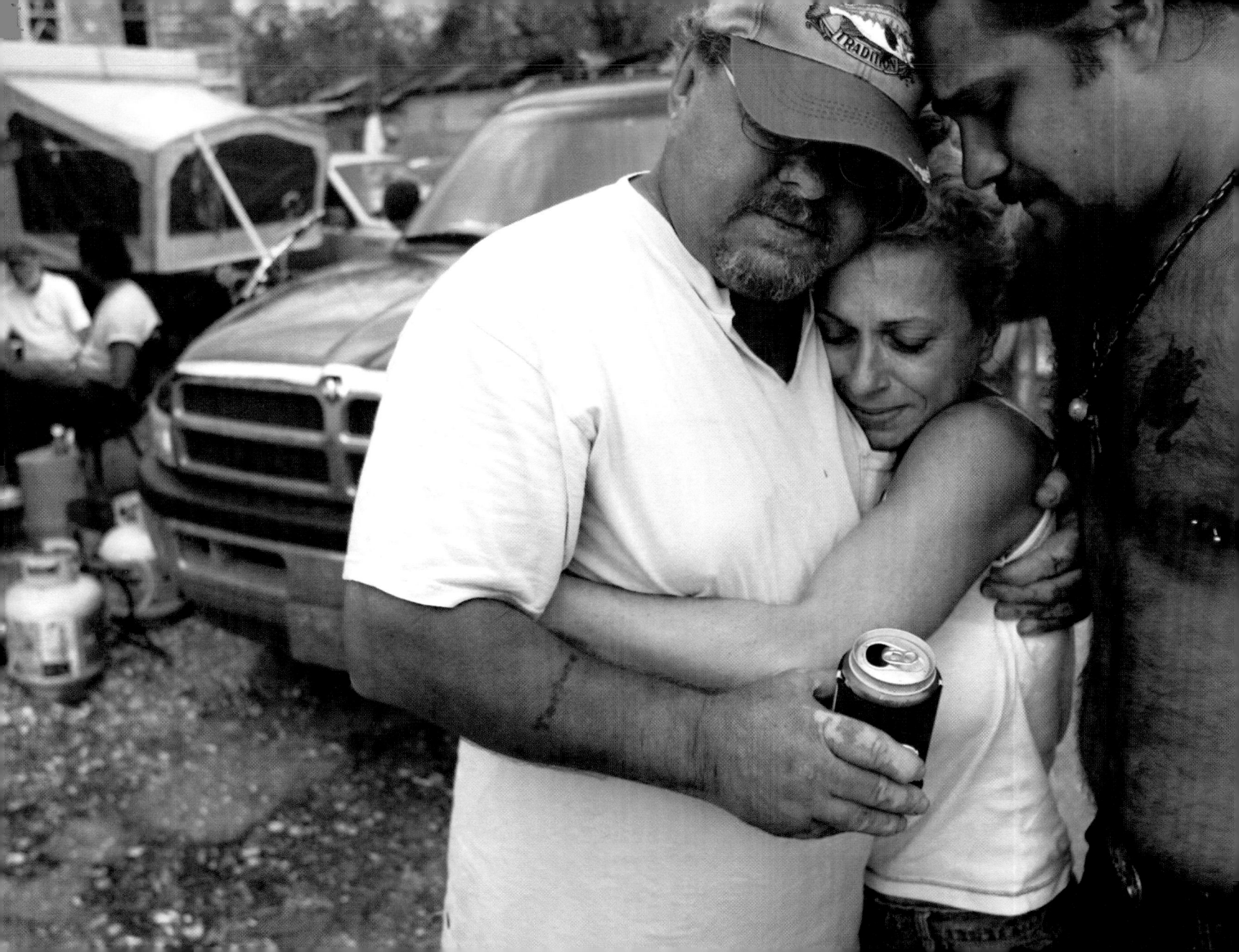

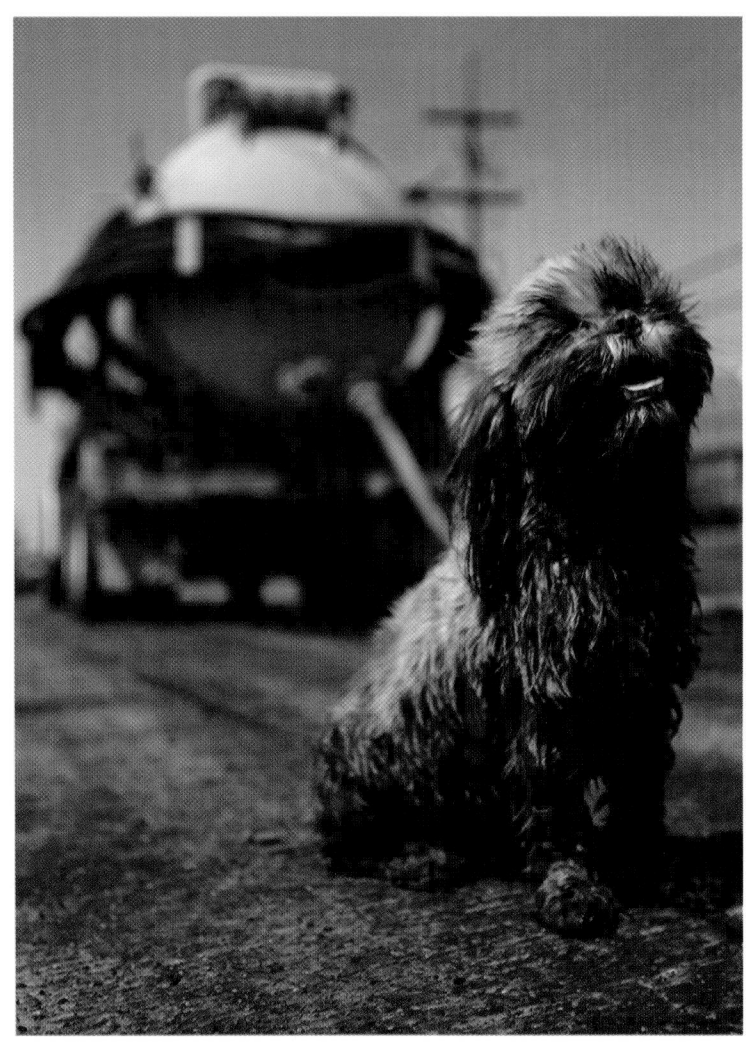

09.06.05 - Chalmette, LA - A small dog covered in oil that was found wandering warmed the hearts of workers cleaning up oil from a ruptured Murphy Oil USA refinery tank.
• TOM FOX

RIGHT
09.06.05 - Chalmette, LA - Cleanup workers Mike Gilfour and Jesse Coffman vacuumed up oil sludge that contaminated part of a neighborhood. A refinery tank owned by Murphy Oil USA ruptured, spilling tens of thousands of gallons of sludge and further fouling Katrina's floodwaters. • TOM FOX

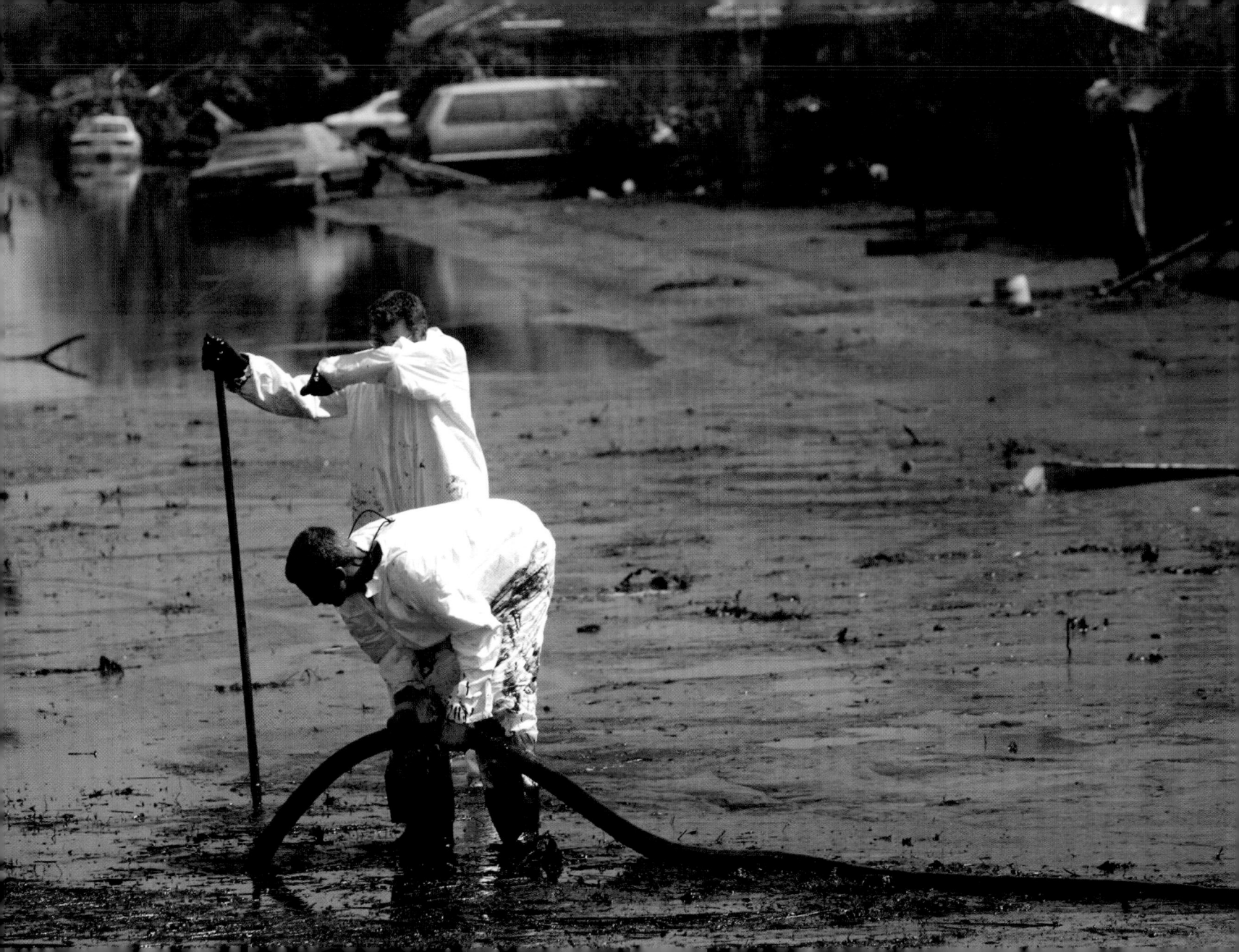

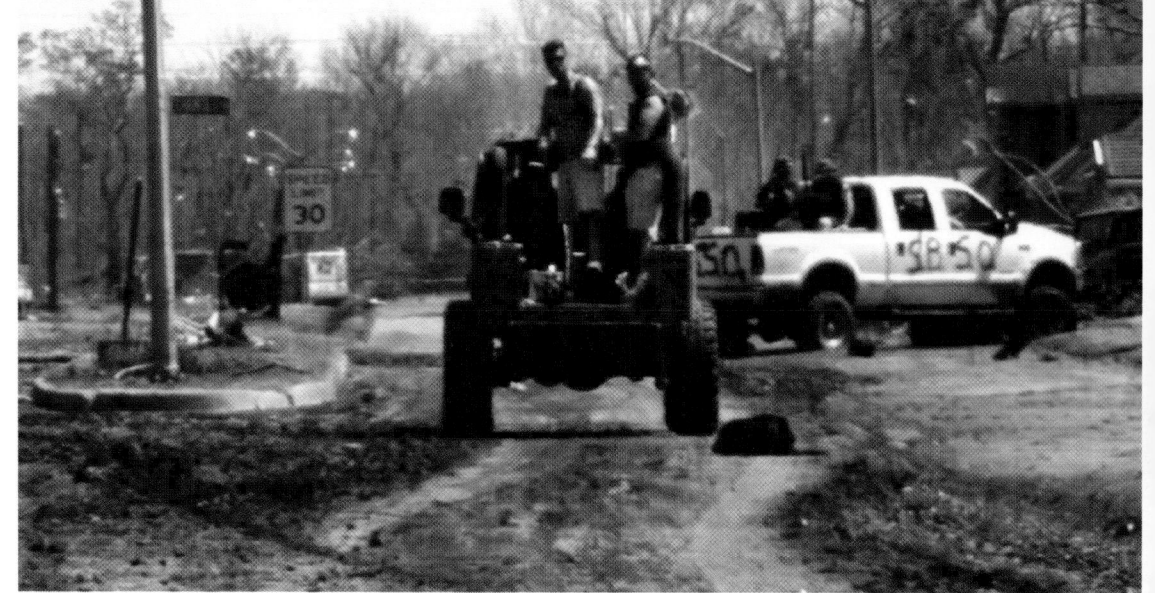

09.07.05 - St. Bernard Parish, LA - A dying black dog lay in the street shortly after the animal was shot by men in a red vehicle, including several members of the St. Bernard Parish Sheriff's Office. Thousands of animals were left homeless without food and care throughout the New Orleans area in the wake of Katrina. The shootings sparked a protest by animal lovers and activists who demanded a stop to the process and disciplinary action against those involved in the shootings. • DAVID LEESON

RIGHT
09.07.05 - St. Bernard Parish, LA - Sgt. Mike Minton (center, in blue shirt) of the St. Bernard Parish Sheriff's Office eyed the video camera, then admitted that he and other officers were shooting dogs. He said the dogs were aggressive and posed a threat to rescue workers and law enforcement in the area. • DAVID LEESON

OPPOSITE PAGE
09.07.05 - St. Bernard Parish, LA - A dog lay in a pool of blood after having been shot by members of the St. Bernard Parish Sheriff's Office. The dog was still alive when this image was made. • DAVID LEESON

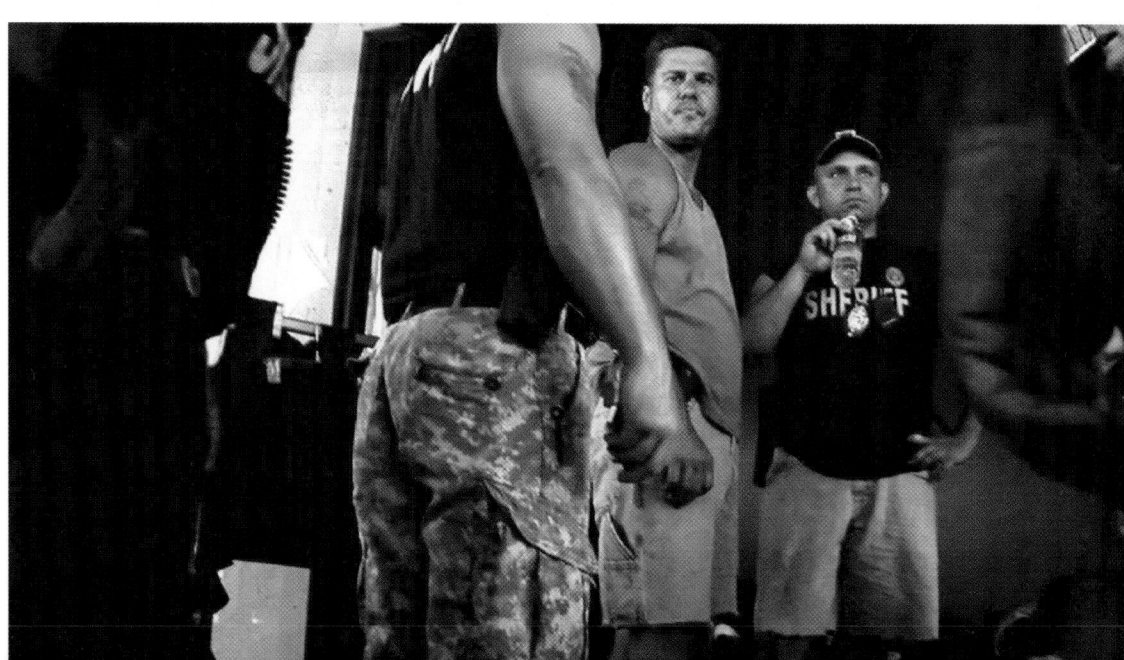

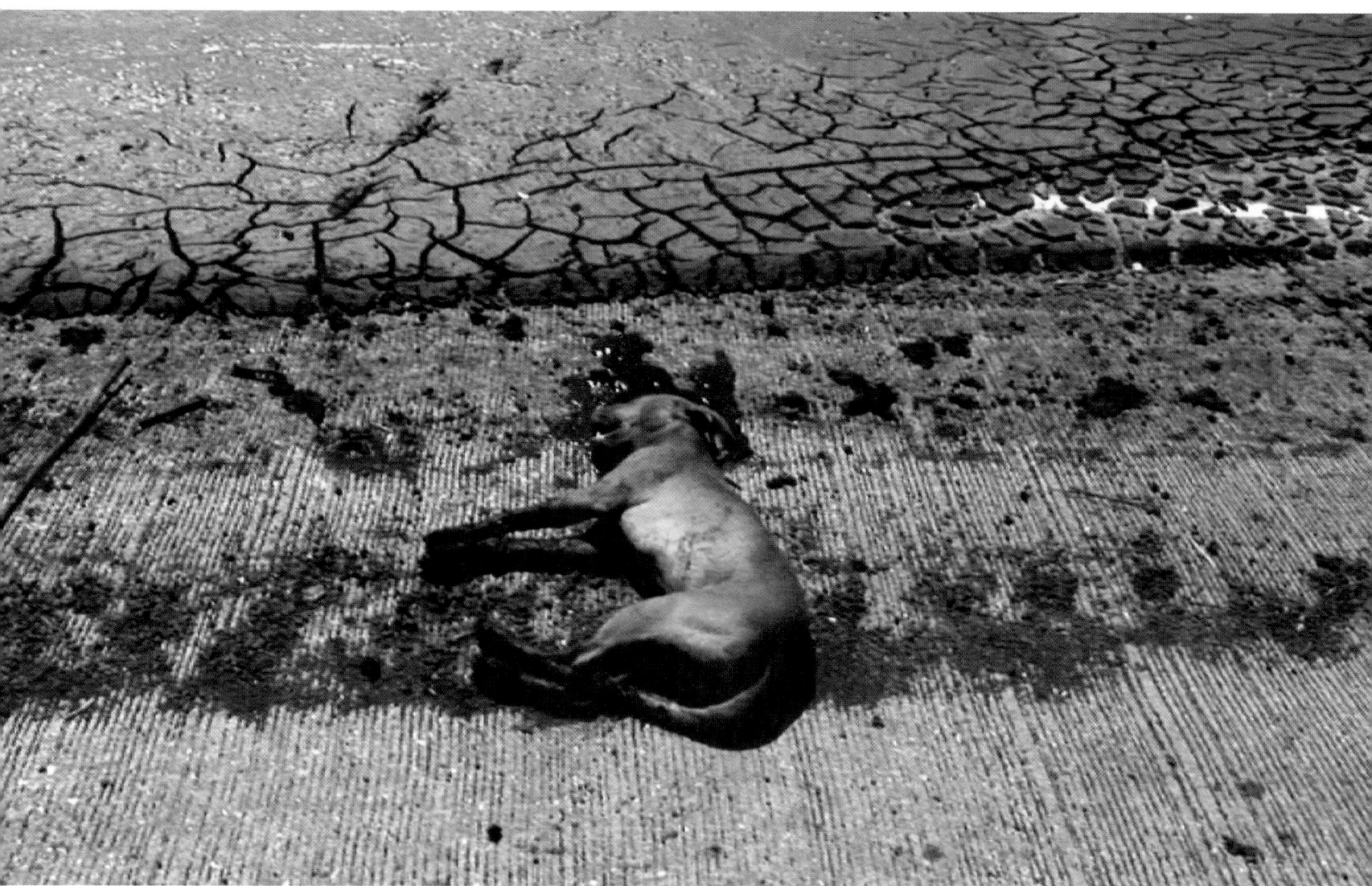

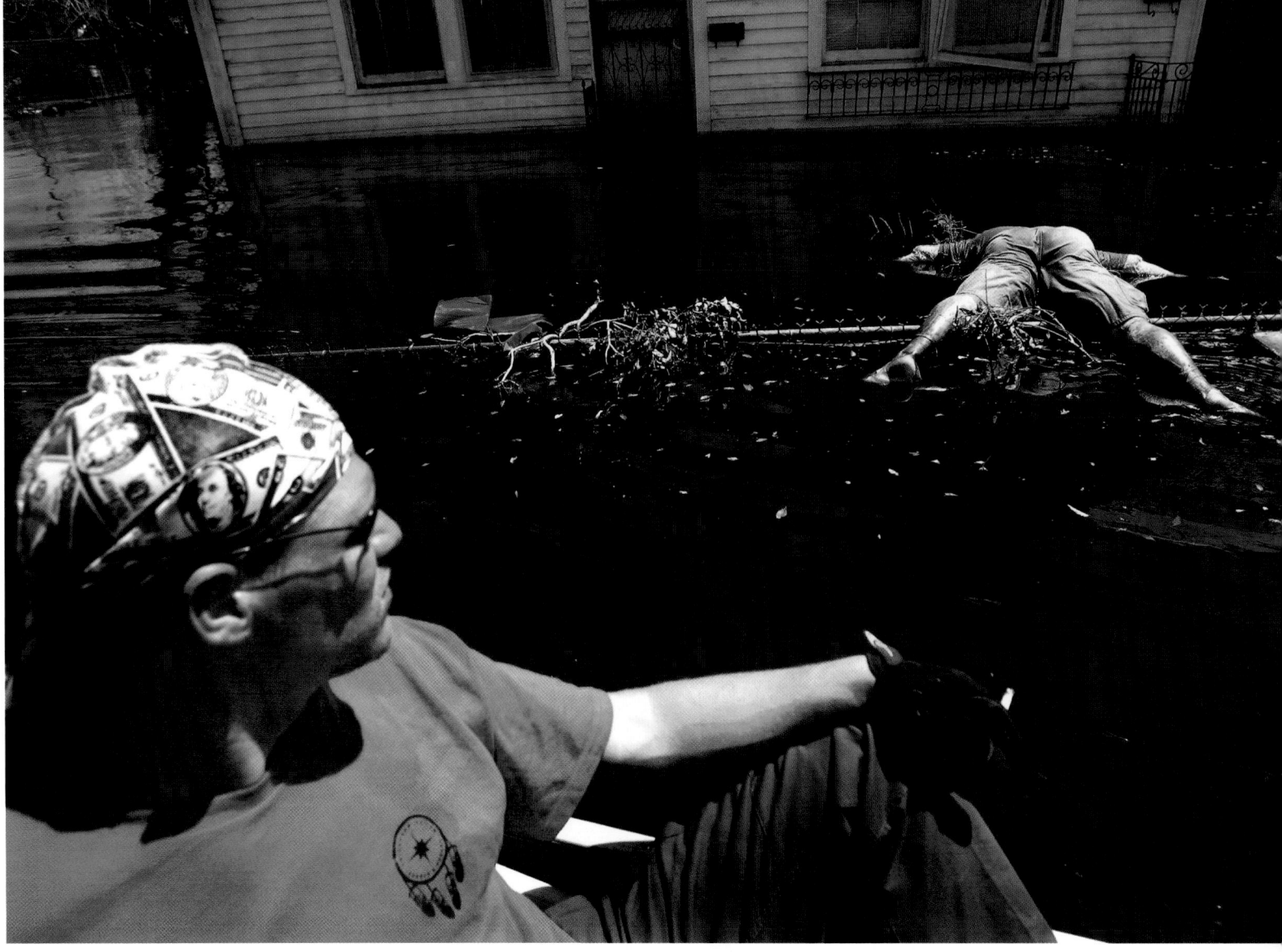

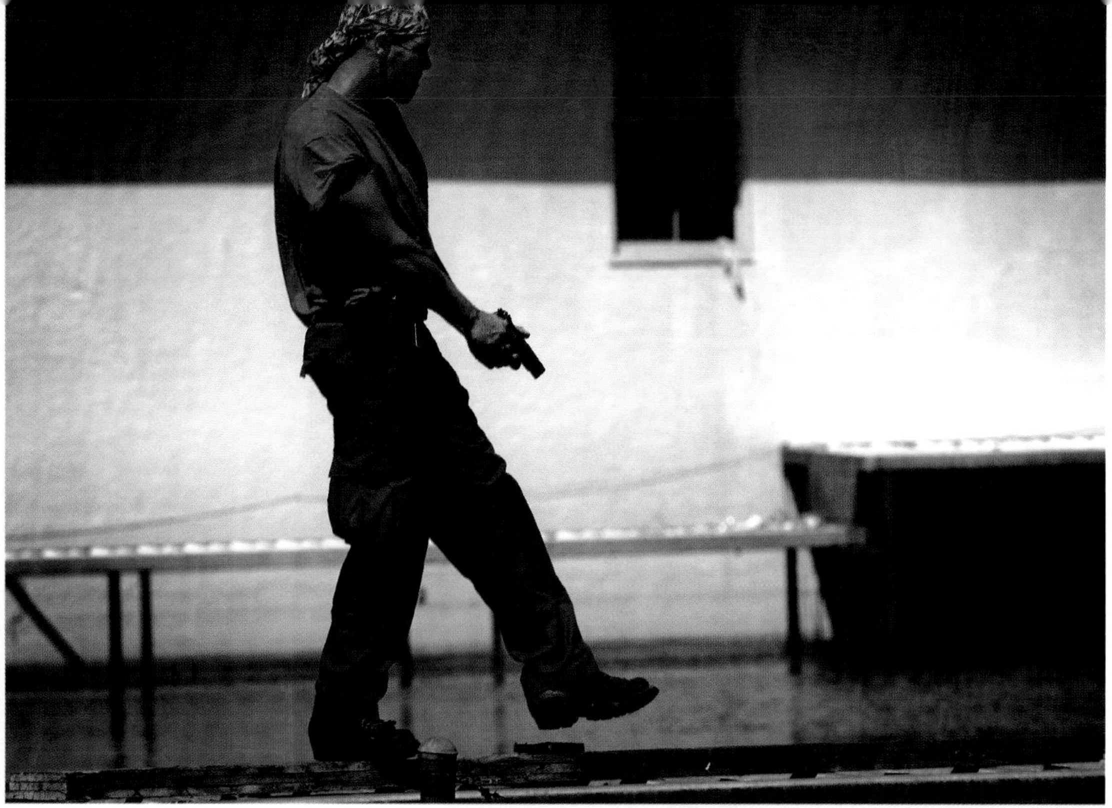

09.07.05 - New Orleans, LA - Oklahoman Casey Kelley of the Chickasaw Nation Search and Rescue team looked for survivors. Although Mayor Ray Nagin authorized the use of force to evacuate residents, most groups were trying to exhaust their other options first. "We'll make that decision when we get there," one official said.
• BARBARA DAVIDSON

LEFT
09.07.05 - New Orleans, LA - Mr. Kelley could only watch as he passed a body floating in a front yard. At that stage, efforts were focused on finding the living. • BARBARA DAVIDSON

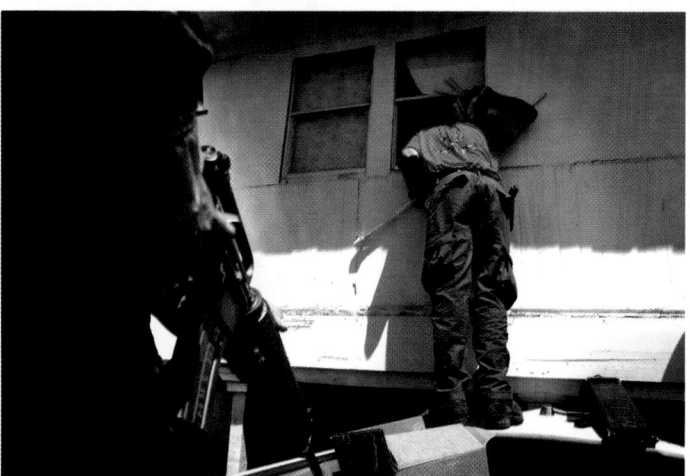

09.07.05 - New Orleans, LA - Mr. Kelley (right) and David Guerrero of the National Guard went house to house looking for holdouts. Officials said it was simply not safe to remain. CDC chief Julie Gerberding said, "If you haven't left the city yet, you must do so." She warned that no one should even touch the water. • BARBARA DAVIDSON

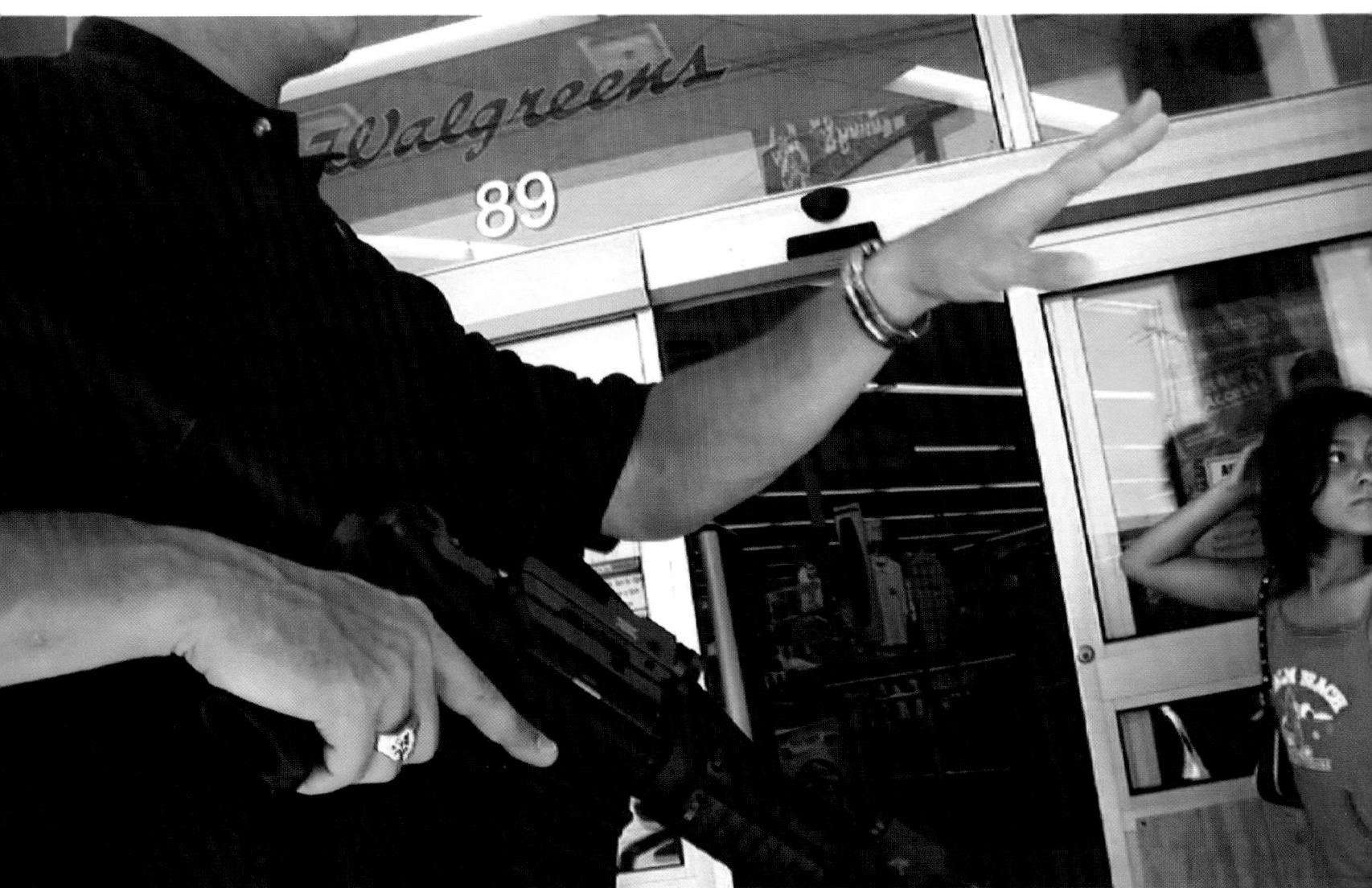

09.08.05 - Gretna, LA - A heavily armed police officer monitored a peaceful crowd outside a Walgreens store, one of the first to reopen within a week of Katrina. Residents formed lines to purchase food, medicine and cigarettes. Shoppers were admitted entrance in small groups to keep the situation inside manageable • DAVID LEESON

09.06.05 - New Orleans, LA - Two men who were driving a vehicle with U.S. Air Force license plates used bolt cutters to loot Bourbon Street signs. The New Orleans Police Department launched an investigation into whether its officers participated in the giant looting spree that overtook the city after Hurricane Katrina. "Out of 1,750 officers, we're looking into the possibility that maybe 12 officers were involved in misconduct," police spokesman Marlon Defillo said. • IRWIN THOMPSON

09.08.05 - Empire, LA - Cowboys on horseback and airboats rounded up stray cattle in rural areas south of New Orleans on State Highway 23 in Plaquemines Parish. Earl Armstrong, a local rancher, lost 1,500 head of cattle grazing on land near the mouth of the Mississippi during Hurricane Katrina. • ERICH SCHLEGEL

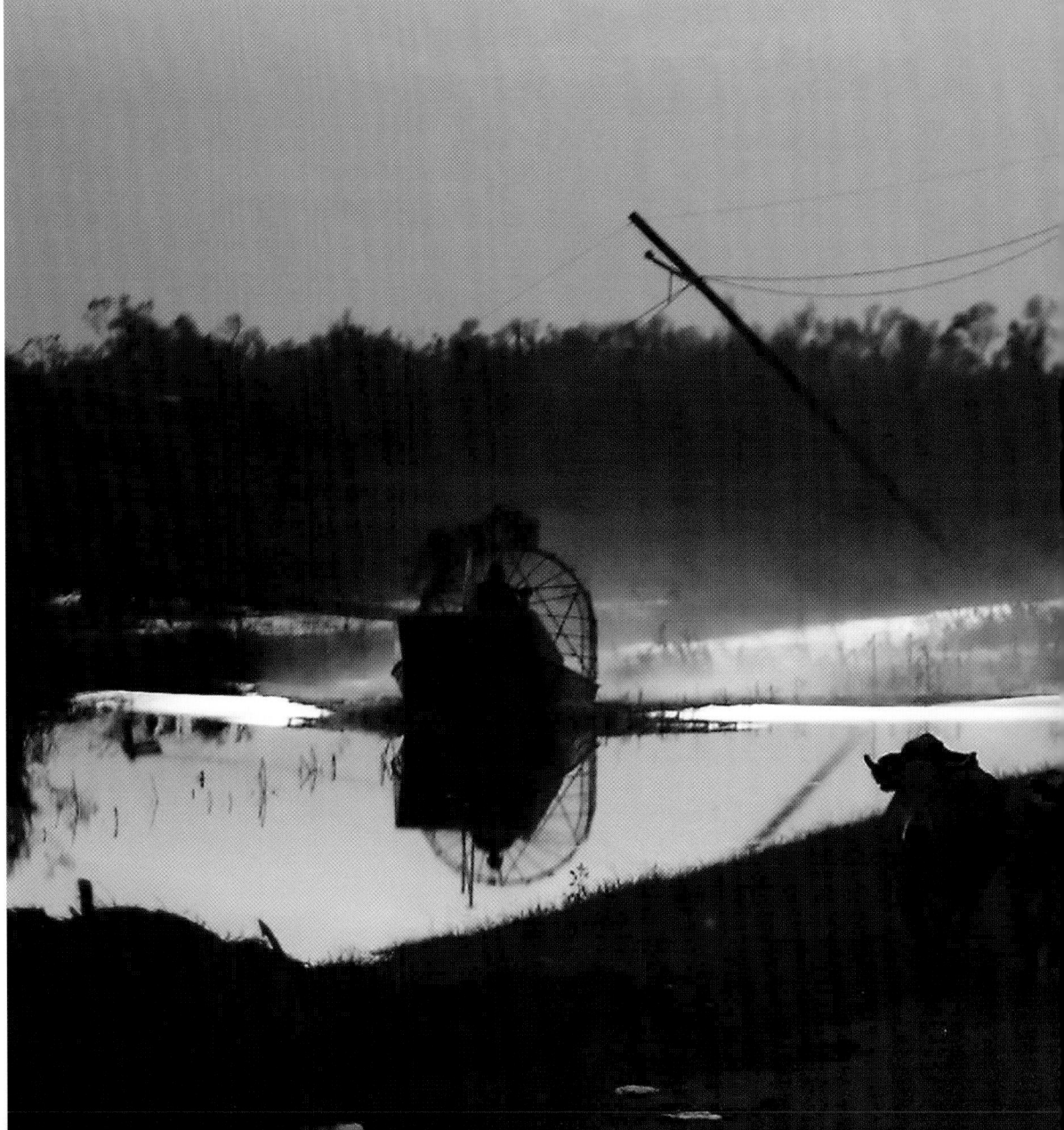

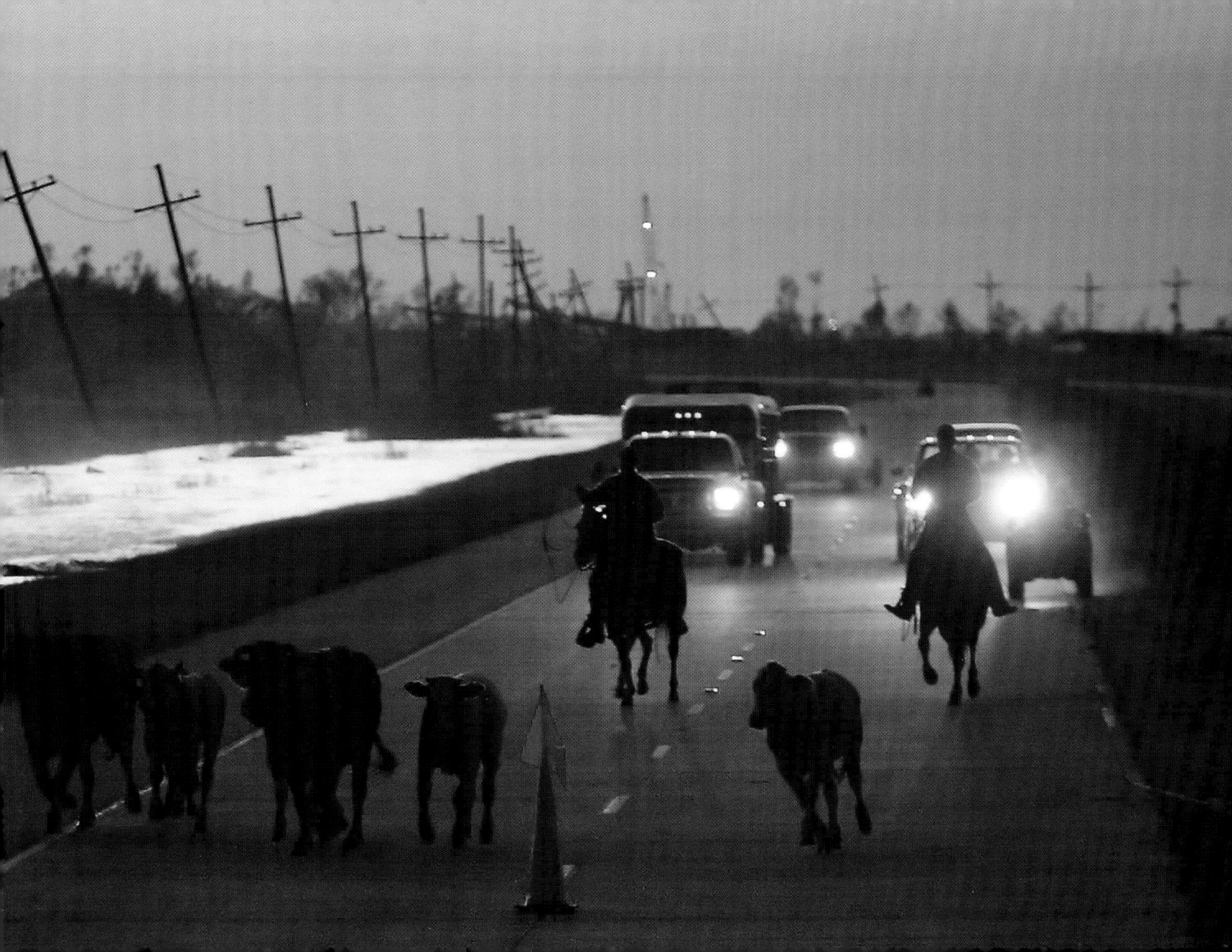

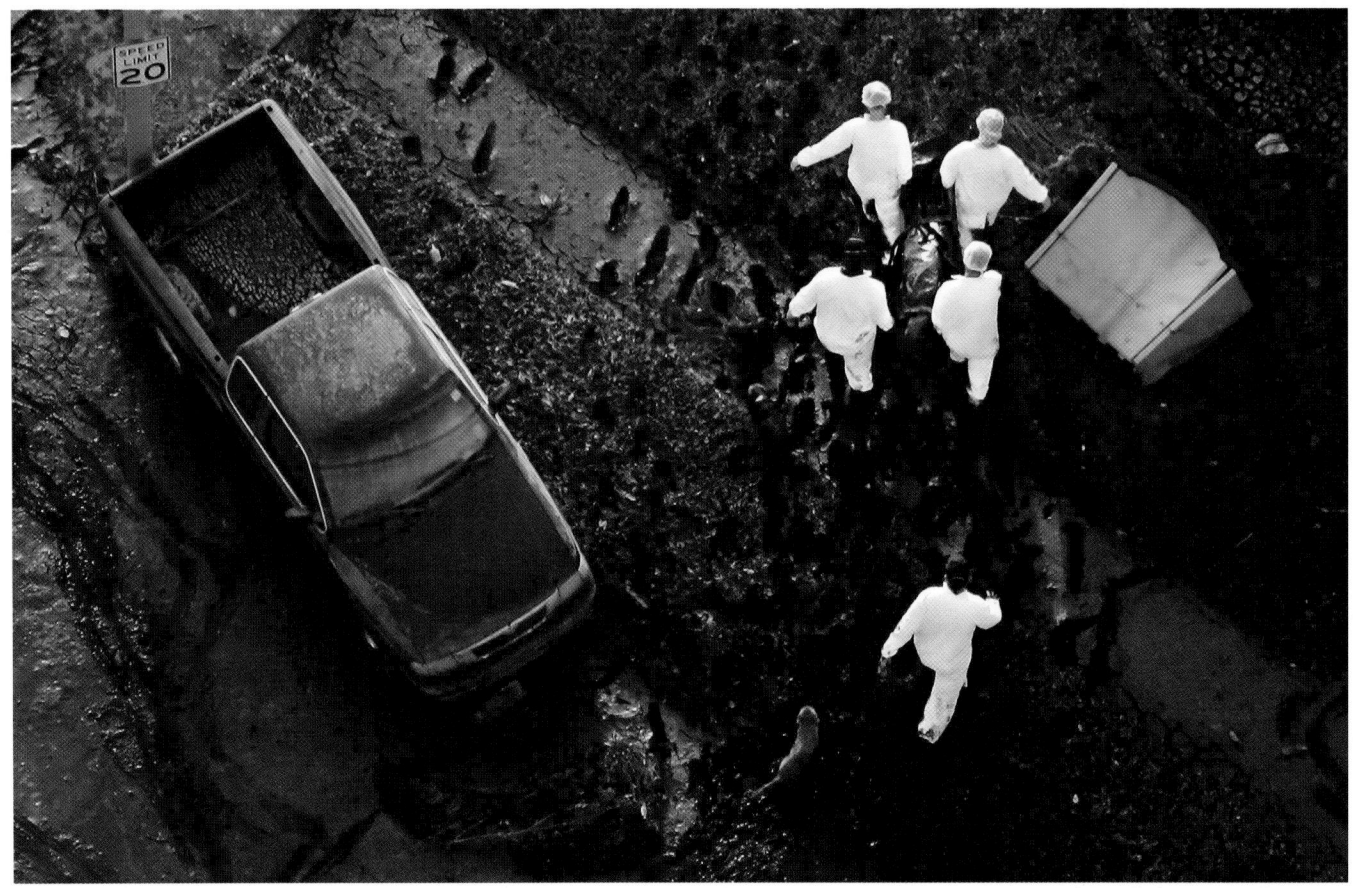

09.08.05 - St. Bernard Parish, LA - Recovery workers wearing protective suits trudged through the mud from receding floodwaters as they carried a body from a house. • SMILEY N. POOL

RIGHT
09.08.05 - New Orleans, LA - Toni Miller, 58, cried as state Trooper Cameron Douglas coaxed her to evacuate. Days before, she had been adamant about staying in her home, which had escaped flooding. "I'm not going anywhere unless they drag me out at gunpoint," she said. When officials came by to tell her she had no choice, she tore the U.S. flag from her porch and called the order un-American. Then she had a change of heart and agreed to evacuate. "There's nothing for me anymore; I understand that now," she said. She put the flag back up. • BARBARA DAVIDSON

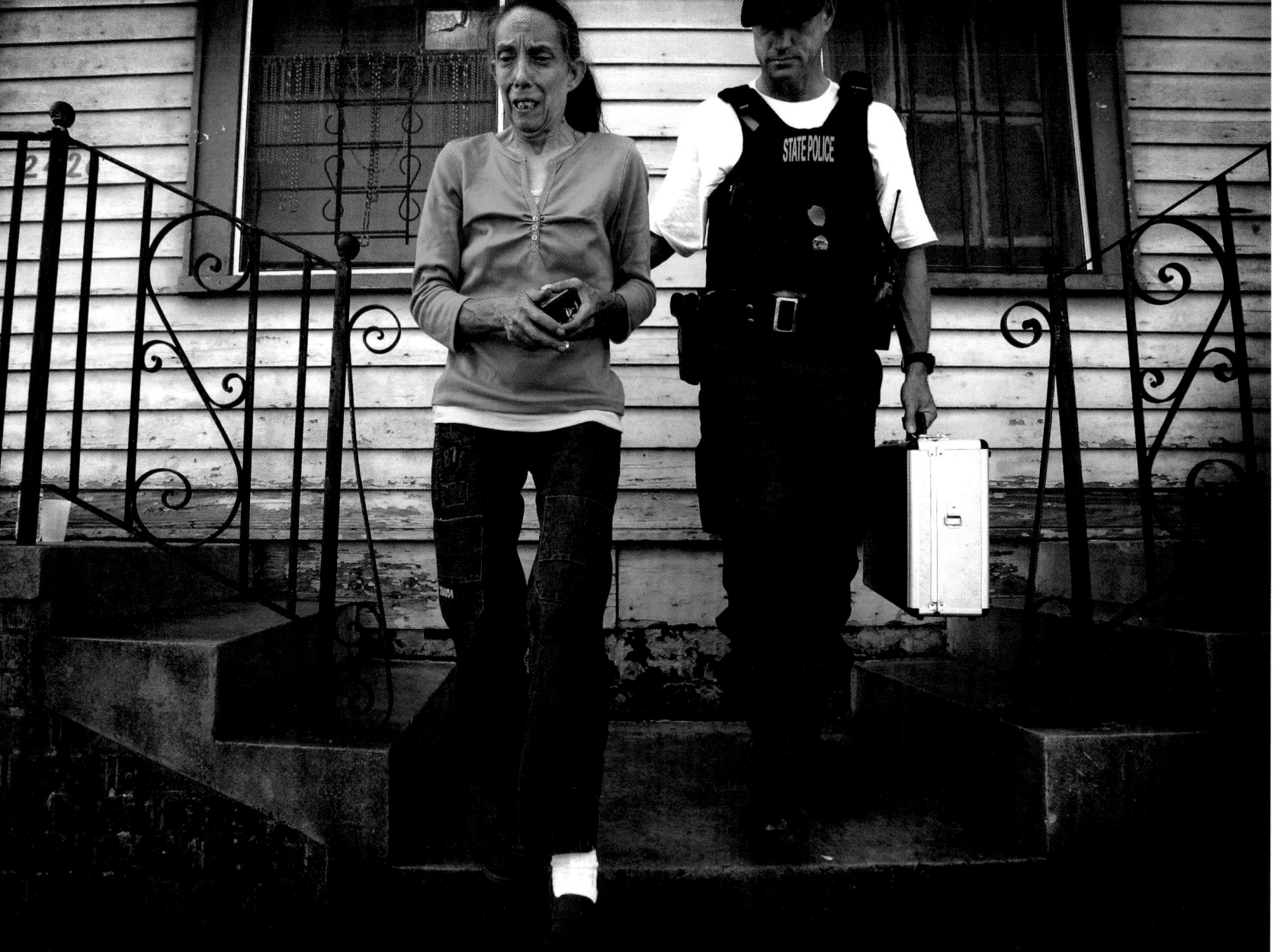

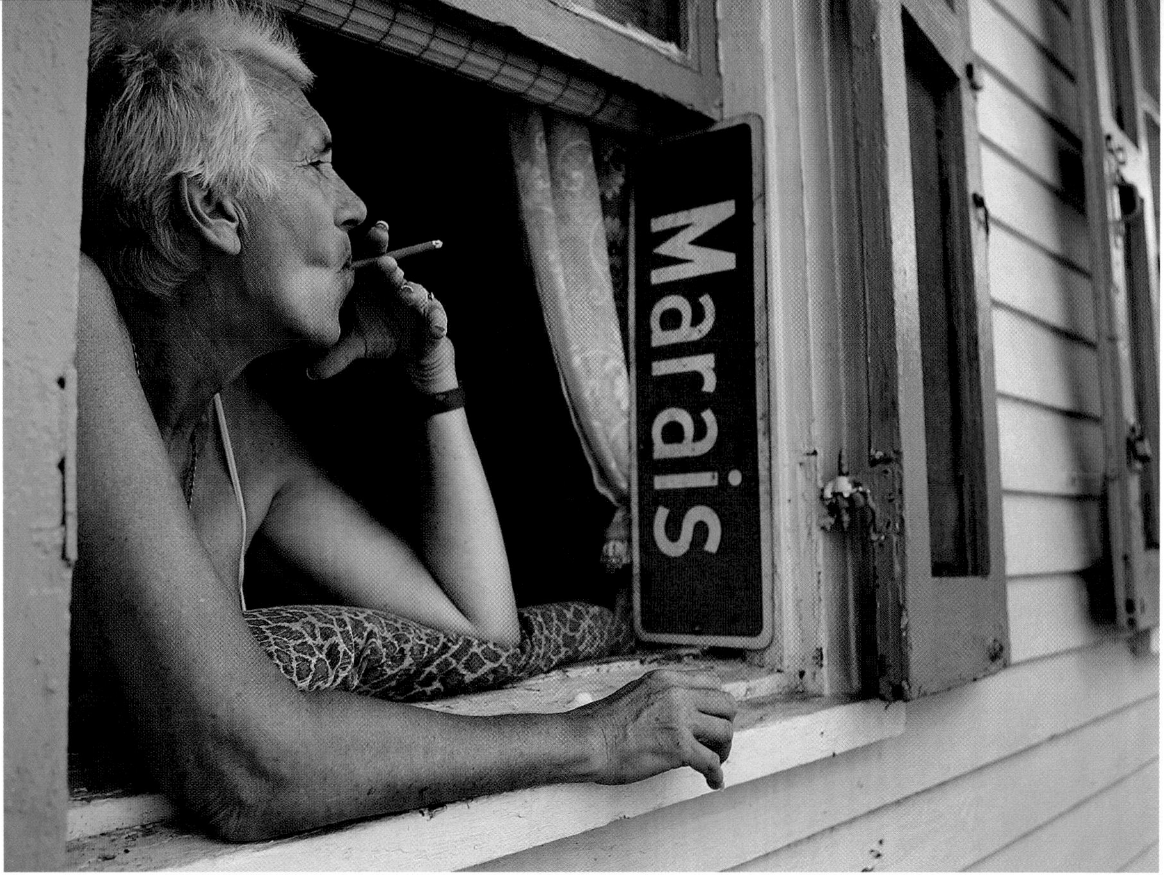

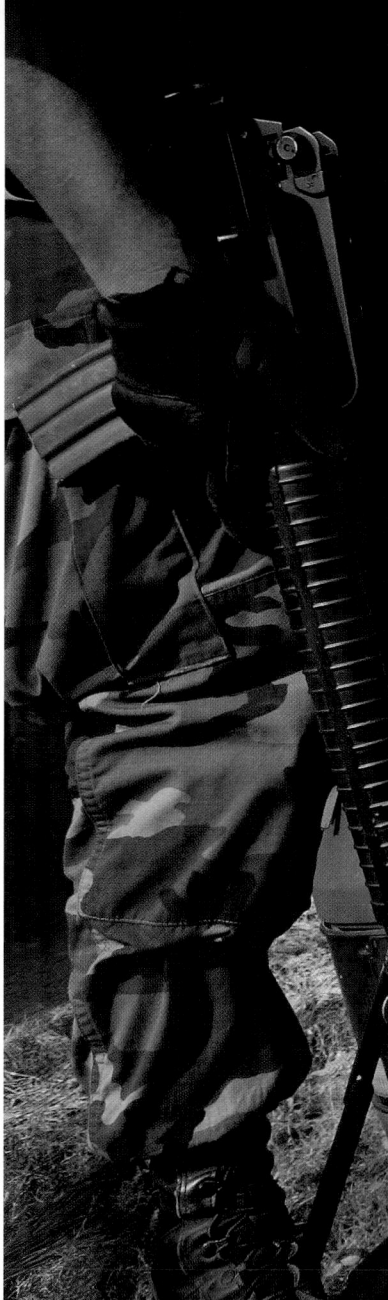

09.09.05 - New Orleans, LA - Ginger Lucci, 55, took in the activity on her street in the Marigny Triangle neighborhood where she has lived for 35 years. She said no hurricane would drive her away. In the music district near the French Quarter, a group of neighbors banded together to help one another after the storm. With each surreal day in the Marigny Triangle, they protected the vulnerable from looters and shared supplies. The neighborhood came to be known for Radio Marigny, a homespun station started by local performer Kenny Claiborne, who broadcast Louisiana music and Bruce Springsteen daily via loudspeaker. • CHERYL DIAZ MEYER

Right
09.08.05 - New Orleans, LA - Marietta Duming rode out Hurricane Katrina in her home and then waited 12 days for help. It finally came down her street in the form of a Louisiana National Guard engineering unit when a soldier heard her cry for help. She climbed into one of the trucks to be taken for medical treatment. • BARBARA DAVIDSON

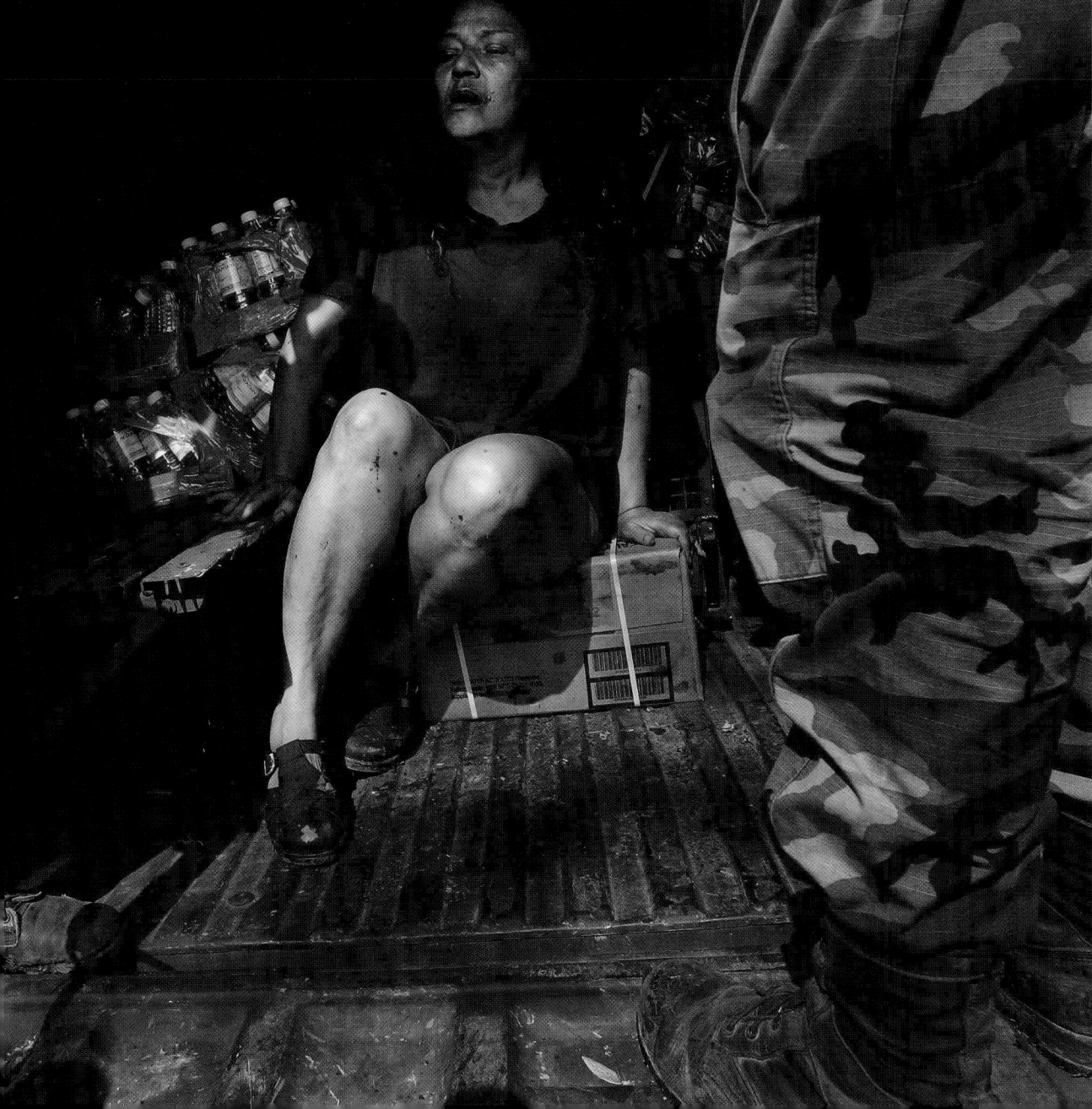

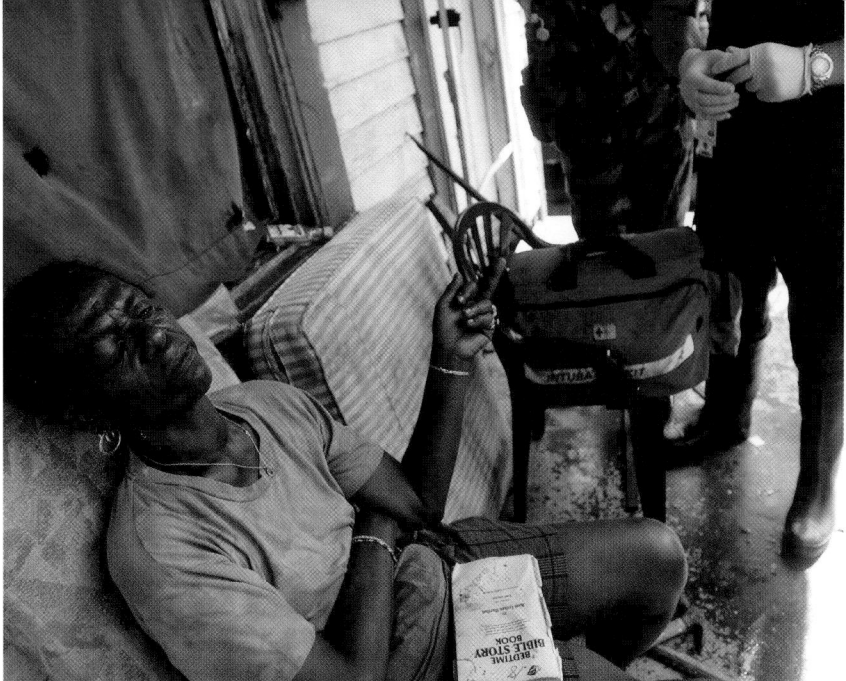

09.08.05 - New Orleans, LA - Cheryl Cook, who has a heart condition, was defiant and determined to stay on Desire Street, where she lived nearly her entire life. Repeated attempts to get her to evacuate initially failed but finally prevailed. • MONA REEDER

RIGHT
09.08.05 - New Orleans, LA - Cheryl Cook spent long, hot days on Desire Street by reading a book of Bible stories - one chapter a day since Katrina hit • MONA REEDER

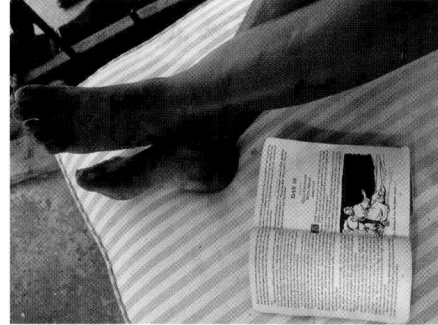

OPPOSITE PAGE
Melvin Johnson, whose Desire Street home was flooded, paddled ahead to check on a friend who refused to leave despite many dangers, including water filled with chemicals, fuels, bodies and human waste. Mr. Johnson and girlfriend Frances Malone moved to drier land, but he returned for belongings and to check on friends in his Ninth Ward neighborhood. • MONA REEDER

A STREET CALLED DESIRE

After Hurricane Katrina's hit on New Orleans a small group of re-dents with homes on a street called Desire in the city's infamous Lo Ninth Ward loosely banded together and refused to evacuate. They sw to stay until forced out - despite knee-deep water filled with chemic fuels, corpses and fecal matter that grew blacker with each passing da

Cheryl Cook sent her children out of harm's way before the hurric hit but wouldn't leave her precious rottweiler, Trouble; her two parake Love and Joy; and her 10 fish.

Melvin Johnson and Frances Malone have lived together for eight ye and couldn't bear to part with their two dogs, Sam, a terrier mix, and B a Shar-Pei. Mr. Johnson, a Vietnam veteran, said he's seen a lot of hearta in his life, and while this was bad, he didn't plan on going anywhere w out the dogs. "They're part of the family," he said, "and you don't aban your family."

But one evening, Mr. Johnson and Ms. Malone met with a Louisi SPCA official and worked out a deal to be evacuated with their dogs.

Mr. Johnson decided to make one last trip through the toxic waters ing Desire to tell Ms. Cook and others about the SPCA deal and to p suade them to leave that morning.

Ninety minutes later he was pulling an orange canoe with a few ite he grabbed quickly from his home on Desire, along with a puppy he fo on a porch across the street. Ms. Cook, Trouble and a few other holdc followed in a green, flat-bottom boat, paddling with rotted, splintered by-4s.

"I used my 'soft' voice," he said, "Then I told them their friend across street [Lionel] was found dead in the hallway."

Ms. Cook cried and hugged Trouble as they were both hoisted into Oregon Army National Guard amphibious vehicle. Mr. Johnson and Malone were in good spirit, with their belongings and beloved Sam Buff, and Ms. Cook calmed down quickly.

As the vehicle carried them away to shelter, Ms. Cook waved good to the remaining holdouts and Desire Street.

•MONA REEDER

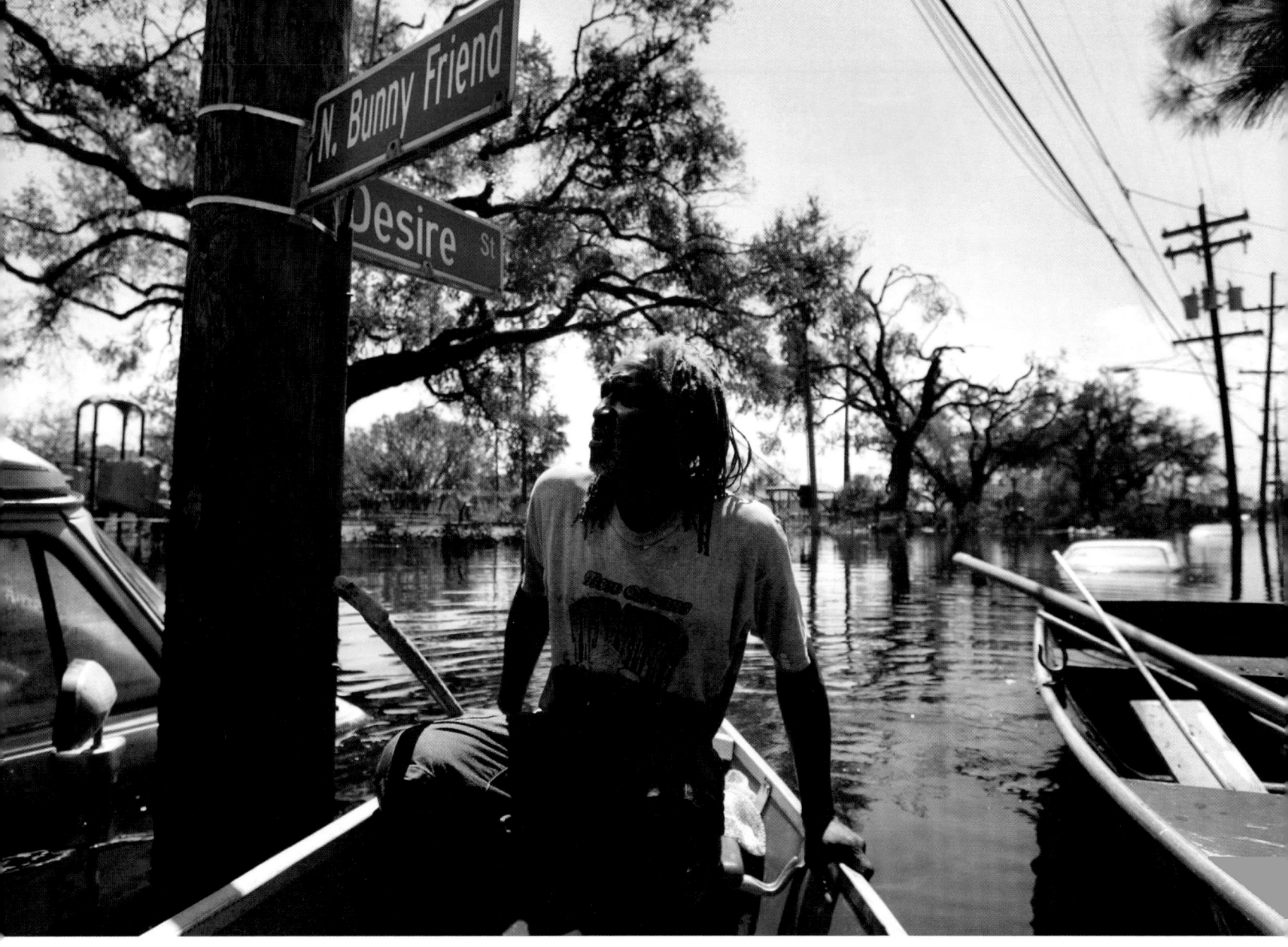

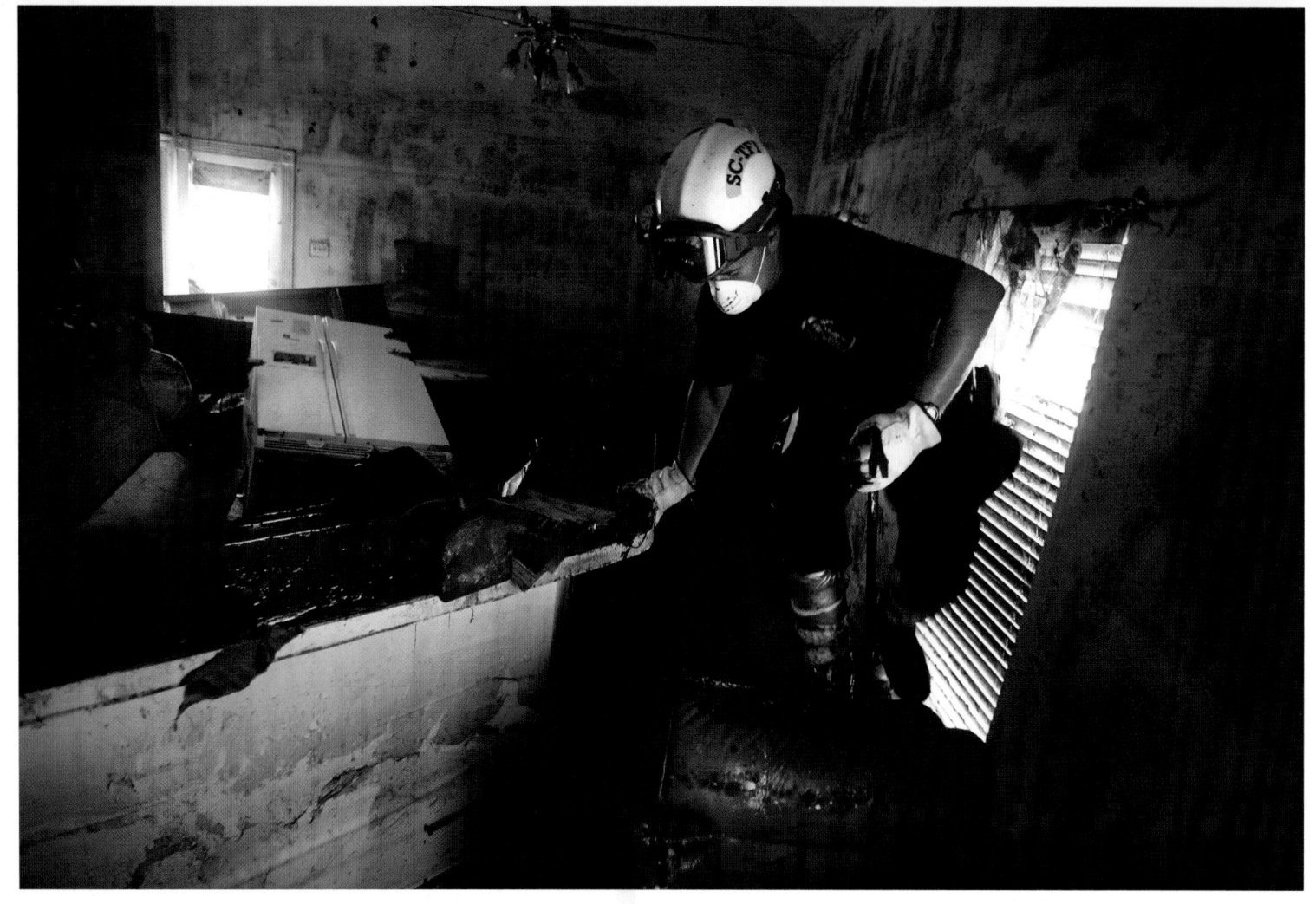

09.09.05 - Meraux, LA - South Carolina Emergency Response Task Force One member Ray Citrone crawled over furniture strewn about in the kitchen of a two-story home in St. Bernard Parish. The water line in the house was up past the second floor. • TOM FOX

RIGHT
09.12.05 - New Orleans, LA - The temporary resting place of 83-year-old Alcede Jackson - a front porch bench in the Uptown section of New Orleans - was marked by a poster board tombstone and a bouquet of flowers. Mr. Jackson's body was recovered nearly two weeks after his death. • BARBARA DAVIDSON

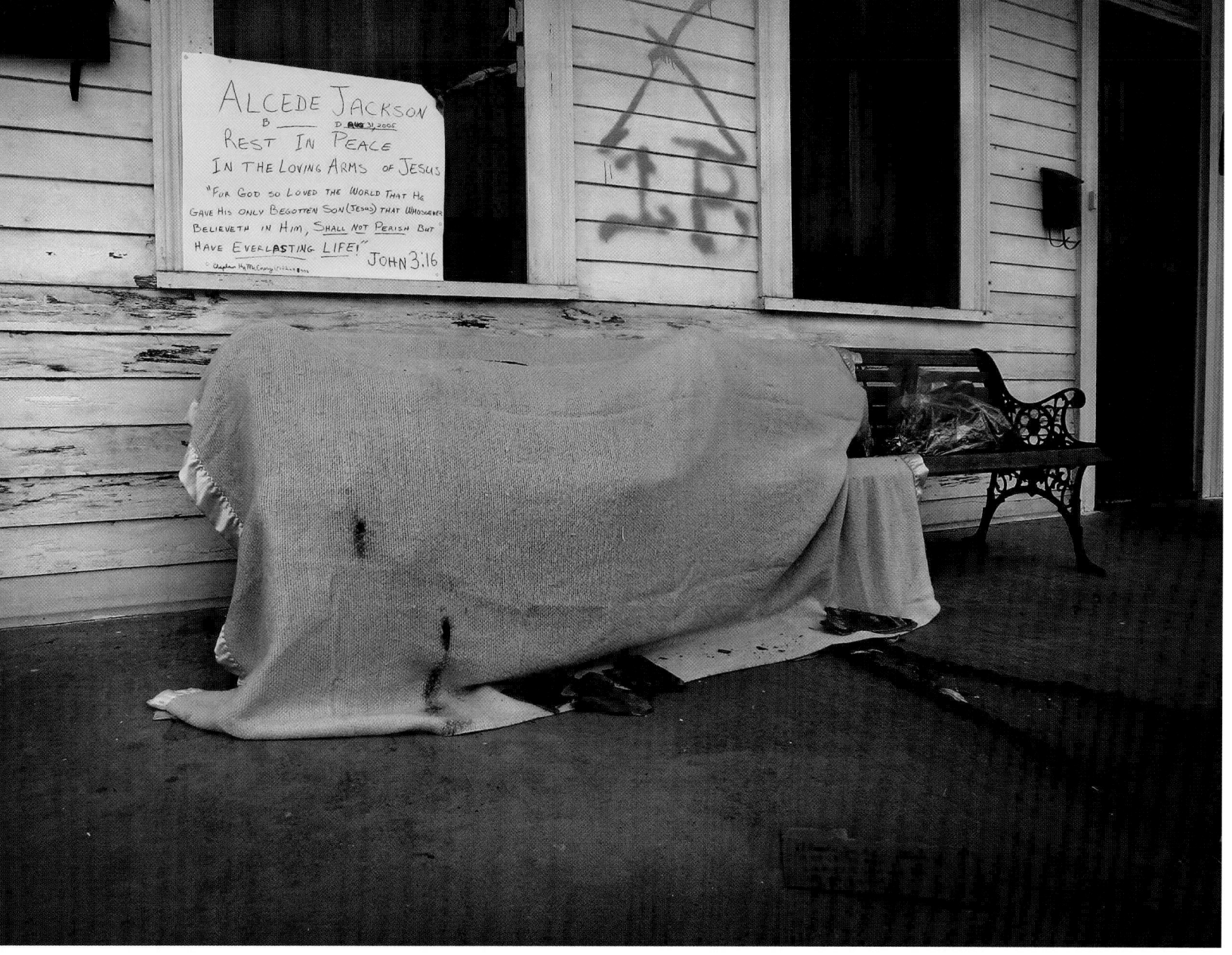

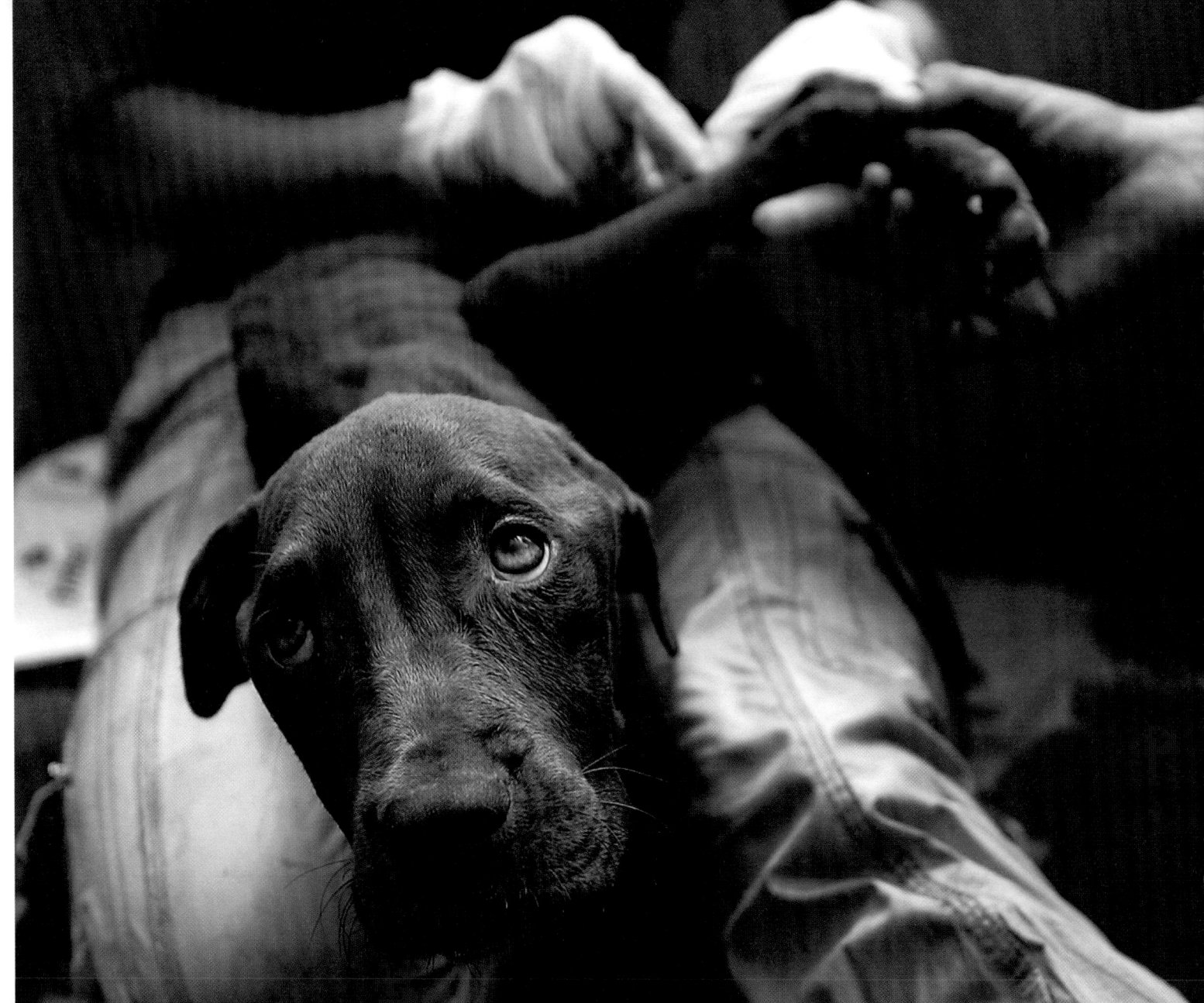

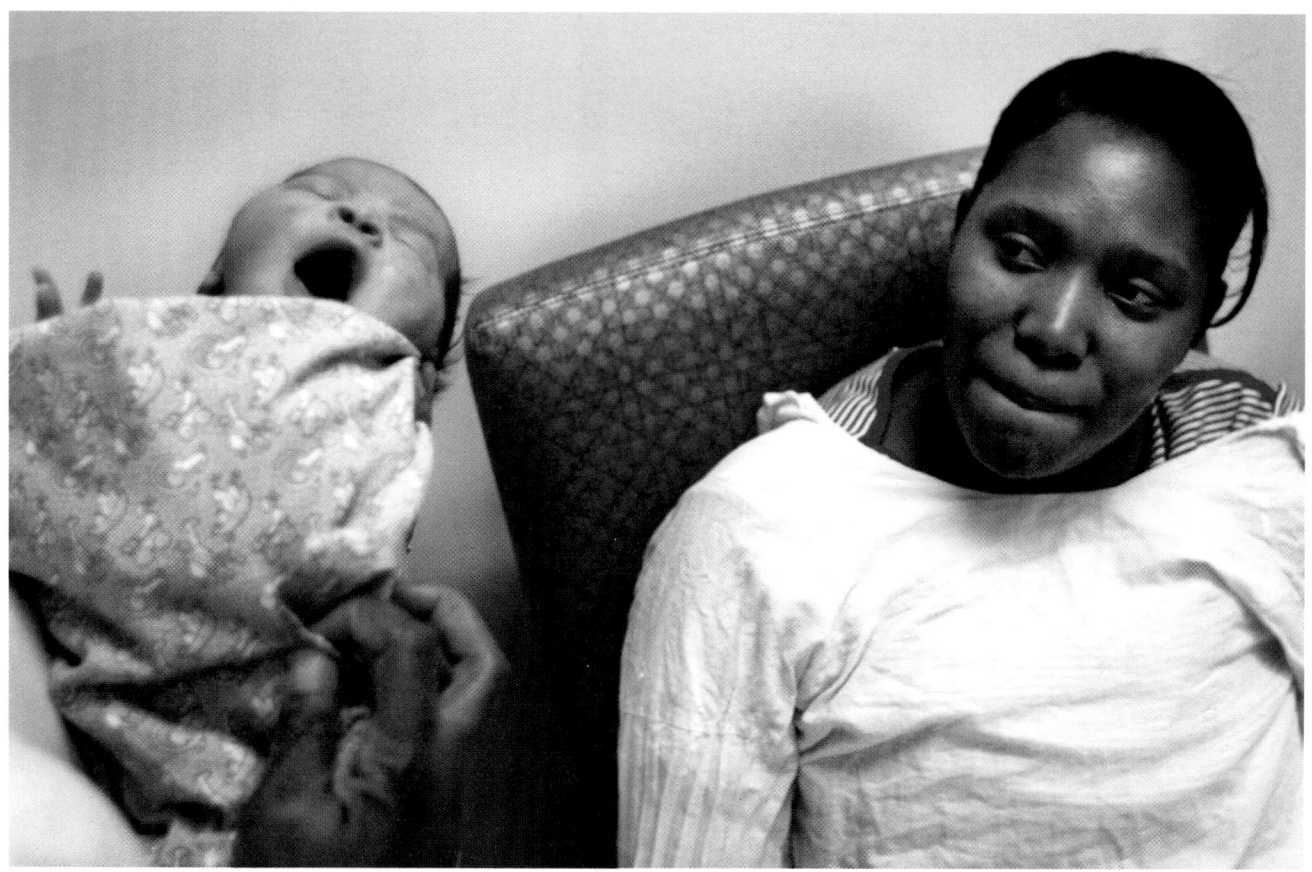

09.07.05 - Dallas, TX - Chalonda Cross' new daughter, Dallas Janae Ducro, yawned in the arms of her godmother Deneen Anderson, a member of Community Missionary Baptist Church in DeSoto. Ms. Cross named her baby after the place where she and her family were treated kindly after being evacuated from their Harvey, La., home. • RICK GERSHON

Left
09.10.05 - New Orleans, LA - Dr. Julie Manly attached an IV to one of seven pit bulls that had survived in a cage. • CHERYL DIAZ MEYER

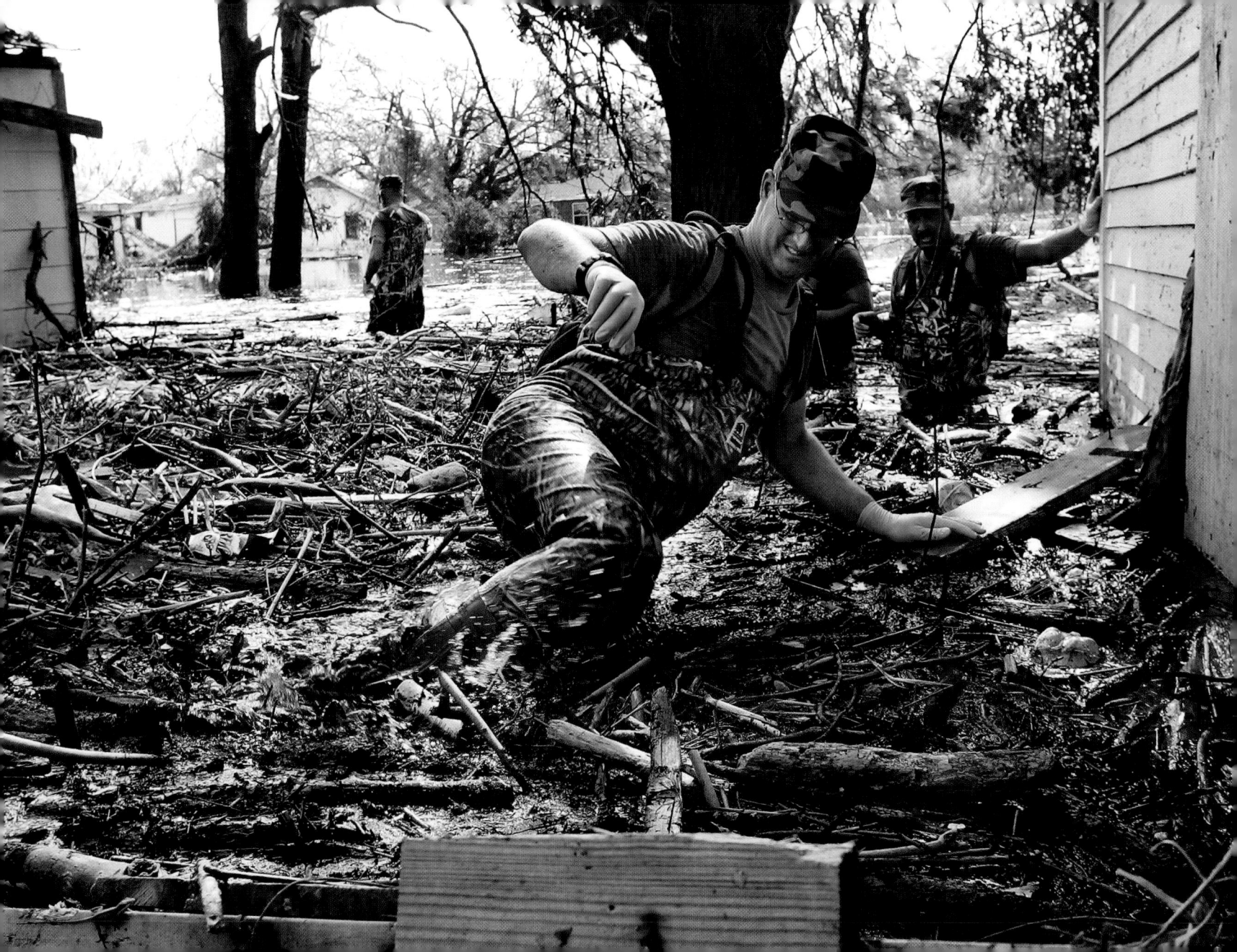

09.08.05 - Empire, LA - New Mexico National Guard members ripped out a steel guardrail to make a passage around two 150-foot "Hogie" boats on State Highway 23 in the bayou country south of New Orleans.
• ERICH SCHLEGEL

LEFT
09.10.05 - Port Sulphur, LA - New Mexico Army National Guard Sgt. 1st Class Chris Andrews pushed his way through filthy, debris-filled water during a house-to-house check. • ERICH SCHLEGEL

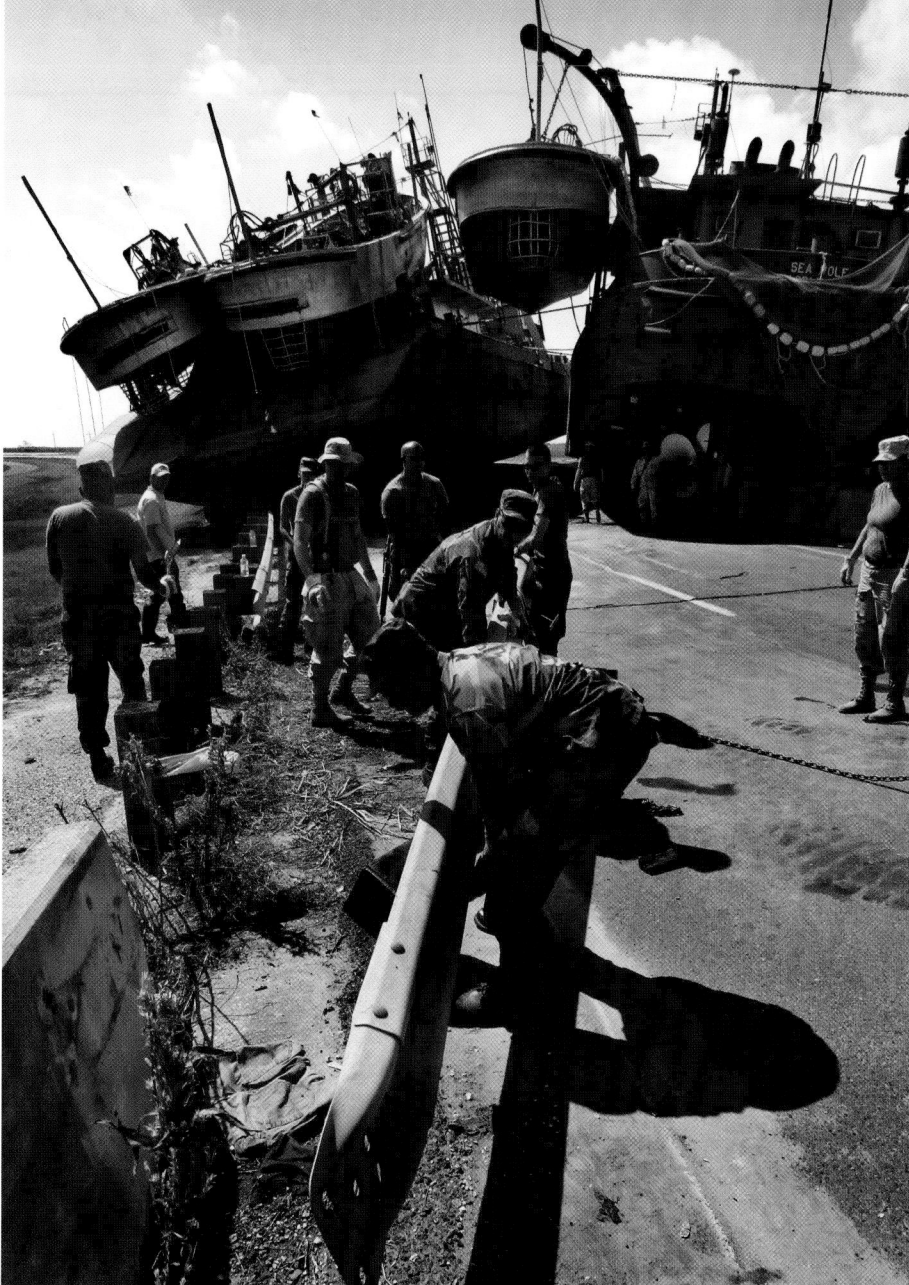

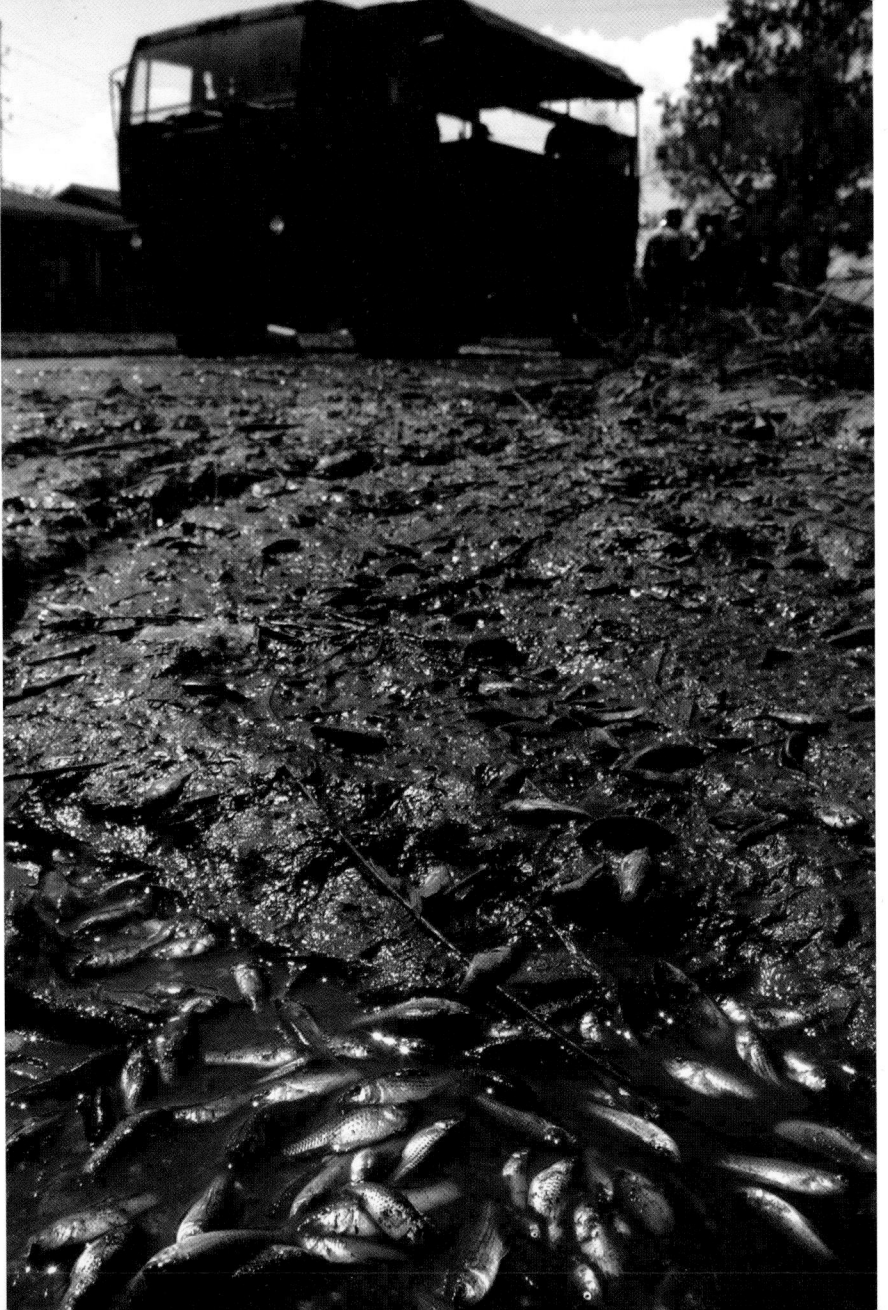

09.09.05 - Meraux, LA - Small fish died in several inches of sludge as floodwaters receded. • TOM FOX

RIGHT
09.10.05 - New Orleans, LA - Texas National Guardsman Spc. Brian Jimenez of Richardson, Texas, was fully armed as he and his North Texas platoon searched for survivors in an area west of downtown. • TOM FOX

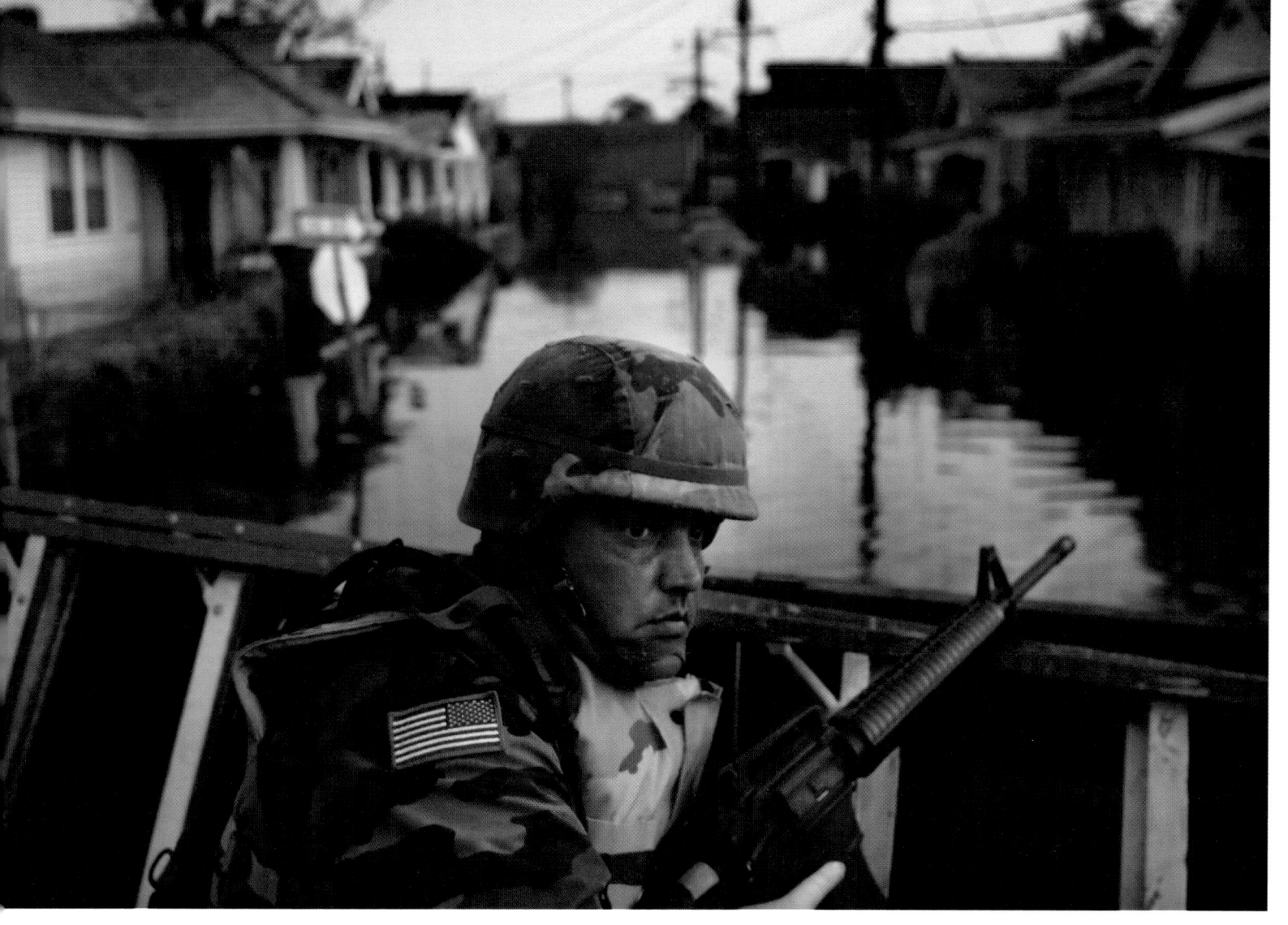

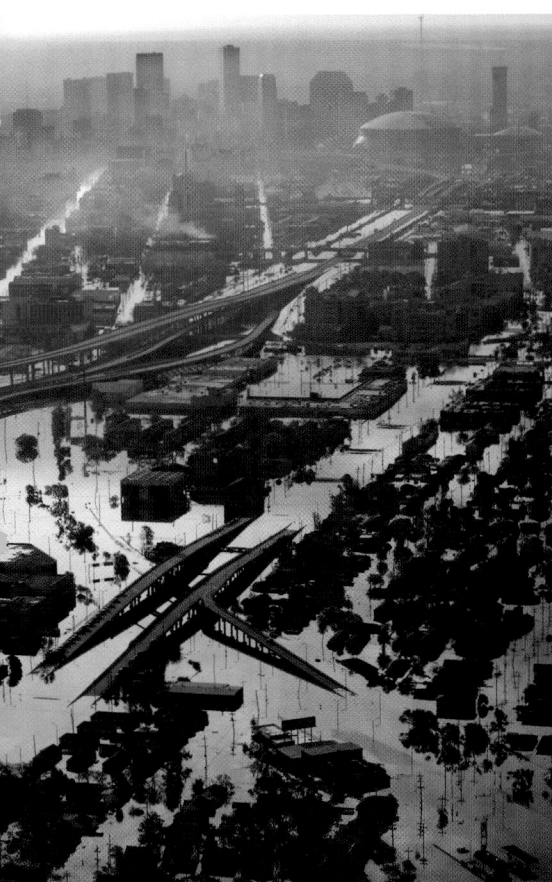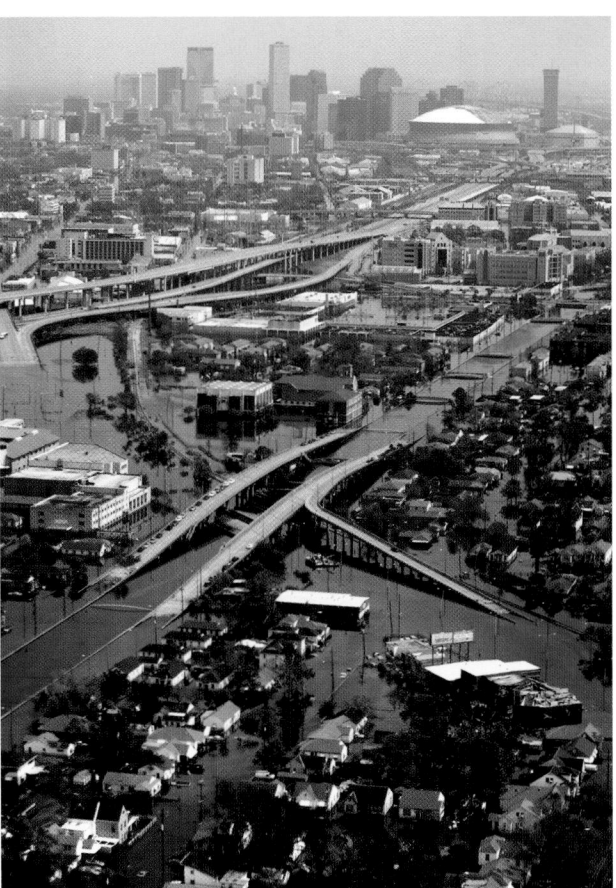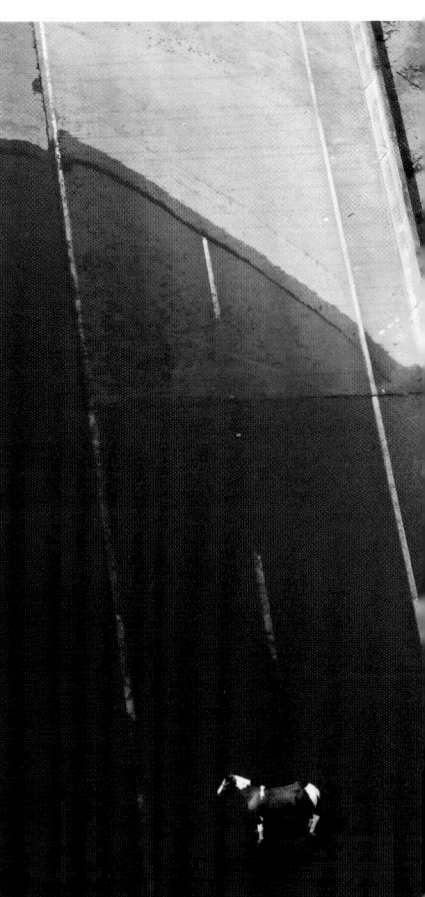

08.30.05 and 09.11.05 - New Orleans, LA - Before and after: A city slowly dries out. At left, a soggy view of damage looking from the west toward downtown the morning after the storm. At right, the same scene almost two weeks later, only a bit drier. • SMILEY N. POOL

09.02.05 - St. Bernard Parish, LA - A horse stood in floodwaters five days after the storm.

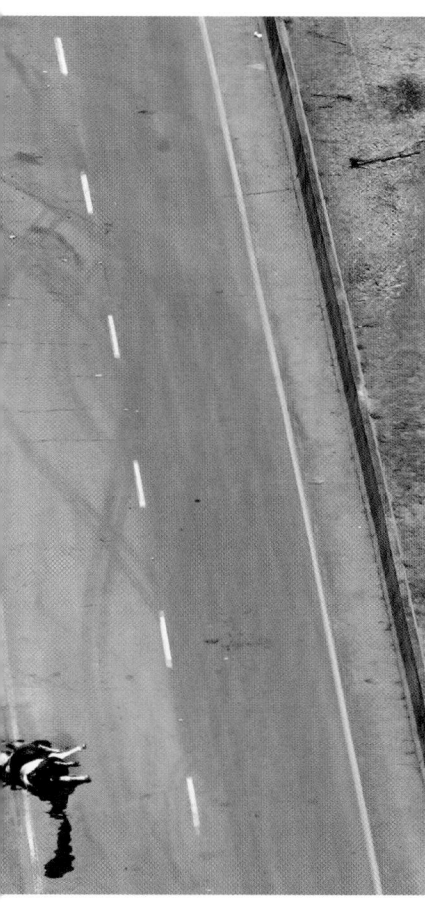

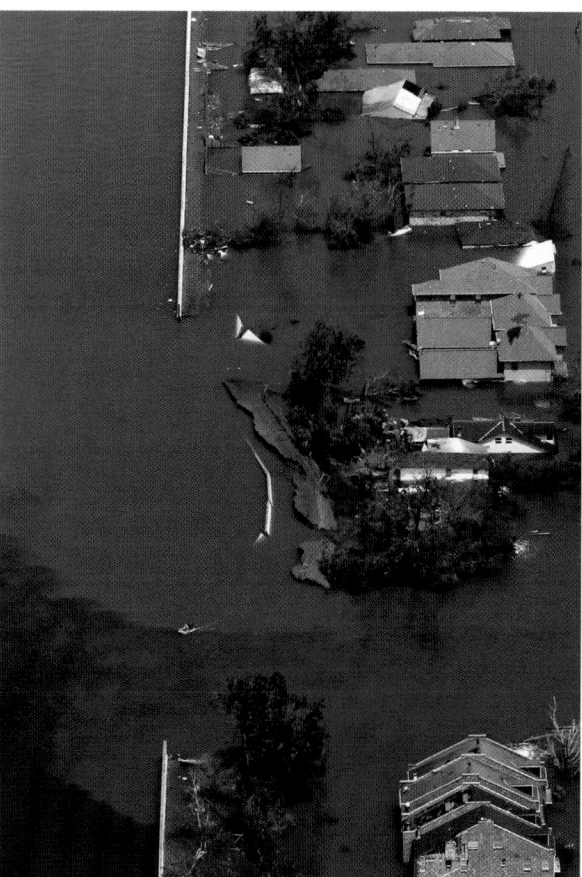

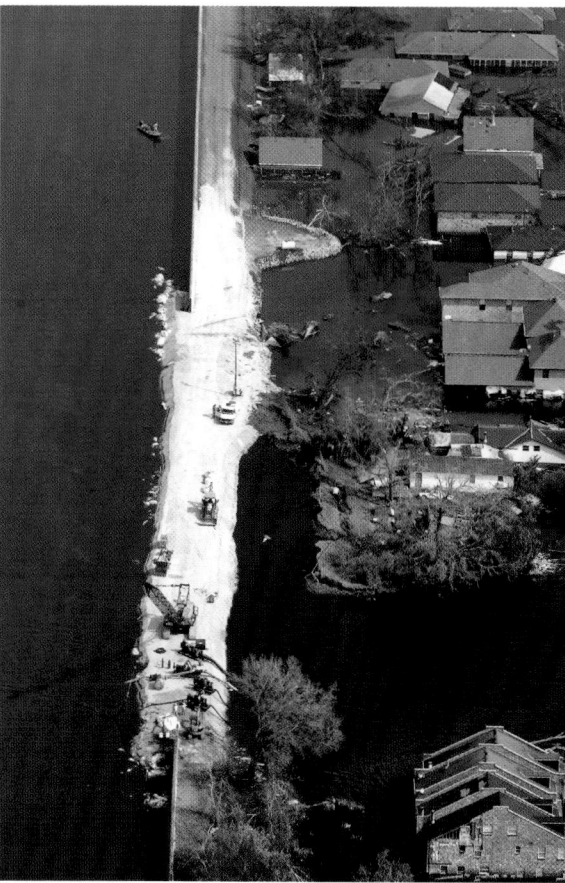

09.10.05 - A week later when the water had receded the horse was dead. • SMILEY N. POOL

08.30.05 and 09.10.05 - New Orleans, LA - At left, a break could be seen in the 17th Street Canal levee the morning after Katrina struck. At right, repairs were evident almost two weeks later. The break in the levee was more than 400 feet long. Corps engineers initially said they believed water flowed over the steel and concrete walls and eroded their earthen base, causing the collapse. • SMILEY N. POOL

09.12.05 - Dallas, TX - James McCray Jr. (left) kissed his daughter Ja'Nya McCray, 3, while they waited for Trinell McCray (center) and Linda McCray, to register with the Red Cross at the Dallas Convention Center. • MELANIE BURFORD

BELOW
09.10.05 - University Park, TX - Sue Sandford (back left) held Kyla Landry as Lawrence Washington prayed before dinner at her house. • MELANIE BURFORD

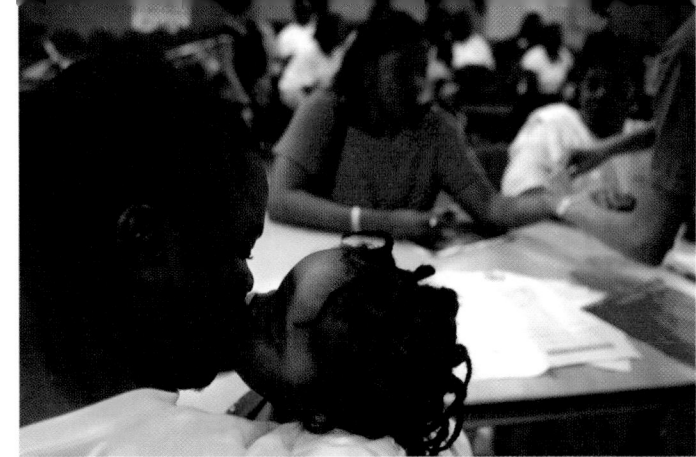

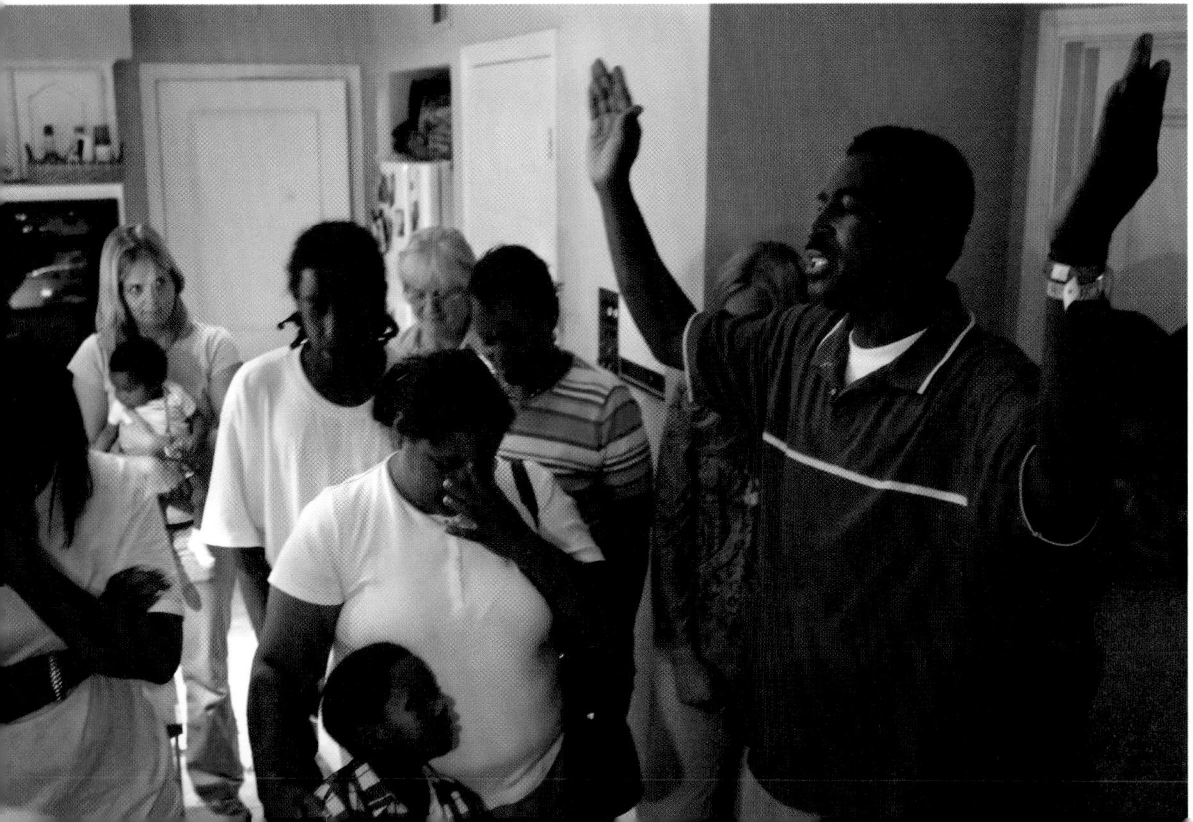

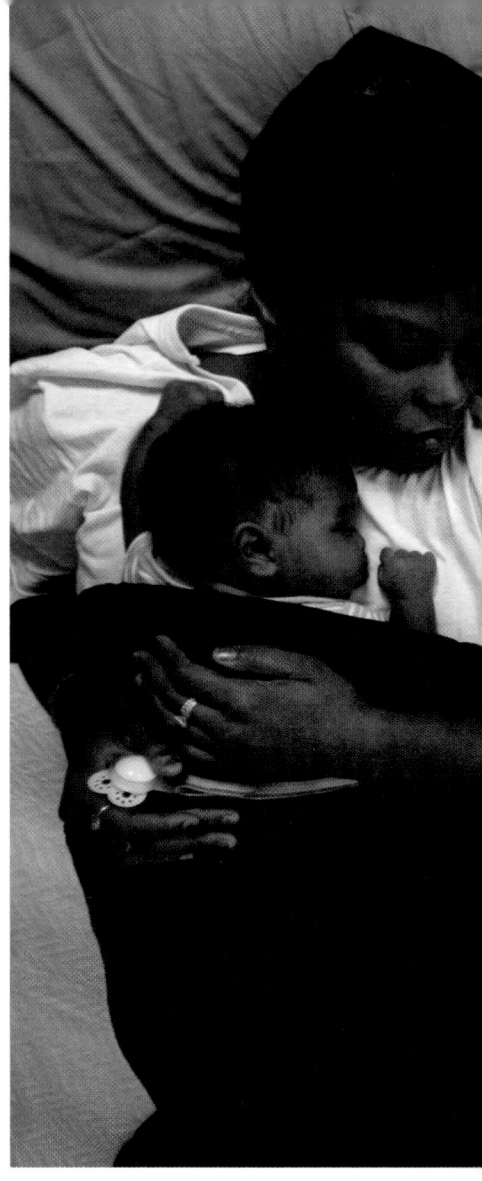

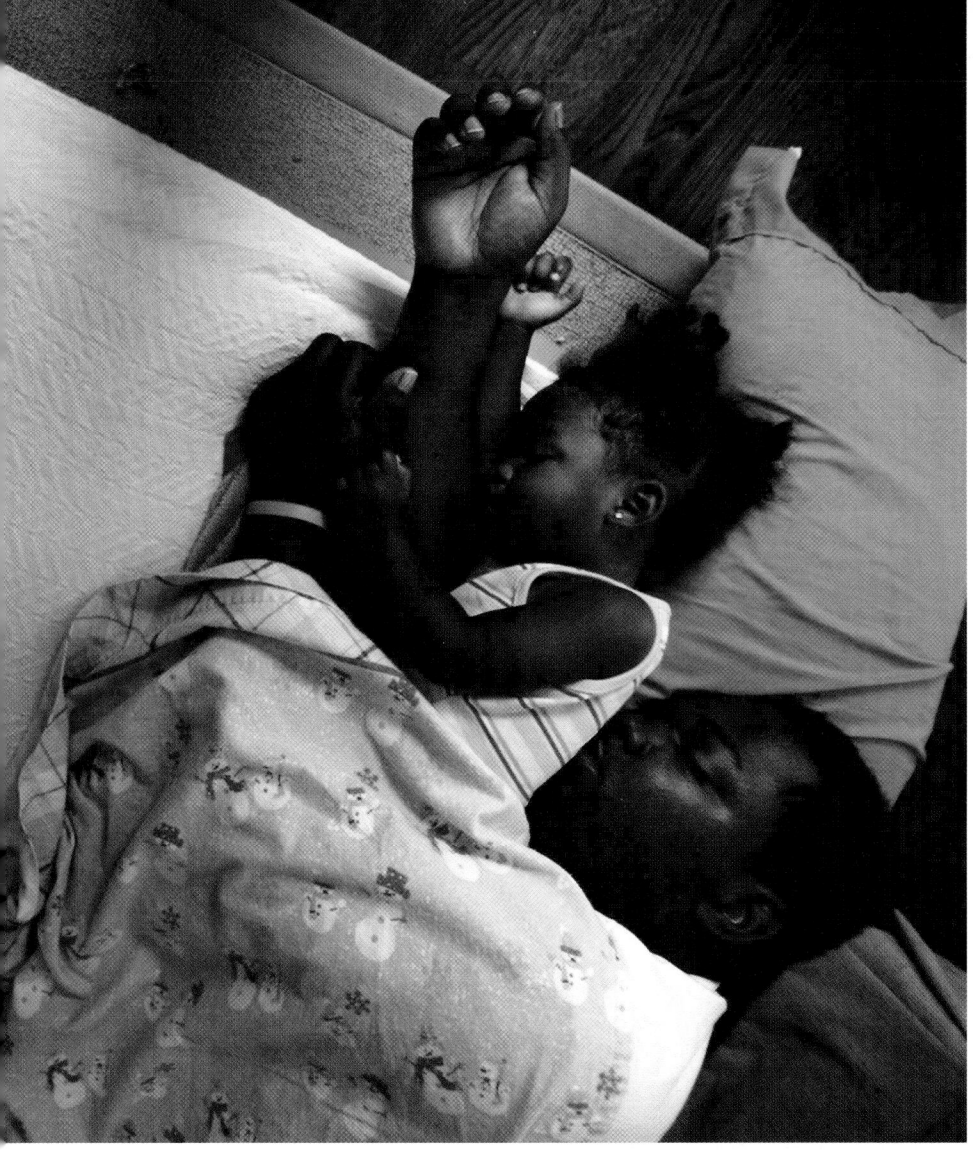

A NEW LIFE, A NEW PLACE

They stood on a rain-stained interstate bridge and watched dark waters rise.

Perhaps a half-mile in the distance stood the family home, its light blue siding visible above the floods. For more than two decades, the McCrays stitched identities here in the Upper Ninth Ward.

They were New Orleans' black middle class, ascending from humble histories in housing projects with names like Desire and St. Bernard.

But on that Monday afternoon, they knew they weren't coming back. The family of 20 was embarking on a search for a new home.

They drove to Dallas and were taken into an affluent University Park home by a single white woman. By mid-September, they had moved into a suburban subdivision in McKinney, signing a six-month lease. They would enter new schools, try out new churches and look for jobs.

In time, they would return home to New Orleans to survey the damage.

•PAUL MEYER

09.09.05 - University Park, TX - Trinell McCray (left) held her baby Kyla Landry while Joshua Landry sleptwith their daughter Sage Landry, 1, on the living room floor of Sue Sandford's house. Twenty members of the McCray family stayed there in the wake of Hurricane Katrina. • MELANIE BURFORD

09.10.05 - University Park, TX - Sue Sandford (left) hugged Linda McCray at the end of a long day at Sue's house. The combined Sandford and McCray families became one extended family, brought together through the tragedy of Hurricane Katrina. • MELANIE BURFORD

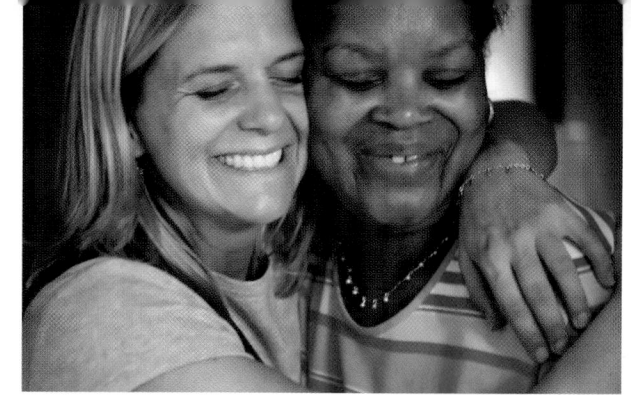

BELOW
09.09.05 - University Park, TX - Brandon Forte, 14, (center) watched television with Emma Garrison, 4, (left) and Josh Garrison, 7, at Sue Sandford's house. With the arrival of the 20-member McCray family, Ms. Sandford installed cable television to keep the children entertained. • MELANIE BURFORD

OPPOSITE
09.13.05 - McKinney, TX - Linda McCray joyously rolled on her new carpet after signing a six-month lease on a house. • MELANIE BURFORD

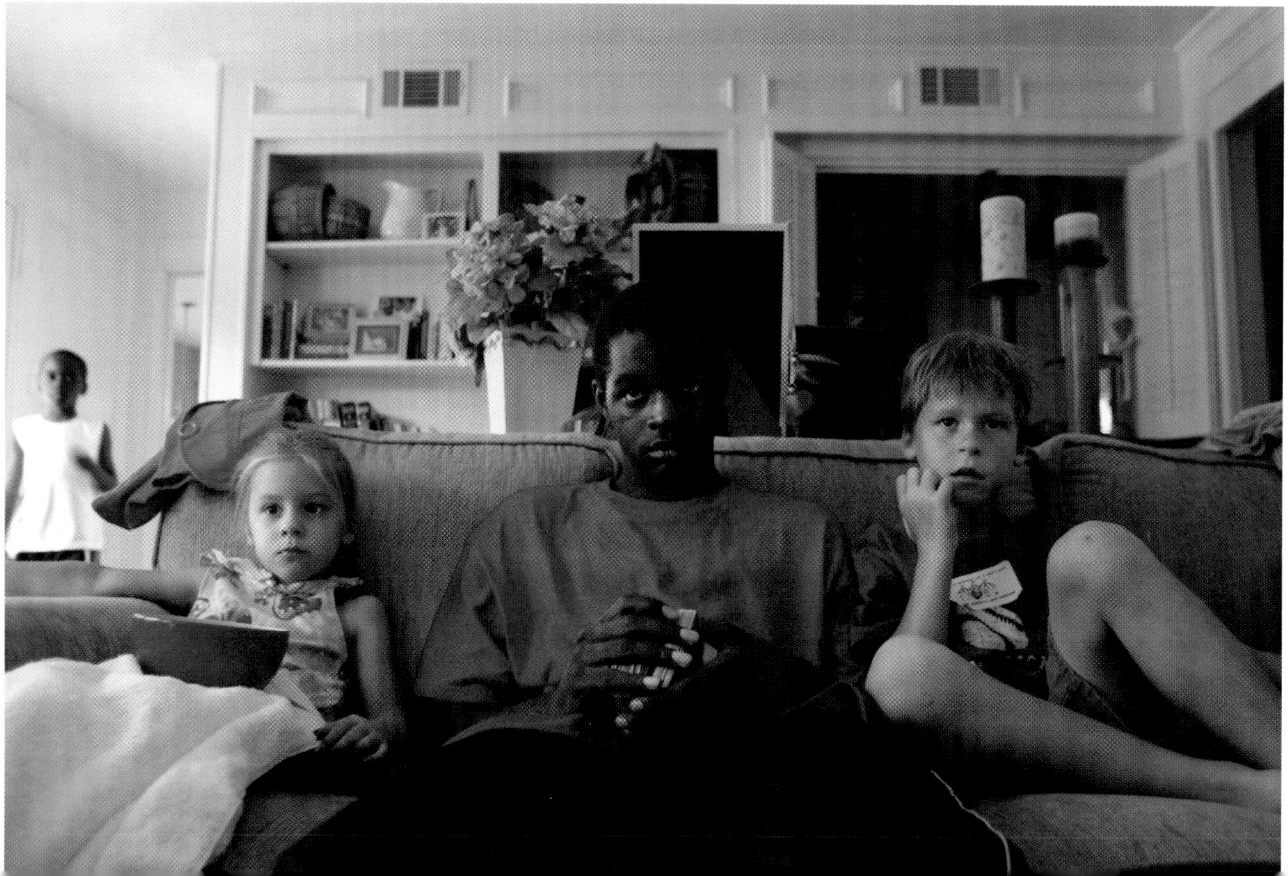

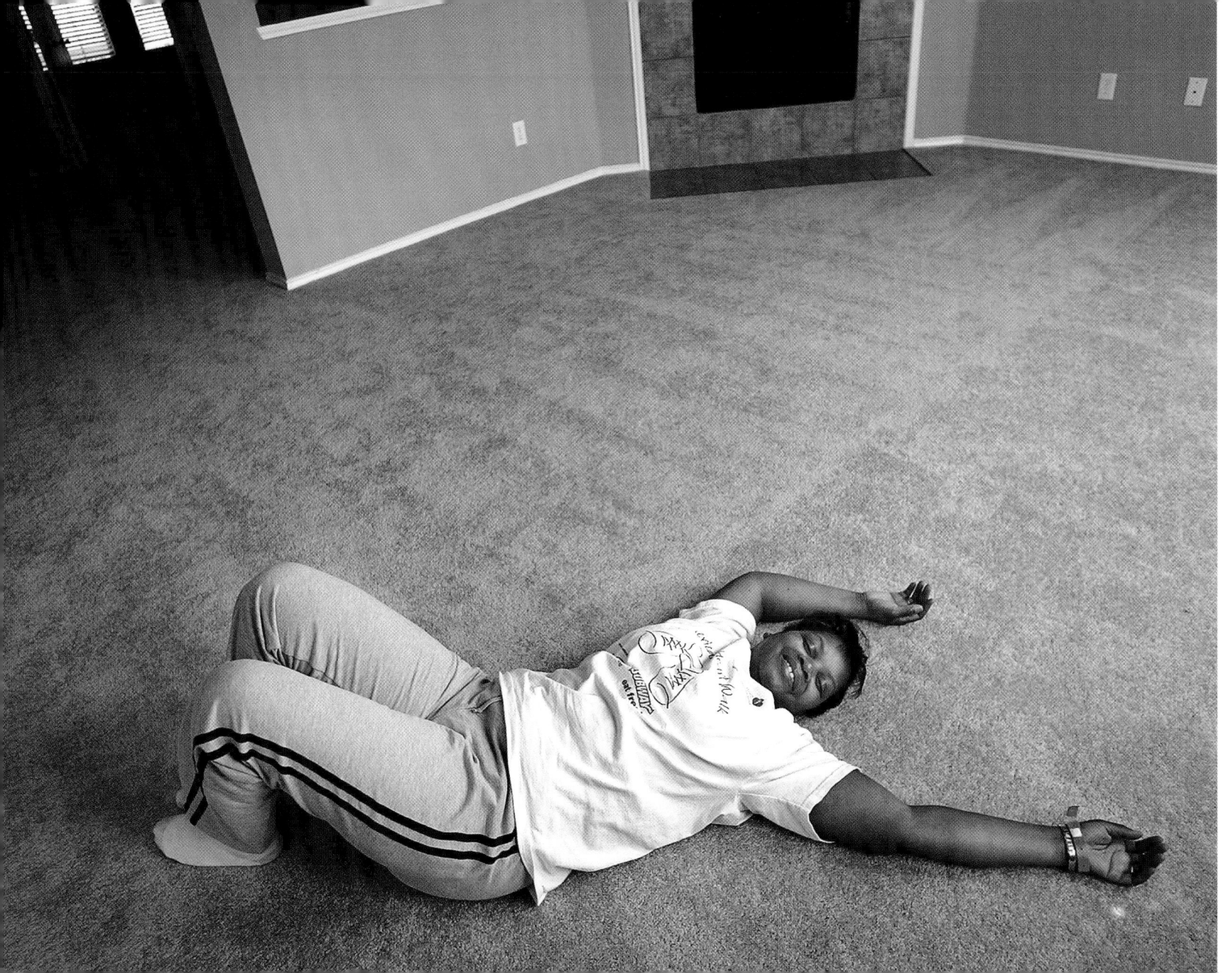

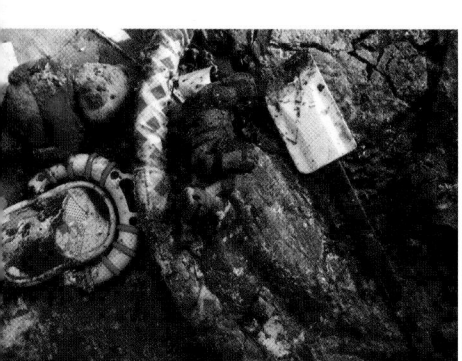

09.29.05 - New Orleans, LA - Debris lay on the kitchen floor of the McCrays' Upper Ninth Ward house a month to the day after Hurricane Katrina devestated the city.
• MELANIE BURFORD

RIGHT
09.29.05 - New Orleans, LA - James and Linda McCray walk through their home. Battling the overwhelming stench of rotting furniture and food, flies, and stiffling temperatures. The McCrays worked for hours salvaging clothes. • MELANIE BURFORD

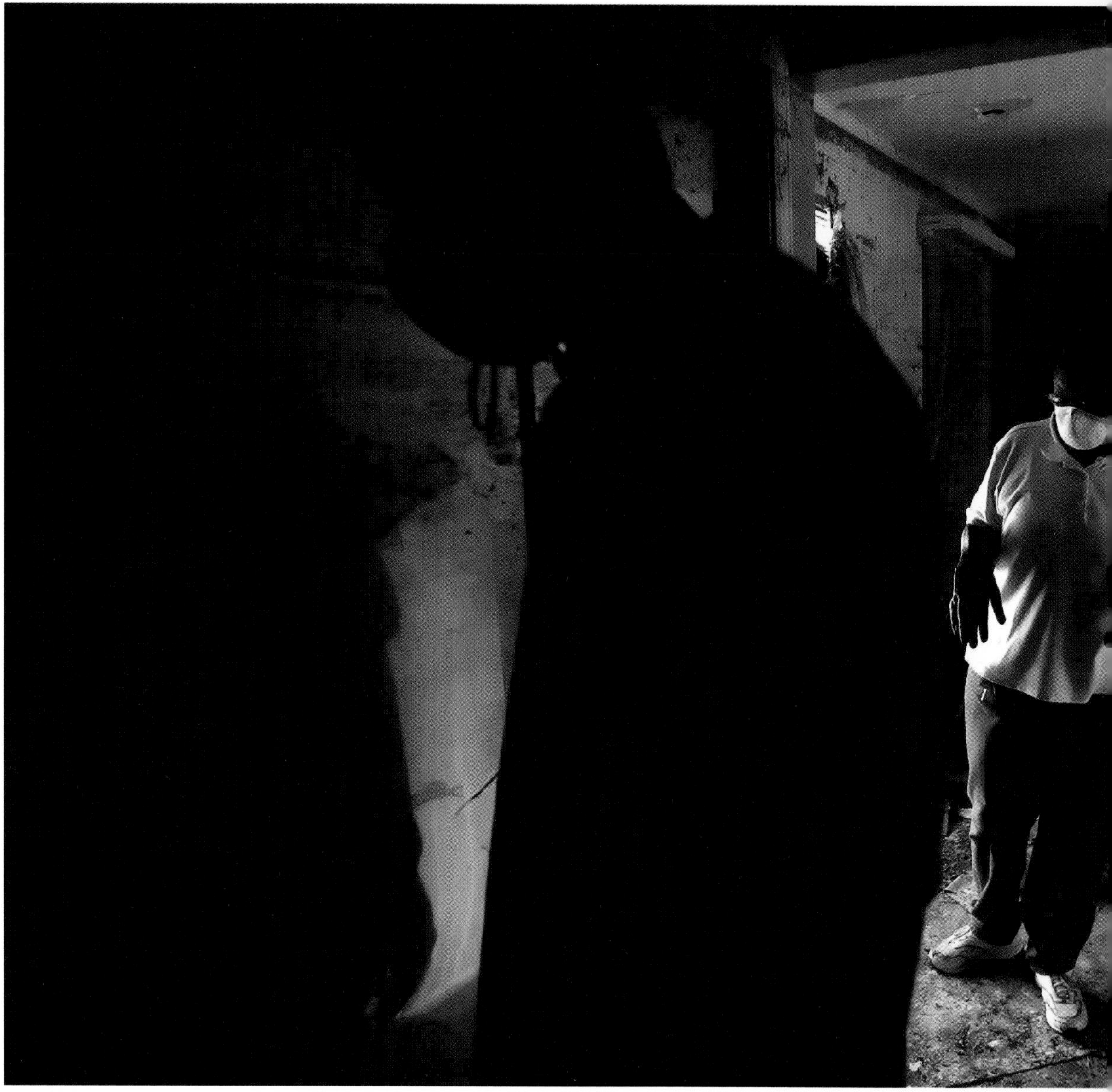

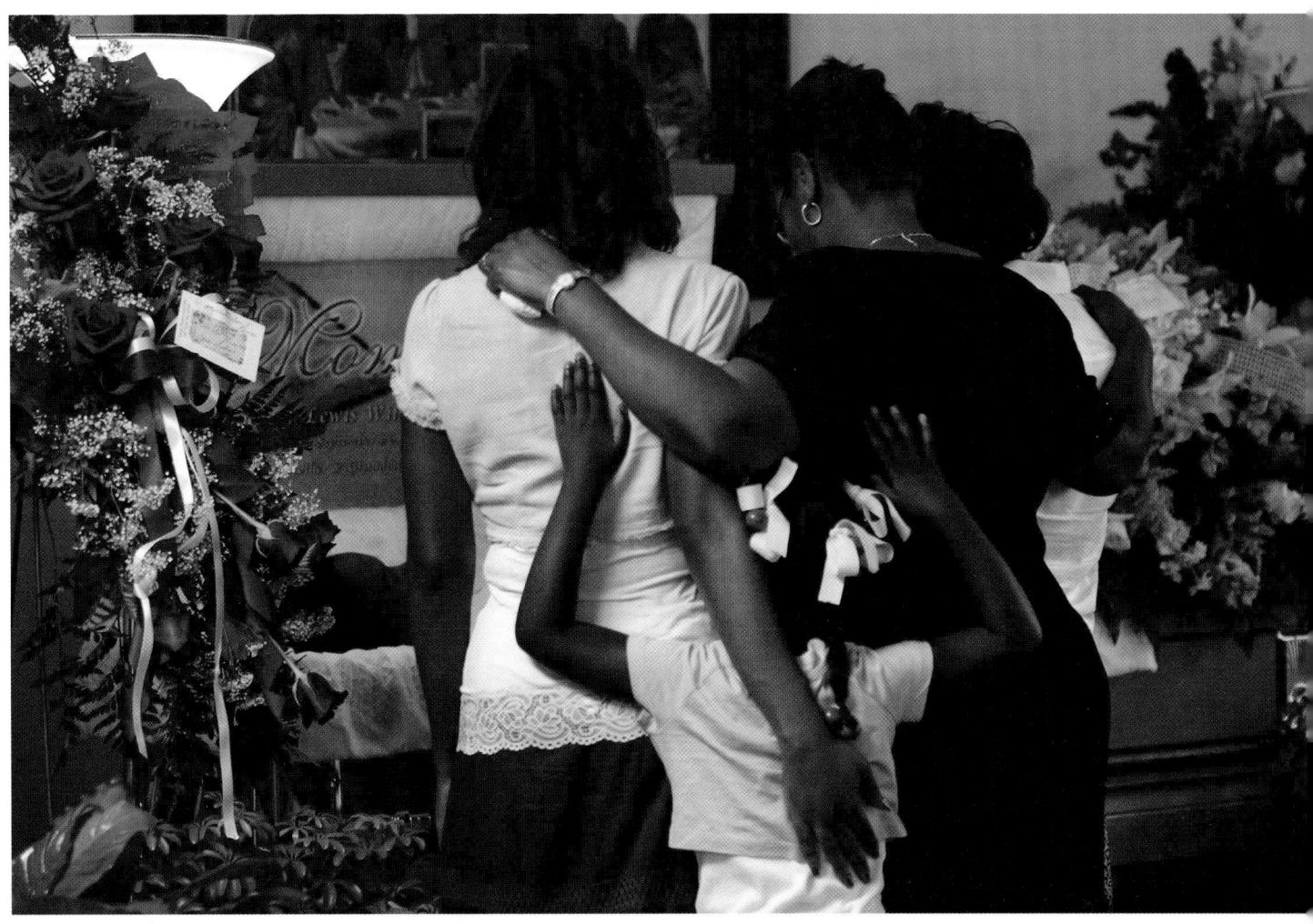

09.30.05 - New Orleans, LA - Members of the McCray family attend a friend's funeral while making a return trip home to their damaged house.
• MELANIE BURFORD

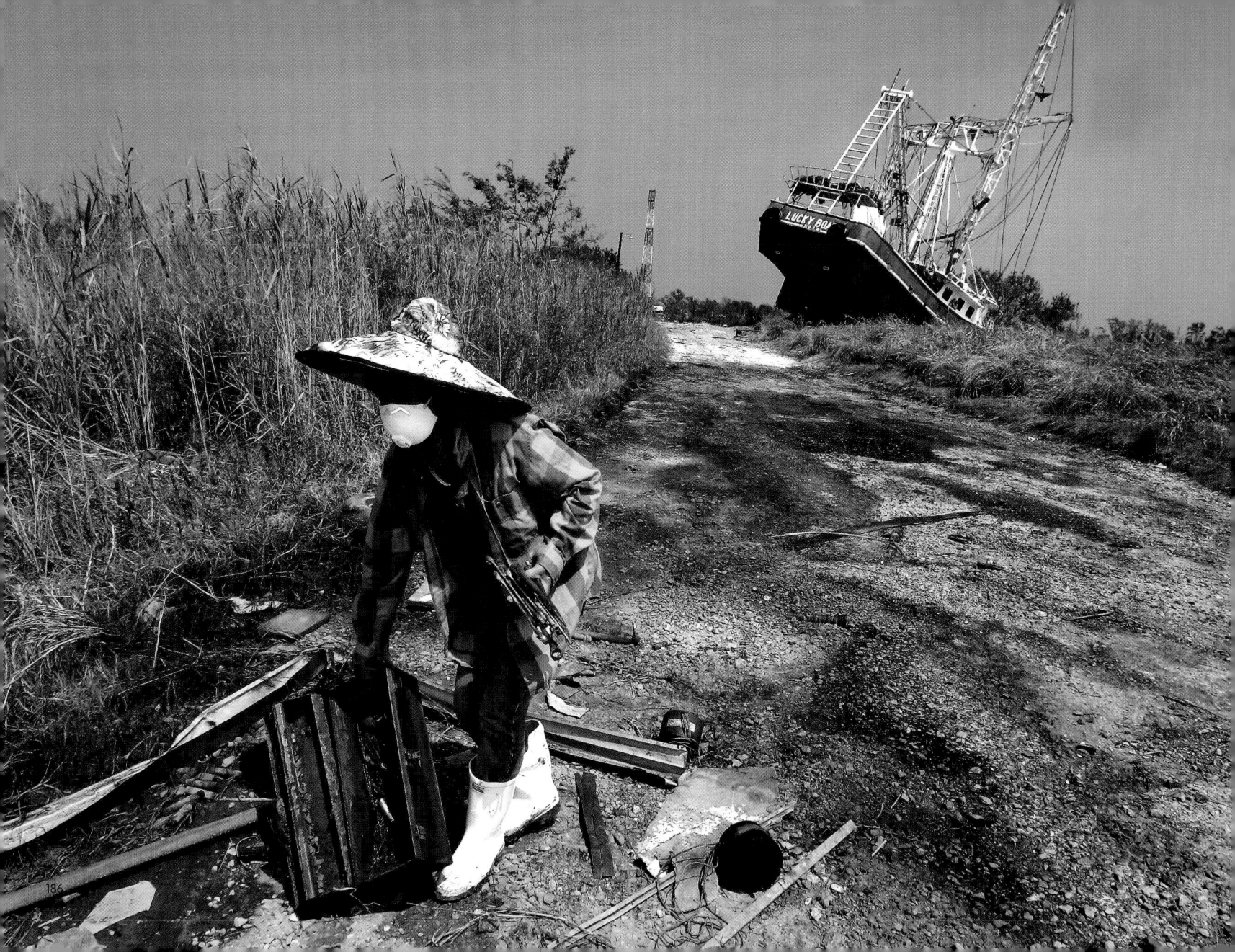

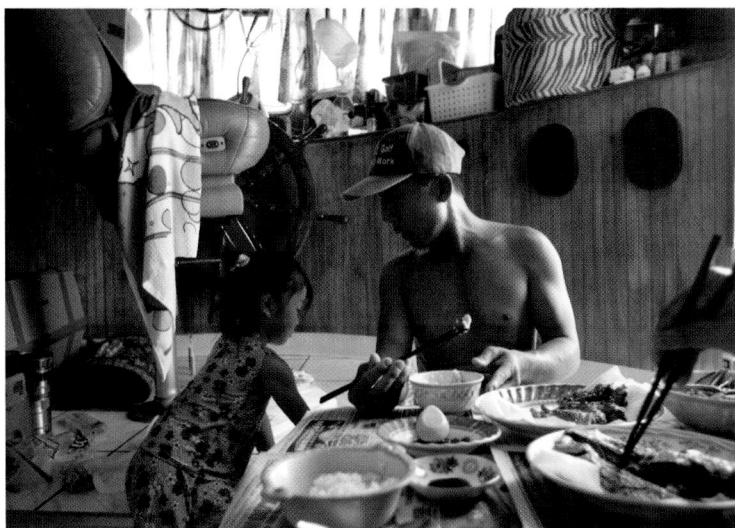

09.21.05 - Biloxi, MS - Shrimper Tam Tran, his wife Thu, and their daughter, Vanna, 4, lived on their shrimp boat after their home in East Biloxi was destroyed. Shrimping in the area may not be able to return for more than a year because of pollution. • ERICH SCHLEGEL

OPPOSITE PAGE
09.21.05 - Biloxi, MS - Dieu Ha Loung salvaged a friend's toolbox near a harbor in Empire. Plaquemines Parish is one of the biggest producers in Louisiana's $2.6 billion-a-year seafood industry, which has been devastated by hurricanes. • ERICH SCHLEGEL

IS SEAFOOD HISTORY?

Fishermen and state officials fear that Hurricane Rita may have dealt a mortal blow to Louisiana's $2.6 billion-a-year seafood industry.

The industry had already been reeling from Hurricane Katrina. Losses from both storms could reach more than $2 billion.

Katrina slammed into southeastern Louisiana and Mississippi on Aug. 29, smothering oyster beds, scuttling fishing fleets and wrecking vibrant melting-pot communities where coaxing a living from the sea has long been part of the culture. Then Rita swamped coastal areas of southwestern Louisiana that had escaped Katrina.

That has heightened uncertainty about the future of an industry that provides nearly 30,000 jobs and lands almost half of the shrimp, 26 percent of the crabs and 37 percent of the oysters caught in the United States.

• LEE HANCOCK

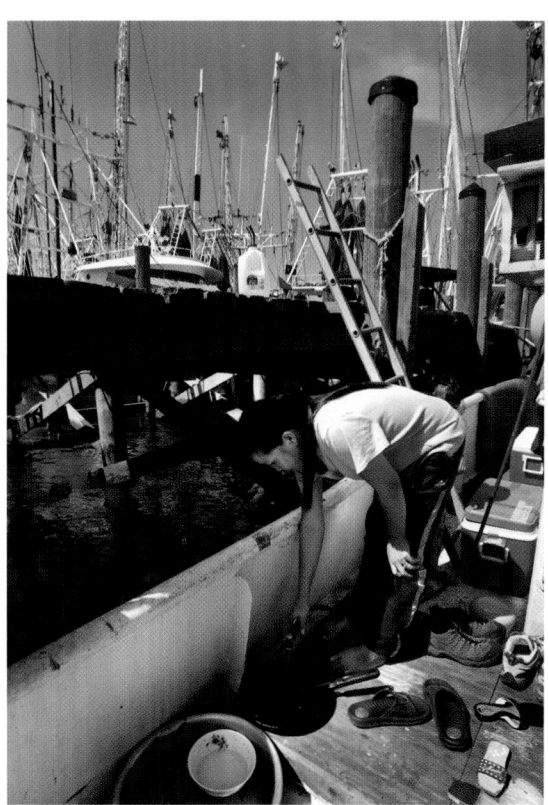

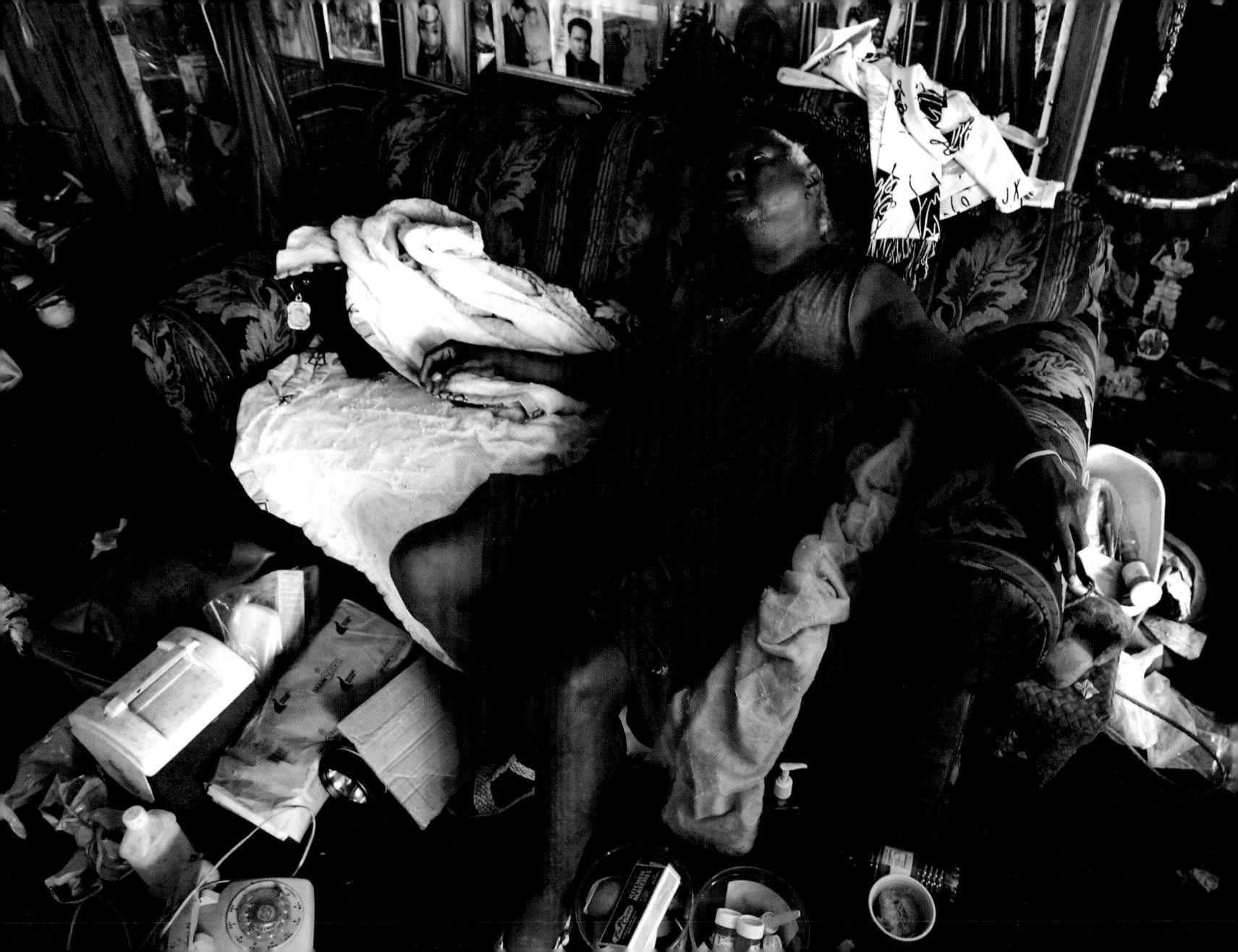

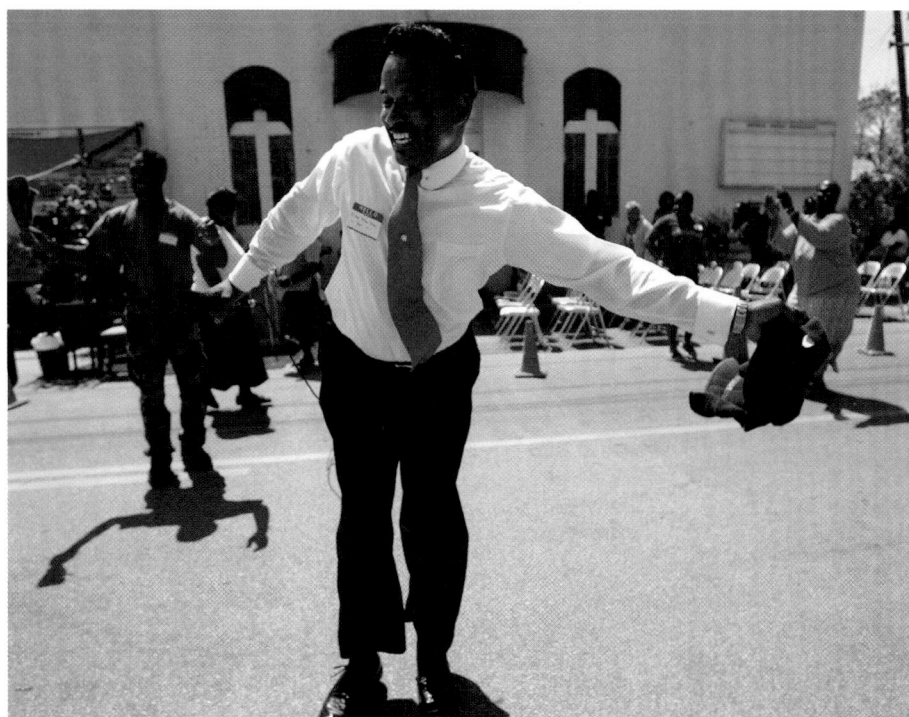

09.11.05 - Biloxi, MS - Bishop DeBruce Nelson danced in the street near his Lighthouse Apostolic Church. Services were held outside in the parking zone, and the bishop often took his preaching into the street during the Sunday service. • MICHAEL MULVEY

Opposite page
09.11.05 - Biloxi, MS - Eddie Mae Smith, 75, collapsed in her home, which was flooded by Hurricane Katrina and infested with mold and mildew. Bishop Nelson came to check on Ms. Smith and found her in dire condition. Nelson said he needed trailers for people such as Ms. Smith, who can't wait for FEMA aid. • MICHAEL MULVEY

REJOICING AMID THE AGONY

Bishop DeBruce Nelson conducted his first service since the devastation of Katrina on an important day in U.S. history: Sept. 11. But the focus of this service wasn't related to what happened on that day in 2001. It centered on rebuilding lives in Biloxi, Miss., after a terrible storm.

Katrina had roared ashore some 13 days before. The church, which had filled with 6 feet of water and was still drying out, was not able to hold worshippers on this day. All the walls had been stripped of sheetrock.

They held a service on the median in front of the church, set up just like any other Sunday except outside in the sun. No covering overhead, little shade, but it didn't matter. Bishop Nelson belted out prayers and offerings of hope. He took his preaching into the street, dancing past cones set up to divert the trickle of traffic.

Many National Guard members would pass the church and stop to take pictures.

The church prayed for those who were lost and those in need. And amid the agony and suffering, they reunited and celebrated.

• MICHAEL MULVEY

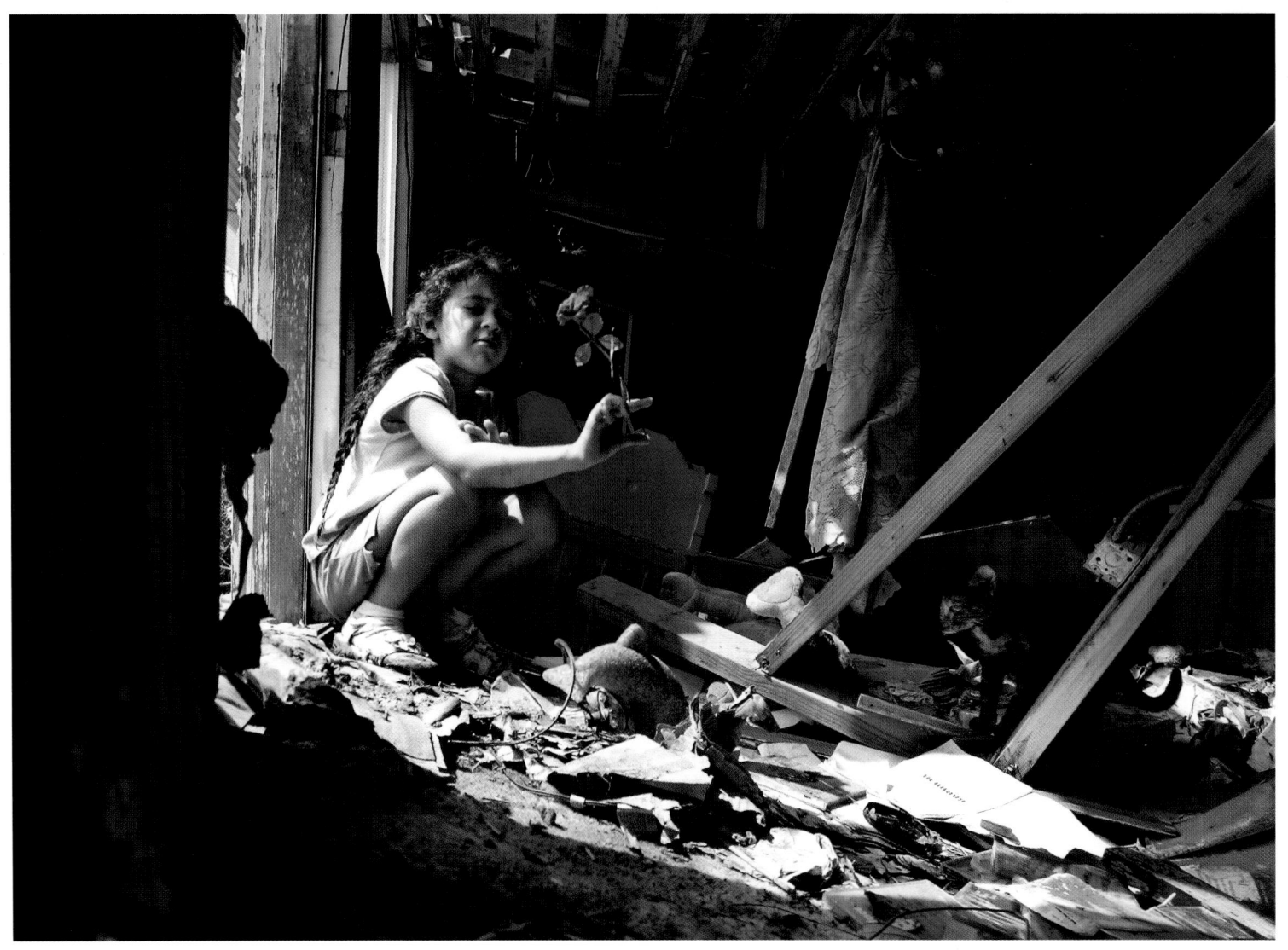

09.12.05 - Port Sulphur, LA - Seven-year-old Britney Sylvie used a rose to play with her cat Pinky while her parents went through their house gathering what belongings they could salvage. • ERICH SCHLEGEL

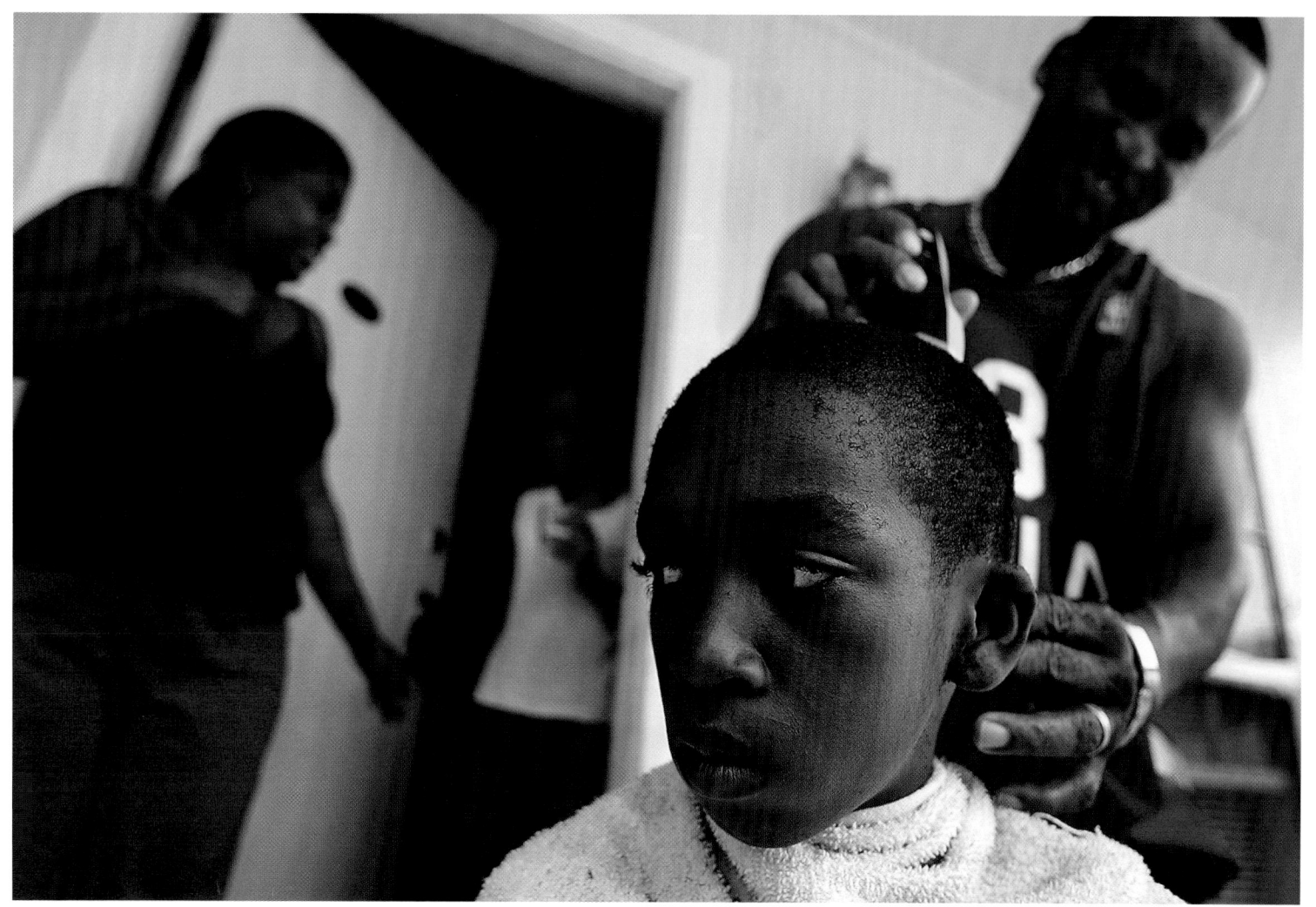

09.14.05 - New Orleans, LA - Davante Johnson, 7, got a haircut from his father, Tyrone Johnson Sr., after returning to their home in the New Orleans suburb of Algiers, which was largely spared from storm damage. • CHERYL DIAZ MEYER

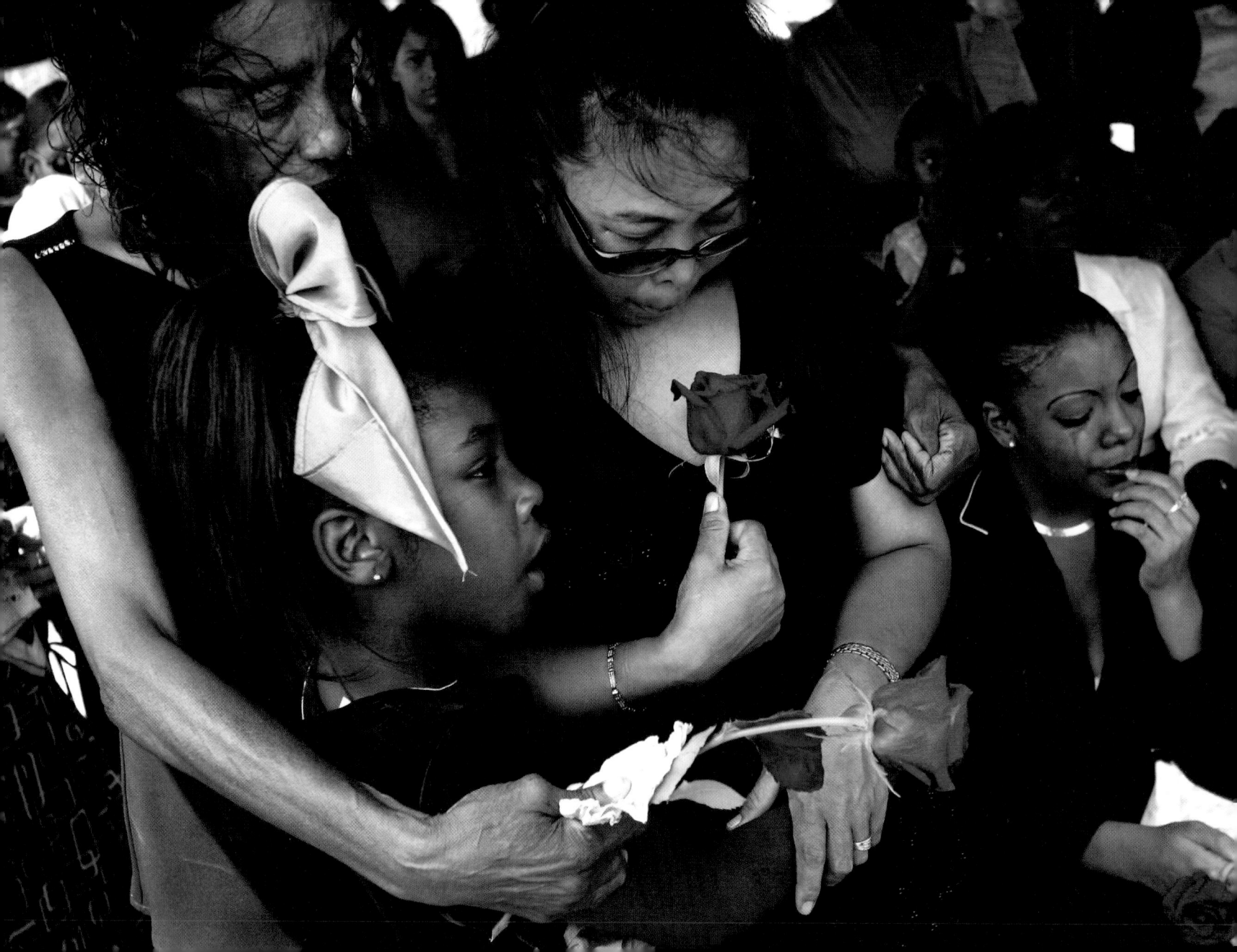

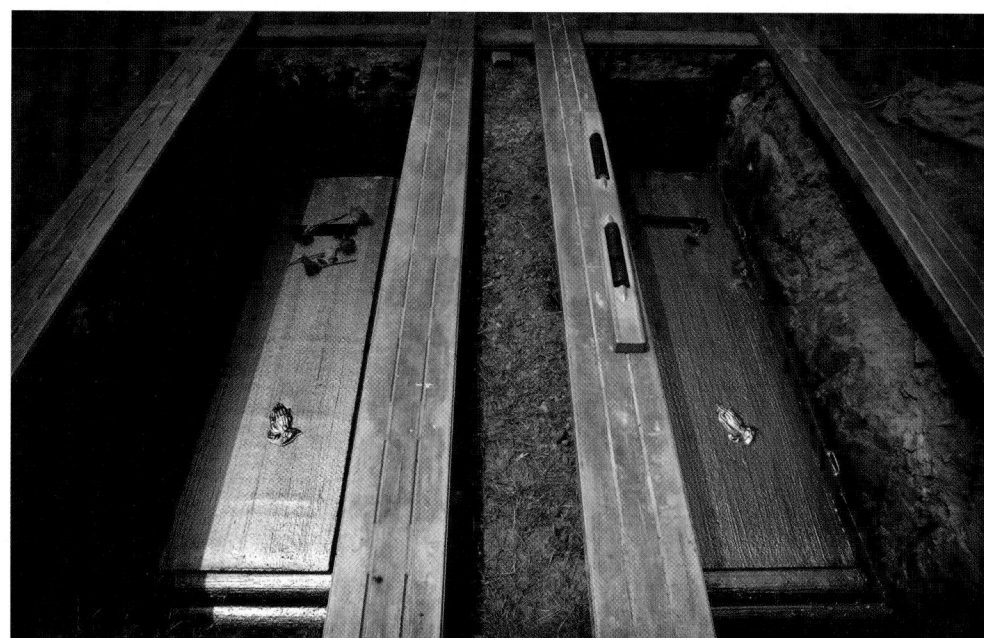

09.16.05 - Gulfport, MS - The coffins of Sam and Mattie Tart rested side by side at Pine Ridge Gardens. Mattie turned 2 the day Hurricane Katrina struck, and Mr. and Ms. Tart were only a week away from their 10th anniversary. • BARBARA DAVIDSON

LEFT
09.16.05 - Gulfport, MS - Genoveva Tart (center) was comforted by Akia Huddleston, 7, and Barbara Tart Shepard as the coffins of Ms. Tart's husband and son were lowered into graves at Pine Ridge Gardens. Sam Tart and the couple's son, Mattie, died after a storm surge swept through their home. • BARBARA DAVIDSON

HAPPINESS, WASHED AWAY

Sam Tart knew from the moment he saw the lovely Genoveva that she was The One.

"I want to marry you," he told her 15 years ago in Singapore. The young Filipino was cleaning houses - even though she held a bachelor's degree in business administration - so she could travel the world.

A short, happy lifetime later, Geno was stumbling through the ghastly streets of her Pass Christian, Miss., neighborhood with the couple's only child, Mattie, lifeless in her arms.

"Please help me. My family's dead!"

Her husband was dead in their home, drowned while trying to save Mattie from Hurricane Katrina's storm surge, which had pounded their town on the little boy's second birthday. All Geno could think was, "I have no one left."

The bodies of her husband and child were lowered side by side into a cemetery surrounded by broken trees in nearby Gulfport.

Geno prepared to go back to the Philippines without her husband and son, three weeks after that peaceful Sunday afternoon when Mattie danced happily around his birthday cake and batted at the blue balloons, the looming storm temporarily forgotten.

One week later, Geno and Sam would have been married for 10 solid years.

And now, Geno is alone.

• KAREN BROOKS

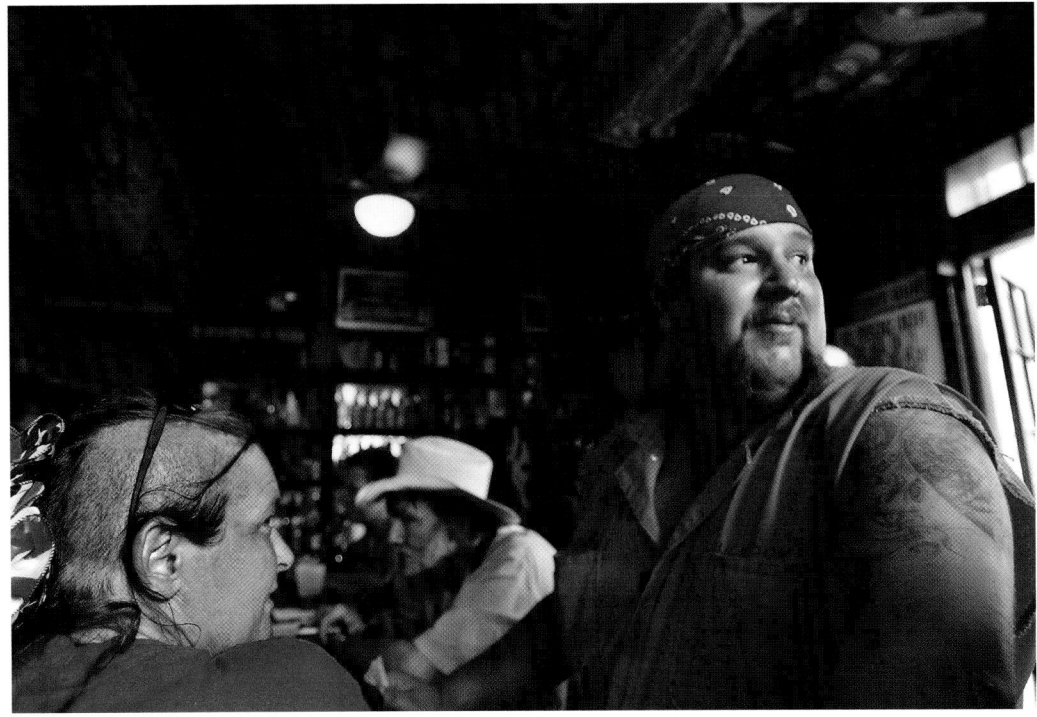

09.16.05 - New Orleans, LA - Marguerite Smith and Kevin Sharrock waited for a drink at Johnny White's Sports Bar & Grill in the French Quarter. The bar remained open after Katrina struck. • CHERYL DIAZ MEYER

RIGHT
09.16.05 - Metairie, LA - Nell Fatland, 88, cleaned up her home after it was hit by Hurricane Katrina and later flooded with 5 feet of water in Metairie. She said that in 55 years, her home had never flooded. • CHERYL DIAZ MEYER

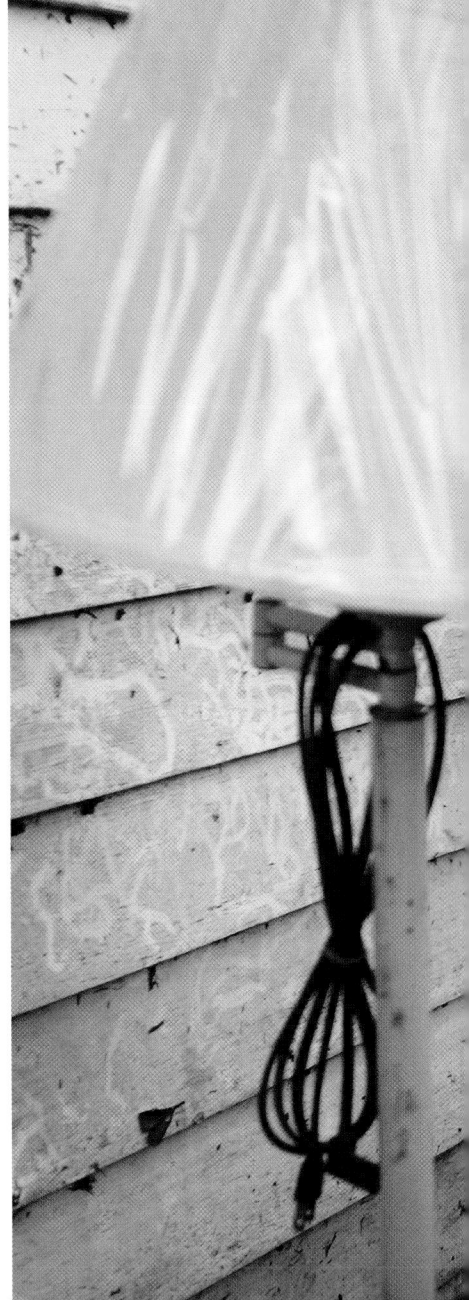

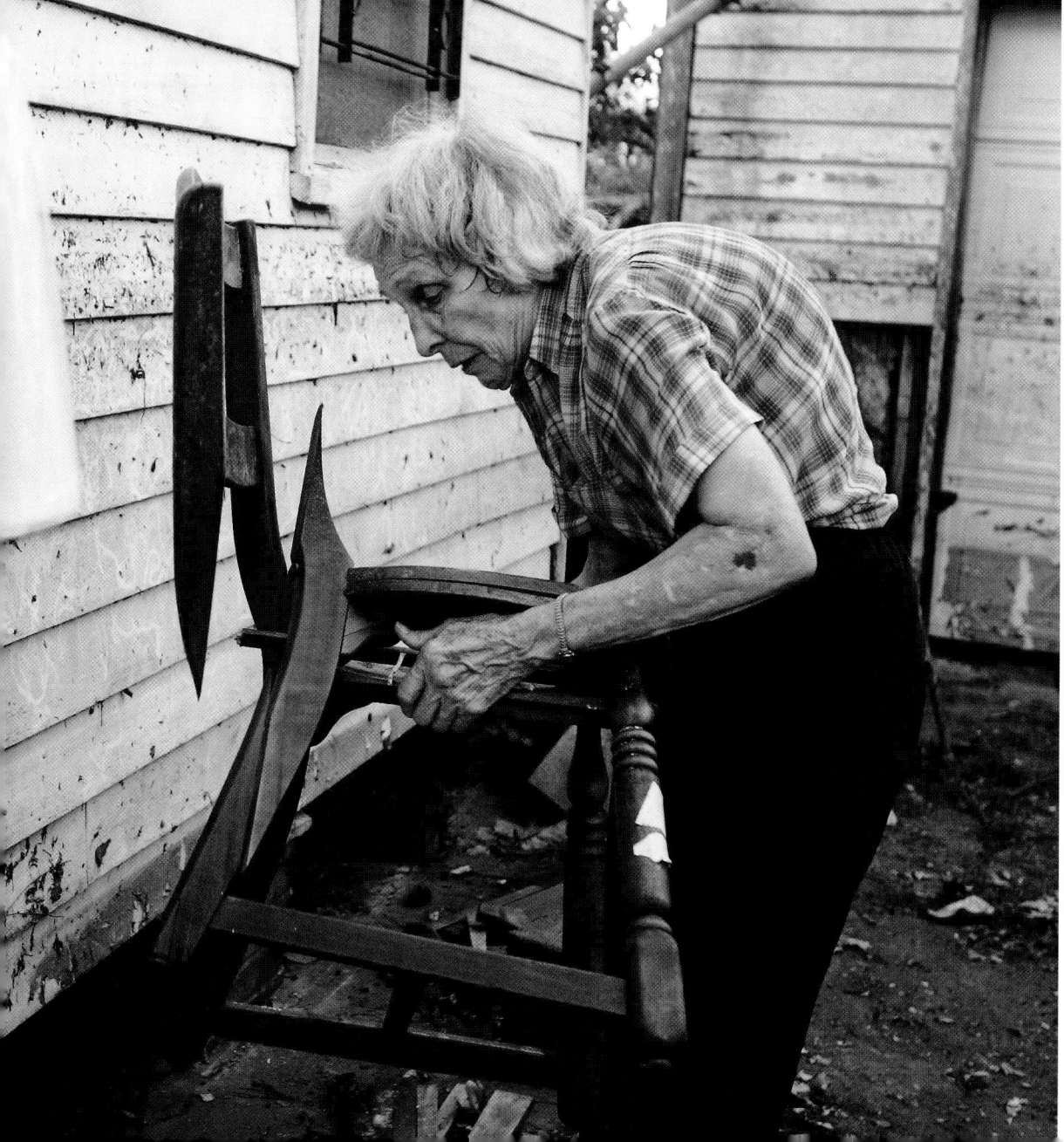

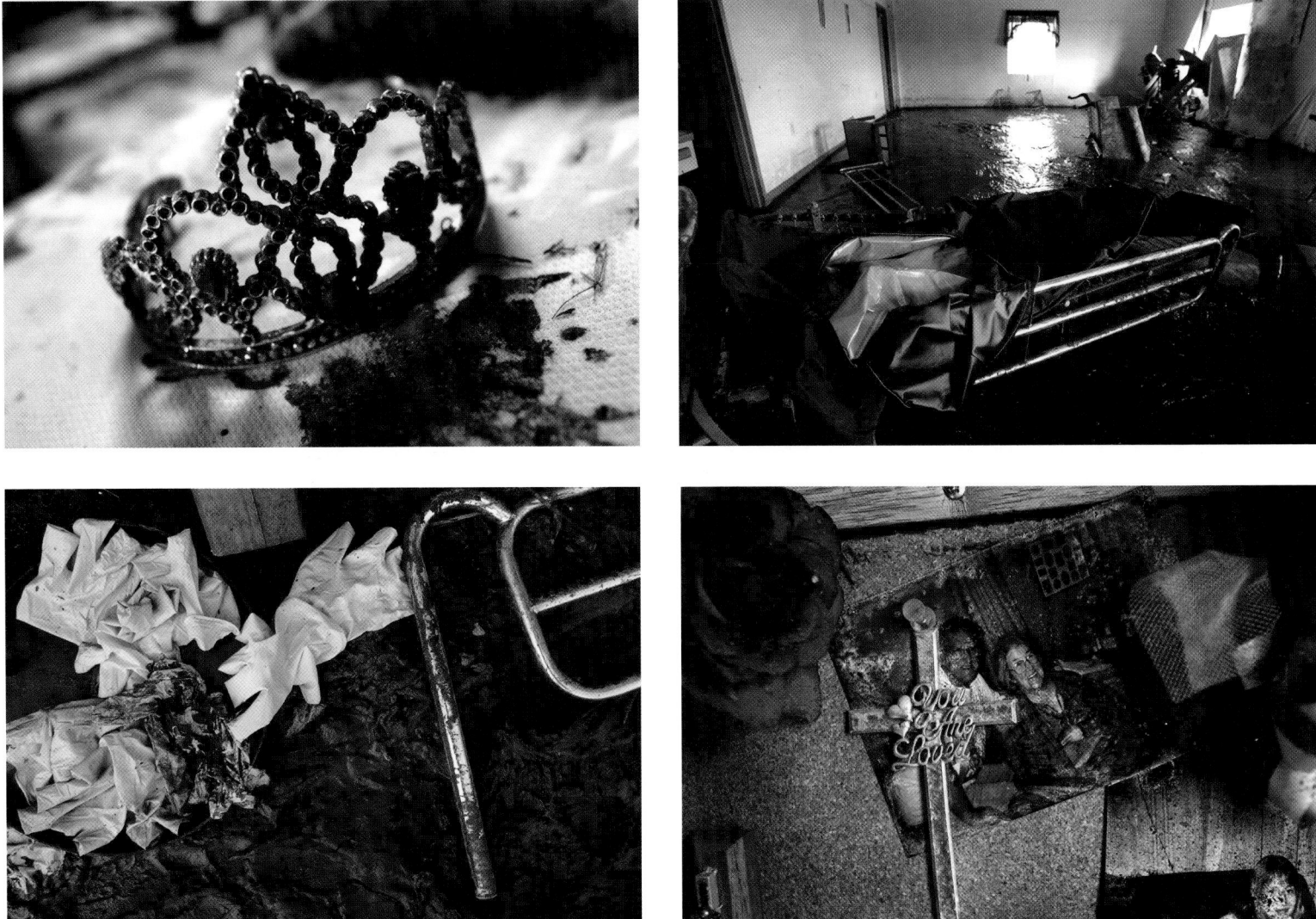

09.15.05 - St. Bernard, LA - No one knows for sure why officials of St. Rita's, a privately owned nursing home, chose not to evacuate. The owners have been charged with negligent homicide. Items left behind include (clockwise from top left) a tiara, extra body bags, family pictures and crosses from the room of Helen Perret (pictured), and used gloves. Neighbors said the home had been a happy place. • ERICH SCHLEGEL

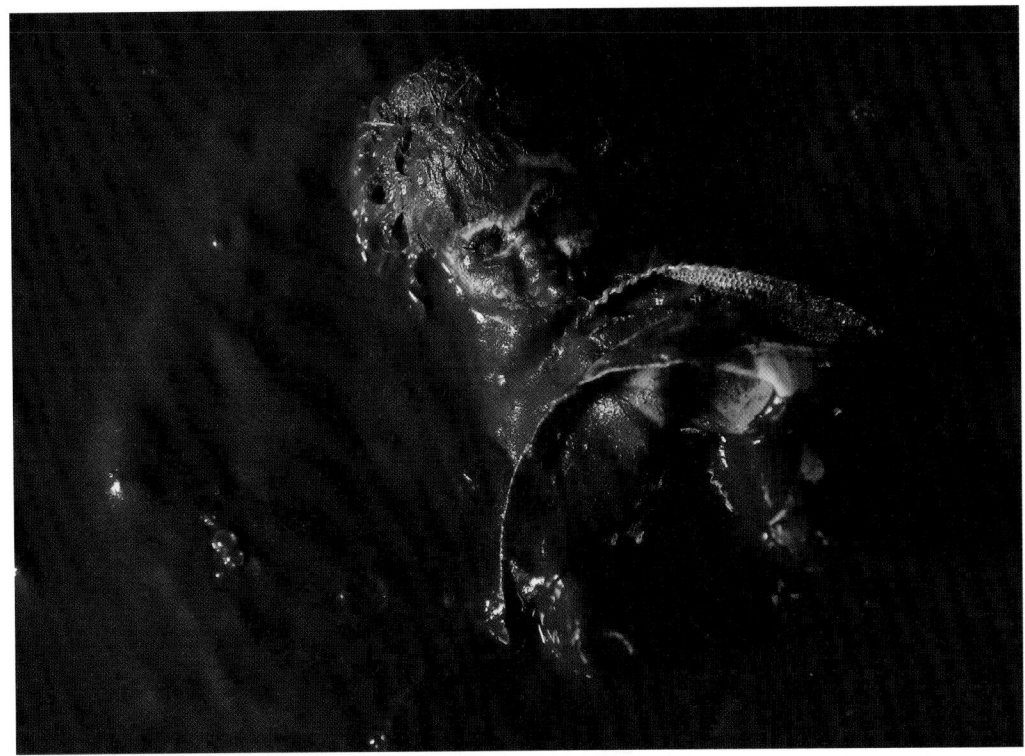

LOST AND FORGOTTEN

The agony of St. Bernard Parish lies in a stinking, mud-choked nursing home named for the patron saint of the lost and forgotten.

The wall of water and misery unleashed by Hurricane Katrina came up hard and fast, wreaking biblical horror at St. Rita's Nursing Center as it rolled across this working-class suburban parish southeast of New Orleans.

Patricia Buffone, a licensed practical nurse, worked at St. Rita's and was among the survivors. "The water came up so fast, and we were grabbing everyone we could," she said. "We just couldn't reach everyone in time."

Authorities finally removed 34 bodies from the home 10 days after the hurricane, and the nursing home sits abandoned, filled with the belongings of those who lived and died inside its brick and steel walls.

• LEE HANCOCK

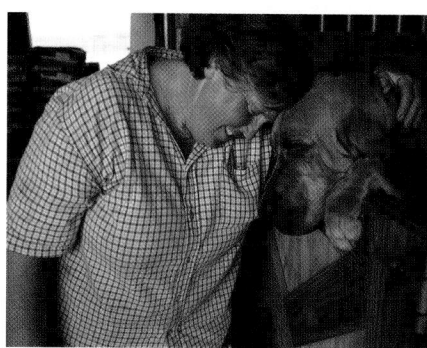

09.16.05 - Home Place, LA - Patty Vogt leans on a friend's bloodhound for consolation after a hard day of trying to rescue her stranded cattle. • ERICH SCHLEGEL

SACRED COWS: A PROMISE KEPT

PORT SULPHUR, La. — Patty Vogt is a red-faced fighter with a pistol in her pocket and an attitude, ready to take on all that a killer hurricane left behind to save what's left of her beloved family farm.

To an outsider, the battle seems quixotic: How can saving a small herd of 60 cows matter to a family that lost almost everything it owned, in a region that has seen so much unvarnished human misery?

For the Vogts and their sister Monica Wertz, the battle is about something bigger. It's about compassion and promises to those who came before, about wresting shreds of meaning from a world that they no longer recognize.

An agriculture man from the federal government flatly told Miss Vogt that the herd that somehow stayed alive for weeks in the stinking green water wasn't worth one of the bags of feed he'd grudgingly handed over.

"I pull my .25 on him," she tells anyone who will listen, patting the front pocket of her grimy blue jeans where she carries a worn Beretta .25-caliber automatic. "I tell his boss, 'Don't send him back down here, 'cause I'll knock his lights out'."

"We get a few more cows out, then I can have peace of mind. I don't care if it's six cows. I'm gonna fight to save them," said Miss Vogt, 51. "When we caught the first, just the other day, we had to rassle it, and we nearly flipped the boat in 30 feet of water. But I said, 'At least we got this one. And we gonna call this calf Baby Katrina'."

Her brother John, 55, says: "To leave 'em there, that's cruelty. All they doing is suffering. You can't stand by."

• LEE HANCOCK

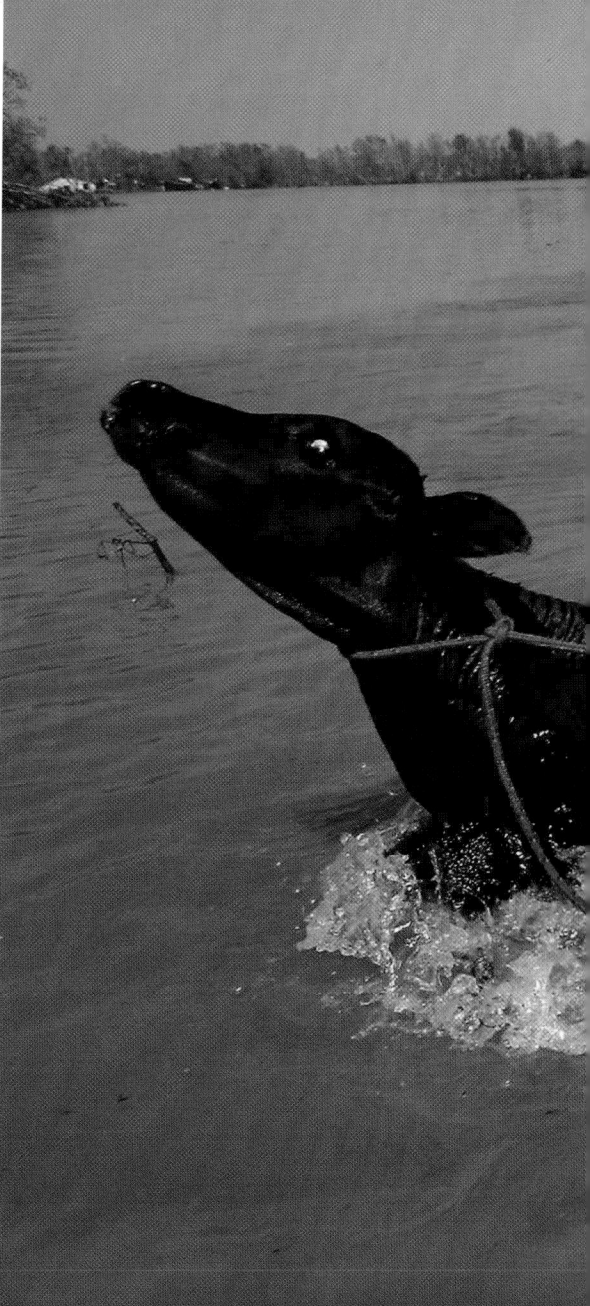

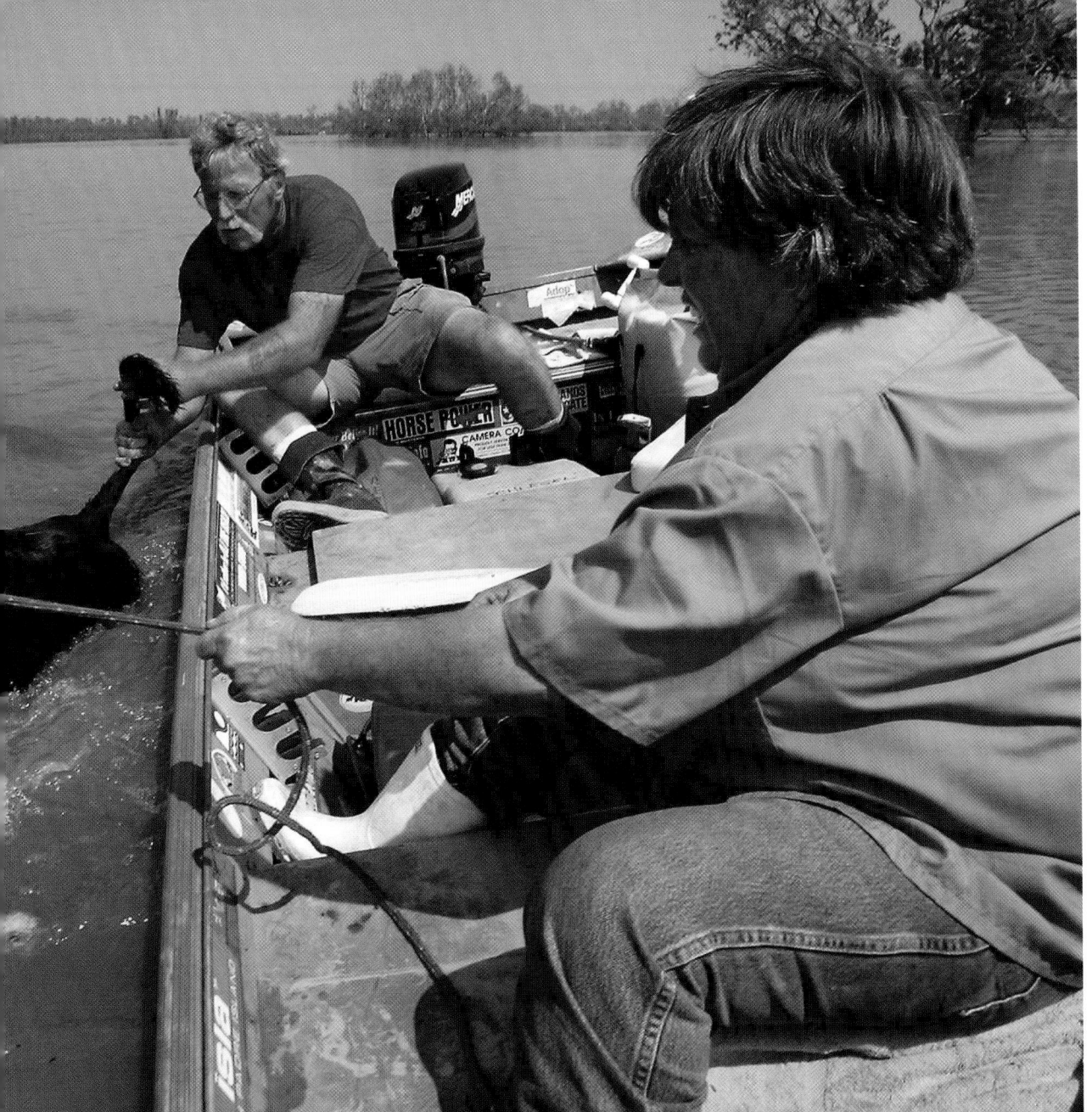

09.12.05 - Port Sulphur, LA - Patty Vogt tried to get some answers from Rusty Berry, a U.S. Department of Agriculture veterinary inspector. Mr. Berry was trying to get the necessary equipment to save Ms. Vogt's cattle, but government bureacracy was slowing things down. • ERICH SCHLEGEL

BELOW
09.14.05 - Port Sulphur, LA - Ms. Vogt and Mr. Morris brought feed to her cattle stranded on the bayou levee, trying to keep them alive.
• ERICH SCHLEGEL

BELOW RIGHT
09.16.05 - Home Place, LA - Ms. Vogt got a hug from neighbor Margaret Bulot, who had heard a report that t Ms. Vogt had been declared dead.
• ERICH SCHLEGEL

OPPOSITE PAGE
09.18.05 - Home Place, LA - Ms. Vogt took a breather from cleaning out her damaged house.
• ERICH SCHLEGEL

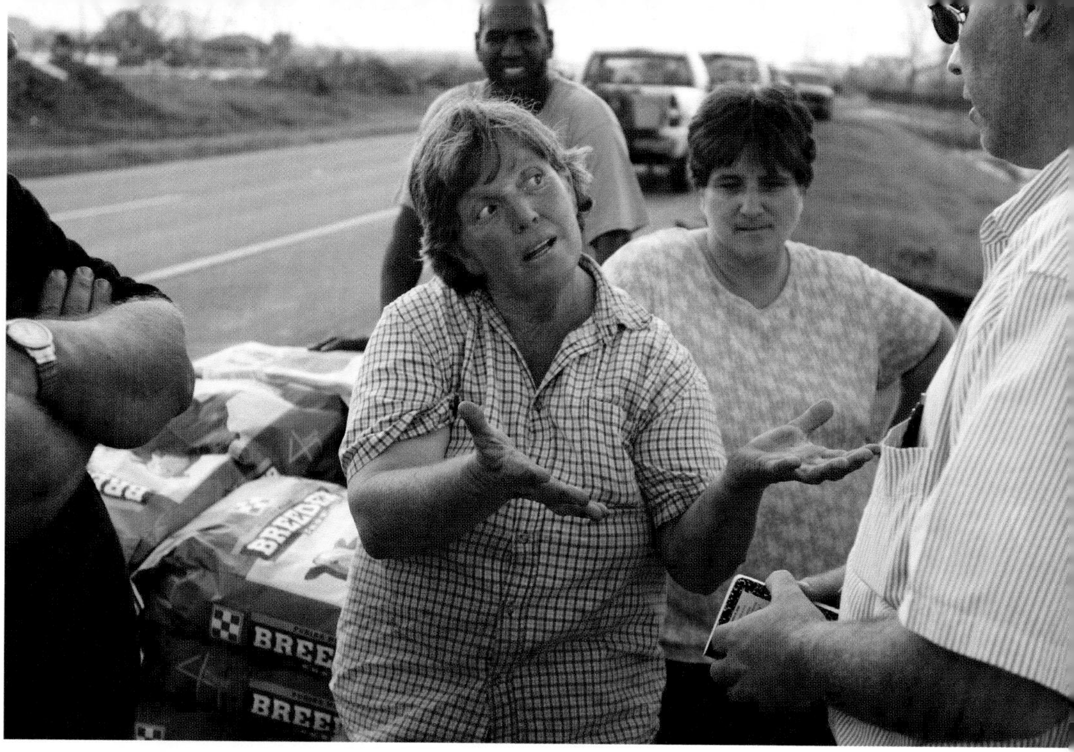

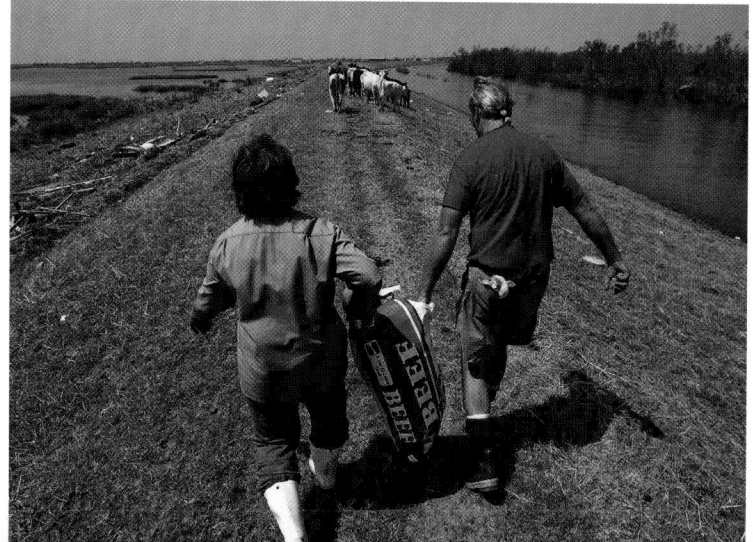

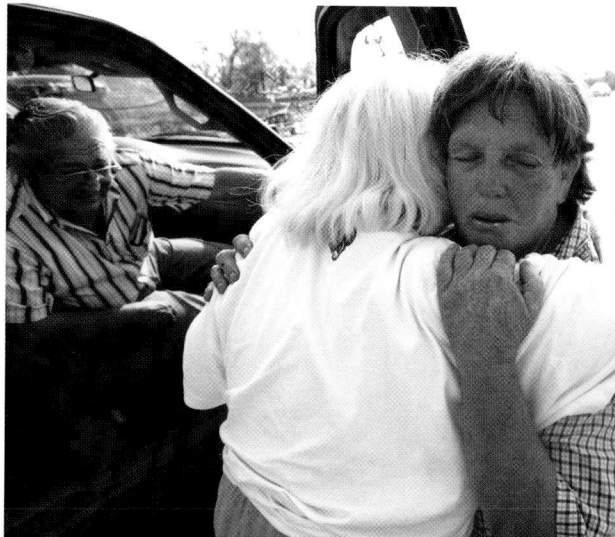

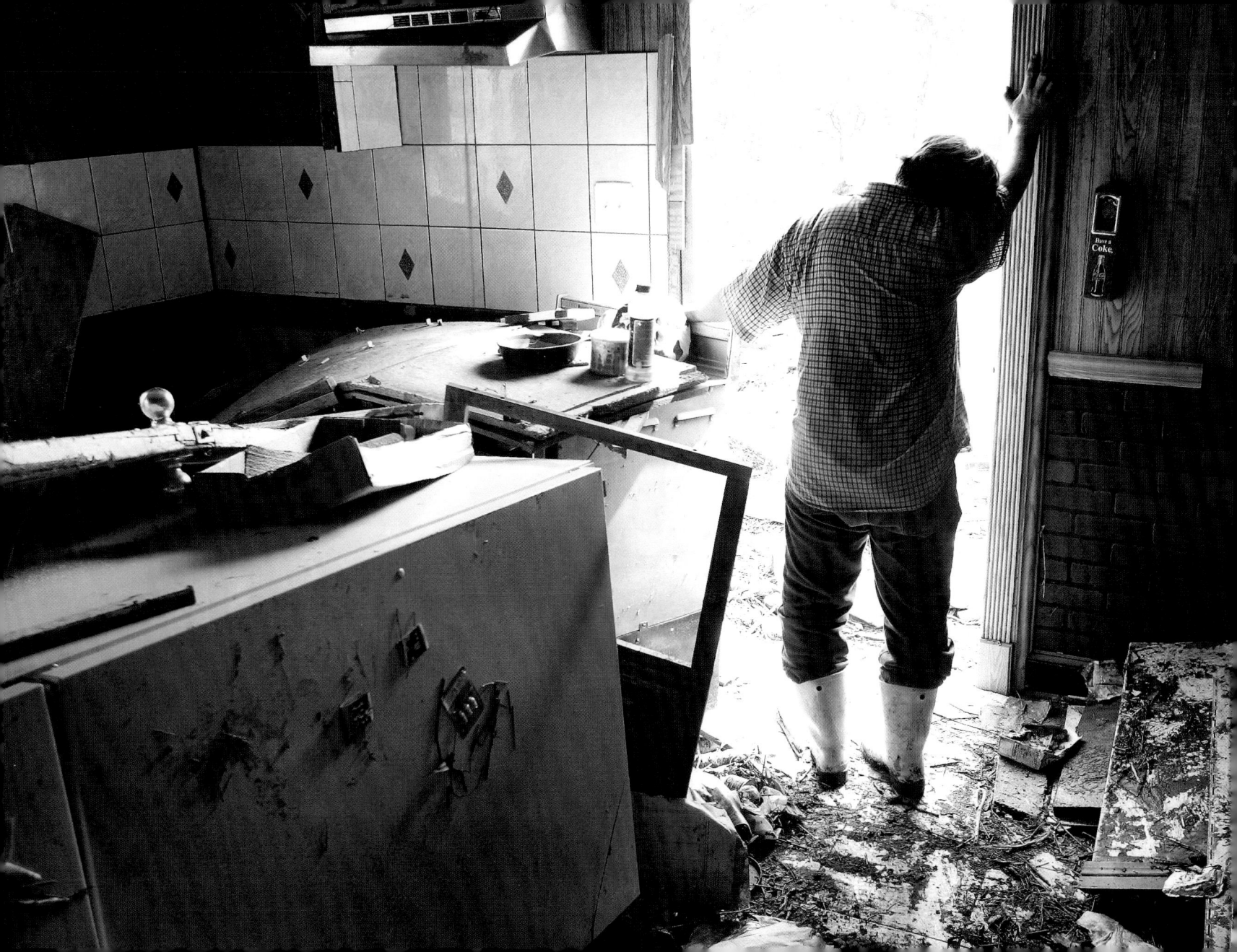

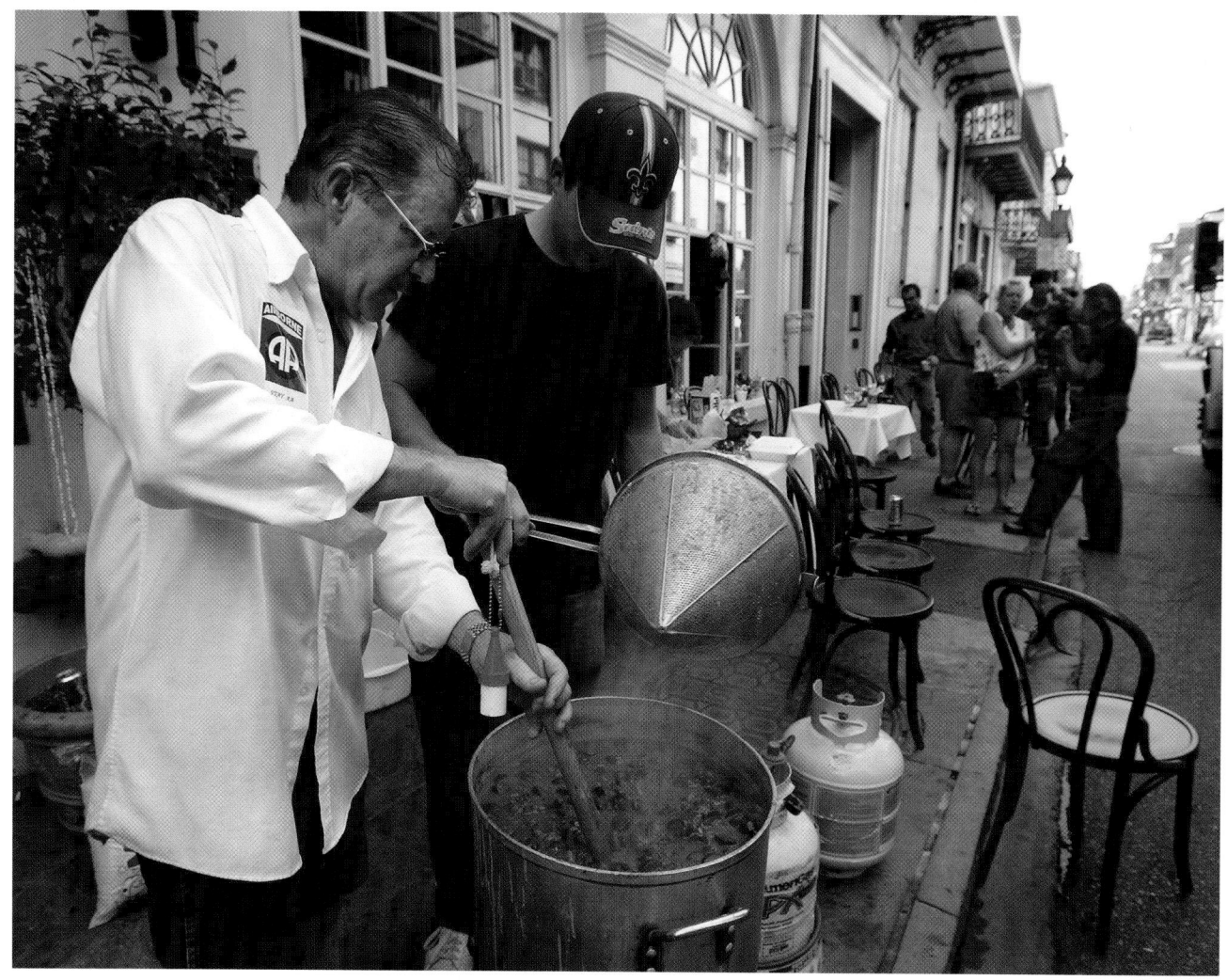

09.17.05 - New Orleans, LA - Finis Shelnutt (left) got help from friend Tim Shirah as he cooked red beans and rice on the sidewalk outside his club on St. Louis Street. He was giving the food away and planned to reopen his club as soon as the electricity was back on. • RICHARD MICHAEL PRUITT

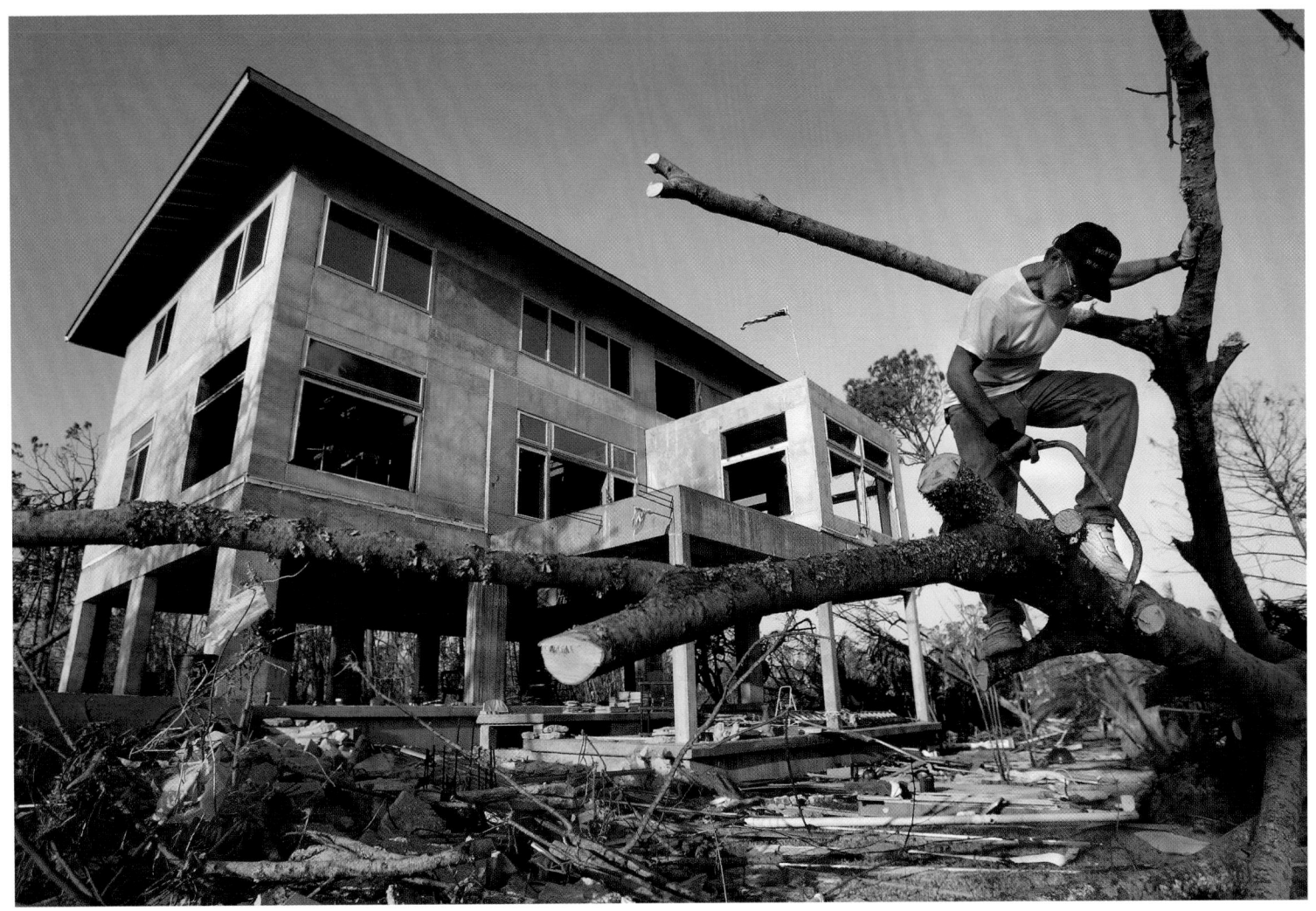

09.21.05 - New Orleans, LA - Scott Sundberg trimmed a limb from a water oak in front of his home under construction in Pass Christian. Mr. Sundberg and his wife, Caroline, were in the process of building their dream home along East Scenic Drive when Hurricane Katrina hit. Their concrete and stucco home was mostly untouched, but the condos in front of their home and most of the structures in their neighborhood were leveled. • BRAD LOPER

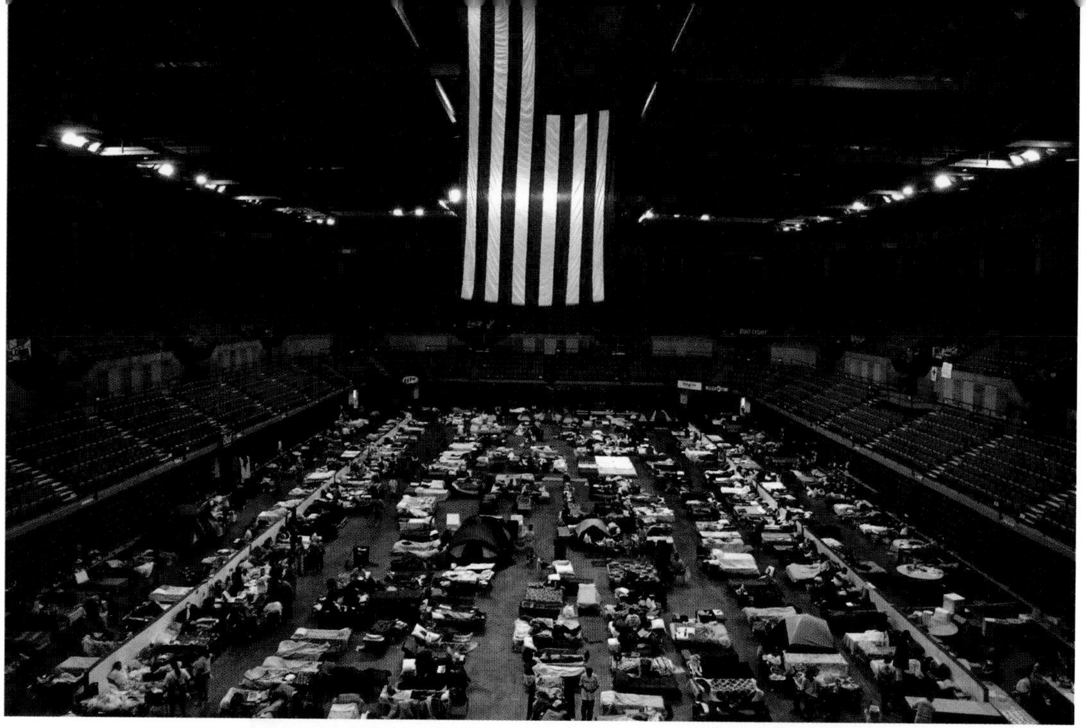

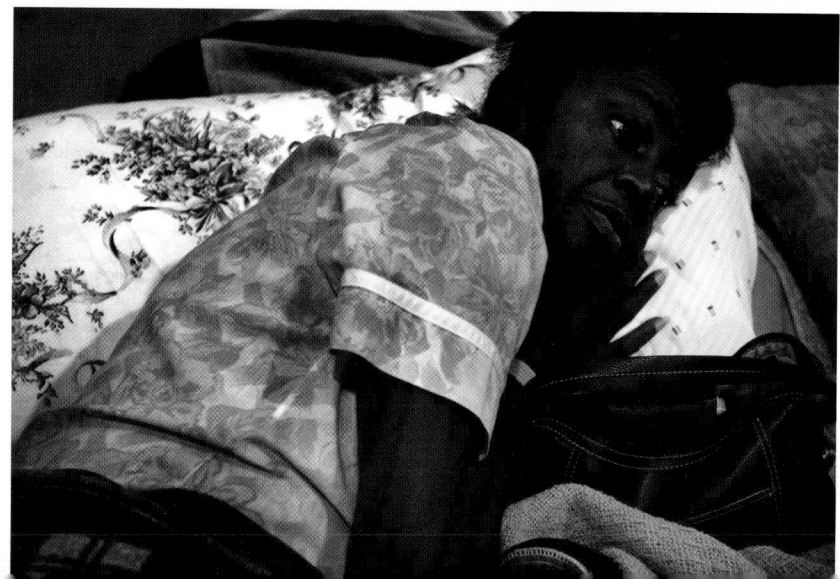

09.15.05 - New Orleans, LA - At its peak, the River Center shelter (above) housed 4,000 to 5,000 evacuees, including a weak Diane West, 58 (right), who was enduring dialysis three times a week. In the shelters closest to New Orleans, frustration and anger were setting in - over the living conditions, the situation and what evacuees and volunteers alike said was a lack of answers. • BARBARA DAVIDSON

<small>OPPOSITE PAGE</small>
09.21.05 - New Orleans, LA - Starting over, together: The Rev. Diane Baker took the rings from New Orleans evacuees Ricky and Tamika Smith, who married at the Dallas County hurricane center, where they had been living with their five kids. They didn't plan to return to Louisiana. • TOM FOX

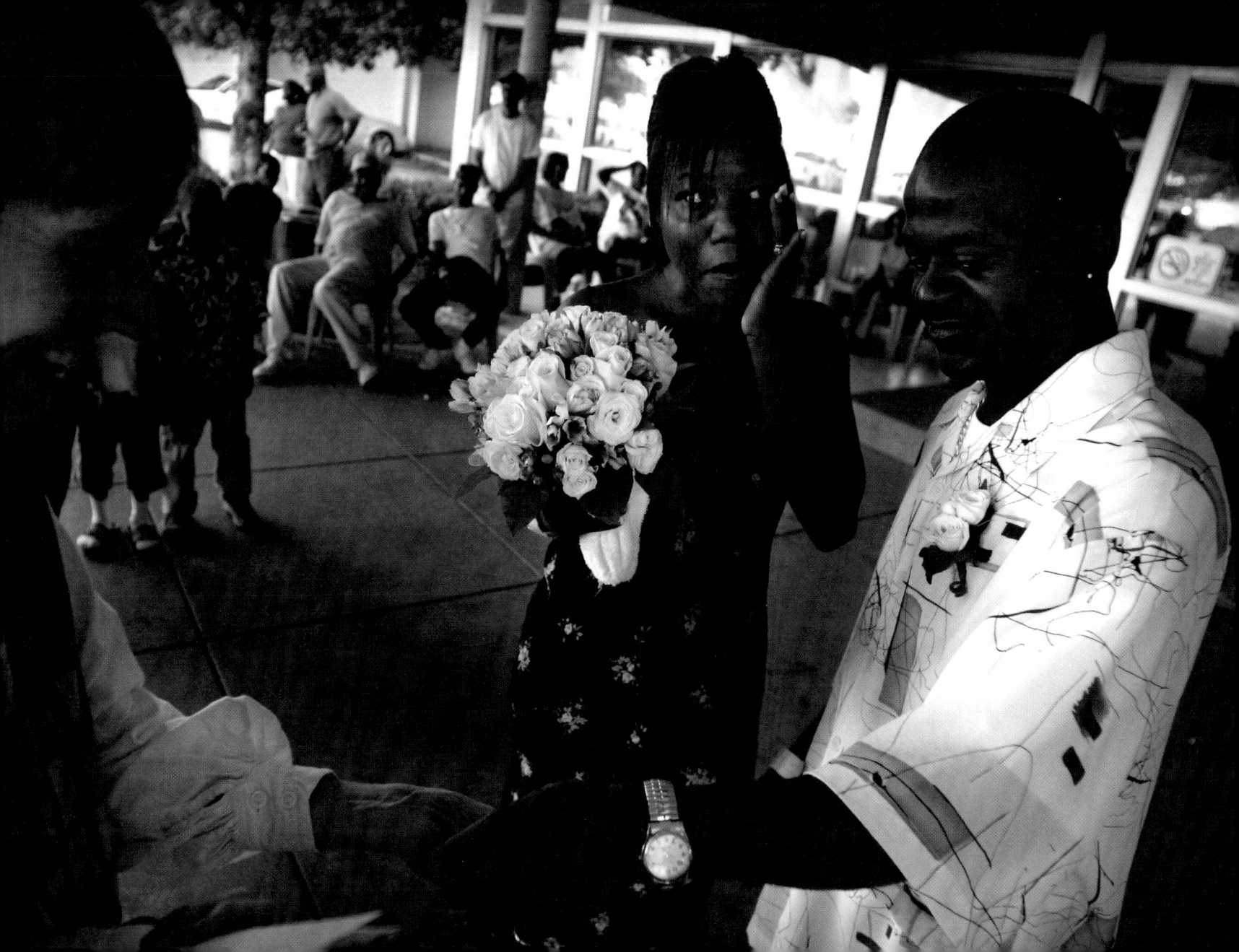

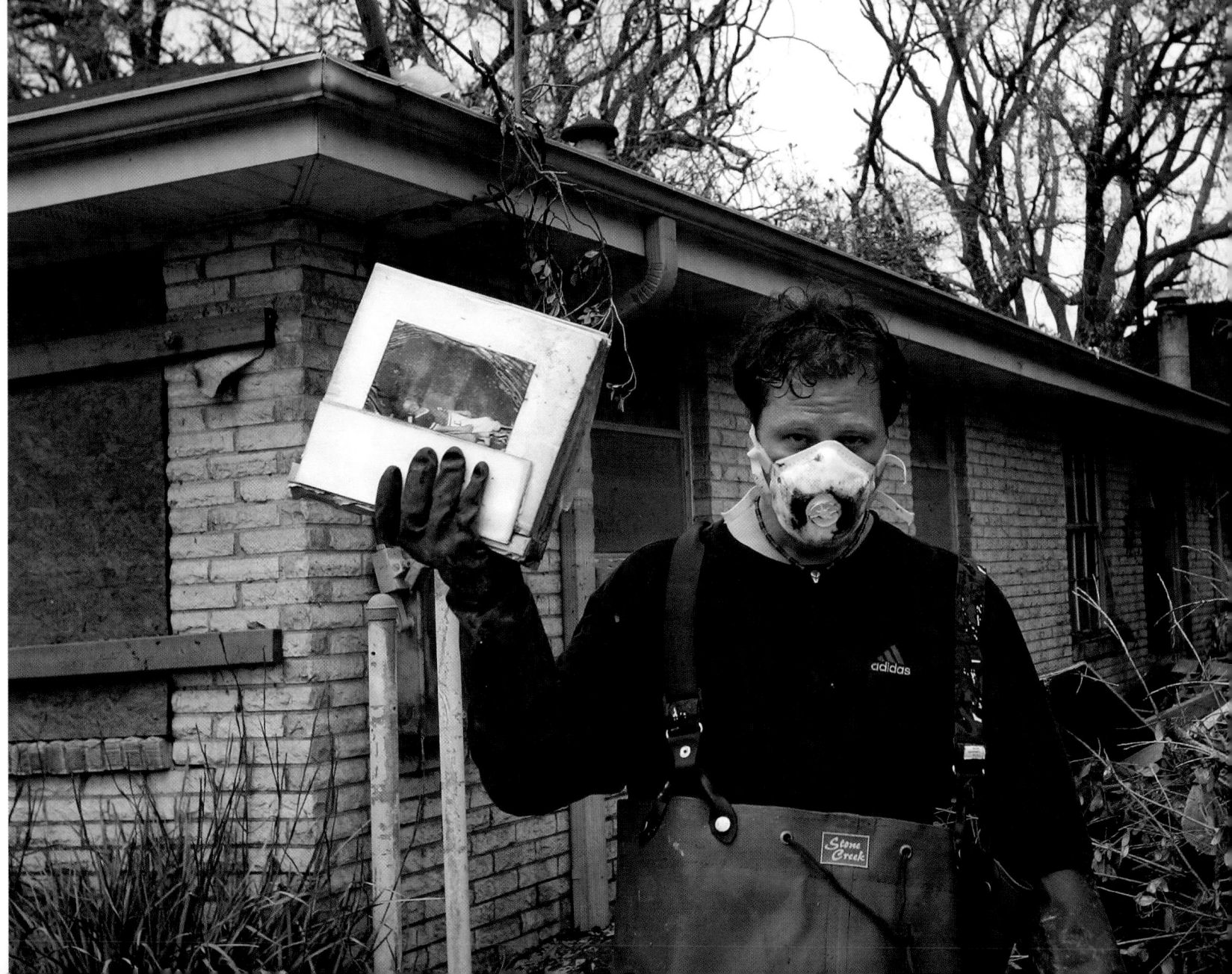

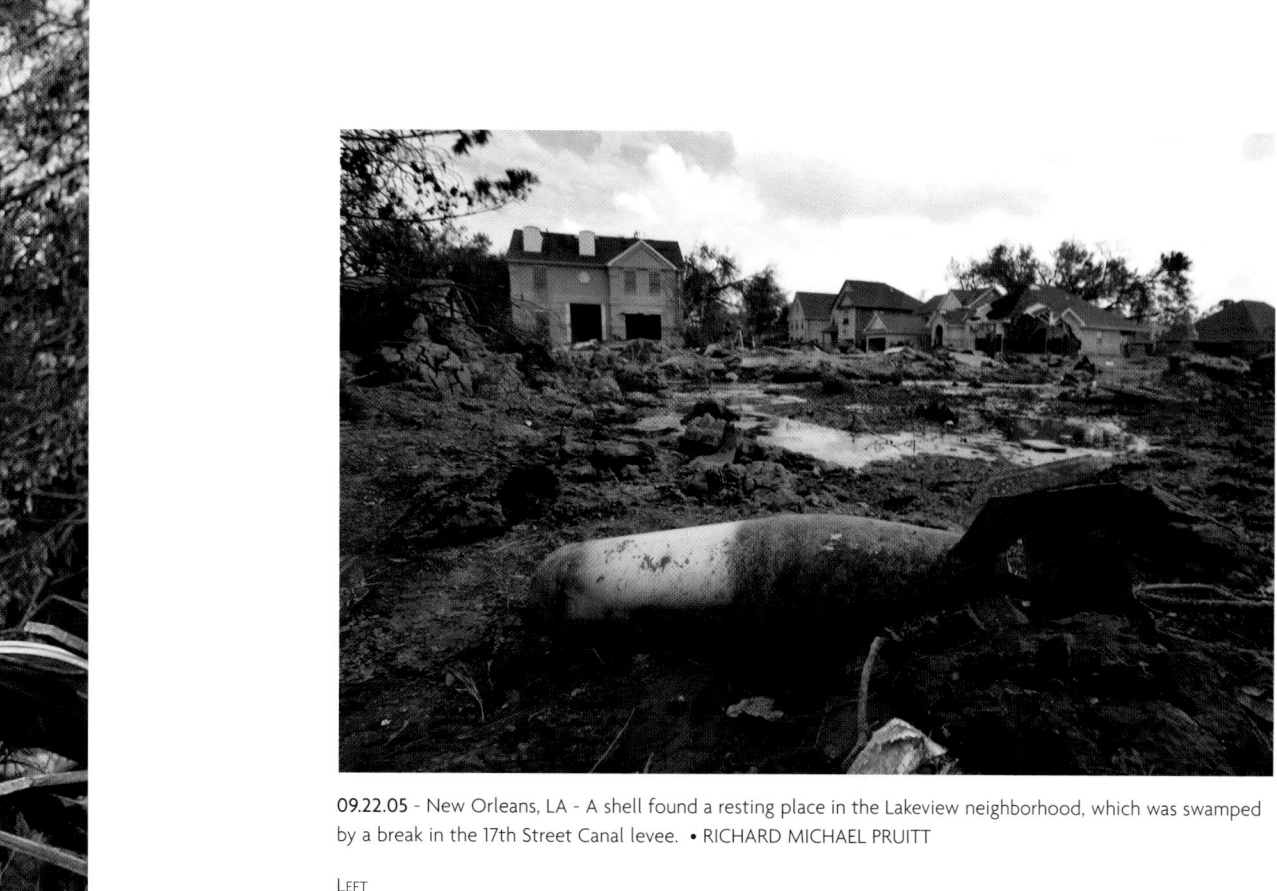

09.22.05 - New Orleans, LA - A shell found a resting place in the Lakeview neighborhood, which was swamped by a break in the 17th Street Canal levee. • RICHARD MICHAEL PRUITT

<small>LEFT</small>
09.22.05 - New Orleans, LA - When Mark Maggio returned to his childhood home in the Lakeview neighborhood, he had to pull on chest-high waders, thick gloves and a medical mask to face the unseen dangers brewed up during the house's three weeks under water. Then he came upon his biggest find - a scrapbook filled with photos from his team's run at the Babe Ruth League World Series title when he was 13. "I get to go through it like buried treasure," he said. • BRAD LOPER

OUT OF HARM'S WAY

More than 1 million people took to the highways and booked every available room inland as Hurricane Rita - one of the most powerful storms ever to threaten - continued on a collision course with the coastline.

Gas stations were running dry as roads filled with outbound traffic. Officials estimated that more than 1 million people, a fifth of the Houston metro area, were headed for higher ground.

Texas' ability to cope with Rita was strained by the thousands of evacuees who were escaping Hurricane Katrina's rampage in Louisiana and Mississippi.

In Houston, Mayor Bill White and Harris County Judge Robert Eckels requested the evacuation of low-lying areas and mobile home parks and said areas along Galveston Bay would be first on the list for mandatory evacuation.

• BRUCE NICHOLS

09.22.05 - Corsicana, TX - Now it was Houston's turn: Motorists from the Houston/Galveston area, threatened by Hurricane Rita, crawled north out of harm's way on Interstate 45. All southbound traffic on the highway was halted 200 miles north of Houston. • SMILEY N. POOL

OPPOSITE PAGE
09.22.05 - Houston, TX - Horses belonging to Roger McMillon of Houston got a view of the thousands of Houstonians trying to flee Hurricane Rita by heading west on FM 1093. • ERICH SCHLEGEL

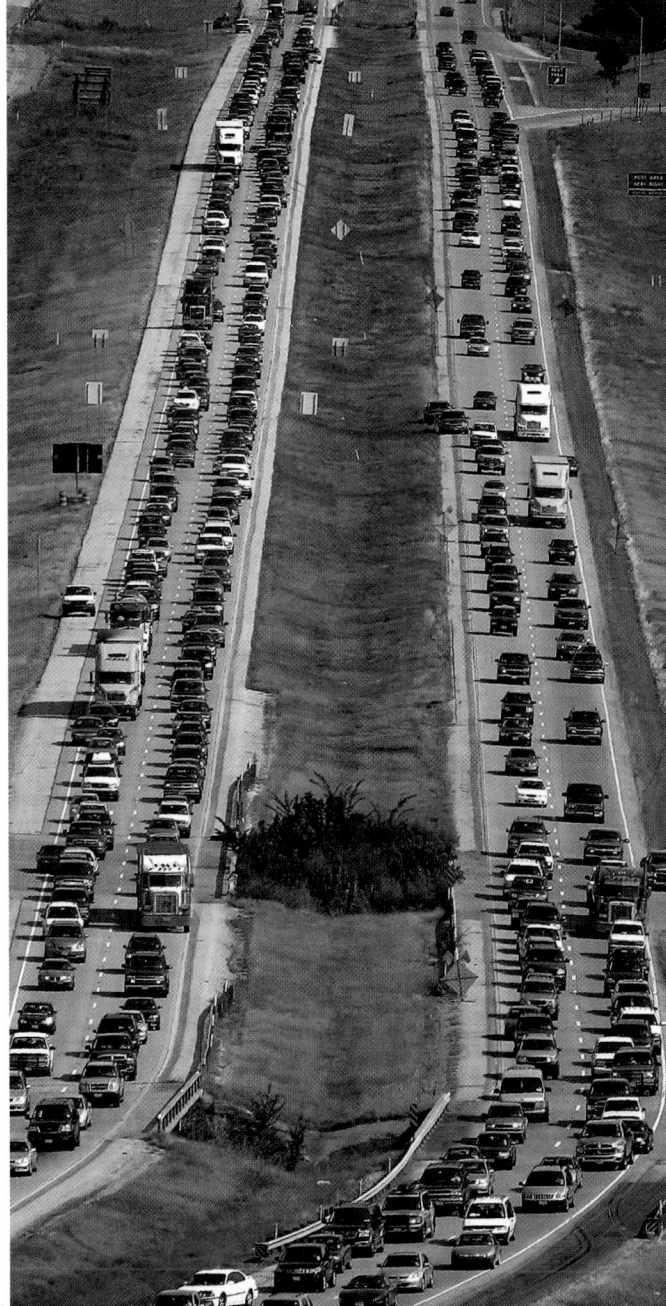

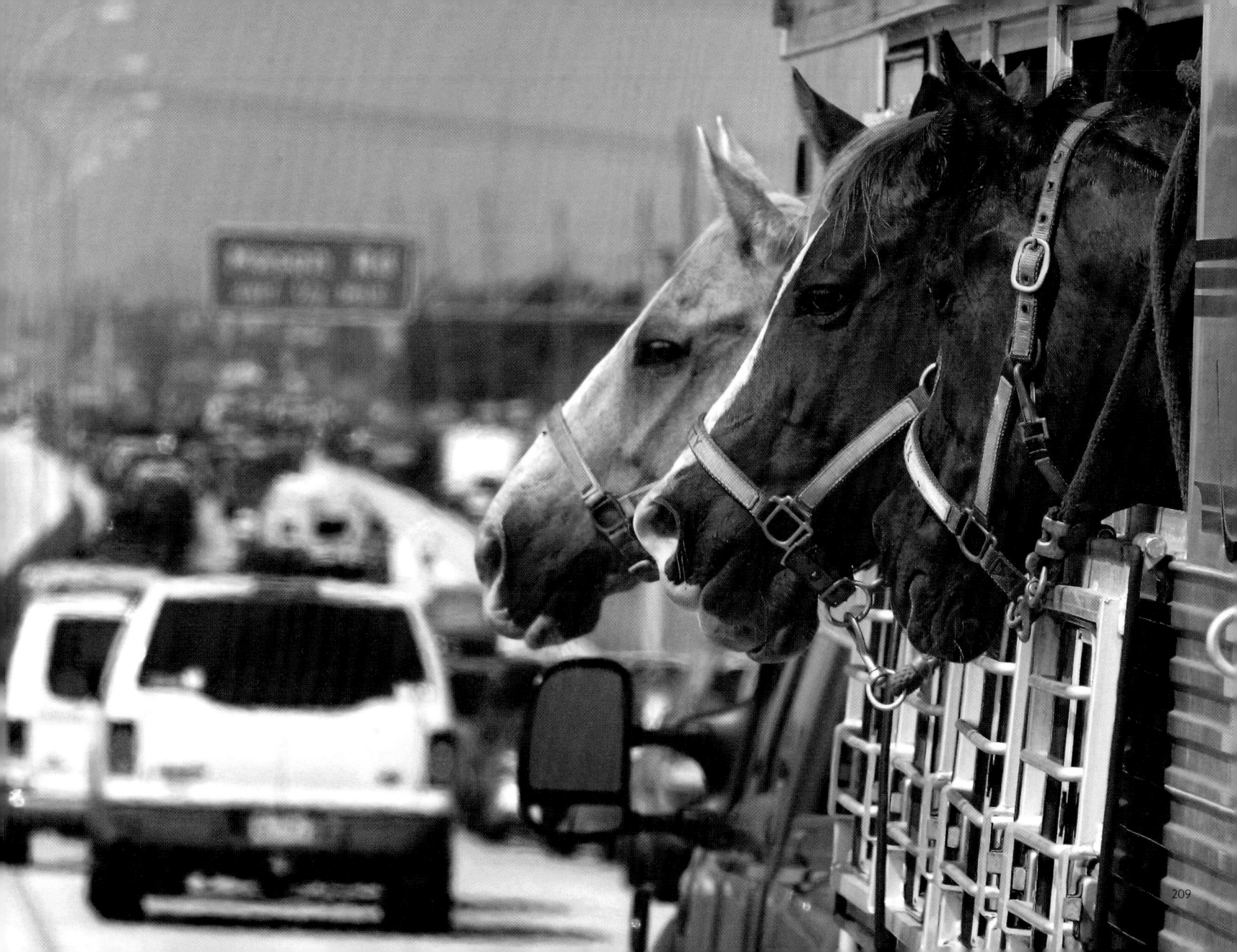

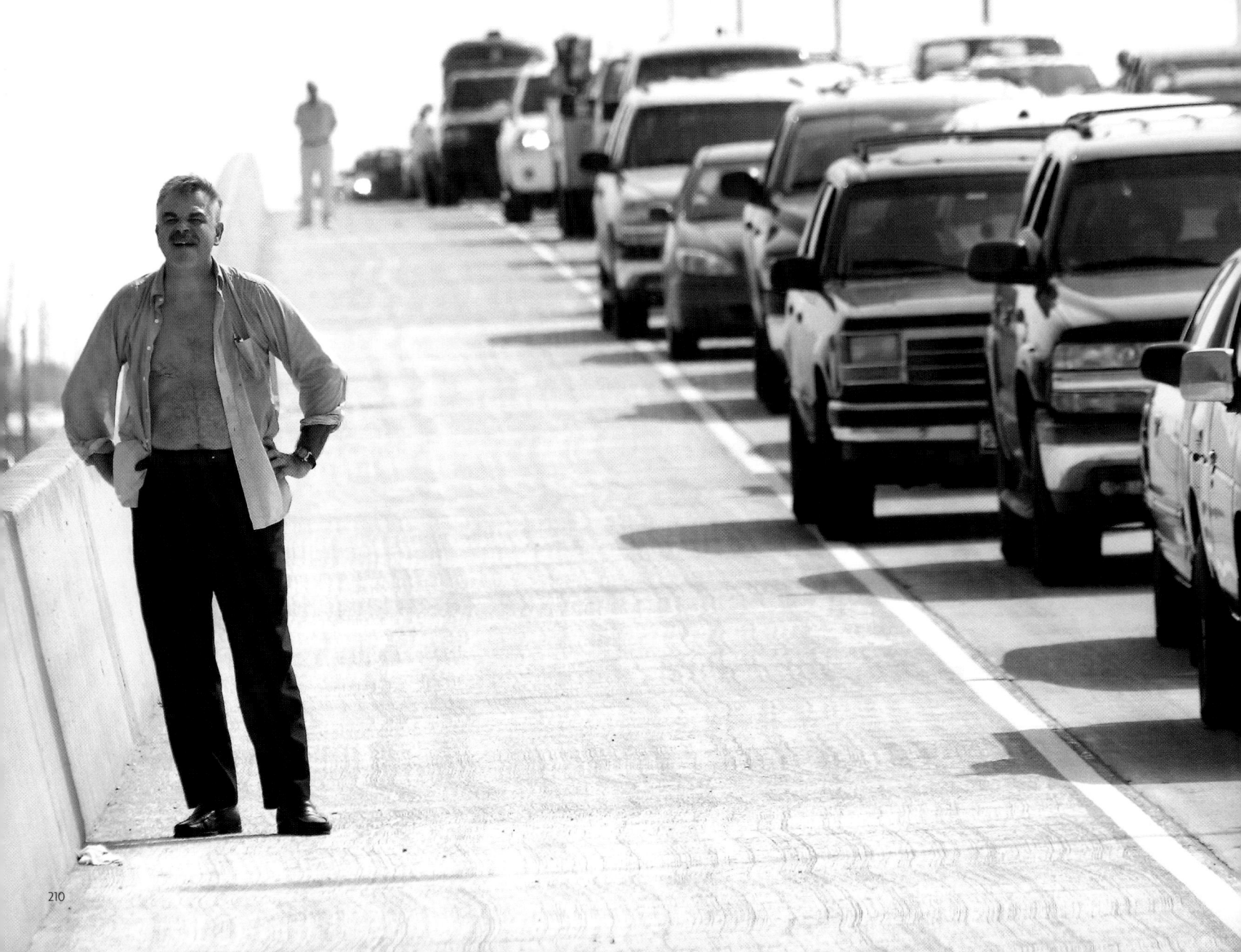

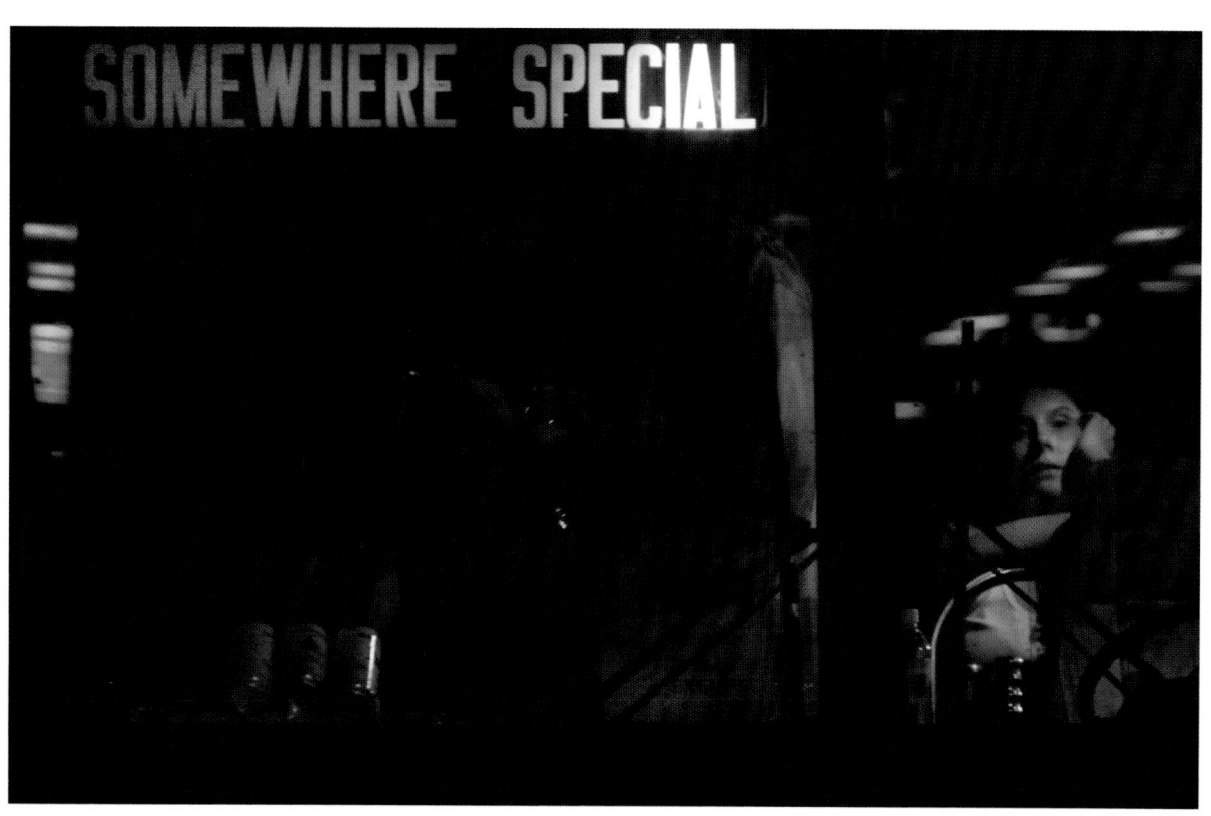

09.22.05 - Houston, TX - Walter Hirka went to Houston on business, then got caught in the exodus. Thousands of Texans spent hours sitting in traffic while trying to get out of Hurricane Rita's way. • ERICH SCHLEGEL

LEFT
09.22.05 - Lake Charles, LA - Residents boarded an evacuation bus at the Lake Charles Civic Center that promised to take them "Somewhere Special." • RICK GERSHON

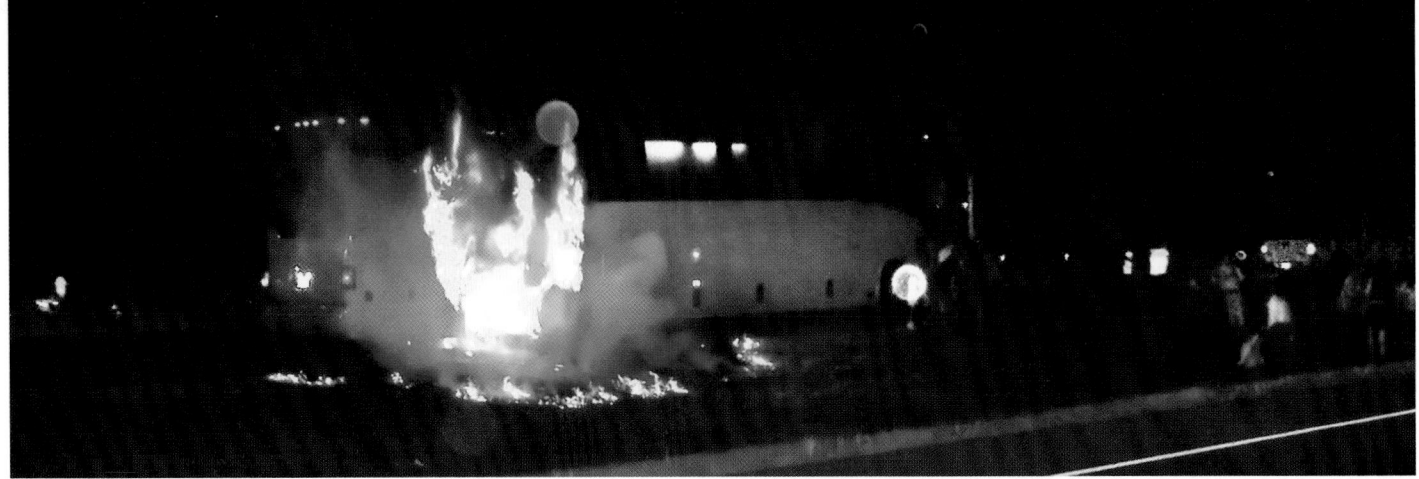

HEADLONG INTO DEATH

All they wanted was to escape death by drowning. Instead, they were consumed by fire.

The 38 nursing home patients from the Houston area used Interstate 45's gray ribbon of pavement to leave Hurricane Rita behind on the Gulf Coast.

Despite advanced age and myriad infirmities, none of them wanted to chance drowning at Brighton Gardens, their home in the low-lying Bellaire area of Houston. They had seen that happen to Louisiana nursing home residents who stayed put during Katrina.

Along with six caregivers and a driver, they boarded a chartered bus and headed to Dallas-area nursing homes that were to provide temporary shelter from the storm.

Two dozen of them never made it.

Flames apparently erupted around the right rear brakes and spread into the cabin, causing several oxygen tanks used by passengers to explode. State officials say it was the worst bus accident in Texas since 1952.

• MICHAEL GRABELL, SCOTT PARKS and DONNA WISDOM

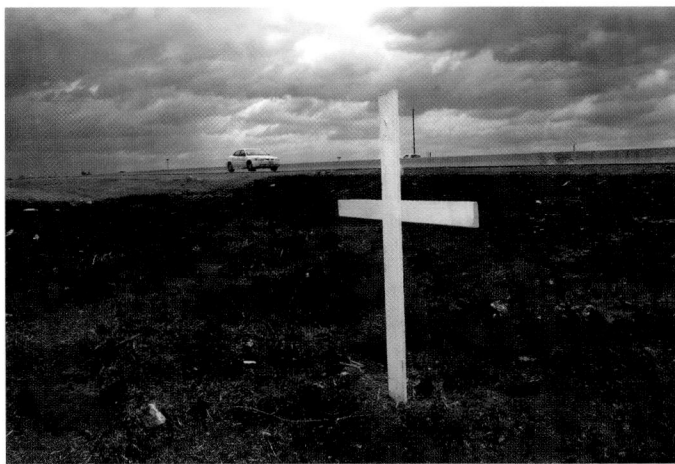

09.23.05 - Wilmer, TX - Thirty-eight infirm nursing home patients from the Houston area, six caregivers and a driver were fleeing Hurricane Rita and were just miles from their Dallas destination when their bus caught fire on Interstate 45 in Wilmer, killing 24. • WAYNE D. COWEY

BOTTOM
09.24.05 - Wilmer, TX - Rest in peace: A cross on Interstate 45 stands in memory to the 24 nursing home patients who died on the bus evacuating them from Houston. • RON BASELICE

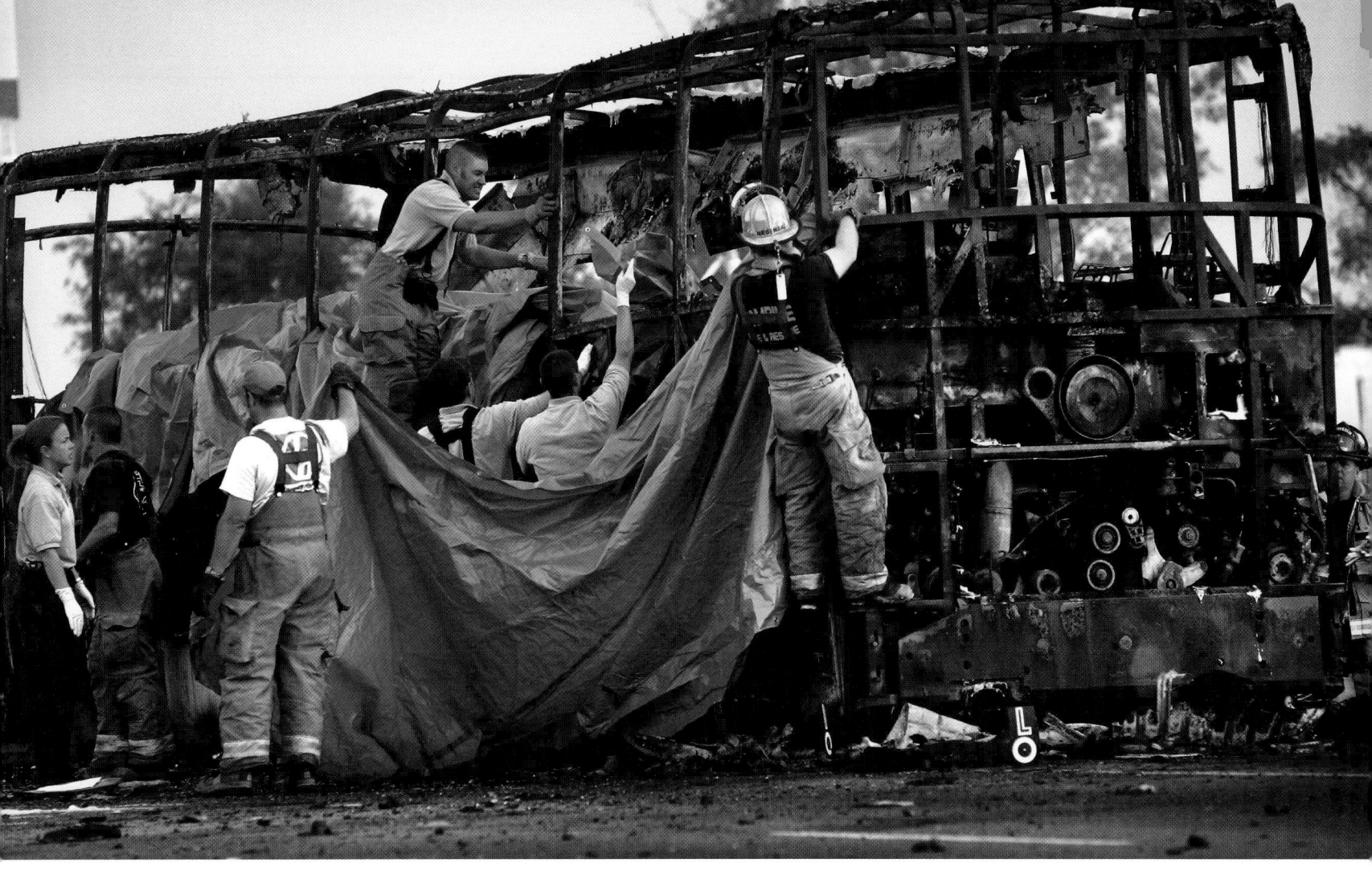

...er, TX - Tarps were used to cover bodies on the bus' charred skeleton. Investigators from the National Transportation Safety Board planned an extensive investigation. • JIM MAHONEY

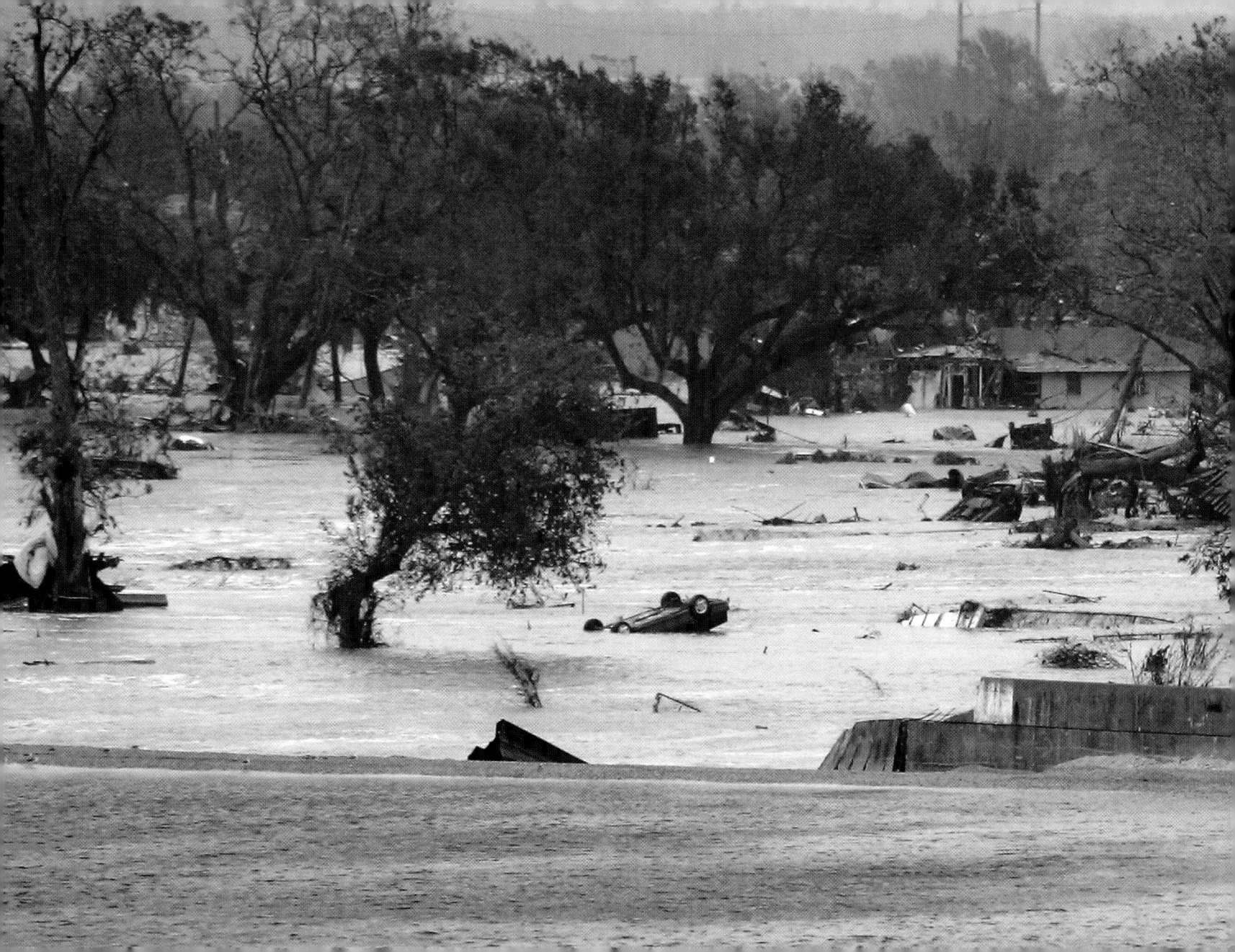

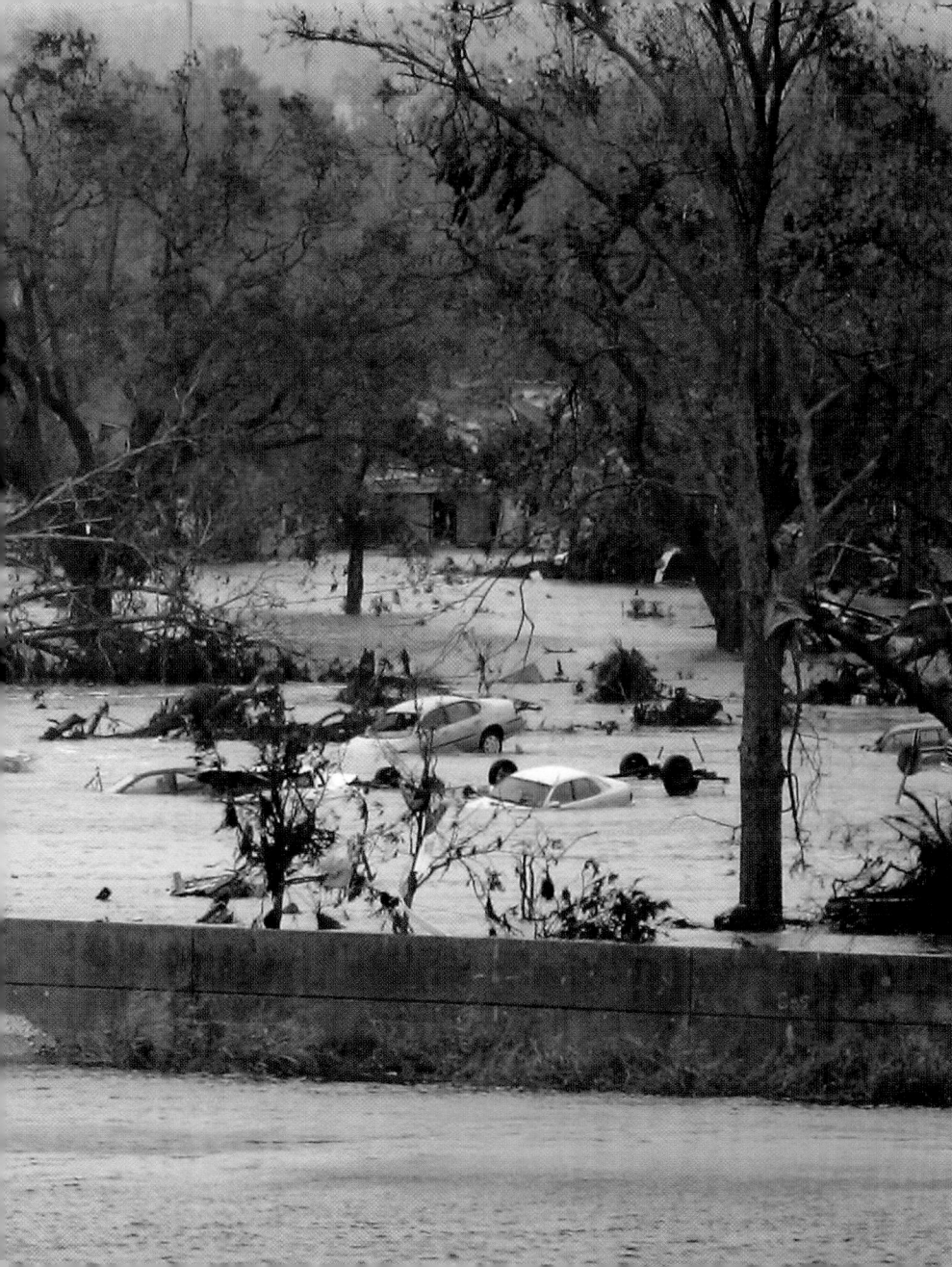

09.23.05 - New Orleans, LA - First Katrina, then Rita: Water poured through gaps in the Industrial Canal levee, again flooding the Ninth Ward following tidal surges from Hurricane Rita. Hurricane-whipped waves also pushed water from Lake Pontchartrain over a seawall.
• BRAD LOPER

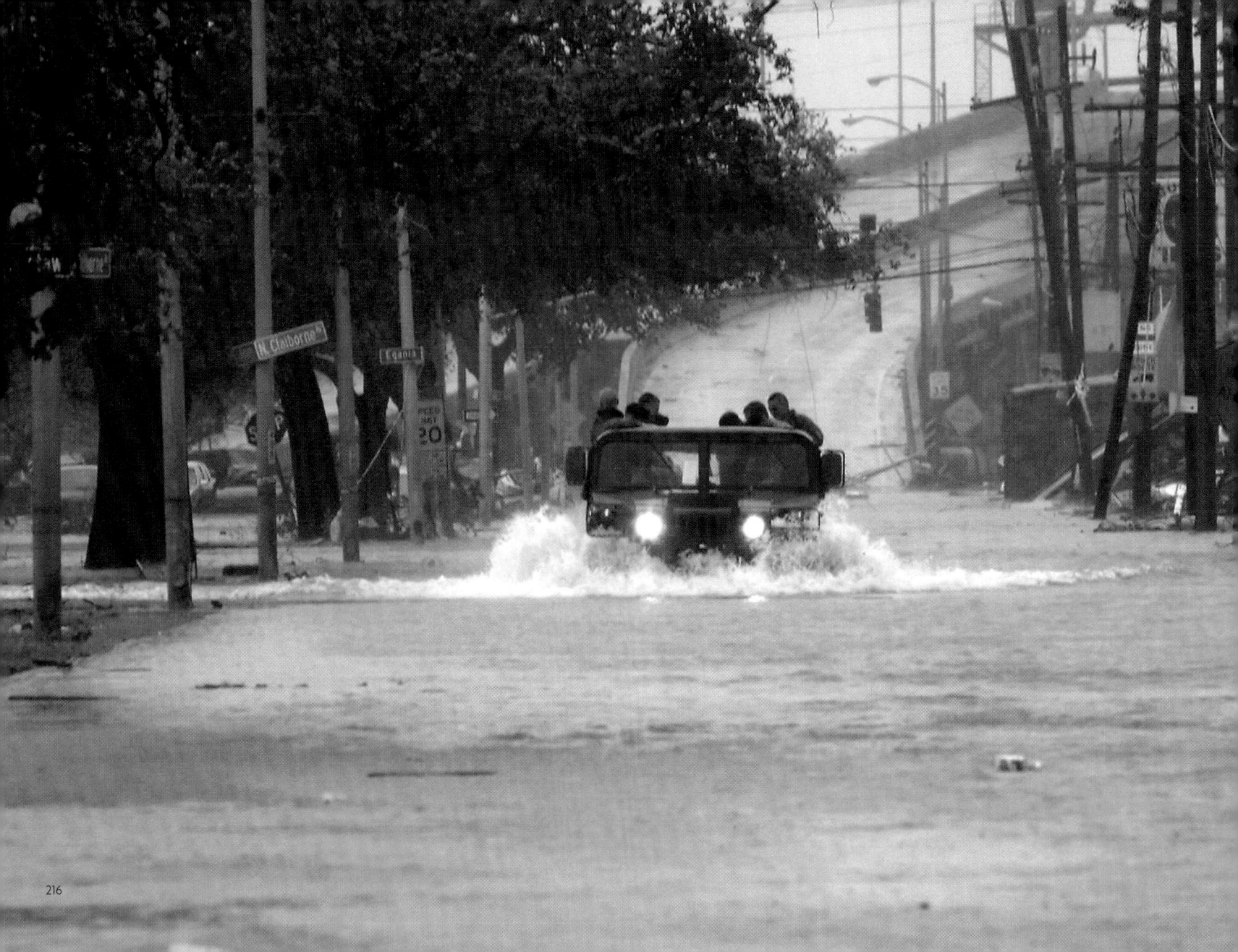

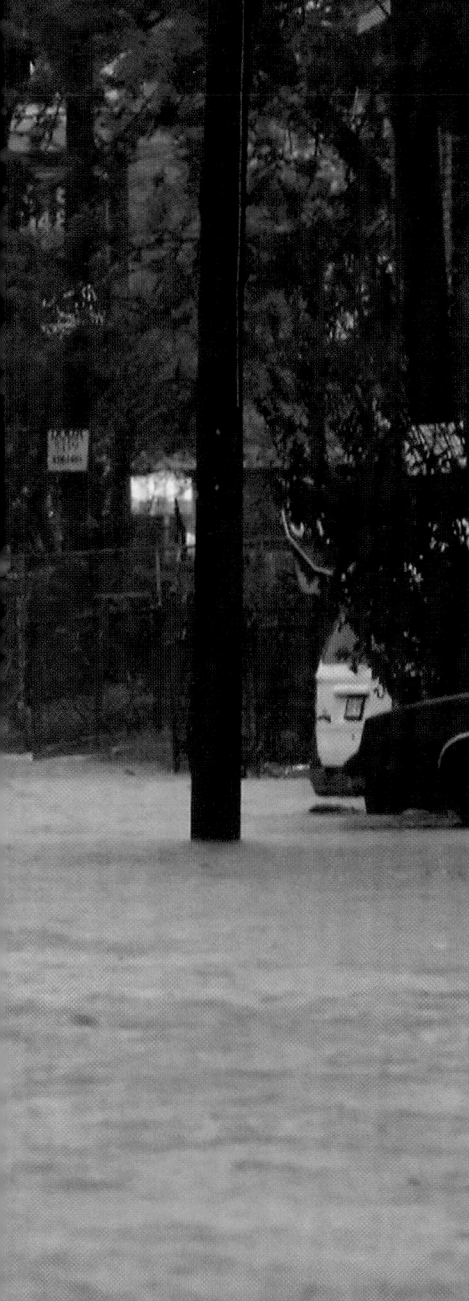

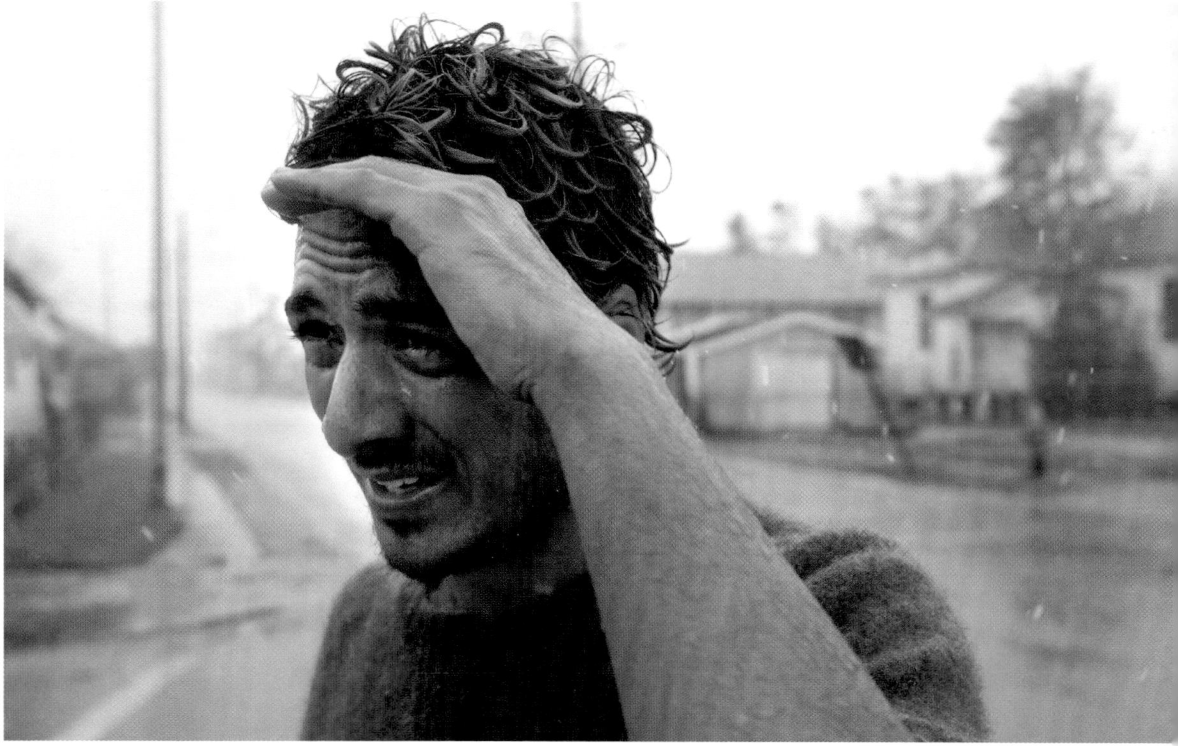

09.23.05 - New Orleans, LA - In the Ninth Ward, Francisco Disantis withstood sweeping sheets of rain and wind courtesy of Hurricane Rita. He was joining a few anarchists and artists who snuck back into the city to begin gutting the flood-damaged ground floor of the L'art Noir gallery on St. Claude Avenue. • RICHARD MICHAEL PRUITT

LEFT
09.23.05 - New Orleans, LA - A military vehicle drove through water as it rose on North Claiborne Avenue by the minute, as water again started flowing over the levee into the Ninth Ward. • BRAD LOPER

09.23.05 - Lake Charles, LA - Eleven-year-old Christopher Thomas clung to his dog Harley as other residents pleaded with him and his mother to leave the dog and evacuate their home.
• RICK GERSHON

RIGHT
09.24.05 - Cedar Hill, TX - Matt Kieschnick, 10, of Evadale, Texas, rode out Hurricane Rita with several family members at Cedar Hill State Park. Many of the families in the park were from some of the most heavily damaged areas.
• VERNON BRYANT

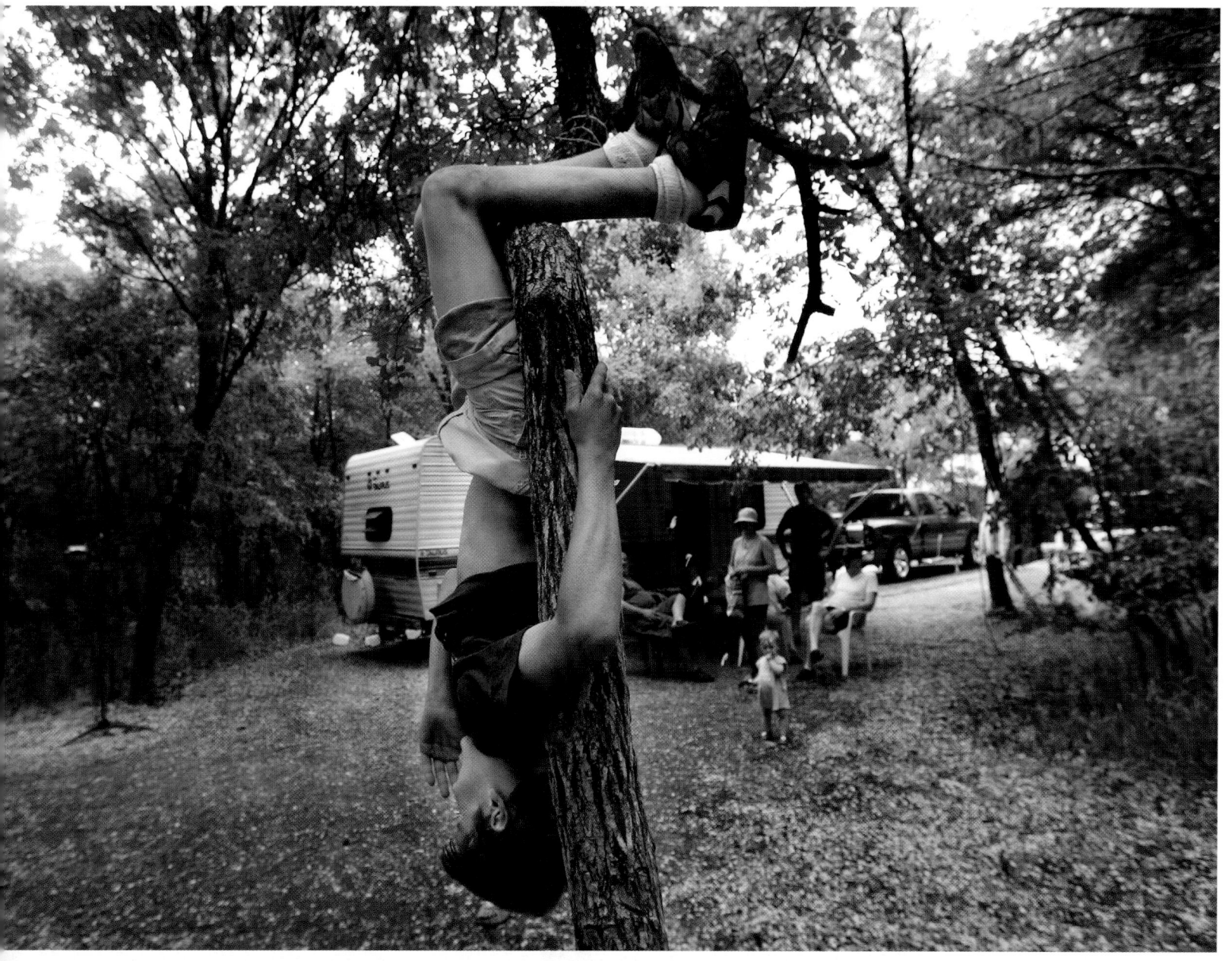

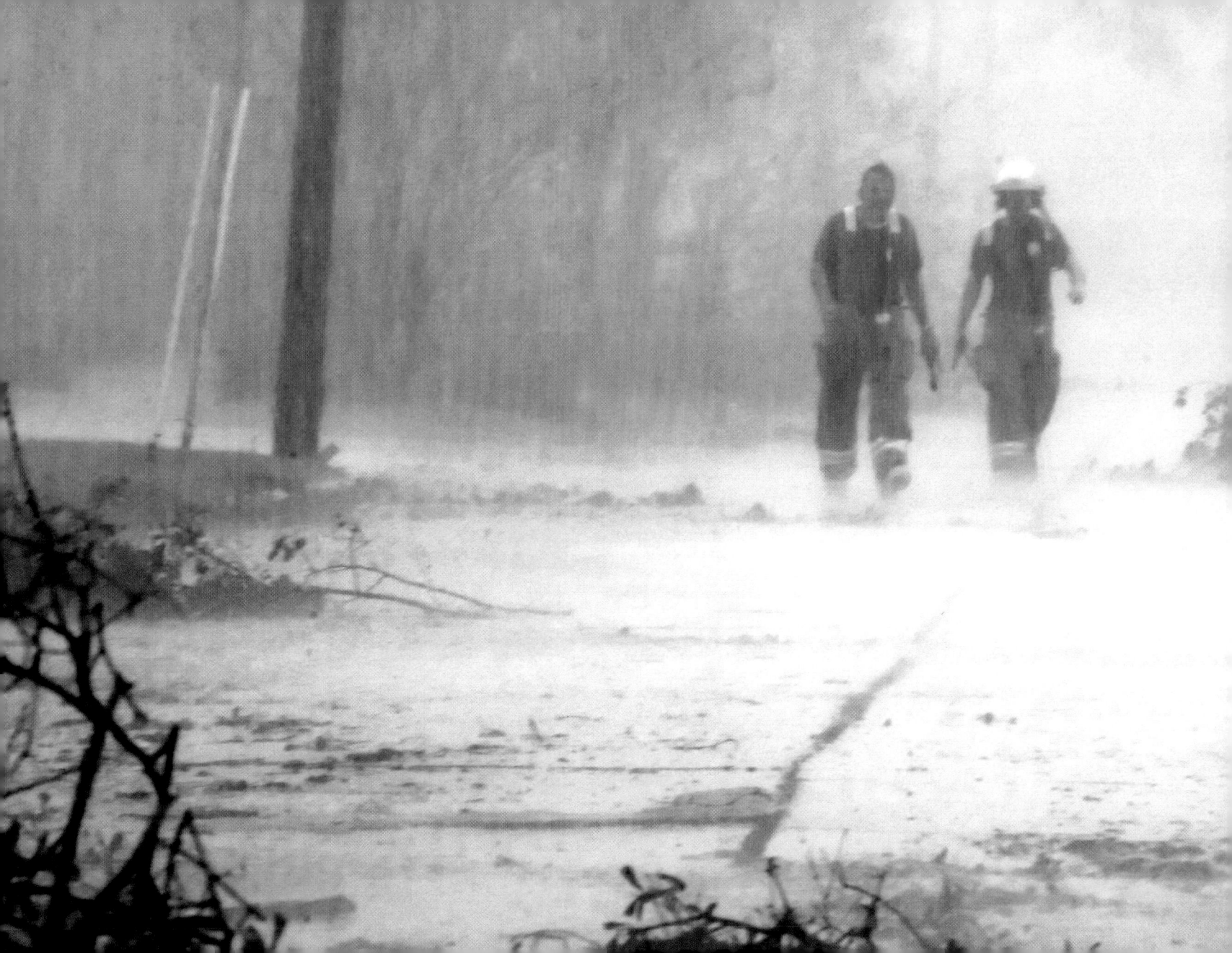

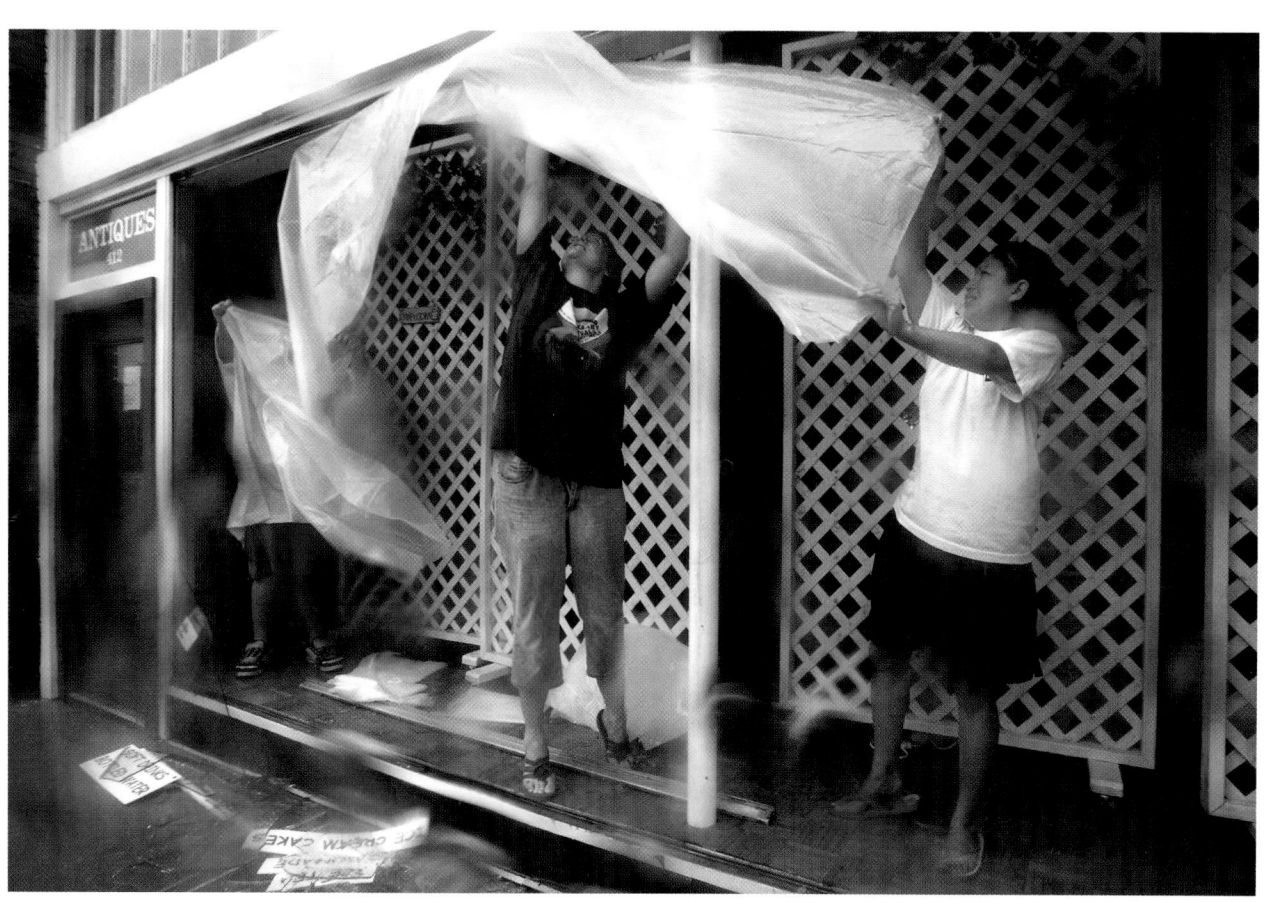

09.24.05 - Nacogdoches, TX - Texans Brian Hart (from left) of Baytown, Michelle Smith of Nacogdoches and Carolina Vargas of Nacogdoches sealed up the hole where a window was before Hurricane Rita ripped through the Nacogdoches Antique Market on Main Street. • LARA SOLT

Left
09.24.05 - Lake Charles, LA - Fire Department Capt. Mike Hebert (left) and firefighter Josh Fountain sloshed down the street in a downpour from Hurricane Rita to check homes for stranded residents. Rita came ashore near the southwestern Louisiana town, but evacuations appeared to have prevented any deaths or serious injuries. • IRWIN THOMPSON

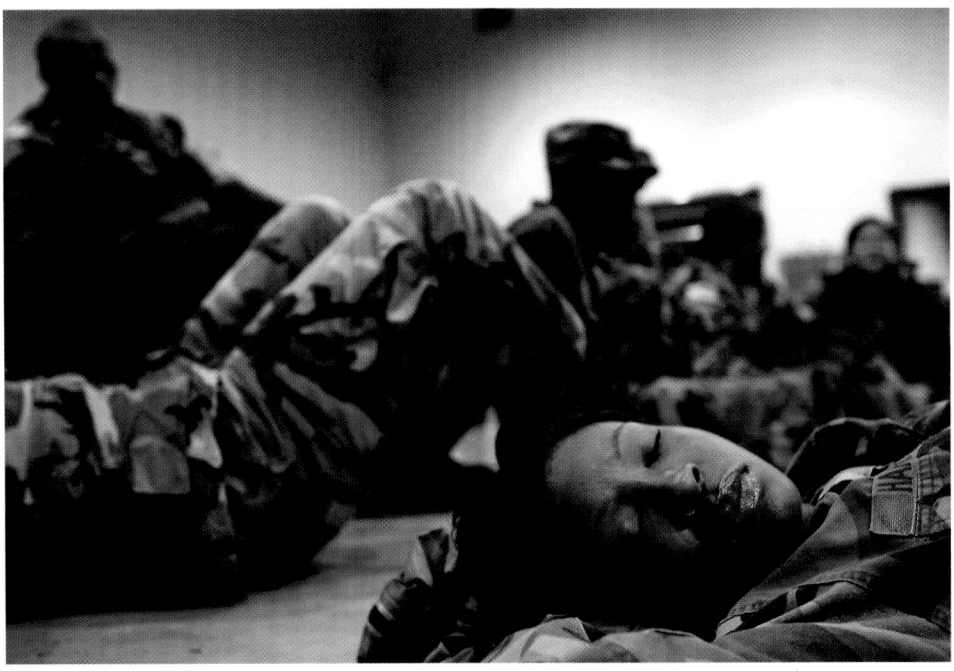

09.24.05 - Houston, TX - National Guardsman Spc. Demechtria Harris managed to sneak in a little nap. Hurricane Rita sent her and other troops from Dallas to Austin and on to San Antonio and Houston. • CHERYL DIAZ MEYER

RIGHT
09.24.05 - Woodville, TX - Pam Selman of Spring, Texas, watched traffic try to maneuver around fallen trees on U.S. Highway 190 between Livingston and Woodville after Hurricane Rita passed through. Woodville is in Deep East Texas, southeast of Lufkin. • LOUIS DELUCA

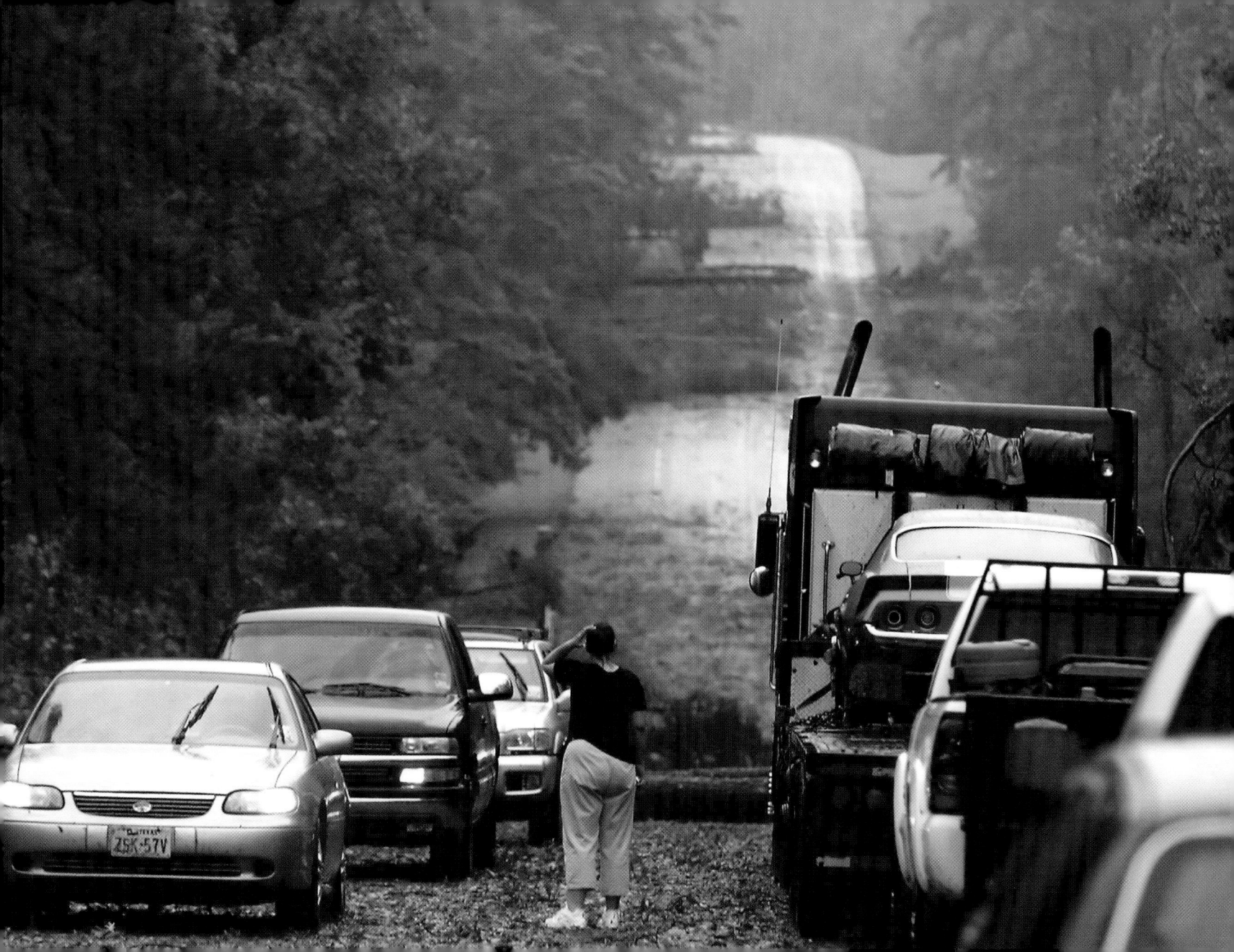

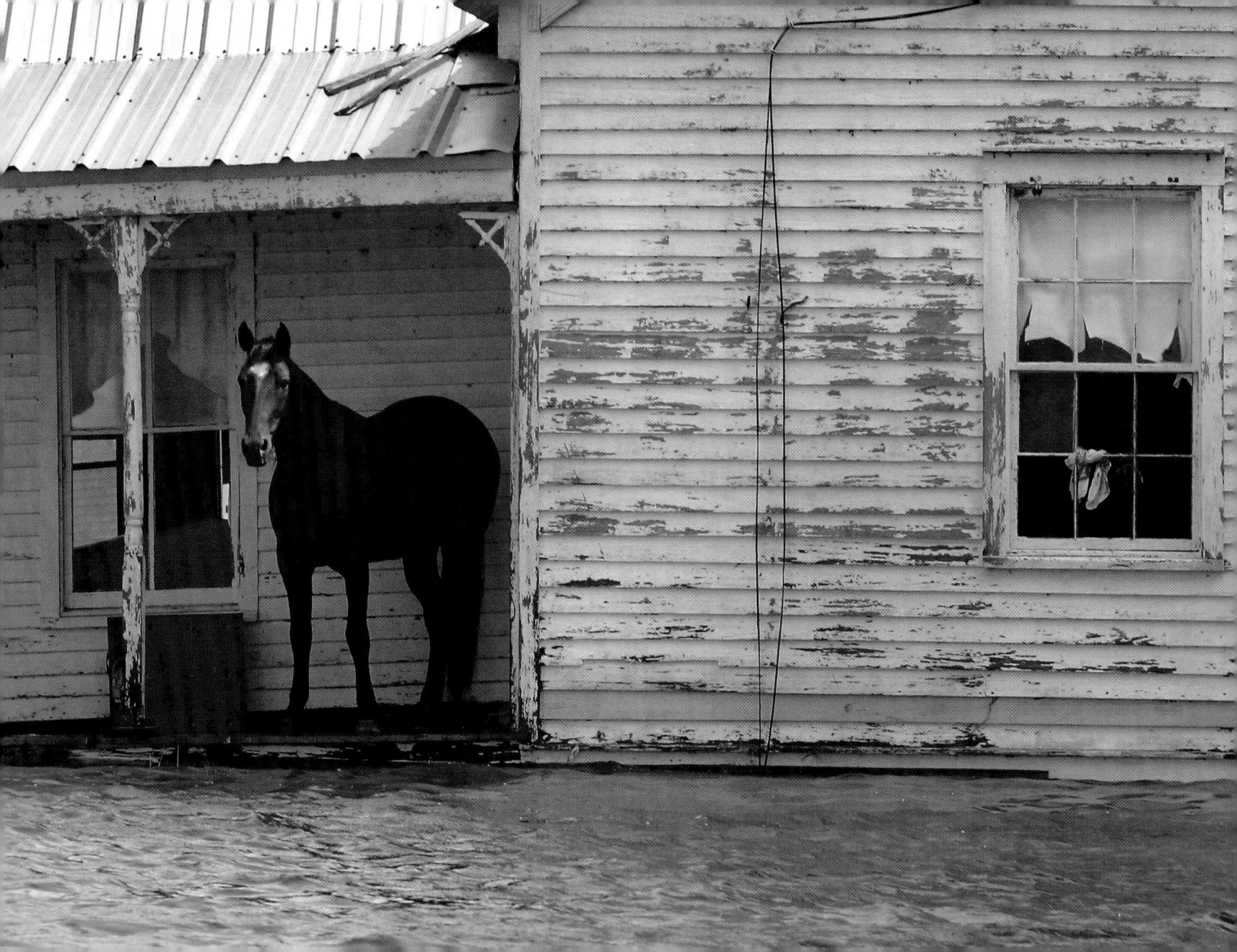

09.25.05 - Henry, LA - A horse took to a porch to keep dry in the already battered Vermilion Parish.
• RICHARD MICHAEL PRUITT

Right
09.25.05 - Abbeville, LA - Floodwaters from Hurricane Rita surrounded a home near Abbeville, leaving a ring of debris just feet from the doorstep. • SMILEY N. POOL

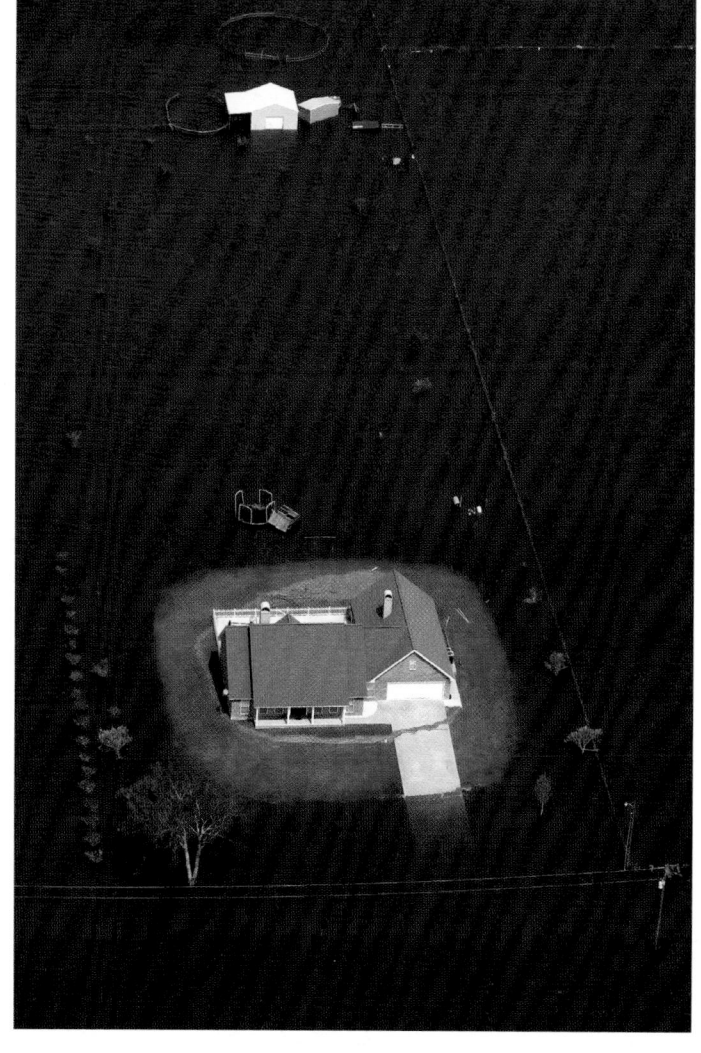

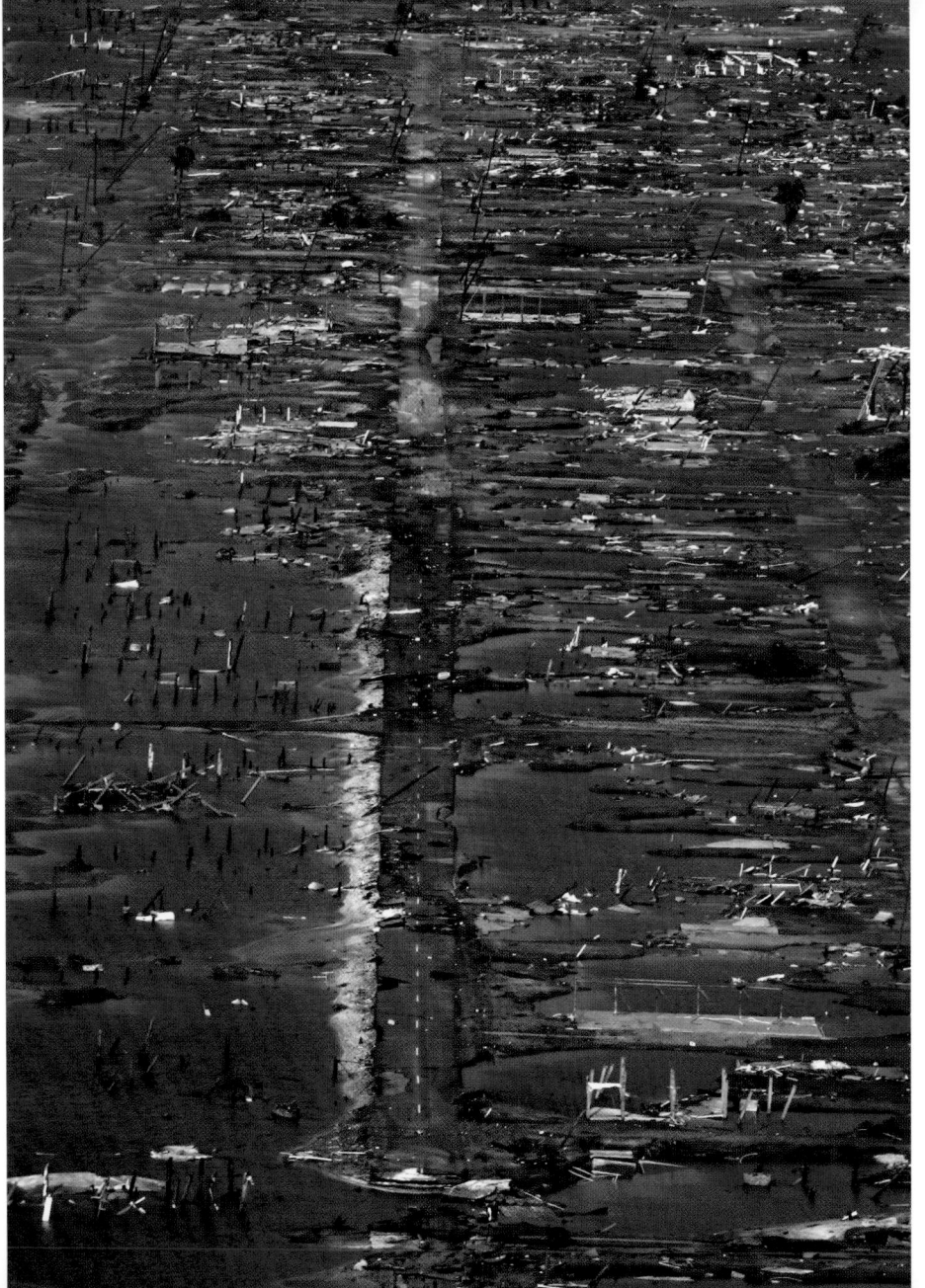

09.25.05 - Holly Beach, LA - Cameron Parish's Holly Beach, a fishing village and popular vacation spot, was reduced to splinters by Hurricane Rita, with concrete slabs the only evidence that homes once stood there. • SMILEY N. POOL

RIGHT
09.24.05 - Port Arthur, TX - Barbara Harrison took a long look at the flooded streets of her city after her husband survived a long night as Hurricane Rita blew through.
• MICHAEL AINSWORTH

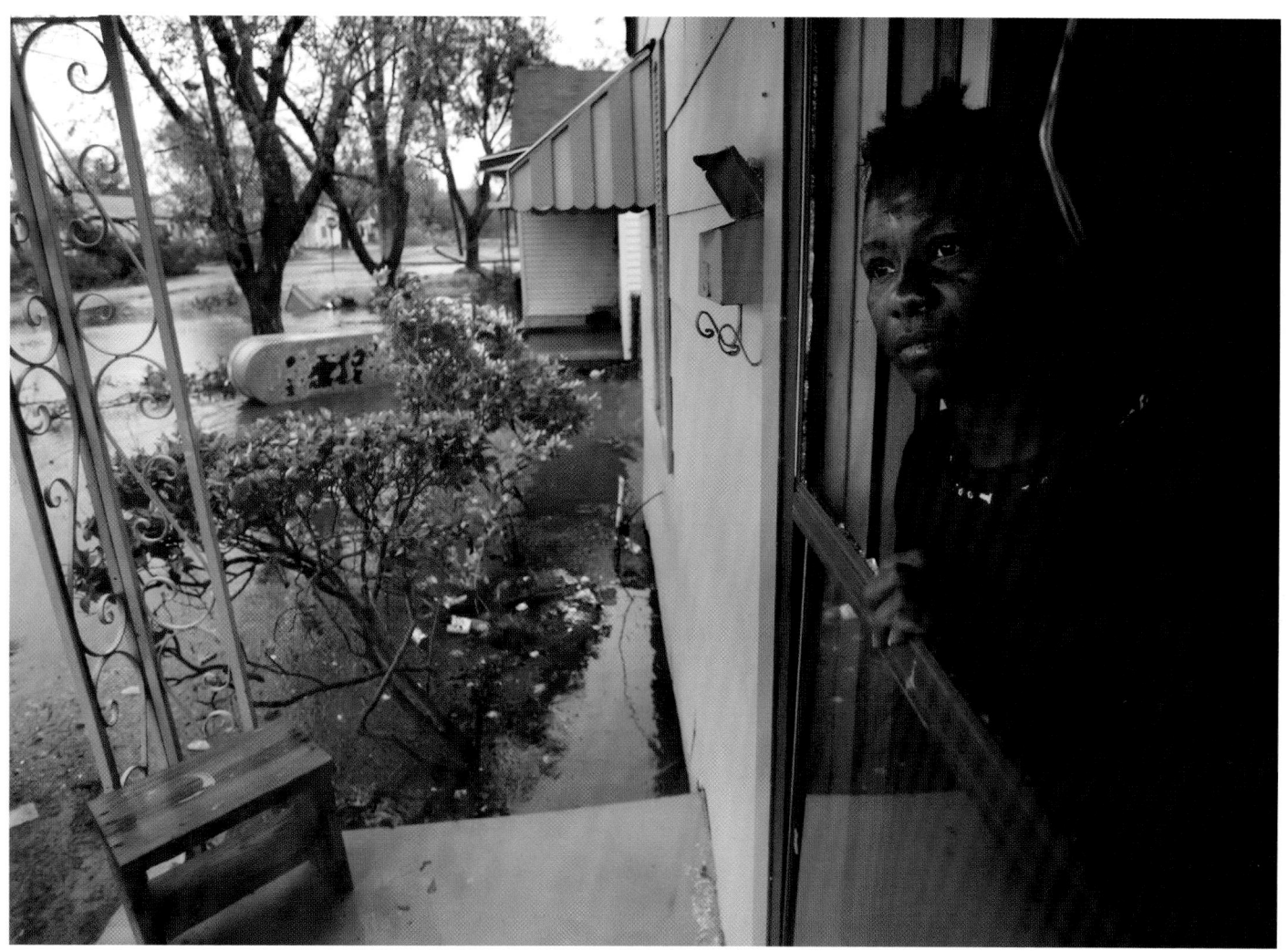

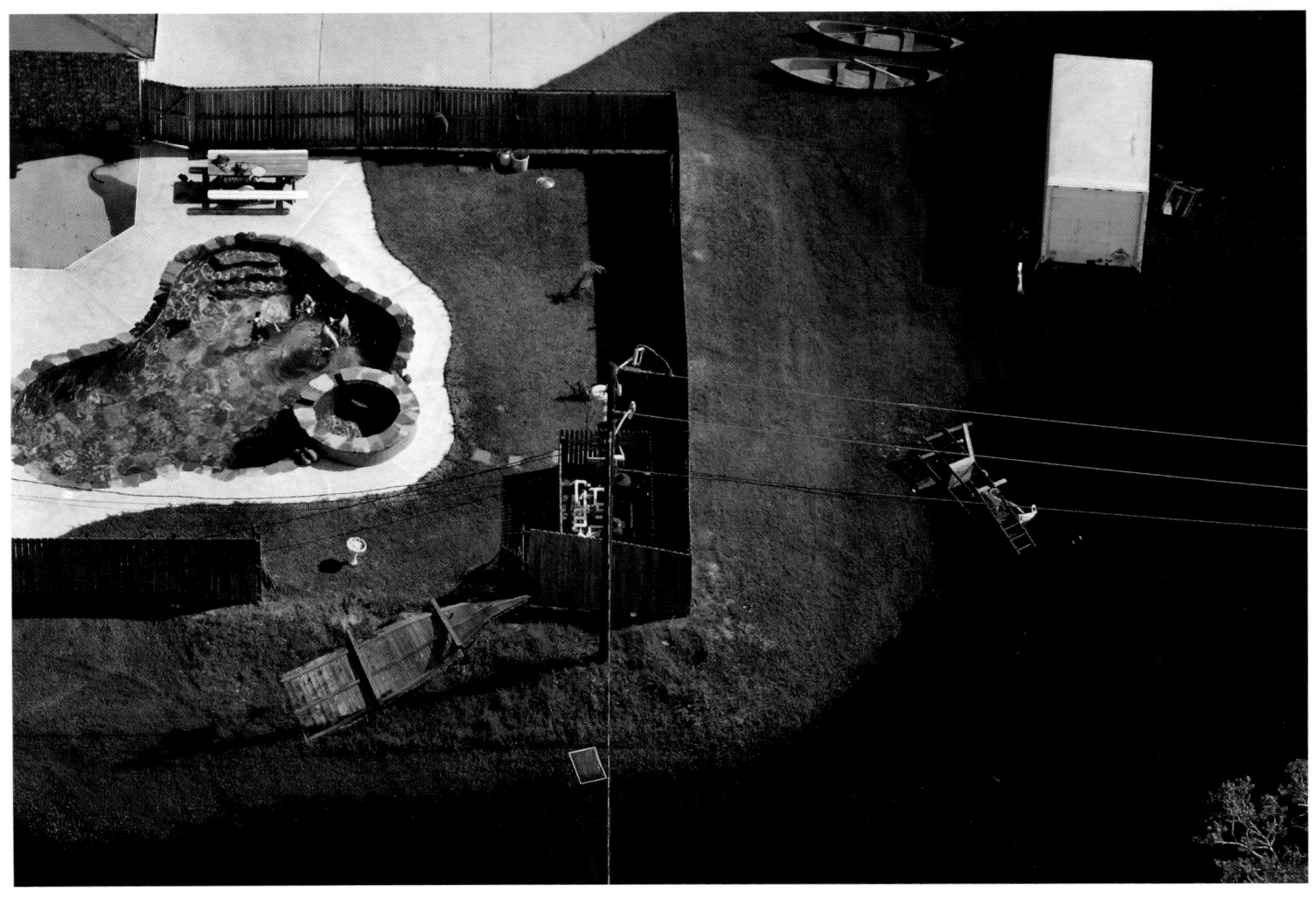

09.25.05 - Chauvin, LA - Children swim in a backyard pool as surrounding floodwaters brought by Hurricane Rita slowly retreat. • SMILEY N. POOL

RIGHT
09.25.05 - Jean Lafitte, LA - With her home surrounded by water dumped by Hurricane Rita, Catherine Howk, 81, worked on a quilt for her grandson. Ms. Howk, who has lived in the fishing village south of New Orleans for most of her life, said she rode out Hurricane Katrina as well and didn't want to leave now. • BRAD LOPER

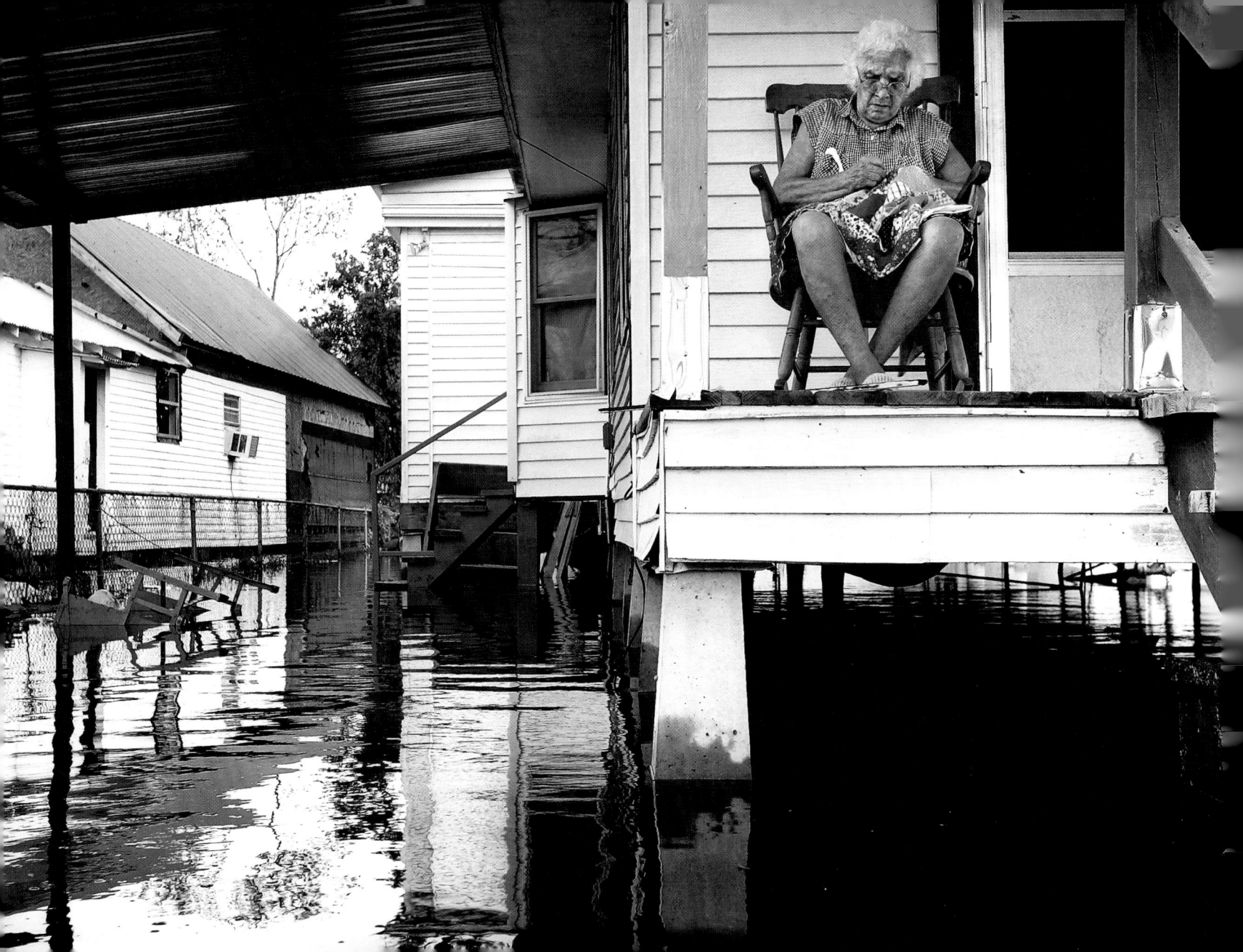

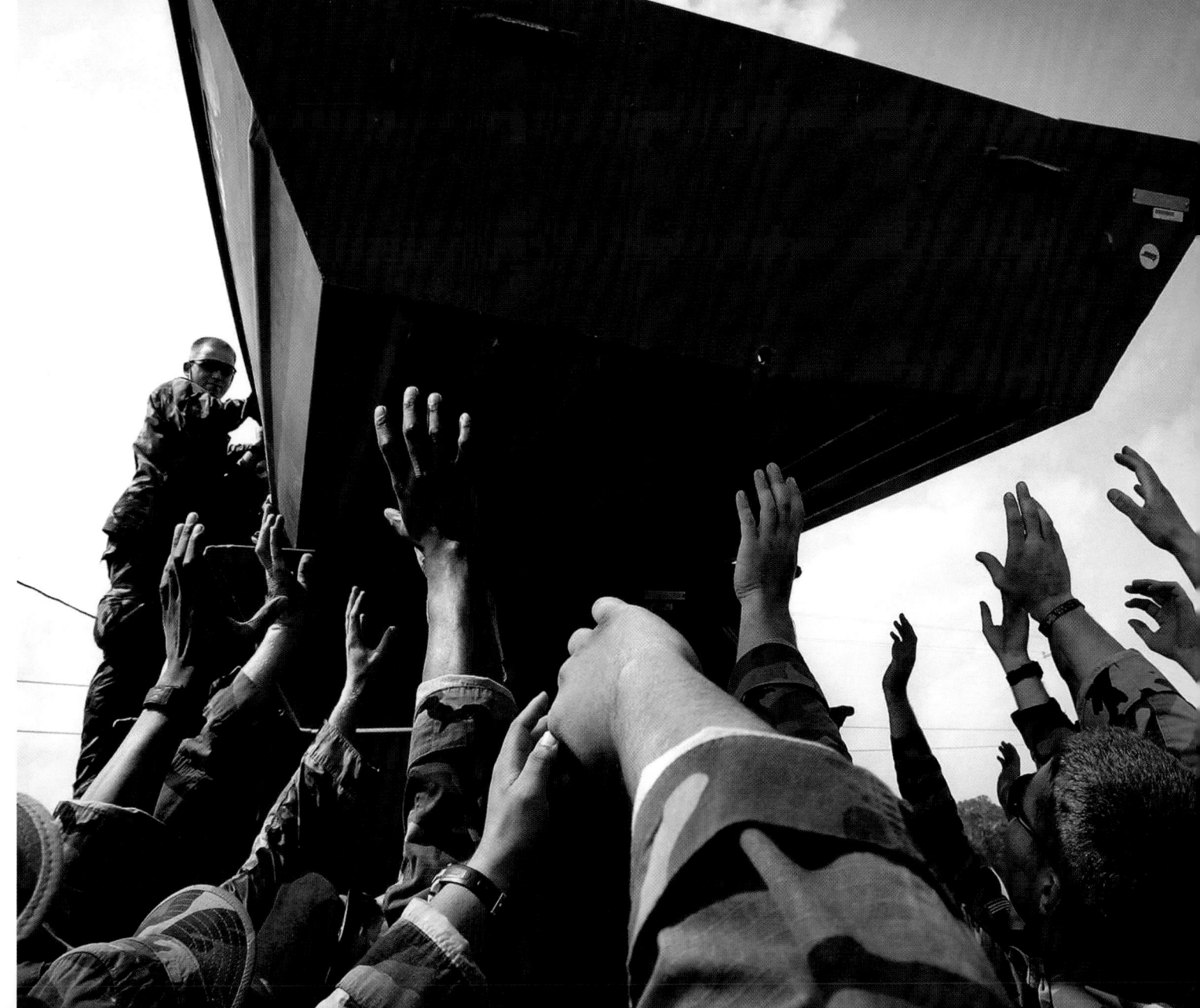

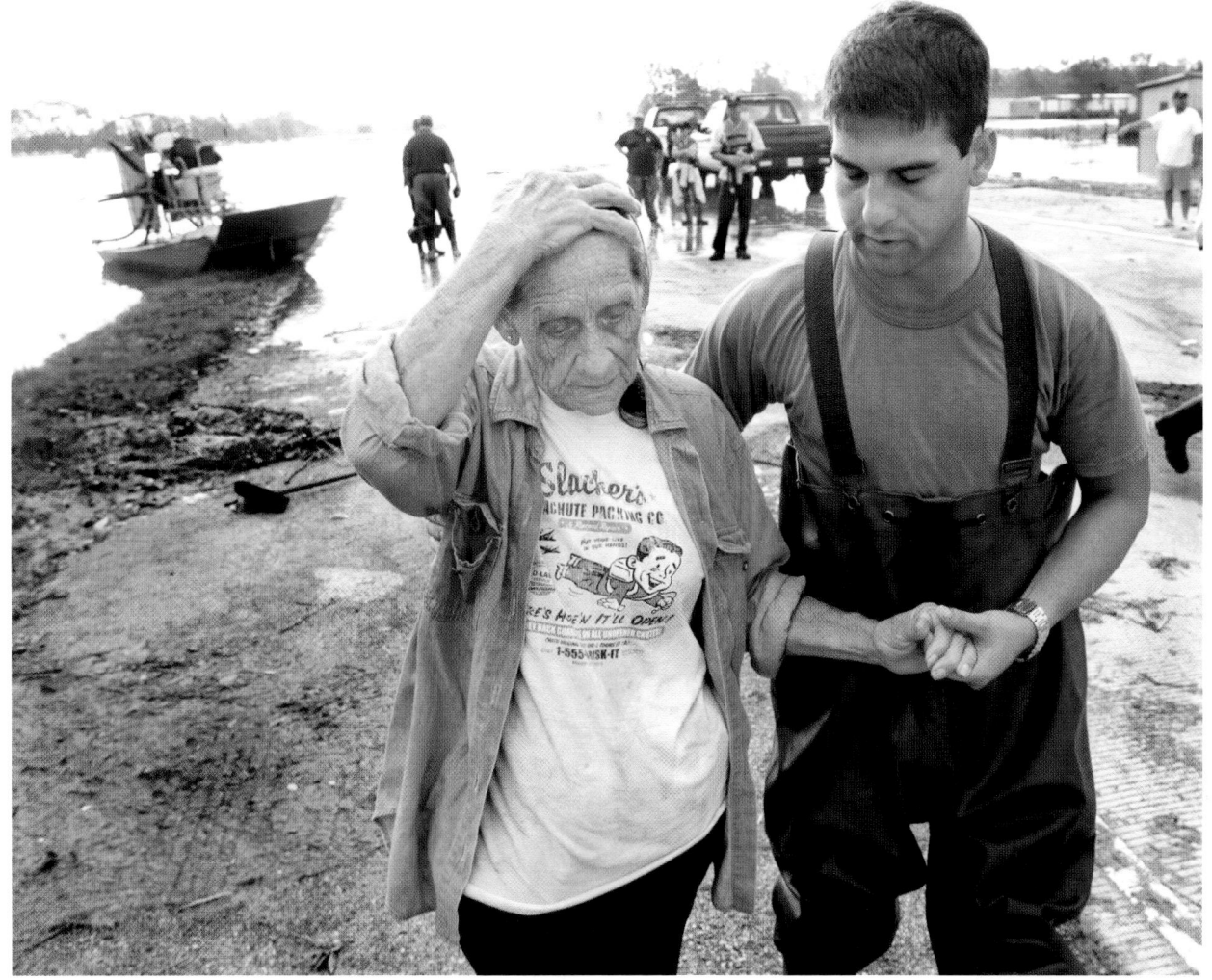

09.25.05 - Erath, LA - Bell Vaughn was rescued from her home by grandson Jon Erick Miletello, a Louisiana National Guardsman. Ms. Vaughn was able to bring her four dogs along, too. • ERICH SCHLEGEL

Left
09.25.05 - Delcambre, LA - Soldiers from the Army's 82nd Airborne Division based at Fort Bragg, N.C., unloaded boats to search for survivors in Delcambre and Erath. Hurricane Rita stranded many residents of Vermilion Parish, in the southwestern part of the state. • ERICH SCHLEGEL

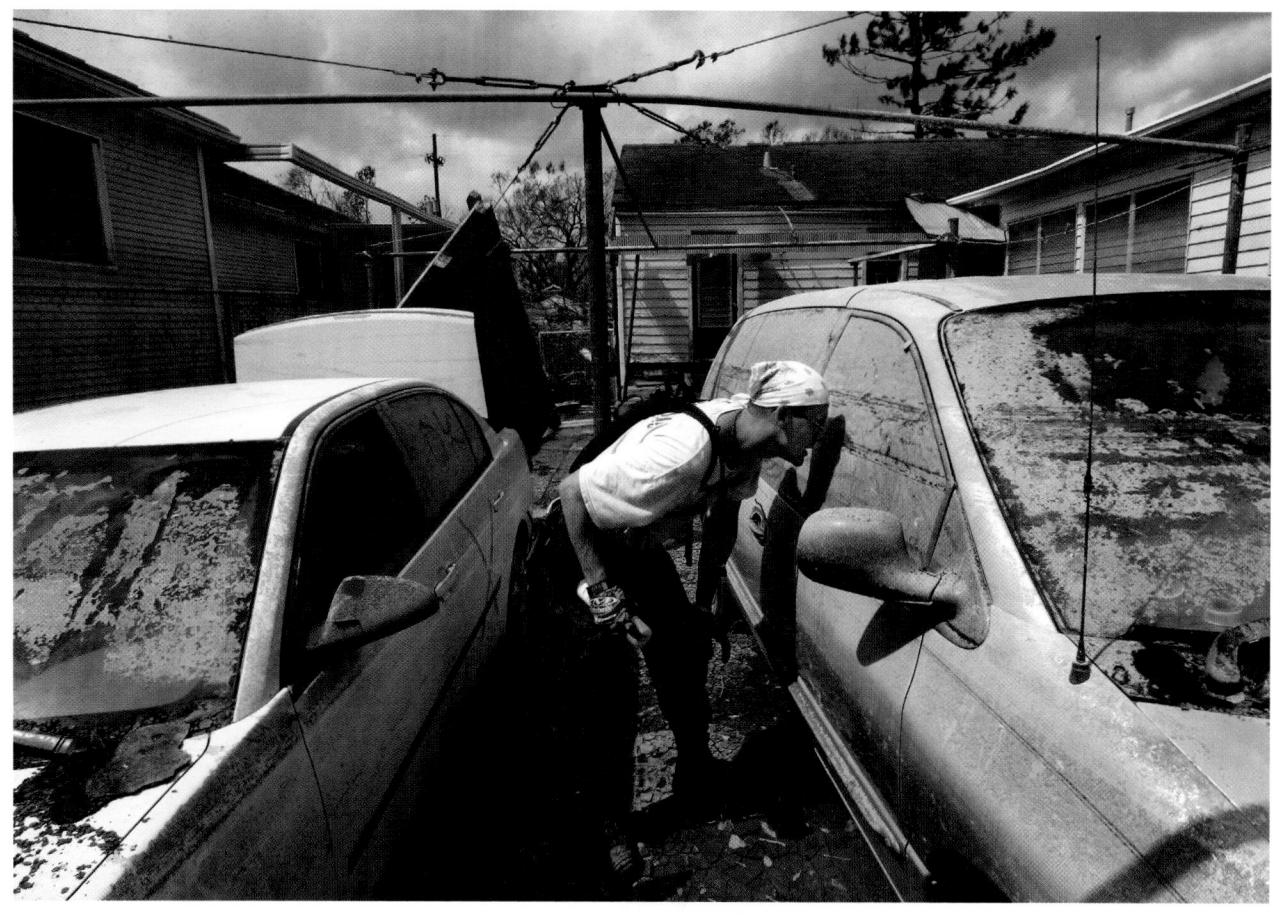

09.25.05 - New Orleans, LA - Floyd Wise of Pennsylvania Task Force 1 peered into a van in the Gentilly neighborhood. Just weeks after Katrina, much of the city was flooded again by Rita, and search-and-recovery operations ground on. • BRAD LOPER

RIGHT
09.25.05 - Erath, LA - Bob Swett (from left), Troy Touchet, Ronald Faulk and Blaine Broussard muddled through the flooding in Erath on barstools outside Shoot's Lounge. The bar was flooded by Hurricane Rita but stayed open. • RICHARD MICHAEL PRUITT

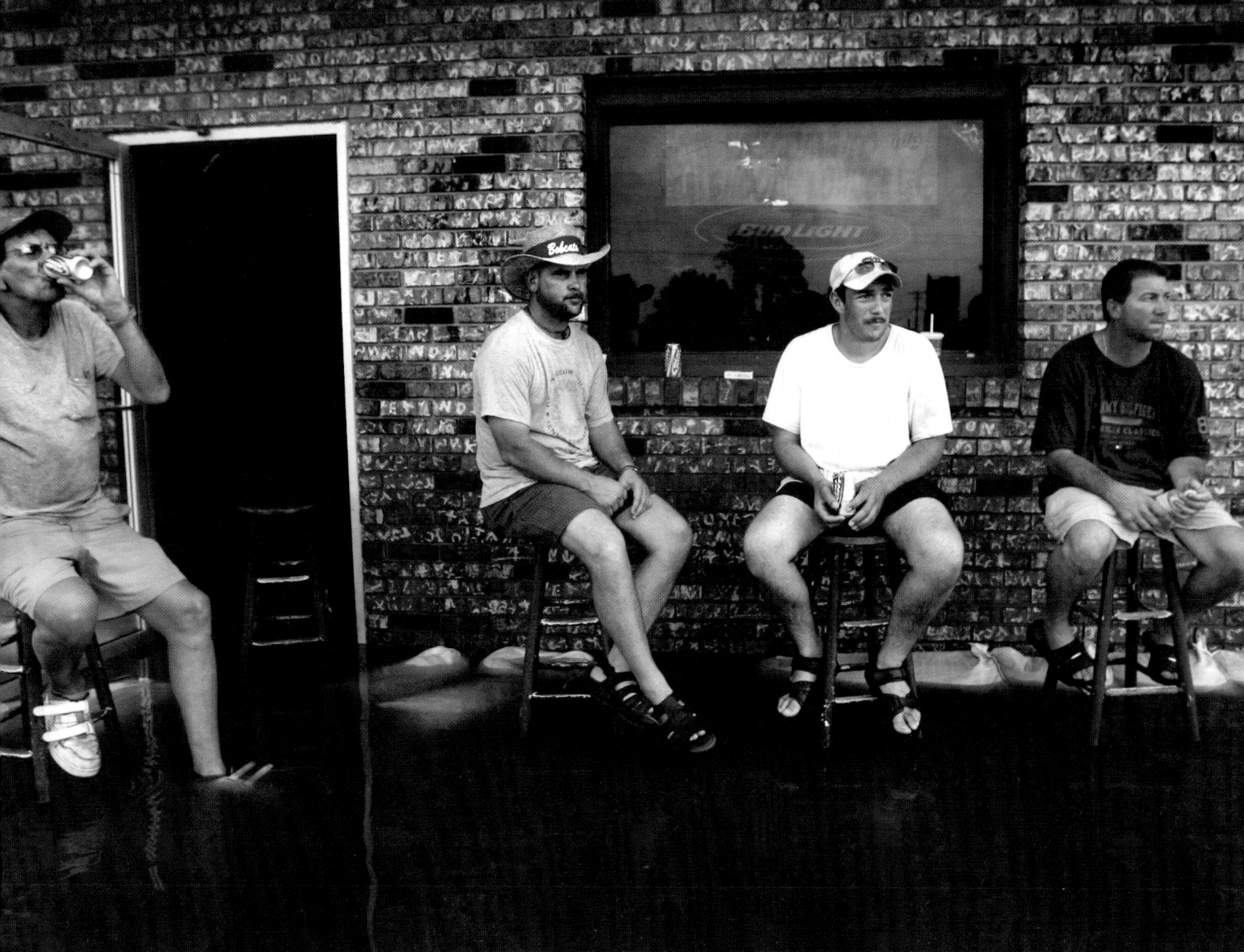

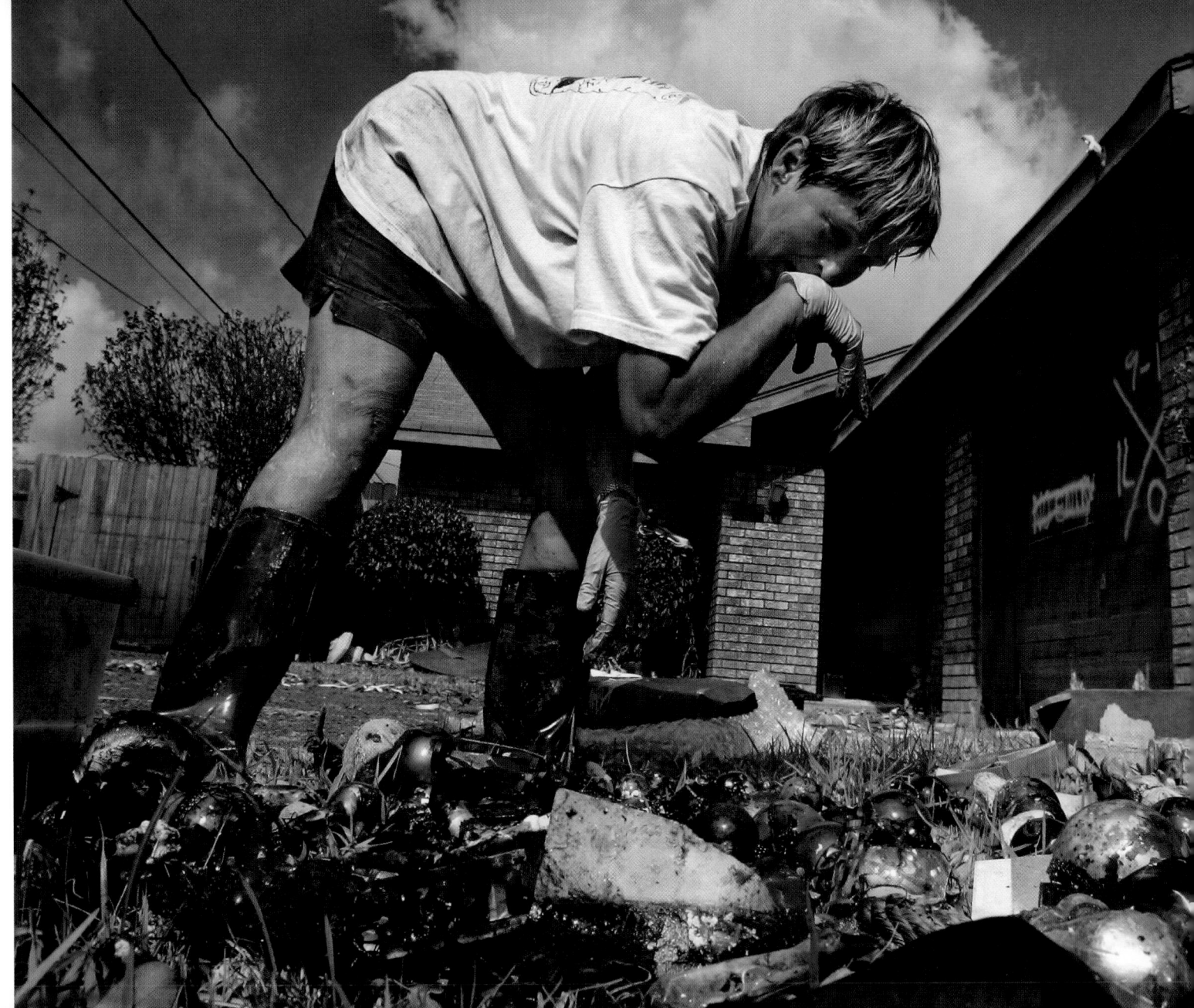

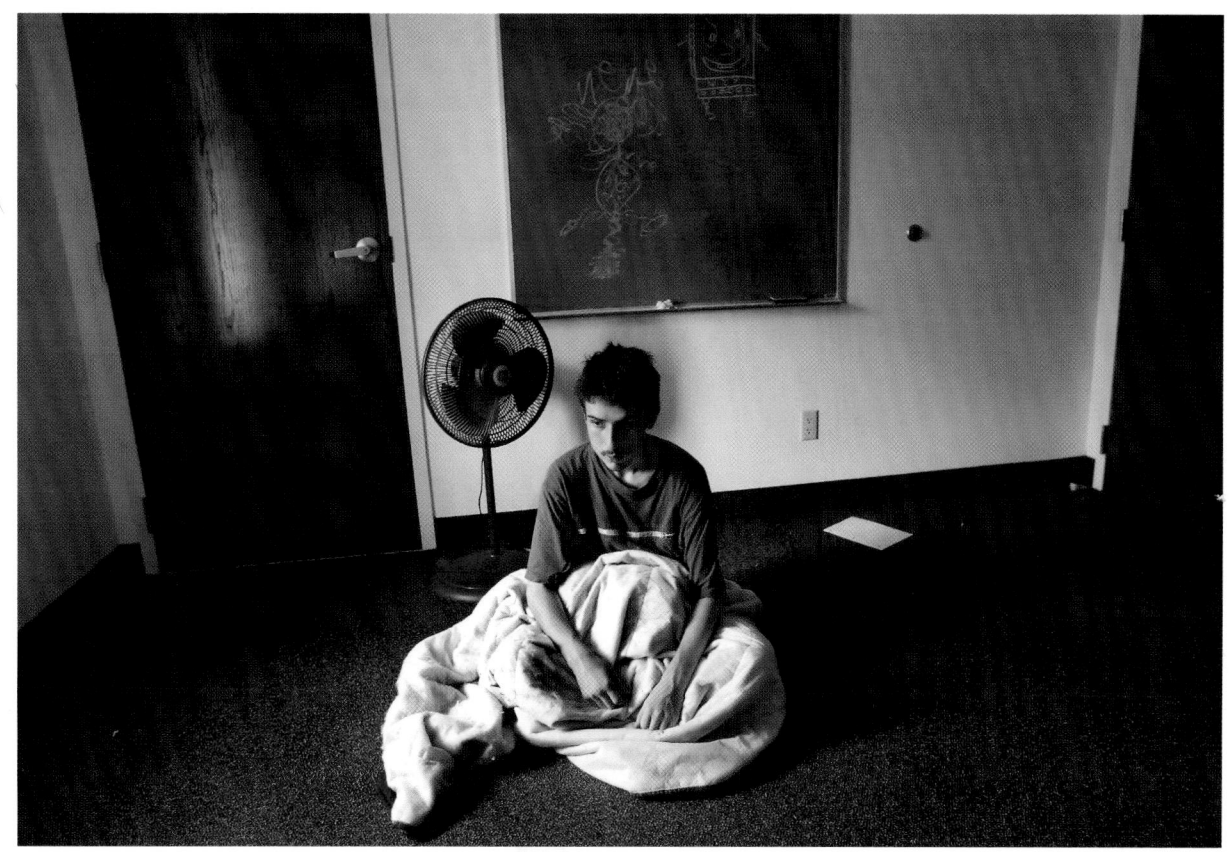

09.26.05 - Nacogdoches, TX - Junior Arellano awoke from a nap at the Nacogdoches Ward of the Church of Jesus Christ of Latter-day Saints, where he took shelter after fleeing Vidor, Texas, with his family. • LARA SOLT

LEFT
09.26.05 - St. Bernard Parish, LA - St. Bernard Parish resident Darlene Sixkiller tried to hold back tears while searching for Christmas ornaments made by her children. • BRAD LOPER

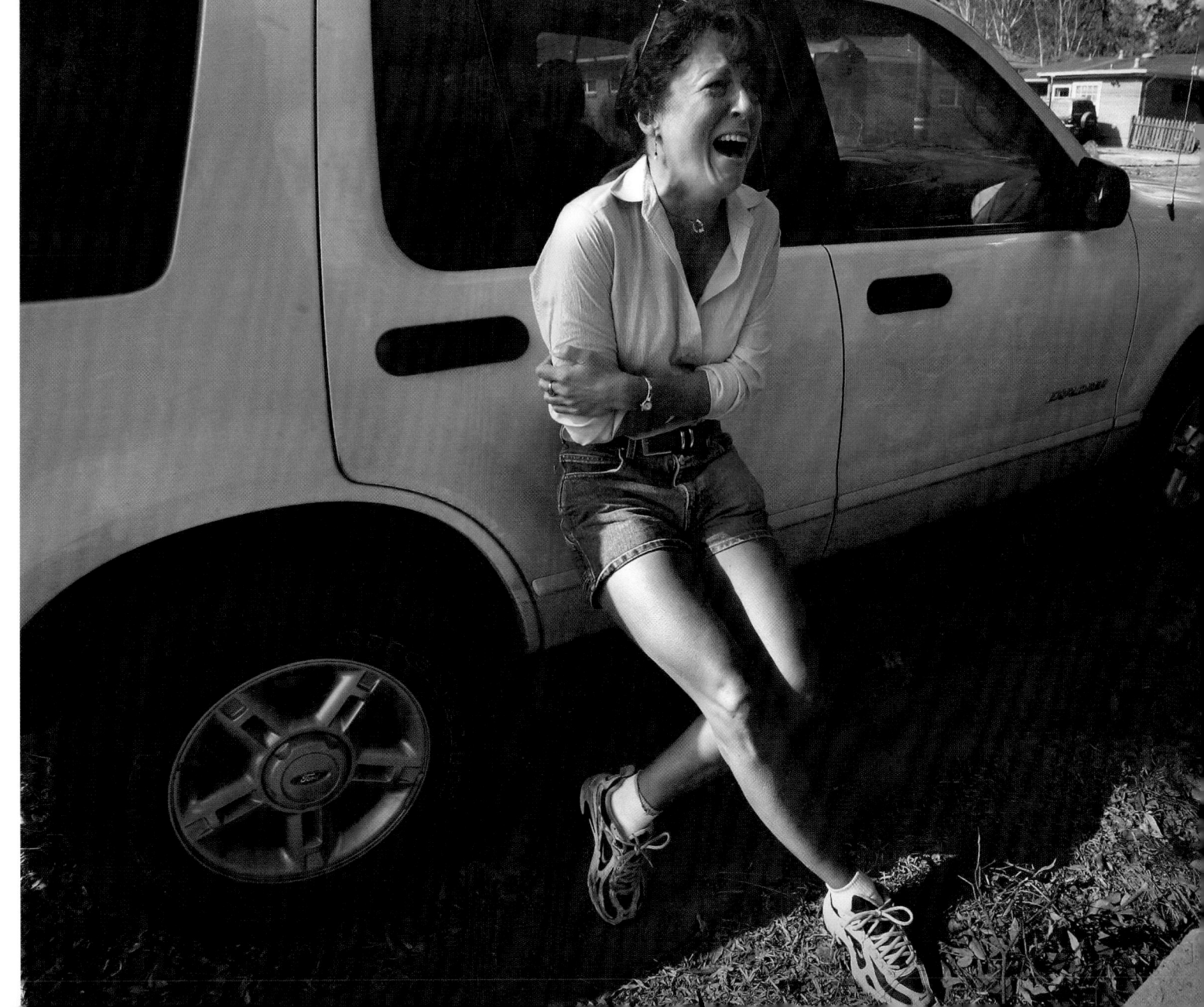

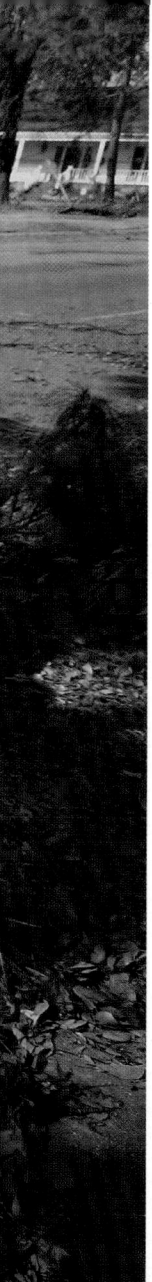

09.29.05 - New Orleans, LA - Lee Elliott was overcome with grief while getting a first look at her damaged home in the Lakeview area. A break in the 17th Street Canal levee had put her house under 10 feet of water. • RICHARD MICHAEL PRUITT

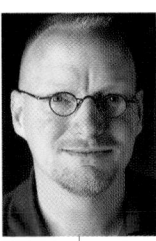

MICHAEL AINSWORTH

Michael Ainsworth was born in Houston and spent his childhood in Bogota, Colombia, and Fort Worth.

He graduated from the University of Texas at Arlington in 1991 with a bachelor's degree in journalism and interned at the Greensboro News & Record in North Carolina and the Hartford Courant in Connecticut.

He has worked at The Dallas Morning News since 1990 and has won numerous awards for sports photography.

•   •   •   •   •

You can't do this job without showing a little compassion. While I was trying to get to the Superdome, a crowd pointed out the body of an 80-year-old man who had fallen to his death from one of the overpasses. Cynthia Scott had been looking out for the frail man.

Ms. Scott despaired that the man had to die in such a way. She was trying to keep her family safe from shootings, heat and dehydration. I photographed her and listened to her story, letting her vent her frustration. "A whole city in ruins and no one doing nothing," she said.

I was getting emotional while taking the photos, and a man nearby said, "I can tell that you really care about people by the look on your face." I can't imagine anyone not showing compassion and understanding in such a horrific situation.

The next day, this picture ran, and I got a call from a woman in South Carolina who wanted me to find this family so she could adopt them. She said she was moved by the woman and the fact that her own twin babies had the same names. But I knew I would never see the family again. I hope they found some comfort through all the chaos.

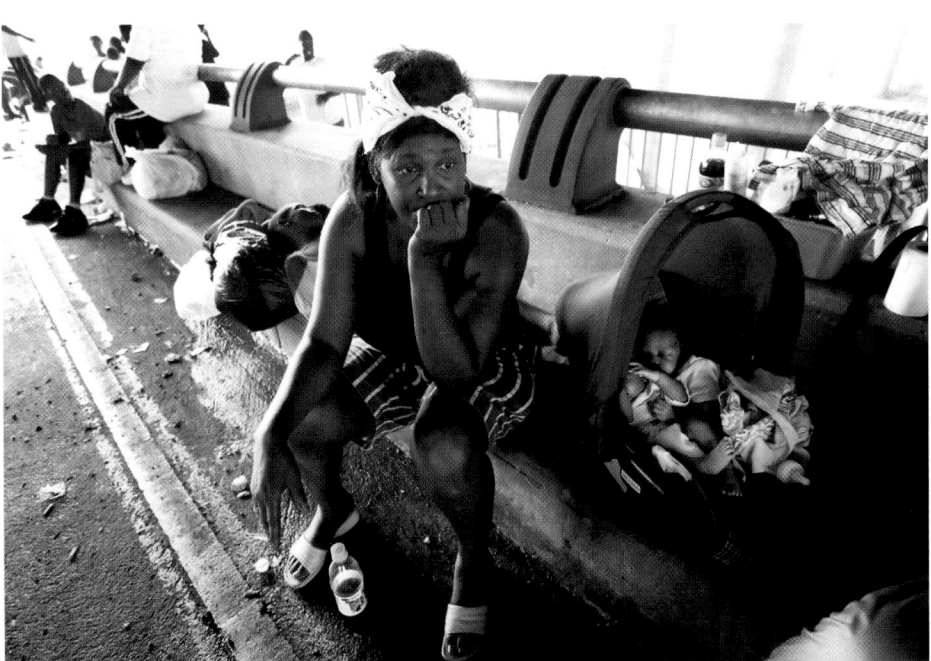

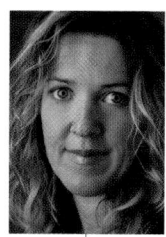

Melanie Burford

Melanie Burford has worked at The Dallas Morning News since 2003.

Her career began in New Zealand in 1990 at the Ashburton Guardian, where, as a staff photographer, she was named Qantas Junior Photographer of the Year. She traveled to America and attended the 1992 Missouri Photo Workshop, where she won the Spirit of the Workshop award. Back home in New Zealand, she worked as a staff photographer at The Evening Post from 1992 to 1999, winning news and sports awards.

During her time at The Evening Post, she was a guest lecturer at the National Journalism School in Wellington, New Zealand. She also led photojournalism workshops and spoke at conferences. For the international photography festival, Fotofest '98, she was director of the Photojournalism and Sports Convention, creating the workshop and one-day seminars.

In September 1999, she traveled to America to attend Ohio University. She worked for Sun Publications in Chicago before moving to Washington, D.C., where she freelanced for The Washington Post, National Geographic Traveler, The Sunday Times and The Daily Telegraph in London.

In 2002, she won the NPPA Best of Photojournalism Cliff Edom New America Award.

•   •   •   •

It is during times of great suffering that we catch glimpses of purity, of the human spirit, of generosity so great that words seem inadequate.

Sue Sandford, of University Park, Texas, shined with such a light. A single mother of four, she embraced a family of 20 strangers flee-ing Hurricane Katrina. Below is a letter to Sue from James McCray, head of the New Orleans family, who within hours of the hurricane lost his home, his livelihood, his community. He had nothing left to offer Sue but words.

9.09.05

Our Holy Spirit helps us with our thoughts. I woke up with these thoughts this morning.

After the first day in your house, I knew God wanted us to meet one of his angels on earth. I've been thinking every day of what I could do for you to show our appreciation for your unimaginable generosity of turning your home over to twenty strangers, but nothing seems to be good enough.

Maybe these words from my heart will be good enough.

I feel like all the people we've met in Texas has been so nice to us and you have been our angel. I feel like you should be Mrs. Texas to illustrate what Texas is all about. I feel like if you represented Texas, everyone would be trying to live here. For this reason I have changed my mind and I will live in Texas.

Thanks Sue,

From the McCray Family

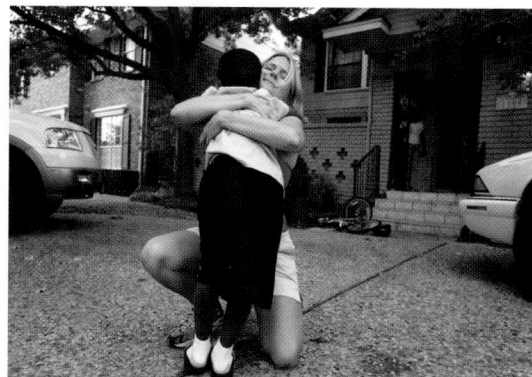

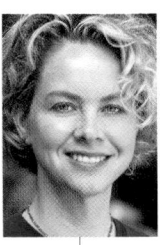

Barbara Davidson

Barbara Davidson grew up in Montreal, Canada, and graduated from Concordia University with a bachelor's degree in photography and film studies. In 1996, she crossed the Canadian border, moving to Washington, D.C., to work for The Washington Times. In 2000, she joined the staff of The Dallas Morning News.

Her first foreign assignment for The News was to document civil strife in the Democratic Republic of Congo. Since then, she has covered conflict in the West Bank and Gaza, Israel, Iraq and Afghanistan. She has also done photo essays about Rwanda, Nigeria, Yemen and Mexico.

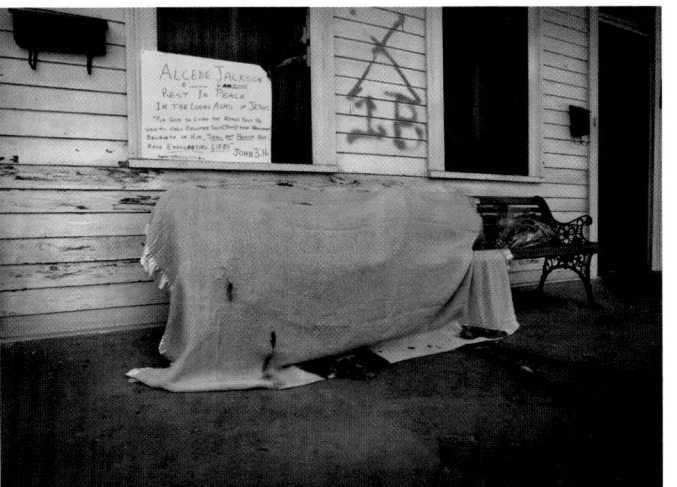

She recently covered the tsunami disaster and the death of Pope John Paul II. In addition to her foreign assignments, she has covered the presidential campaign, the Republican National Convention and unique Texas stories. She has received numerous awards for her work from organizations such as The White House News Photographers Association, The National Press Photographers Association and Pictures of The Year International.

• • • • •

What I saw in Mississippi and New Orleans was disturbingly similar to the war zones I have covered in Iraq and Afghanistan. That level of human suffering, and the complete breakdown of infrastructure, is not supposed to happen in the United States. The lack of government preparedness in dealing with the hurricane's aftermath made this part of the nation seem like a Third World country. It was completely heartbreaking to see the lack of aid.

One poignant memory I have is finding the body of 83-year-old Alcede Jackson, who had lain for 14 days on a wrought iron bench on the front porch of his shotgun house in the Uptown district of New Orleans.

I took pictures of the unreal scene: the baby-blue blanket shroud, the bouquet of wilted flowers, the glow-in-the-dark green poster board tacked, tombstone-style, over his resting place. Neatly placed near the body was a piece of cardboard with handwriting bearing his name and address. Here was a dead man left for two weeks on his front porch - a place where he probably spent hot summer evenings with his wife, talking to neighbors and watching the world go by, until finally FEMA contractors took him to the morgue.

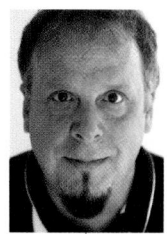

LOUIS DELUCA

Louis DeLuca is a senior staff photographer for The Dallas Morning News, where he has worked since 1992. He has been named National Press Photographers' Regional Photographer of the Year five times and has been awarded runner-up five times. He has also worked at the Dallas Times-Herald, the Chicago Sun-Times, the Shreveport Journal, and the Marshall (Texas) News-Messenger. He is married and has four children.

•   •   •

"Please tell our story." The words, spoken in a beautiful Jamaican accent, caught me by surprise. These three women had lost everything. Their Gulfport, Miss., beachfront apartment no longer existed because of Hurricane Katrina.

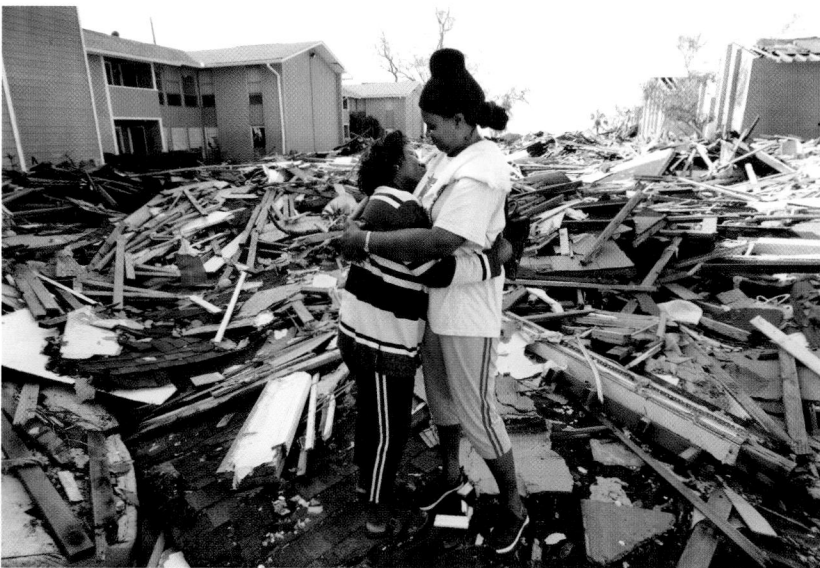
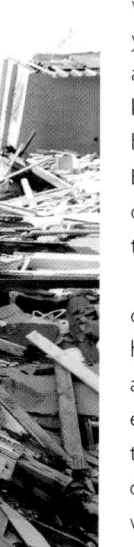

woman started to cry. "Roxona, at least we are alive," Avis said as she offered the comfort of a hug to her friend.

I continued to take photos as we passed another apartment building, guarded by a man with a rifle. "Don't worry," Avis said. "He is our friend." The man with the rifle offered me some bottled water. "What are you going to do?" I asked her. "I don't know. Maybe go back to Jamaica. But for now ..." She didn't finish her thought.

Our exploration of the ruins of their home had come to an end. They decided to go back down the beach to the damaged hotel where they had waited out the storm. "Thank you again," the three women said almost in unison. Avis gave me a hug and walked away with her friends.

I had been expecting some resistance as I accompanied the women through through the piles of wood and bricks that used to be their home. But there was none. "You are so patient ... thank you," one of the women, Avis, said. Another softly sang a hymn. The third

That night I prayed that their story, at some point, would have a happy ending. I am still praying.

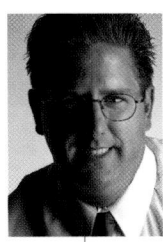

Tom Fox

Staff photographer Tom Fox, 37, returned to The Dallas Morning News in 2001 after a five-year stint as chief photographer and photo editor of the start-up daily Arlington Morning News, sister paper to The Dallas Morning News.

In addition to covering Hurricane Katrina this year, he has covered the Breeder's Cup, the presidential inauguration, Terri Schiavo's fight for life and space shuttle Discovery's return to flight.

He also worked as a staff photographer at the Corpus Christi Caller-Times from 1994 to 1996.

He is a graduate of the University of Texas at Arlington, where he earned a bachelor's degree in photography and worked as a photographer and photo editor at the university newspaper, The Shorthorn. While in college he served photography internships at the Idaho Statesman in Boise and the St. Paul Pioneer Press in Minnesota.

Born and raised in Austin, Minn., Tom grew up in several states across the Midwest before settling and graduating from high school in Duncanville.

•   •   •   •

In the blur of Hurricane Katrina photos, this one stood out: a shaggy dog covered in oil in flood-wrecked Chalmette, La.

Dallas Morning News photographer Tom Fox took the picture of the dog Sept. 6, 2005, but was unable to rescue him.

The animal, referred to throughout as "Oily," was found along Judge Perez Drive in Chalmette by me and another staff photographer while covering a massive oil spill. Chalmette, like much of New Orleans, was flooded and for the most part a ghost town. The only living beings left were animals, mostly dogs, a few rescue people and the four oil cleanup men we ran across that day. Oily was a little bundle of energy who had the misfortune of being stuck in an oil spill. The dog had been hanging around the oil workers when we drove up. He was in good spirits and took a liking to us. We took photographs of him and the workers in the midst of this environmental disaster.

The thought of helping the dog crossed our minds like it did several other times when we crossed paths with stray dogs. Having to cover this huge catastrophe, we couldn't do justice to all of these dogs. At the time, there were no pet-rescue people in these flooded communities. These dogs needed professional help, and we weren't in a position to provide it.

Along with several other photos I took that day, Oily's was the one that put a face to the disaster. His picture made it onto the wires and several Web sites the next day. There was such an outpouring of response from the public to Oily's plight.

There were those who thanked us for highlighting the plight of these animals. And there were those who faulted us for not doing enough.

Days later, pet rescuers picked up dogs along Judge Perez Drive in Chalmette. They drove to Gonzales, La., where most pets were taken to be reunited with their owners. It hasn't been confirmed whether Oily was rescued. A Pennsylvania reverend e-mailed that he thought Oily was taken home by one of the oil cleanup crew members working on the street that day. He thought that made sense since Oily didn't show up on any of the rescue lists.

In the 17 years I've been covering news, I haven't received a fraction of the response from a photo as I did from Oily - both good and bad.

DAVID LEESON

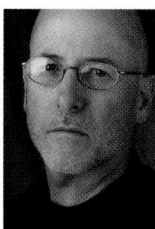

Pulitzer Prize-winning photojournalist David Leeson has been on staff at The Dallas Morning News since 1984. He has also worked for the Abilene Reporter-News and The Times-Picayune in New Orleans.

His assignments have taken him to more than 60 countries and numerous world conflicts in 20 years.

He was a finalist for the Pulitzer three times before winning the award in 2004 with colleague Cheryl Diaz Meyer for photographs taken in March and April 2003 on the front lines with the U.S. Army 3rd Infantry Division during the invasion of Iraq. He has also won two Robert F. Kennedy Journalism Awards and numerous regional, state and national awards.

In fall 2000, he began shooting video for The Dallas Morning News, becoming the first staff photographer in the nation to shoot video full time for a newspaper. Since then he has completed more than seven documentary films.

Two of his documentaries from the war in Iraq won honors. "War Stories" (2003) won a National Headliners award, a national Edward R. Murrow Award and a regional Emmy Award for best television documentary. "Dust to Dust" (2004) was named a finalist for best short film at the USA Film Festival.

• • • •

There was something unusually awful about being in New Orleans in the aftermath of Katrina. I've been to many terrible places in my career and seen things I wish I hadn't. I'm a 30-year veteran of news photography and the often gritty view of daily life.

Katrina made me feel like a newcomer to the business. More than two decades ago, I covered a devastating tornado that struck Wichita Falls, Texas. I was working at the Abilene Reporter-News. It was my first major news event, and I couldn't sleep the night before. Upon arriving, I drove the broken streets and saw people picking up the pieces of their daily existence like someone vainly pasting together a broken heirloom, knowing it will never be the same.

I could not have predicted the wars, disasters, crime, social injustice, starvation and pestilence I would see in the coming years. But I never expected to be as disturbed as I was by what I saw in New Orleans.

In some ways, I was a beginner. It was my first time to go to any news event, big or small, without a 35mm still camera. I carried only a new Sony high-definition video camera and used it to produce video for the Web and still photos taken directly from the raw tape.

But new technology wasn't what disturbed me. There were two things that came to the surface. First was that the wind and water had produced a near apocalyptic society in their wake. I was not alone in my dismay at the failure of government to come to the aid of victims.

The fact that an estimated 15,000 residents were left without food and water at the New Orleans convention center, where they had been told to go for shelter, is a shameful indictment of the system. It was the only time I fought back tears.

But the most disturbing moment, when everything changed for me, was when I witnessed the apparently indiscriminate shooting of stray pets by sheriff's officers in St. Bernard Parish, downriver from New Orleans. That represented everything that had gone wrong in this post-hurricane society. Every failure punctuated with each dog killed.

Sure, New Orleans will rebuild. The party will go on. But the so-called "Katrina Effect" will resonate well after the water recedes.

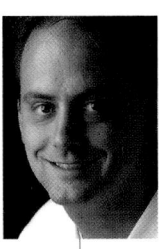

Brad Loper

Brad Loper, 35, joined The Dallas Morning News in July 2001 after a five-year stint as a photographer/special projects page designer at the Arlington Morning News.

Born and raised in Amarillo, he moved to the Dallas-Fort Worth area in 1990 to attend the University of Texas at Arlington, where he received a bachelor's degree in communication with a minor in criminal justice in 1993. He was named College Photographer of the Year (Third) by the National Press Photographers Foundation and the University of Missouri School of Journalism in 1992.

Following graduation, he interned at the Topeka Capital-Journal in Kansas and the Palm Beach Post in Florida, then worked at the Amarillo Globe-News before returning to the Dallas area.

He has won numerous awards from the National Press Photographers Association, the Society for News Design, the Press Club of Dallas Katie Awards, and the Texas Associated Press Managing Editors Association for his work as a photojournalist and page designer.

He and his wife, Adrienne, have three children, Nathaniel, 8, Ian, 5, and Gabriel, 2.

•　　　•　　　•　　　•

Reporter Sudeep Reddy and I flew to Hattiesburg, Miss., then boarded a helicopter to New Orleans to cover the evacuation of patients and staff from Memorial Medical Center. Watching the doctors, nurses, kitchen and housekeeping staffs toil together was amazing. Titles and seniority disappeared as everyone pitched in to get the job done.

The scene that stays with me was that of patients laid out in the parking garage waiting for evacuation in the sweltering heat and humidity. On the upper level, nurse Mary Jo D'Amico used a piece of cardboard to fan patients. She, like the rest of the staff, was there for several days and nights with little food and water and no electricity. Yet they all continued to do their best to take care of the patients and one another.

On my second trip, I spent eight days in New Orleans and a day in Mississippi.

I learned that humor presents itself even in tragic situations. A pawnshop in Biloxi was leveled, but propped up on the slab was the front door, positioned where it originally stood, with glass broken out and a "No Trespassing" sign.

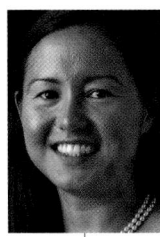

Cheryl Diaz Meyer

Cheryl Diaz Meyer has been a senior staff photographer at The Dallas Morning News since 2000. She was awarded the 2004 Pulitzer Prize with fellow staffer David Leeson for their work covering the war in Iraq.

In 2001, she traveled to Afghanistan to photograph the war on terrorism and its effects on the people trying to free themselves from the Taliban regime. She has received numerous awards, including the John Faber Award from the Overseas Press Club.

In April 2002, she traveled to the Philippines and Indonesia, where she photographed Muslim and Christian extremism and the violence caused by religious hatred.

She was born and raised in the Philippines and immigrated with her family to Minnesota in 1981. She attended the University of Minnesota, where she graduated cum laude with a bachelor's degree in German in 1990. Later she attended Western Kentucky University, where she graduated with a bachelor's degree in journalism in 1994. She worked as a photo intern at several newspapers around the country, including The Washington Post.

•　　　•　　　•　　　•

Step into the Marigny Triangle near New Orleans' French Quarter after Hurricane Katrina and witness a neighborhood quietly bursting with energy. Despite the mass exodus of residents, an eclectic collection of musicians, jazz bar and club owners, restaurant waiters and disc jockeys lived as if they were the last human beings on the planet.

They were the holdouts of the evacuation - men and women of all ages who were caring, hospitable, resilient, a little crazy and ultimately dedicated to their community. The area sustained little damage from the hurricane and no flooding. Many felt they could survive until the city began to rebuild.

Joel Moody, a young restaurant worker, kept watch over the Alley Katz bar. Like so many others, he refused to evacuate without his dog. But slowly, the not-so-subtle threats from the National Guard began to wear on him. The message: You must evacuate now or be forced to evacuate without your pet.

After much reflection, Mr. Moody sadly made the decision to leave. His best friend, Camille Penny, an emergency medical technician who continued to work in New Orleans after the disaster, bid him farewell. Their tearful embrace weighed heavy with emotion, and I could only imagine how much they had shared in the days following Hurricane Katrina. The fear, the chaos, their ultimate survival ... a friendship bonded in pain.

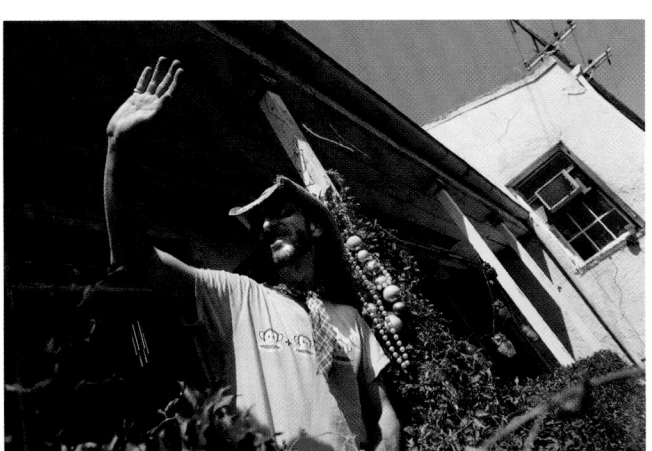

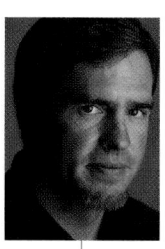

Michael Mulvey

Staff photographer Michael Mulvey has worked for The Dallas Morning News since March 1997. He was the Dallas-based contract photographer for the Reuters news agency before arriving at The News.

He has also worked for The Boston Globe, The Associated Press, The Augusta Chronicle in Georgia, and The Bryan-College Station Eagle. Most recently, he was part of the award-winning team covering the 2004 Olympics in Athens, Greece.

He is a native Texan and a graduate of Texas A&M University with a bachelor's degree in journalism. He is also a former member of the Texas A&M Corps of Cadets and was a photographer for A&M's student newspaper, The Battalion.

•   •   •

The moment was gripping as Bishop Nelson knelt down to hug Eddie Mae Smith of Biloxi, Miss., who was weeping on her sofa in a living room covered with mold and the stench of mildew. He kept telling her that he was going to get her help as he took on all the weight of her pain.

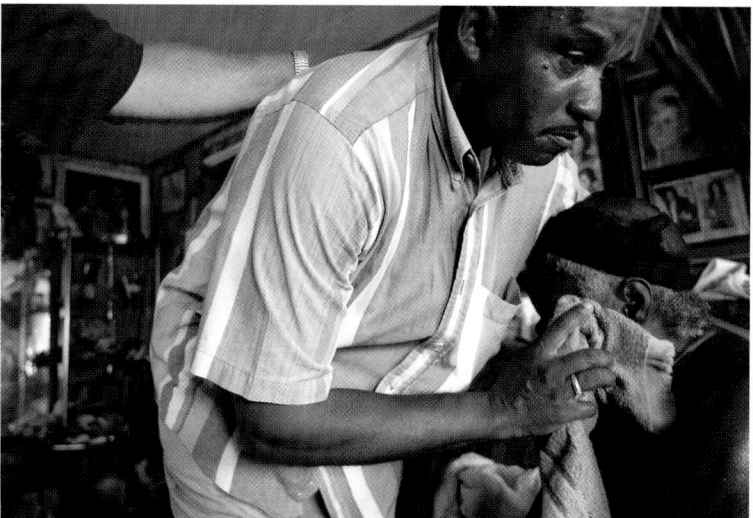

The moment was drastically different from the time I spent hours earlier with Bishop Nelson. I had photographed him as he preached outside his church, and he had been very animated during the service. He made sure everyone near the church heard his message as he belted out Scriptures into a microphone. Often he would dance into the street near traffic, praising God in front of his congregation.

It was devastating for him to find Ms. Smith in her condition, 13 days after the storm hit. The 6-foot floodwaters had receded, leaving everything in her home wet and molding. Not knowing what to do, the 75-year-old continued to live in her home. She dried her wigs on the chain-link fence and tried to salvage personal items. When Bishop Nelson found her, she was sifting through garbage left on the street outside her home. I held hands with Bishop Nelson and Ms. Smith as the bishop prayed for help.

SMILEY N. POOL

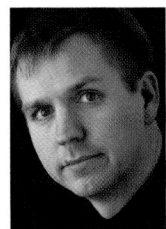

Smiley N. Pool joined the staff of The Dallas Morning News in August 2003 after eight years at the Houston Chronicle. Over his 20-year newspaper career, he has covered five Olympic Games; stories on pediatric AIDS in the U.S., Europe and Africa; street children in Romania; and many major local, national and international news events.

A native Texan who was born in Galveston, he also worked at the Colorado Springs Gazette and the Austin American-Statesman. He interned at the Austin American-Stateman while a college freshman and worked at weekly newspapers in St. Louis during high school.

He is a seven-time winner of the National Press Photographers Association regional photographer of the year award, as well as numerous local, state and national awards.

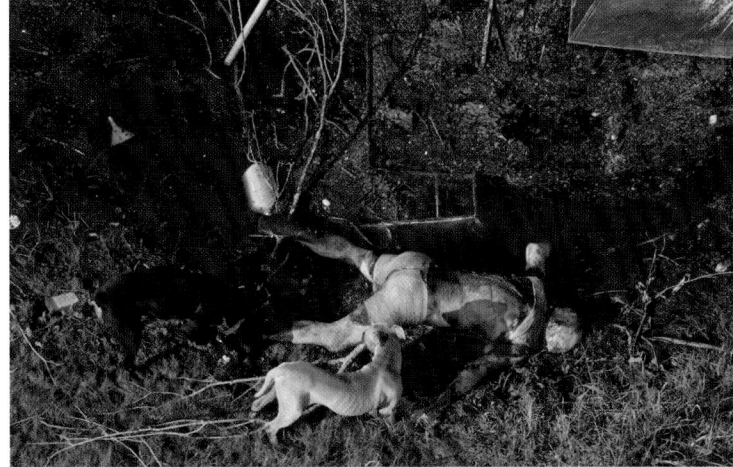

before I could bring myself to tell her what I'd seen. I still haven't shown her the photograph.

More times than I can remember in my career, I've been moved to tears. Sitting in the back seat of a helicopter after photographing dogs feeding on a human corpse in New Orleans, I was moved to prayer.

I took a deep breath, closed my eyes and silently asked for forgiveness for taking the photograph. I asked that peace come to the soul of the man whose remains had floated to that single dry spot of land. I asked for comfort for his family. I asked that the dogs find safety. I asked that strength guide the rescue workers as they continued tirelessly to pull more and more of the living from those floodwaters.

Finally, I asked that we all cherish the blessing of life that has been given to everyone who survived Katrina.

· · ·

"The most horrible photograph I've made in my career." That was my answer to the simple question, "What did you see today?" which my wife asked in one of our brief phone conversations during the aftermath of Katrina. The phone fell silent.

It was two more days

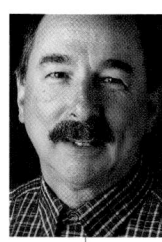

Richard Michael Pruitt

Richard Pruitt is a senior staff photographer at The Dallas Morning News. He went to school in the East Texas town of Marshall and attended East Texas State University in Commerce, now Texas A&M University-Commerce.

He served as president of The National Press Photographers Association, the only national organization dedicated to the advancement of photojournalism through education for newspaper and television photographers.

He has received numerous awards for his work from The Associated Press, United Press International, Dallas Press Club, Texas Headliners and the National Press Photographers Association.

Most national magazines have published his photographs, including Life, Time, Newsweek and People.

He and fellow Morning News photographer David Woo produced the book "Texas Women" in the late 1970s. It was on the top 10 list of books sold in the Southwest for more than two months. They are working on a book about Texas celebrities and their pets, "Top Dogs of Texas With Their Pets."

•   •   •   •   •

You could say my day started at midnight. I was sleeping in the driver's seat of my car, listening to Army trucks and fire engines pass while trying to get a little rest in front of the Vermilion Parish Sheriff's Department in Abbeville, La. The day before, officials had rescued more than a hundred people from flooded farmhouses and small communities. More than half of the parish was under water from Hurricane Rita. They were scheduled to start search and rescue efforts again at daybreak, and I wanted to record these heroes being heroes. I had seen the pictures from Hurricane Katrina: people

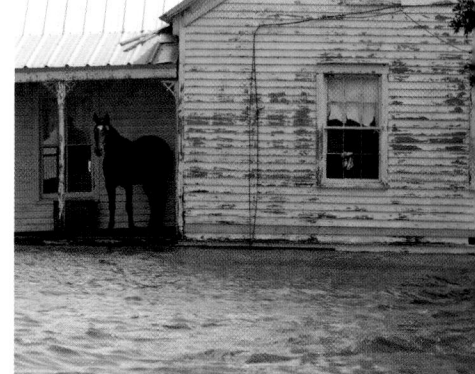

begging for help while camped on the roofs of their waterlogged homes.

As the sun was rising, I hitched a ride on a boat with Senior Agent Gabe Guidry of the Louisiana Wildlife Department. His boat was larger than most going out on the rescue mission. We had two smaller boats in our team along with two television crews. We went from farmhouse to farmhouse checking for signs of life.

We were slowly moving around to the front of a white house when I saw a horse standing on the front porch. It raised its leg a few inches as if asking for help. Agent Guidry assured me that the water would be down enough in the next couple of days and that the horse would be fine.

The picture of the horse on that farmhouse porch surrounded by water was published in The Dallas Morning News and sent around the world by The Associated Press. I received more than a dozen e-mails from horse lovers around the world wanting to know the animal's fate.

When fellow staffer Irwin Thompson took my place in the area, one of the first people he met was a man who told him that after he saw the picture of the horse, he went out and got the horse off the porch.

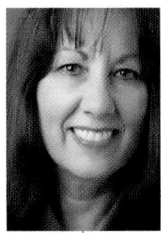

MONA REEDER

Mona Reeder graduated from California State University, Sacramento in 1989 with a bachelor's degree in journalism and art. After working at papers in California, Ohio and Arizona, she joined The Dallas Morning News as a senior staff photographer in 1999.

While at The News, she has covered many major international and national news events, including the Iraq war and the war on terrorism in Afghanistan.

Her photographs have won numerous awards, including World Press, Pictures of the Year International and the Robert F. Kennedy Award of Excellence for her documentary work on the diabetes epidemic of American Indians. She was named Arizona Photographer of the Year in 1998.

•   •   •   •

It was on a street named Desire in New Orleans' flooded Ninth Ward that I first saw his face peeking out between iron porch rails. He was one of thousands of animals abandoned during Hurricane Katrina. And the folks who were determined to stay in their homes despite the toxic floodwater lapping at their front doors would wade through chest-high water to feed him as he sat alone on that porch. They called him Day By Day since all of them were surviving one day at a time.

As I paddled my canoe down Desire Street, I would tie up to the porch and climb over the railing to give him fresh water each day that I had it to give, and I wondered if he was going to make it. Silently I vowed that if he was still on that porch when my assignment was nearing an end, I would take him with me. I was sick of seeing so much death and destruction.

Nearly two weeks after Katrina hit, the folks on Desire Street who had loosely banded together to stay, because they couldn't bear to leave their own pets, were persuaded to evacuate. One of their friends down the street had died during the night. And when they waded up to St. Claude Street pulling a flatbottom boat filled with their pets and a few precious belongings, Day By Day was with them.

He had made it to higher ground and relative safety, but the National Guard wouldn't take him, and he was going to be left behind to run loose in the area. It was at that moment I decided to take him home with me, although I was sleeping in a tent behind Nine Mile Point fire station and had no idea how a puppy would go over in already crowded quarters.

My worries were soon over as the firefighters and Morning News colleagues adored him and even offered to baby-sit while I continued to work the next two days.

After surviving the hurricane and toxic floodwaters, the puppy was terribly sick, and a veterinarian in the Dallas area didn't think he would make it. He thought he had distemper. But after six days in puppy ICU and isolation, lots of antibiotics, vitamins and fluids, Day By Day pulled through and was promptly nicknamed Heyday by my family.

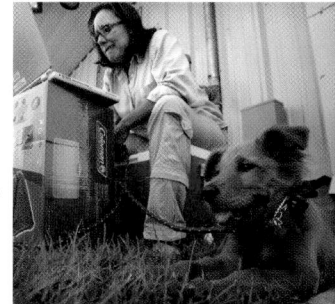

When I look at this photograph taken by friend and colleague Tom Fox on the afternoon I brought Heyday to our camp, it reminds me of the wonderful firefighter friends I made, the caring people of Desire Street, the bond and camaraderie shared with my co-workers, and my new best friend, Heyday.

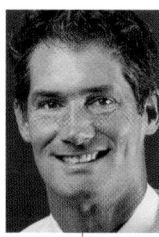

Erich Schlegel

Senior staff photographer Erich Schlegel has worked at The Dallas Morning News since 1988. He has also worked at The Brownsville Herald and the Corpus Christi Caller-Times. Born in Monterrey, Mexico, he lived throughout Latin America before moving to Texas in 1973. He is a graduate of Southern Methodist University with a degree in business. While at The News, he has covered seven Olympic Games, three Super Bowls, and conflicts in Bosnia, Albania, Zaire and Sri Lanka. He favors assignments in Latin America, where he has covered stories in Cuba, Mexico and Central America. He has won awards from World Press Photo, Pictures of the Year International, Society of News Design, APME and other national and regional competitions. He is The News' bureau photographer in Austin, covering assignments in Central Texas, on the Mexican border and special projects around the world. He lives in Austin with his wife, Karen, and daughter, Thira.

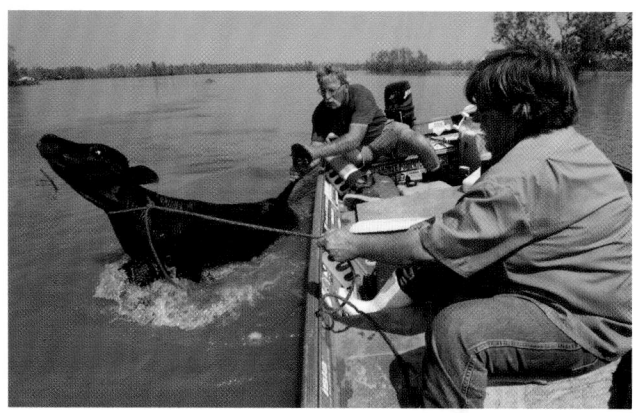

• • • •

I had been working on a story about Patty Vogt, a rancher and citrus farmer in Plaquemines Parish south of New Orleans. Hurricane Katrina first made landfall here, and the eye of the storm destroyed the area. Out of 300 head of Patty's cattle, only about 56 were left, stranded by water on a levee. Seven of those were trapped in flooded ranchland. Patty was getting no help from authorities and was relying on the kindness of neighbors and friends. Trucker Don Morris had come from North Carolina to help Patty. His trucking route brought him through the area regularly, moving oranges and oysters. Boats were needed to access the levee. Every day someone would lend a hand, offering their boat so she could get feed and water to the stranded cattle. I had brought my 14-foot flat boat to the area knowing it would come in handy in the flooded areas around New Orleans. I took Patty and Don out to make a feed run that turned into my first cattle roundup by boat. With us was Mandi Wright, photographer for the Detroit Free Press, who was also following Patty.

In Patty's authoritarian manner, she instructed me to check out the cattle stranded in the water. Instead, I gave Don control of the motor so I could shoot Patty up front with Mandi. Several cows got out of the brush into open water. Don brought us up to the half-running, half-swimming cattle. He was able to grab onto one of the calf's ears and pass the head to Patty. She called for rope, and I handed her some red climbing rope I had on hand. "What's this, designer rope?" she barked. "Just use it!" I yelled. Patty was finally able to get control of the calf, and Don brought us to the levee, where they tied up the young cow and brought us to the road, calf in boat.

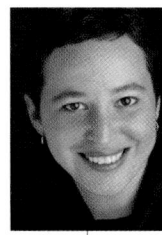

Lara Solt

Lara Solt joined The Dallas Morning News as a staff photographer in 2003. Before coming to Dallas, she freelanced in the New York City area for The New York Times, The Star-Ledger in New Jersey and National Geographic Traveler.

Previously, she worked as a staff photographer for Copley Newspapers/Sun Publications in the Chicago area. She has won national and international awards in Pictures of the Year, World Press Photo and other competitions.

She is a graduate of Ohio University's School of Visual Communications.

•   •   •   •   •

I'm standing in front of a church in Slidell, La. Katrina was here just days before. I am here to document a small group of people who drove from Sachse, Texas, with trailers full of donations to help in any way they could.

We arrived here after nearly everyone else scrambled to get out. It is a ghost town. Those who stayed have no power, no running water, no food.

Everyone is scurrying around, organizing the beginnings of a relief effort. An elderly woman pulls up in a car with a toddler crying in the back seat. She asks if I have anything to eat. All I have is some smushed-up peanut butter and jelly sandwiches, so I put as many as I can on a paper plate. When she sees what I have brought, she bursts into tears. She is so choked up she cannot speak, overwhelmed by the smallest act of kindness.

I cannot forget this moment because it drove home the level of desperation that people were reduced to by Katrina. I want to acknowledge the volunteers I traveled with and everyone who looked beyond their own lives to reach out to those in need.

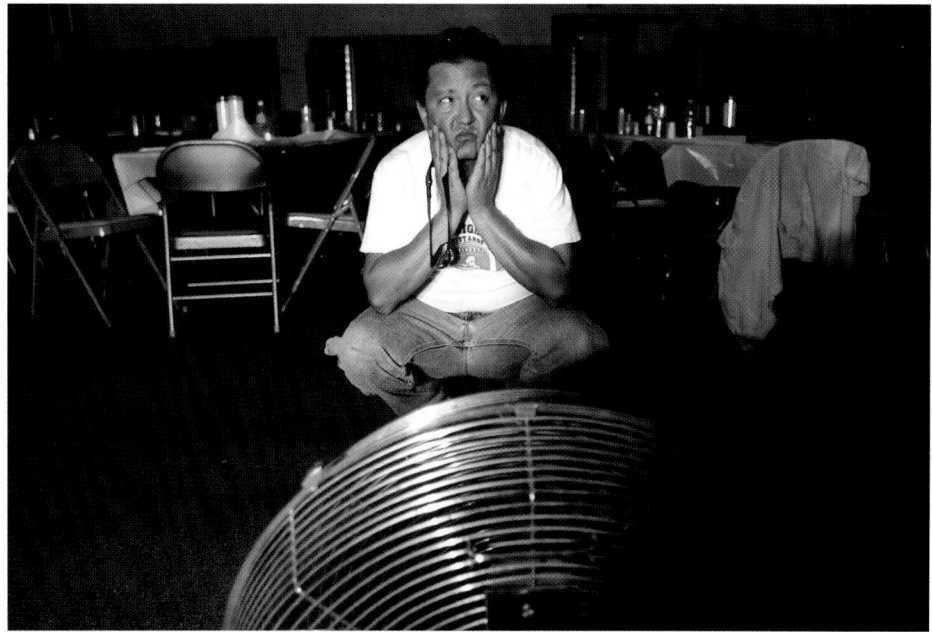

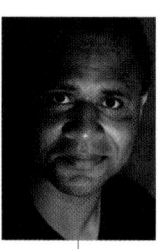

IRWIN THOMPSON

Senior staff photographer Irwin Thompson has worked at The Dallas Morning News since April 1990. Before coming to Dallas, he was a staff photographer at the Times-Picayune in New Orleans and the Monroe (La.) News-Star. He has won numerous awards, including recognition from the Texas Associated Press, the Louisiana Associated Press, Texas Headliners, the Press Club of Dallas Katie Award and the National Press Photographers Association. He grew up in DeRidder, La. He graduated in 1984 from Northeast Louisiana University with a bachelor's degree in photojournalism.

•   •   •   •   •

When I look at the pictures I took in New Orleans during and after Hurricane Katrina, I'm drawn to the image of evacuee Jeremiah Ward, sitting on a rescue boat in the Ninth Ward, wearing his makeshift shoes. Two hastily torn cigar boxes imprinted with the words "Keep Moving" were attached to Jeremiah's feet by three large rubber bands. The image shows the sense of urgency and improvisation on the part of residents of the historic, low-income area as they escaped from their homes when floodwaters abruptly rose. By the time they were rescued, most had narrowed down possessions to items that fit in small trash bags and carrying cases, or to the clothes they were wearing, leaving a lifetime of memories and belongings behind. The simple picture sums up the plight of New Orleans evacuees, their desperation, hopelessness and despair after Hurricane Katrina and the ensuing chaos after the levee broke. The images are forever etched in my memory.

Ron Baselice

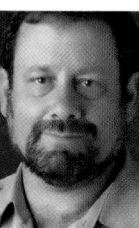

Ron Baselice grew up in the Philadelphia area and discovered photography in the ninth grade, when he and a neighbor came across a black-and-white developing kit while cleaning out a basement. He attended Brooks Institute of Photography in Santa Barbara, Calif., and moved to the Dallas-Fort Worth area after college. He was hired as a staff photographer at the Irving Daily News in 1982 and joined The Dallas Morning News after the Irving paper became a zoned section of the Morning News. He lives in Arlington with his wife, Janet, and their daughters Holly and Paige.

Vernon Bryant

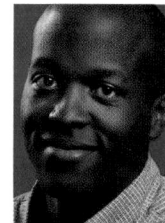

Vernon Bryant was hired at The Dallas Morning News after completing an internship in 2000.

He was born in Plano and spent eight years in San Jose, Calif., before returning to Texas to finish high school and attend college. He graduated from the University of North Texas with a bachelor of arts degree in photojournalism and a minor in art photography.

He interned at the Austin American-Statesman for two summers and USA Today.

Jim Mahoney

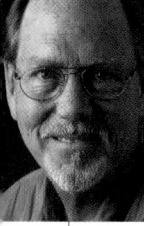

Jim Mahoney came to The Dallas Morning News in 1979 after eight years at the Denton Record-Chronicle. In 1981, he assumed the newly created position of photo editor, working with other newsroom editors to coordinate photo coverage and improve the use of photos in the newspaper. Over the next 18 years, he worked as assignments editor, night photo editor and assistant director of photography. In 1999, he returned to the position of photographer.

He has received awards from The APME Association, the NPPA and UPI, including a 1989 Katie Award from the Dallas Press Club for his work on the newspaper's special section 25 years after the assassination of President John F. Kennedy.

Rick Gershon

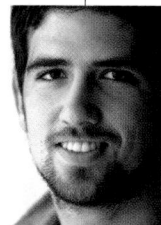

Rick Gershon grew up in Pilot Point, Texas, and attended the University of North Texas to pursue his dream of playing Division I college football. But after his freshman year, he discovered photojournalism and left football to dedicate himself to learning the art of visual storytelling. After he graduated in August 2004 with a bachelor's degree in photojournalism, he was named College Photographer of the Year by the University of Missouri and received an Award of Excellence as Photographer of the Year in the Pictures of the Year International competition. He joined The Dallas Morning News in August 2005.

CREDITS

The Dallas Morning News Staff

Photographers: Michael Ainsworth, Ron Baselice, Melanie Burford, Vernon Bryant, Evans Caglage, Natalie Caudill, Barbara Davidson, Louis DeLuca, Tom Fox, Juan Garcia, Rick Gershon, Randy Eli Grothe, Milton Hinnant, Nathan Hunsinger, Mei-Chun Jau, Kye R. Lee, David Leeson, Brad Loper, Jim Mahoney, Michael Mulvey, Cheryl Diaz Meyer, Smiley Pool, Richard Michael Pruitt, Mona Reeder, John Rhodes, Erich Schlegel, Lara Solt, Irwin Thompson • **Photo Editors:** Rick Choate, Anne Farrar, Michael Hamtil, Alysia Oglesby, Guy Reynolds, Andrew P. Scott, David Woo • **Lab, Imaging and Librarians:** Lab Manager John Zak, Gary Barber, Walter Cruz, Mike Gibson, David Guzman, Leila Hill, Ahna Hubnik, David Leeson II, J.D. Vega, Lisa LeVrier, Doug Stjernholm, Henrietta Wildsmith, Chief Librarian Jerome Sims, Cris Miller • **Assistant Directors of Photography:** Leslie White and Chris Wilkins • **Director of Photography:** William Snyder

The Book Staff

Photo Editing: Leslie White, Michael Hamtil, Chris Wilkins, William Snyder • **Layout and Design:** Anne Farrar • **Photo Imaging:** Gary Barber, John Zak, Ahna Hubnik • **Copy Editing and Proofing:** Laura Ehret, Allison Stewart, Becky Williams, Keith Campbell

Literary Agent and Publicity Expert

Farris Rookstool, III, CEO of Powerhousepr, Inc., who envisioned the concept and title for the book, secured a publisher, and helped produce it in record time

ACKNOWLEDGMENTS

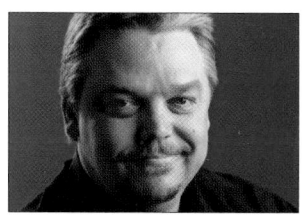

• WILLIAM SNYDER, DIRECTOR
OF PHOTOGRAPHY

Personal thanks to ...

The Dallas Morning News Photo Department for your incredible energy, journalistic skills and artistry. You brought the many stories, great and small, of Hurricanes Katrina and Rita to our readers. It is an honor to work with you every day. • **The DMN photo editors** for their time, energy, sacrifice and grace under pressure while producing this book - especially **David Woo** for his tenacity. Without him, there would be no book. • **Cokie Roberts** for joining us in this venture and her beautiful introduction. • **Keith Campbell and the News Desk** for their fantastic photo display. • **Mark Miller and Cindy Smith** for those superb Sunday papers. • **Mark Edgar, Mike Drago** and their crew on **the State Desk**, especially Bruce Nichols, Lee Hancock, Karen Brooks, Pete Slover, and Arnold Hamilton for their wonderful stories and essays for this book. • **Dwayne Bray, Leona Allen, Ed Timms, Eric Nelson** and their crews on **the Metro and Suburban Desks** for all their local coverage. • Our brothers and sisters at **WWL in New Orleans** for their generosity during their own time of crisis. • **The firefighters of Nine Mile Point Fire Department, Station 79** for their hospitality, generosity and showers. • **Senior Deputy Managing Editor Walt Stallings, Vice President and Managing Editor George Rodrigue and Editor Bob Mong** for their encouragement, guidance, support and trust. • Most importantly, I'd like to thank all **the DMN spouses, significant others and children** for their love, support, and sacrifice that enables, strengthens, and allows us to do the work we love.

Special thanks to ...

The following people, for making our coverage and this book possible: **Patricia Blair, Ed Dufner, Lisa Kresl, Sue Smith, Bob Yates, David Deutch, Chris Morris, Ana Barrera-Waggoner, Chuck Stewart, Denise Beeber, Will Pry, Cindy Smith, Terry Kelly, Rebecca Stumpf, Alma Lozoya, Carol Taylor, Cheri Shipman, Kevin Lueb, Jill Houston, Erik Schutz, Cindy Bagwell, Sheri Baxter, Noel Gross, Dan Koller, Ryan Rusak, Paul Meyer, Gretel Kovach, Sudeep Reddy, Wendi Greene, Rolando Rivero, Joshua Markham, Amanda Franklin, Greg Brown, Gino Jensen, Wanda Brown, Ken Pyatt, Jim Rossman, Avia Green, Kerri Hunter, Dolphus Williams, Valerie Helewa, Amy Lewy, Cameron Snyder, Scott Snyder, Ramsey and Eugene Jabbour, Diane Hamilton, Sandra Smith, Dirck Halstead, Ken Geiger, Chris Johns.**

And last, but not least, I want to give a *very special thanks* to **Belo Chairman, President and CEO Robert Decherd** and **The Dallas Morning News Publisher and CEO Jim Moroney**. Without their commitment to and support for quality journalism, none of this would have been possible.

CORPORATE SPONSORS

Canon U.S.A., Inc.

Canon supports the photographers of the Dallas Morning News and the "Eyes Of The Storm" project. All photographs in this book, except the video capture on pages 135, 146 and 157, are the product of the photographers' visions and Canon EOS-1D and EOS-1D Mark II digital cameras and lenses.

Powerhousepr, Inc.

Tenet Healthcare Corp.

Verizon Wireless

The Dallas Morning News has designated the net proceeds from this book to benefit The Dallas Morning News Charities and the hurricanes Katrina and Rita relief efforts.

DallasNews.com

For more information on Hurricanes Katrina and Rita, and to obtain additional copies of this book or the photographs within it, please visit DallasNews.com